The Management Process

A Selection of Readings for Librarians

Ruth J. Person, editor

American Library Association

Chicago, 1983

Designed by Ellen Pettengell

Composed by FM Typesetting Co. in
Linotype Melior

Printed on 50-pound Antique Glatfelter,
a pH-neutral stock, and bound
in 10-point Carolina cover stock
by Edwards Brothers Incorporated

Library of Congress Cataloging in Publication Data

Main entry under title:

The Management process.
    Includes bibliographies.
    1. Library administration—Addresses, essays,
lectures. 2. Library personnel management—
Addresses, essays, lectures. I. Person, Ruth J.
Z678.M277   1983   025.1   83-3788
ISBN 0-8389-0381-9

Contents

Acknowledgments

Gathering and shaping the variety of writings represented in this book into a cohesive collection was greatly facilitated by several individuals. First, I would like to recognize the efforts of my colleague, Charles T. Townley, in getting this collection underway. The direction taken by this book represents our many hours of discussion about the need to provide a supplement for those students and practitioners who wish to move beyond textbook approaches toward a deeper analysis of the managerial process in libraries. I am particularly grateful for his ideas, his comments and suggestions, and his willingness to discuss ideas about management on an ongoing basis.

Second, I appreciate the long-standing assistance that the staff members of the Industrial Relations Library at the University of Michigan's Graduate School of Business Administration, have provided me. Their help made the search for relevant management literature an easier task.

Third, I would like to acknowledge the support of my friend and colleague Margaret Taylor in our many discussions of the writing and publishing process, and the help of my husband George H. Person in the final organization of this book.

Fourth, I am most grateful to Rose Vainstein, both for helping to shape my ideas about library management and for serving as a catalyst for the development of a book such as this. Her ideas about the teaching of library management and the use of readings

viii   **Acknowledgments**

to support teaching and learning have been invaluable to me in developing this book.

Last, and most important, I would like to acknowledge the help of my research associate Sally Sartain, who was absolutely indispensable in keeping this project running smoothly. Her good humor, sense of order, ability to search out vital but "fugitive" information, and support in clearing the way for the completion of the project were invaluable.

RUTH J. PERSON

Introduction

Understanding the management process as it relates to the library is essential in the increasingly complex environment, both internal and external, in which today's library exists. Those first entering the library workplace must understand how this environment is managed. Development of increasingly sophisticated management knowledge and skills by would-be library managers, and a continuous "fine tuning" of these skills by practicing library managers is also necessary. Thus, there are several categories of individuals who have a particular reason to examine the management process in libraries. Students in library education programs who undertake course work that focuses on management issues are an obvious example. But practitioners who aspire to managerial responsibilities or who already hold managerial positions also need to examine this process in order to cope with the many changes taking place in the library environment.[1]

Several texts present library management and its major elements; numerous business and public administration texts also cover management in a more general sense. By examining these, students of management can obtain the framework necessary to begin their studies. But a text cannot present detailed analyses of all of the elements of management, nor can it cover all approaches or represent all of the changes taking place in the field. Thus, individuals who look for supplementary reading at a more advanced level may eventually turn to the more specialized monograph and periodical literature in business, public, and library management. During the past two decades this literature has grown in size and scope, reflecting the many changes taking place in the study and practice of management. A growing direction toward specialization in management literature has also developed. Although library management literature does not approach the scope of that in business and public administration, it demonstrates many of the same characteristics.

The individual who embarks upon a further study of library management through the literature may find that this growing and sometimes fragmented body of material hampers efforts to develop a coordinated approach to advanced management study. Drawing together illustrative materials from the universe of business, public, and library management literature into a book of readings provides one way of approaching this problem.

The Process Approach

Numerous approaches to the study of management are available. In looking for the most general and all-encompassing way of structuring a means of studying management in the library setting through the literature, the "process" approach seems especially viable. If we define management as "the process by which a cooperative group directs actions toward common goals,"[2] we can in turn use this definition to analyze the development of intentions and the "transforming of intentions into results"[3] while also providing a framework for the study of management in libraries.

One way to examine this process is to break it down into certain functions that make up the process. These functions, often given different names by different authorities, can be represented as: planning, decision-making, controlling, organizing, communicating, staffing, and directing. Although these functions are closely interrelated, they can be further broken into separate processes in order to examine important management concepts.

Although these processes exist in the organization as a means of "transforming intentions into results," it must be understood that individuals may adopt a particular role structure and approach the job of management in ways that do not fit neatly into this process framework. As Mintzberg[4] has demonstrated and DeGennaro and Thomas and Ward[5] have supported in the library environment, what managers *do* in interpreting and carrying out the management process may not precisely correspond with the "functions" of management. Second, "task" aspects of management required at a specific time to solve a particular problem may also color the view of the management process. Faced with financial exigencies, increased demands for services, and an information explosion, it is tempting to neglect process.[6] But it is the management process and its functions that provide a framework for individual interpretation of the manager's job and a means of developing and maintaining the library as a responsive organization.

The Structure of This Book of Readings

Articles and excerpts from books that present a variety of viewpoints about the management process are collected in this book. By incorporating a variety of views, we avoid the "lure of the universal theory"[7] that can so limit the study and practice of management. Regardless of viewpoint, however, every effort has been made to incorporate readings that demonstrate ways in which the process of management can be applied and improved.

The seven sections of the book represent the important functions within the management process. Each section is introduced by a brief essay that explores the nature of the readings included and the relationship of the managerial function being discussed to the overall process of management. Following the reading selections, a brief discussion of additional sources that will help to interpret or add to the topic being presented is provided. Readers who wish to expand their study of the topics beyond the essays in the collection will find these additional sources particularly helpful.

In summary, this book is designed to serve both students and practitioners in its approach. Students might use it as a supplement to a management text and as a source for directed readings. Practitioners might use it as a source of self-directed management study in which the readings provide a framework for examination of the management process and a suggestion of various elements to be studied in greater depth. It is hoped that it will serve as a stimulus for continued examination of management in the library setting.

Building a Collection of Readings

This collection of readings is intended to provide a general framework for the study of library management. The book is designed to reflect a concern with management as a process and the ways in which that process is applied to a library setting. It has been developed with two assumptions in mind: (1) that organizations, *including different types of libraries*, share certain common properties that make the management process applicable in the general sense to all of them, although its interpretation in each may be different; and (2) that process has both internal and external aspects, and that the focus here will be largely internal.

The intent of the selection process for this collection of readings was to find articles or excerpts from books that would be both descriptive of some element in the managerial process and prescriptive of some ways of enhancing that process. At the same time, the selections were to be suggestive of new approaches and future trends in management, intellectually stimulating, and related as far as possible to library management or at least to a service environment. They were to be part of a cohesive whole and yet had to stand alone as essays. With these criteria in mind, selection became a difficult task. The literature of management, while enormously expanded, has become more specialized. Library management literature often seems weighted in the direction of academic libraries. In addition, it is also fragmented in some areas— for example, "control" as a topic receives little discussion in the library literature compared to "staffing." By careful examination of the literature, readings were found that would meet the stated criteria and contribute measurably to a book of essays.

Management
in the Library
Setting

In order to study the process of management in a particular organizational setting, it is necessary to examine the relationship of key elements in this process to environmental, organizational, and performance constraints. Two factors are necessary to this examination. One is the identification of salient characteristics in the type of organizational setting in which the management process takes place. The other is the establishment of some kind of framework or model of management. Keeping these two factors in mind, ideas for the enhancement and improvement of the management process in the library can then be explored.

The selections in this chapter have been chosen to establish a framework for this examination of the library management process by presenting a progression of ideas from general to specific. All in some way identify functions of the management process used as a structure for this book, and all illustrate the complexity of the management process—the interrelationship of the various management functions, the importance of the environment as an organizational influence, and the difficulty of developing organizational responsiveness in the face of a changing future.

It has been suggested that certain kinds of organizations are particularly vulnerable to external constraints in attempting to reach equilibrium.[1] A service organization such as the library often seems to be subject to such vulnerability. Does this mean, then, that the characteristics of a type of organization affect its management processes in attempting to reach a balanced state? Within this context, Newman and Wallender define the not-for-profit organization, identify constraining characteristics of this organizational type, and elaborate on the impact of such constraints on the management process. Since most libraries can be placed in this not-for-profit category (often termed "nonprofit," "service," or "public service" organizations), such an assessment is particularly useful in exploring library management. The authors point to the particular difficulty of establishing adequate control processes in the not-for-profit organization, where objectives are often hard to measure.

Nitecki moves the reader to a conceptual, holistic model of library management that includes and expands upon a number of the elements identified by Newman and Wallender. His discussion of the environment in which the library operates and the necessity of understanding such an environment in order to carry out the management process helps to link the reading selections in this chapter.

The remaining selections in the chapter expand on both the conceptual framework provided by Nitecki and the analysis of organizational setting offered by Newman and Wallender by identifying specific and critical problems that must be addressed through the library management process. In viewing the library as a professional service organization, Drake argues that the goals of librarians conflict with those of libraries, thus preventing effective services from being provided. The role of management in this setting, then, must be to achieve goal congruence between these two elements by taking an *active* stance toward the planning and implementation of change, by sharing authority, and by integrating professionals into the decision-making process. Martell's article provides a point from which to proceed in looking more closely at each function in the management process as outlined by the remaining selections in the book. Martell offers a reassessment of traditional management practices and a way of viewing the hindrances that often cause management failures when "mechanistic" organizations try to adopt modern management theories. Above all, he stresses the need for adaptability and flexibility in making management changes, a view implied by all of the authors included in this book.

1. Managing Not-for-Profit Enterprises

William H. Newman and Harvey W. Wallender III

Effective management in the not-for-profit sector of society is a growing concern. People's daily lives are increasingly dependent on not-for-profit enterprises, and an ever-increasing share of total national resources flows into them.

Among business leaders and business school personnel a popular theme is "application of business management methods in not-for-profit agencies." Many hospitals, welfare agencies, little theatre groups, and even universities are seeking help from business sources in managing their affairs. *The presumption is that basic management concepts can and should be applied to not-for-profit activities just as diligently as to profit-seeking companies.* Members of the Academy of Management applaud such talk, often with a self-satisfied "that's what we have been saying all along" response.

Nevertheless when moving beyond pleasant generalities, some doubt creeps in. Maybe not-for-profit enterprises are different. Perhaps profit maximization is the keystone in the management structure model. At least business school faculties do seriously consider suggestions for special courses in not-for-profit management—which implies that significant distinctions exist.

The troublesome issue is not whether the underlying processes of managing are found in all sorts of purposeful cooperative endeavors. They are. Studies by sociologists and cultural anthropologists, as well as reports of administrators and consultants, show that planning, organizing, controlling, and activating are essential in not-for-profit and profit-seeking enterprises alike. But wide differences exist among specific enterprises in the manner by which these processes are carried out.[1]

Reprinted from *Academy of Management Review* 3:24–31 (Jan. 1978).

The pertinent question is: Do not-for-profit enterprises have particular characteristics which make inappropriate some managerial concepts that are beneficial in profit-seeking enterprises?

To study this question the authors reviewed the literature on managing such not-for-profit enterprises as hospitals, schools, welfare agencies, and art museums; conducted a pilot study of how 22 diversified not-for-profit enterprises actually are managed; and designed an approach (model) for identifying and better understanding the *distinctive* aspects of managing such enterprises. Avoiding the institutional aspects of big government (separation of legislative, executive and judicial activities; civil service; taxation and other unique funding; etc.), the focus was on self-administered, self-contained organizations which generate and deliver a completed service. The pilot study covered eight health, five art and culture, three social aid, two religious, two scientific research, and two government urban service enterprises of this nature. Such a unit is called an "enterprise."

This report is only a first cut at the problem, for reasons that will become obvious in the outline of the proposed approach. But the basic viewpoint should be useful to others even in its preliminary form.

Impotence of the Not-for-Profit Category

Comparisons of the process of managing in diverse enterprises quickly reveals that the not-for-profit classification is too broad to be useful in management analysis. It fails to flag significant distinctions for several reasons.

First, "not-for-profit" is a catch-all term embracing a heterogeneous array of enterprises. Some feeling for the diversity is suggested by the general groups of not-for-profit organizations listed in table 1. Each group covers widely differing enterprises. The U.S. Internal Revenue Service publishes a list of 293 code numbers for use in classifying organizations applying for tax exemption.[2]

The differences among not-for-profit enterprises—for example, a cancer research institute versus a Harlem street academy versus a cemetery association—are so great that their common negative characteristic of not seeking a profit becomes minor, at least with respect to managing them. Some need elaborate, formal structures; others thrive on high adaptability and informality. Long-range programming is vital for a water supply co-op, whereas a tenants' association rarely plans a year ahead.

TABLE 1. Array of Not-for-Profit Enterprises Grouped by
Services Rendered

Services Performed	Enterprises
Health Services	Hospitals Nursing Homes Clinics
Education	Universities Schools Trade Institutes
Social Services	Welfare Child-Care Family Counseling
Arts and Culture	Orchestras Libraries Museums
Cooperatives	Insurance Savings Banks Utilities Marketing
Other Private	Religious Scientific Research Associations Clubs Unions

Other Government	Uniformed:
	    Military
	    Police
	    Fire
	Civilian:
	    Regulatory
	    Fiscal
	    Justice

Second, in several categories, profit-seeking and not-for-profit enterprises are quite similar in their operations. From a management viewpoint, running a large mutual life-insurance company differs only in minor respects from administering a stock company. Proprietary and not-for-profit nursing homes face substantially the same managerial tasks as do farmer co-ops and private feed companies. This is not to belittle eleemosynary aims; on a few matters they are a major distinction. But in a comparative management study, differences in the nature of business undertaken predominate over ownership differences within the same industry.

More subtle is the fact that profit maximization is highly abstract. It is useful as a value criterion when choosing between alternative courses of action, but by itself it gives little guidance as to which alternatives to examine. Instead, a manager must devise strategies, select technologies, establish policies and programs, mobilize resources, and create a management design which integrates these forces into a "going concern." *It is these instrumental characteristics of an enterprise which set the parameters for a good management design.*[3] To build a good management structure the designer has to appreciate "the nature of the business"; knowing the value placed on profits is not enough.

The profit motive does indeed help shape strategy, programs, etc. The absence of such a clear goal can get enterprises into difficulties. But the profit/not-for-profit dichotomy is too general to be useful. It is impotent in providing leads to good management practice.

Constraining Characteristics Existing in Specific Enterprises

Analysis of the unusual managerial problems in a variety of not-for-profit enterprises reveals several features which affect managerial practice. Instead of a single charactersitic (not-for-profit), a variety of influences may be present, existing in some enterprises and absent in others. They appear in various combinations. The presence of one or more of these constraining characteristics creates distinct difficulties in utilizing widely accepted managerial techniques.

With present knowledge, a preliminary listing can be made of fairly common constraining characteristics, and the approach (model) to not-for-profit management indicated. By identifying features to watch for, and suggesting how they may bear upon the effectiveness of various managerial devices, an approach is set forth to the otherwise amorphous thinking about managing not-for-profit enterprises.

The constraining characteristics which seem to account for unusual managerial problems in the enterprises studied are the following:

1. *Service is intangible* and hard to measure. This difficulty is often compounded by the existence of *multiple* service objectives.
2. *Customer influence may be weak.* Often the enterprise has a local monopoly, and payments by customers may be a secondary source of funds.
3. Strong *employee* commitment to *professions* or to a cause may undermine their allegiance to the enterprise.
4. *Resource contributors may intrude* into internal management—notably fund contributors and government.
5. *Restraints on the use of rewards and punishments* result from 1, 3, and 4 above.
6. *Charismatic leaders* and/or "mystique" of the enterprise may be important means of resolving conflict in objectives and over-coming restraints.

Two potential sources of confusion should be noted. First, even when present, the above characteristics are only part of a total managerial setting. The primary tasks of management, and arrangements for dealing with these tasks, are alike in all sorts of enterprises. Objectives, policies, programs, defined jobs, procedures, information flows, standards, measurements, executive motivation, power, and the like will be useful in every joint undertaking. This approach to not-for-profit management assumes that this general base is widely recognized. The constraining characteristics are *additional* considerations, singled out for attention because they help differentiate one setting from another. They pose *added* constraints to which managers must adjust.

Second, not-for-profit enterprises have no monopoly on these characteristics. They may be found to a greater or lesser extent in a profit-seeking enterprise, but because their frequency of strong impact is much higher in not-for-profit enterprises, they serve as a useful diagnostic tool.

Impact of Constraining Characteristics on Managing

Now comes the central question: If one or more of the six constraining characteristics are found in an enterprise, what is the likely impact on the process of managing? Preliminary answers can be seen in a series of examples, indicating the nature of adjustments to look for in not-for-profit enterprises, and suggesting specific issues that confront managers of particular enterprises.

Impact on Planning

Both rational decision-making and institutional planning are influenced by the constraining characteristics.[4] When present, the constraints add at least four readily observed complications to planning in not-for-profit enterprises.

Goal conflicts interfere with rational planning. Underlying the principles of company planning is the presumption that managers seek to make choices as a single, rational individual would. They try to optimize in terms of a selected criterion (usually long-term profits); and when differences of opinion emerge about what action to take, such conflict can be resolved by using rational judgment about the likely consequences.[5]

In not-for-profit enterprises, such a single criterion which provides a base for rational choice is often hard to find. Divergent goals are likely to persist. A nursery school may aim at day-care for children of working mothers, child socialization, headstart on the three R's, creative expression, psychological counsel, or just plain fun. A labor union has economic, political, and social goals. The aims of particular professions within the enterprise may add to this array of goals. Consequently, a planner must deal with a whole set of values. Goal conflicts may arise in any organization, but unresolved divergence of aims is likely to be more severe in not-for-profit enterprises.

The consumer of the service provided is in a weaker position than the customer of a typical business firm. Customers of not-for-profit enterprises usually pay only a fraction of the service cost, and often there is a presumption that the producer knows best what the customer should receive. Such *reduced influence of customers* in a not-for-profit enterprise may permit the diversity of values to continue without a clear market check.

Our field survey revealed two mechanisms often used in not-for-profit enterprises to provide direction and priority among various goals. Profit ventures also employ these mechanisms, but because of goal ambiguity they play a larger role in not-for-profit enterprises. One is a *charismatic leader.* Especially in smaller enterprises, a dynamic and forceful individual often "calls the plays." This leader has personal convictions about the values to be used in decision-making and either has enough power to make important choices, or is so influential that her or his values are accepted by others who make decisions.

A second way value conflicts are resolved is through a *mystique* that dominates the enterprise—a strong conviction about the importance of a particular service mission and the unusual capacity of the enterprise to provide that service. The Mayo Clinic, Ford Foundation, Rotary Club, and Red Cross each have an internationally known mystique, and many local not-for-profit ventures have comparable traditions. Once established, the mystique defines a respected role in society. The mystique sets the character and values decision makers are expected to follow.

An integrated planning focus tends to shift from results to resources. Not-for-profit enterprises often provide services which are hard to measure: education, zoos, health care, etc. Besides being intangible, these services may be subsidized in a way that removes a market test of adequacy. Integrated planning in terms of results becomes obscure. There is no net "bottom line." Instead, much of the planning deals with performance of activities which presumably will create desirable results. For example, because measuring what students actually learn is difficult, the operating objectives for a professor are often expressed in terms of number of classes, student contact hours, or reports submitted.

Then, because activities of individuals in an enterprise are usually diverse, with no common denominator to serve as the basis for integration of plans, central planning moves even further back in the service-creating cycle to resource inputs. Dollar budgets or personnel assigned become the focus. The implicit assumption is that assigned resources will be used for proper activities which in turn will produce desired results. This is two steps removed from Management by Objectives (MBO)!

Planning in terms of resource inputs is not confined to not-for-profit enterprises. Central decisions regarding advertising, research and development, and internal company services are often expressed as a percentage of sales or some other input figure. It is inability to measure current output that prompts such practice.

Ambiguous operating objectives create opportunities for internal politics. When fuzzy objectives are combined with planning in terms of resources only, operating executives have considerable leeway in what they actually do. Sometimes this uncertainty permeates the entire planning process.[6] Such leeway makes possible political maneuvering for personal ends. It is a tribute to thousands of lower-level managers in not-for-profit enterprises that the potential for maneuvering is not often abused and that results in most instances are reasonably satisfactory.

Professionalization simplifies detailed planning but adds rigidity. As not-for-profit enterprises increase in size, a need arises for standing plans (policies, standing operating procedures, etc.), just as in their profit-seeking counterparts. But a large number of "professionals" may modify this aspect of planning.

Where professionals hold dominant roles, as in hospitals and schools, many standard methods and procedures are dictated by the professions rather than enterprise management. Professional traditions may be so strong that the enterprise managers have difficulty changing conventional behavior patterns to fit new service missions. For instance, established test routines common in hospitals became obstacles in a newly developed family health program. In a high school, the established history curriculum with its well-defined courses virtually blocked an experiment with a combined social issues/English writing "seminar." The availability of *professional methods and standards* does simplify local planning of normal activities, but it also imposes rigidity in adjusting to new needs, such as the education of hard-core unemployed, or modern birth control.

In summary, the planning process in not-for-profit enterprises is basically similar to planning in profit-seeking companies. Missions, operating objectives, budgets, scheduling policies, procedures, etc., all have a similar role. But there are constraints which muddy the process. Multiple goals, hard-to-measure results, intrusion of resource contributors, weak customer influence, and professionalization make clean-cut, rational planning more difficult. Where these constraints are found—in either profit oriented or nonprofit ventures—crisp, integrated planning is likely to be feasible only when a charismatic leader or strong mystique is also present.

Impact on Organizing

This same cluster of constraints—to the extent that they prevail in a specific enterprise—may also affect the organization. Three examples stood out in our pilot study.

Decentralization is complicated. While the usual pros and cons of delegating authority to make decisions are present in not-for-profit enterprises, additional pressures may be felt. If employees have strong professional training and standards—as do most medical doctors and teachers—then decisions about work embraced within the professional code can be safely decentralized. In fact, professionals probably will insist that they make their own local decisions.

But most of the pressure runs in the other direction. For intangible, hard-to-measure services not covered by clear professional standards (ranging from art selection to zoo-keeping), important decisions have to be centralized. For such matters, senior executives have difficulty communicating to subordinates the meaning of enterprise objectives, and consequently they do not dare make broad delegations.

Full delegation may be obstructed by two other characteristics often present in not-for-profit enterprises. Because judgment about good or poor performance is necessarily subjective, the use of rewards and punishments tends to be restricted. Sales and productivity bonuses, or their equivalent, are not feasible (or are illegal in many cases). Instead, promotion, discharges, and the like are traditionally made on the basis of external training or seniority. This separation of rewards from performance of assigned tasks weakens the influence of managers on subordinates; lacking confidence that their instructions will be carried out, managers are reluctant to delegate.

In addition, private donors, government agencies, and other suppliers of resources to not-for-profit enterprises often impose special conditions on their continuing support. Senior managers must always be alert to how these outside interest groups will view the enterprise's action. This leads to "defensive centralization"; managers retain decision-making themselves, to avoid actions which outside interest groups find objectionable.

Linking pins for external-internal integration become important. Not infrequently, contribution of funds and other resources is so important to a not-for-profit enterprise that special jobs or sections are established to maintain favorable relationships. Most obvious is the need for a donation-raising organization in a venture heavily dependent on private contributions or a government contract unit in a venture supported by public grants.

But the critical task is integration. The interests and values of contributors may differ sharply from those of scientists, prima donnas, and doctors who actually create the services of the enterprise. As Lawrence and Lorsch[7] point out, the orientation of such special groups makes even communication between them difficult. A special need arises for people in buffer roles, who can relate to both inside and outside groups and can promote agreement on actions to be taken. This integrating task is especially difficult in enterprises where the service is intangible and objectives are multiple and shifting. A good organization will recognize this need.

Job enlargement and executive development may be restrained by professionalization. A large number of "professionals" may interfere with job enlargement and job enrichment. Medicine, education, social work, and other professions have increasingly narrow specializations—nerve specialists, psychiatrists, pediatricians, vocational counselors, music teachers, speech therapists, choreographers, anesthetists, etc. Each field requires special training, and many have rigid qualification examinations. Such professions develop their own codes of conduct, values, and beliefs; they have rather sharp ideas about what activities are, and are not, within their province.

Members of an established profession often view the enterprise in which they work largely as a place for them to practice their profession, especially when it is a not-for-profit enterprise. Consequently, by expanding job content (job enrichment), managers often encounter the following from their professionals: "That's not my specialty; it is not what I was hired to do." To a large extent, where professionals predominate, a manager has to design his organization to appeal to prevailing professional norms.

A further influence of professionalization, especially when reinforced by traditions transferred from government civil service, is hindrance to promotion-from-within. In private enterprise, many personnel development practices are built around rotation and promotion-from-within. It is assumed that individuals adapt and grow as they gain experience and that this change provides opportunities for people to expand the scope of their activities. This kind of personal career building based on the internal dynamics of an enterprise is difficult when employees are tied to a profession. Some internal movement occurs, but managers have to look harder for people who are willing to step outside their professional roles and adjust their activities to the particular needs of the enterprise.

The presence or absence of the profit motive is not the key consideration. Rather, it is strong professionalization, which can be found also (although with less frequency) in profit-seeking enterprises, such as proprietary hospitals.

Impact on Motivation and Control

The underlying process of control in not-for-profit enterprises involves the same elements as control in profit-seeking firms. An array of control types such as post-action control, yes-no control, and even steering-control fits into the total control structure.[8] Nevertheless, special problems arise.

Several constraints on effective control have been implied in the preceding analysis. Heading the list are *hard-to-measure* objectives of many not-for-profit enterprises. When desired results are ambiguous and judgment of success is subjective, a predictable and impersonal feedback cannot be established. Because quality of services is often judged intuitively by persons of varying expectations, pars lack consistent definition. Some aspects of any activity can be measured, such as number of people served and direct financial expenses; but these aspects are only part of the total picture, and they tend to receive disproportionate attention merely because they can be measured.

Partly because of these measurement difficulties, rewards and penalties in many not-for-profit enterprises are unrelated to individual performance. When pay increases and promotions are tied to seniority and external professional certification, such separation of rewards from performance reduces the impact of any centrally administered control system.

Such severe limitations on output controls lead many not-for-profit enterprises to rely on *control over inputs*—expenses and use of personnel—and over volume of activities. These controls on the use of resources and on rates of activity are typically treated as maximum limits, and there is little or no positive reward for meeting the control standards. Understandably, the personal response of people affected by these restraining controls is usually negative.

Individual managers do give attention to the quality and quantity of output. Certainly orchestra conductors evaluate results and take corrective action. But this kind of control is necessarily individualistic and subjective; especially in medium and large enterprises, it lacks the *consistency and predictability* which is so important in developing widely accepted norms of behavior. And if busy managers are hit-and-miss in their exercise of these controls, employees are likely to feel that corrective action is arbitrary and unwarranted.

For positive motivation, managers in not-for-profit enterprises must rely heavily on personal commitment of employees to shared goals. A great deal of such commitment does exist among professionals and others. Charismatic leaders and enterprise mystique enhance the commitment. This congruence of personal desires and enterprise goals enables many organizations to function despite rather crude and uninspiring control mechanisms.

Unfortunately, as enterprises grow larger this sense of commitment is hard to maintain. One reads daily of welfare agencies, schools, and hospitals having labor disputes and trouble with efficiency. The elite professions may feel strong commitment but the proletariat apparently finds less "joy in serving." It is here that the lack of a tradition of constructive control is taking its toll.

Conclusion

Our analysis to date suggests: (1) Treat managing of not-for-profit enterprises as a variant of the basic management model. (2) The not-for-profit character per se is too ambiguous to indicate the nature of such variations. (3) Instead, see if any or all of several constraints are present. (4) When such constraints are found, be cautious about relying on related managerial devices, examples of which are identified in the latter half of this article.

We have singled out constraining characteristics—intangible objectives, weak customer influence, professionalization, intrusion of resource contributors, limits on use of rewards, and reliance on a charismatic leader or enterprise mystique—and have illustrated how they may modify effective managerial practice. More study of both constraints and their impact is needed, study which we believe will lead to elaboration rather than refutation of the findings reported in this article.

2. Conceptual Dimensions of Library Management

Joseph Z. Nitecki

Introduction

Single pages of a loose-leaf file, scattered around, are of little if any value to anyone, except perhaps for bits of information contained on each page separately. However, when gathered together in a folder for an identified purpose, and organized in some meaningful fashion, the potential informational value of the total file is larger than the sum of information contained on individual pages in that file. It is the management of the file that increases the amount of its information. This can be accomplished by relating the organization of the documents in the file to the file's purpose, and by engaging staff in acquiring, maintaining, and servicing the content of the file to library patrons.

Similarly, what is essential to our study of management are not the objects, events, or activities in the library, but the relationships between them. It is not a part of the library administrator's duty, for example, to catalog books, or to interpret the library resources to its users. He or she is, however, responsible for relating these activities within the library organization in such a way that they will provide both efficient processing and effective services.

A relational approach to library management stresses a value-oriented type of management. It emphasizes the qualitative, and to some lesser degree quantitative, properties and processes of various components in library structure. It is a kind of relationship that can be planned, organized, and coordinated by library managers in their efforts to stimulate, direct, and evaluate library proc-

Reprinted from *Journal of Library Administration* 1:47–58 (Summer 1980).

esses and services. "It is relationships rather than facts that administrators (generically) can change. . . . The most crucial decisions the administrator can make or ignore are with regards to the relationships of the system itself and the role . . . he will take in relation to them."[1]

The present study identifies relationships between fundamental components of management in general, and formulates these relationships in a model expressing the specific managerial environment of library administration.[2] Important in this approach is the overall goal adapted from General Systems Theory to generalize relationships between the whole system and its parts, without destroying a unity of library or the plurality of its component parts.

Definition of Management

Generic Definition

"The most comprehensive definition views management as an integrating process by which authorized individuals create, maintain, and operate an organization in the selection and accomplishment of its aims."[3] This definition covers a wide spectrum of managerial issues and activities, relating them to all types of organizations and to all levels of administration, from the theoretical formulation of managerial principles to their practical applications. In defining management it is also desirable to point out some important and salient similarities among all types of management which are present as much in commercial, profit oriented organizations, as in social, not-for-profit institutions. In all such instances, a manager is responsible for the overall activities of the organization, by creating "a productive entity that turns out more than the sum of the resources put into it," by harmonizing "in every decision and action the requirements of immediate and long-range future," and by integrating all "resources into a viable growing organism."[4]

In essence, managing means "arranging" relations between energy producing things and events. The energy, in an Aristotelean sense, resides in certain configurations as a potential force. A change in these configurations may "actualize" the latent or potential energy into an active force. Hence, properly matched events or data affect each other's inner relational structure. A series of such changes constitutes a process, an activity. These are considered positive if they result in creating new things or data, negative if they weaken existing arrangements.

Each change, whether it affects spatial or temporal arrangements, introduces a novelty: some familiar arrangement or state of affairs has been changed into a new arrangement or set of relations. This results in a tension (e.g., physical instability or psychological concern, anticipation, excitement, etc.), which in a metaphorical sense creates new energy, accounting for new changes, reflected in some new activities.

For our purposes, we may distinguish between the following energy initiated changes: (1) familiar, physical changes, manifested in work actually performed (e.g., shelving books); (2) psychological changes, evident in motivation and persuasion (e.g., rewards and punishments); and (3) the most relevant to our study, philosophical or conceptual changes essential in coordination of managerial activities (e.g., planning to change an arrangement, or making decisions by choosing among available options).

Paramount in the nature of relational analyses of library operations is the concept of synergy, a process in which an aggregated, combined action of different elements together produces more effective or efficient results than each could produce by itself. Synergy accounts for a qualitative output higher than the initial input.[5] In one sense synergy of information constitutes the essence of library organization. It is, for example, often argued that processing and servicing of library resources is more productive if performed as an integral part of a library system, than if each activity would be performed independently of each other. This issue is relevant in considering decentralization of collections and services.

The relationship between information and energy has an added importance in the theory of librarianship, since information can be defined as a content of a message capable of triggering energy (action), while the message itself is a product of energy (physical energy in, for instance, writing a book, and mental energy in formulating the message). "The close relationship between energy and information came to light when it was understood that energy had to be spent in order to acquire information and information had to be used in order to collect energy and put it to use. Every bit of information has to be paid for in energy, and every increase in energy must be paid for in information."[6]

Definition of Library Conceptual Management

The literature on management sometimes fails to make a distinction between administration and operations of an institution, confusing the concept of managing an institution with the actual supervision of its operations. Traditionally defined, "operational activities are those in which effort is exerted directly on the materials with which the enterprise is concerned, while managerial activities are those in which effort is exerted in facilitating the operational activities. . . ."[7]

In our model, we distinguish between conceptual and supervisory activities of a manager, thus further limiting the concept to its relational aspects only. Direct control of operations, institutional politics, public relations, and other similar directorial activities are excluded from this conceptual definition. Conceptual management involves: (1) planning appropriate means-ends relations, (2) designing conditions for work performance by organizing relations between means and ends, and (3) modifying developed relationships in response to feedback obtained by monitoring the behavior of the conceptual relations in library practice.

On the other hand, supervising is an operational, applied management. In this stage: (1) planning involves activities such as scheduling the use of resources, (2) organizing implies using new processing methods and technologies, and (3) coordination becomes a direct control of operations. Emphasis in such applied management is on authority, manifested in a possession of power to govern library resources, including people, by making them work. The end objective of conceptual management is creation of new processes; the end objective of applied management is the product of these processes.

In library practice, a demarcation line between conceptual and applied or supervisory management is difficult to detect. In large libraries, with appropriate staff in the director's office providing necessary support in the performance of the supervisory responsibilities, the two functions are usually clearly identified. In a smaller or one-person library, on the other hand, the two aspects of management are more fused together. The diminishing distinction between conceptual and supervisory management reduces the perspectives necessary for successful leadership. It could result in a myopic conceptual management. Yet an overly pronounced separation between the two types of management can disrupt communication channels between the director and the library staff.

Finally, the overall mission of libraries as social institutions is to optimize knowledge among actual and potential library patrons, by making available and by interpreting to them all records of human knowledge. In turn, the function of a conceptual manager is to act as a catalyst, initiating new relationships within the library organization by creating conditions favorable to constructive relational processes. These functions are reflected in decision-making processes, which determine direction and extent of informational transfer.

Conceptual Model

As already mentioned, our model is based on a holistic view of management. It is considered as a synergic process of interrelating library resources, thus creating and expanding necessary conditions for library operations. It is a system approach, defined as a series of relationships between interacting, dynamic elements, organized together as an integrated, goal-oriented whole.[8] However,

the concept of system is not readily confined. It reveals and enriches itself only in the indirect illumination of the many clusters of analogous, modeled, and metaphoric expressions. The concept of system is the crossroad of the metaphors; ideas from all disciplines travel here . . . (making) possible the discovery of what is common among the most varied systems.[9]

The major impact of a system approach on the proposed model is its stress on the library system as a totality, and on its order and regularity. But most important, "the concept represents a way of thinking, rather than a precise methodology."[10] Its complexity is made up of a variety of autonomous elements, integrated in an elaborate network of relations, constantly interacting with its own environment. The library viewed as a system is thus conceived as a dynamic, mission-oriented, informational system, with "a set of rules and procedures designed to transform data into information."[11] The framework of a system approach allows us "to build up an understanding of the nature of library functioning incorporating layer upon layer of specificity, while at any stage of the analysis, being able to retain the 'totality' of the library as an organization serving the objective of delivering an information service to its community of users."[12]

Main Components of the System

The model depicted in figure 1 synthesizes the relationship between three main components of library management: (1) administrative instruments, the resources, (2) managerial functions, and (3) library goals.

The functions of planning, organizing, and coordinating provide basic conceptual activities in managing the library system,

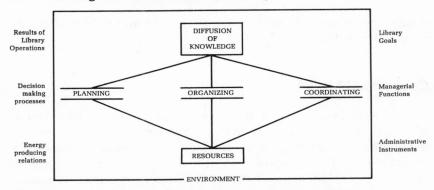

FIGURE 1. General blueprint of library administration

each affecting the total structure through the formulating and re-formulating of various relationships between library resources and goals. The model itself is embedded in and develops within a specific environment. Any changes in the external influences upon the library directly affect internal relationships between its component parts.

The relationships are considered at two closely interrelated levels: (a) intrinsic, inherent relations determining internal properties and values of each component in library organization, regardless of its relations to other components within the system; and (b) extrinsic, external relations between the components of a system, affecting the internal properties, qualities, and relations of each component.

Intrinsic Relations

1. Goals of library management. Dissemination of knowledge, as the library's overall goal, can be defined in terms of relationships between potential information contained in the informational carriers (such as books in the library collection) and the degree of satisfaction of the library patron's need for this information.

In libraries, goals are usually defined generically, allowing for adaptation to social changes. As a rule, libraries do not design, but merely adapt new technologies (e.g., automation). Nor do they generally initiate new social movements, but adjust to them (e.g., changes in book selection reflecting moral permissiveness). Confusing the library goals with those of the individual or his community creates a danger of goal displacement, mixing means with ends (e.g., computerization of processes at the expense of services), or imposing minority group preferences on the silent majority of the library public.

Furthermore, library goals formulated in a vacuum are intangible and unaccessible to conceptual interpretation or empirical analyses. They do become tangible, however, once they are related to their components in the library system.[13]

Thus, for example, broad goals stressing the importance of knowledge in the lives of citizens are too general to be of practical value. However, the same generic goals related to more specific library objectives, such as efficiency in book delivery to the patron, are more meaningful to the library administrator.

It is important that evaluation of library operations as a whole, or of any of its components, should always be made in terms of aspired goals. This requirement is well illustrated by a truism: that a highly specialized library collection, or a very sophisticated library service, is not necessarily always essential or desirable. Take, for example, the undergraduate library. Its resources are specifically designed for a definitive level of students; any in-depth expansion of its collection could destroy or jeopardize the library's primary objective.

This kind of goal-confusion is often experienced by directors of smaller academic libraries who may be pressured by enthusiastic, research-oriented professors for a collection containing everything in their highly specialized field. Another example of goal relevance to other library components is in the administrator's constant effort to achieve a

precise balance which tolerates minimal routine and maximum utility for the library program . . . A university librarian, for example, must provide for the maximum of freedom, convenience, and accessibility in the use, withdrawal, and exchange of books, records and fugitive materials, if the library is to serve the academic community. At the same time he works under the severe necessity of reducing the loss of books, of being economical in the use of staff and supplies, and efficient in ordering, cataloguing, and keeping accounts. The two functions may well be antithetical.[14]

2. Managerial functions. The functions of conceptual management consist of policy selection (planning), development of operational procedures (organizing available resources), and monitoring their behavior in an actual library environment (coordinating and mediating desired end results in actual operation).

The policies relate the actual with the desirable library system. Procedures interrelate activities of various library components into a systematic operation, while their implementation is coordinated with the needs of patrons in mind. Planning identifies library services and the methods by which they can be met. This function is affected by a number of factors, such as educational, cultural, and recreational needs of the library patrons, financial support by the parental institution, curricular activities in university libraries, and specialized subject needs in industrial libraries. Organizing library resources involves formulation of policies and procedures which determine the processing and servicing activities of the library. "Major tenets of organizational structure are to organize personnel, priorities, facilities, responsibilities, and authority in accordance with goals."[15] Coordination interrelates various factors of library operations. In contrast to the organizational function, it cannot be predetermined by rules or regulations, since "any change in the conditions (of operations) may bring about a change in the rules."[16] The coordinating function is thoroughly pragmatic, fully concentrating on end-results of library services.

3. *Library resources.* Library resources represent means available to libraries in accomplishing their goals. They consist of: (a) human resources of library staff, other employees of the organization, and to some extent the users of the library; (b) physical records, such as books and other formats of information carriers; and (c) auxiliary, yet equally important, resources such as the physical plant, furniture, computer hardware, or financial support. Internal relationships within each resource are determined by the resource's own characteristics.

The largest, most important, and perhaps most difficult to supervise is the area of human resources, which covers the whole range of issues, problems, and theories. This is not only the most dynamic but also the most sensitive library resource. It is easily affected by negative changes caused by internal relational imbalances. Thus, for example, job satisfaction may reflect library working conditions, salaries, or idiosyncrasies of individual staff members.

None of the difficulties will be resolved by merely rearranging the components of the library structure, or by reassigning an employee, until the negative relationships between affected components are modified. Searching for causes of problems usually means, in effect, searching for negative relations. Once these are identified, the rest is more a matter of physical, procedural, or organizational adjustment.

The three components of conceptual library management are fully interrelated among themselves. The goals of library operations are influenced by the impact of the content of the library collection, the profile of its users, and the resulting intensity of knowledge dissemination. Each change in the definition of goals, in turn, profoundly affects the planning, organizing, coordinating, and controlling of library operations. The planning function is not only determined by the nature of the organization, but it changes the structure of that organization by actually designing its future course, that is, by modifying existing objectives or by rearranging their priorities.

Processing library resources determines the value of the library itself by increasing or decreasing its utility, and by expanding or deteriorating services of its staff. It significantly impacts on planning and the mission of the library.

4. *Library environment.* The total interrelationship between the three components of managerial functions is directly influenced by the environment in which the organization operates. "Libraries do not function alone; they are dependent on agencies in their environment for support. And for this reason external factors are key determinants in shaping their goals and influencing their success."[17] Among the most frequent influences are the geographical, political, cultural, and economic pressures for inclusion or exclusion of certain titles in the library collection. Conversely, the impact of libraries on the environment is also an important factor; "this implies that, as the external environment changes, the nature of the library's impact on it will also change."[18] Hence, there are no two libraries that could be managed in exactly the same way, even if their resources, functions, and goals were somehow identical.

Extrinsic Relations

Extrinsic relations are of two kinds: spatial (e.g., books, people, and library buildings) and temporal (e.g., as illustrated by age and physical conditions of books, people, and library buildings).

Spatial relations determine the location of various components within the library system. They define physical boundaries of the organization. They also determine its structure, indicating the precise location of books on the shelves, the distribution of service stations throughout the library building, the identification of the relative position of each staff member on the organizational chart, and the like. In isolation, spatial relationships are fixed in time, freezing the organization into a closed, status quo system.

Temporal relations, on the other hand, reflect changes in the

library system. They define the scope of library activities and determine library functions. Processing library material, answering
reference questions, shelving books, and searching indexes are
some examples of temporal processes. Hence, the extent of temporal changes in the library organization determines the degree
of its dynamism. Temporal relations alone, separated from their
spatial components, are fluid and relatively intangible. They have
the potential of ultimately leading to organizational chaos.

Thus, looking at library organization from either of the two
vantage points alone, one would see that library system as either
a motionless structure or would perceive it in motion, resembling
blurring images of fast moving objects on a movie screen. What is
missing, of course, is a link between library structure and functions. It is provided by expanding one's own conceptual vision into
the third vantage point, the perception of library purpose. This
combined approach provides a three-dimensional concept of library system. Each dimension represents not only one of the three
major library subdivisions, but also three significant, although
partisan viewpoints: (1) procedural, involved in library spatial organization, (2) the contextual, concerned about library temporal
services, and (3) the conceptual, merging the other two approaches
into unified spatio-temporal processes and services and fulfilling
the overall mission of the library.[19]

Proceduralism deals with relationships among physical properties of library organization, which can be measured, experimented
with, multiplied, or divided. The common denominator to all library procedural activities is a model of a well functioning machine. All procedural activities are codified in a formal system of
rules and regulations, and are a favored subject of research among
scientists representing contemporary schools of scientific management. (Note, for example, the recent application of probability
statistics, games theory, queuing, and other mathematical approaches in the empirical study of library operations.)

Contextualism is involved in relationships between acts in
their context, adjusting, adapting, and mediating library services
in response to the constantly changing demands for them. Since
the human factor is central in this approach, contextualism is of
interest to psychologists and social and political scientists, many
belonging to human relation schools of management (e.g., McGreg-
or's X-Y theory, Maslow's hierarchy of needs, or Herzberg's hy-
giene and motivation factors).

The conceptual approach connects the library structure with
its functions by relating them to an ideal concept of what the li-

brary ought to be. It creates pressure for continuous improvement, aiming at an ideal library organization. Many studies in library history, philosophy, and comparative librarianship refer to the conceptual dimension of librarianship, since these allow for studying similarities and differences between different structures developed in different cultures, and for different purposes.

In figure 2, proceduralism is identified with library structure ("X" in the diagram). It determines the quantitative aspects of the library by concentrating on the size of the library collection, technology, organizational patterns, etc. Contextualism ("Y" in the diagram) represents library operations, expressed by temporal changes in services and collections. It evaluates the quality and effectiveness of services and it mediates conflicts and balances the contradictory pressures for services. Conceptualism ("Z" in the diagram) represents the coordinating factor, interrelating the structural processes and temporal services in terms of the institutional goals.

In a distinctively service-oriented, public library, its goals will closely relate to expanded library services, with less pronounced technological development ("Zy"). In a highly specialized technical or business library, the goals of the institution will be inclined toward the structural aspects of library organization, providing

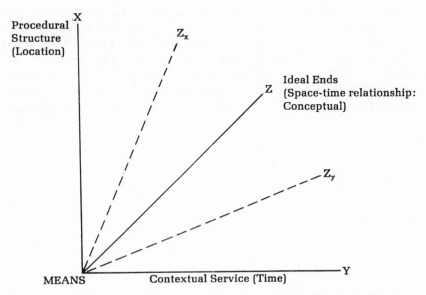

FIGURE 2. The three dimensionality of conceptual management

highly advanced informational technology with much less emphasis on user services ("Zx").

Hence, the interrelationship between procedural, contextual,
and conceptual axes of the library system determine the structural,
temporal, and ideal character of the library. None of the three dimensions by itself can fulfill the managerial requirements. A processing center, concentrating exclusively on processing library materials, is not a library, nor is an information agency answering
questions only, or a library consultant offering advice but not services. It is the interrelationship of the engineering, servicing, and
planning dimensions into one interdependent system, that makes
the library a unique information institution.

Summing Up

We hope that our model will be of value to other librarians,
by providing a conceptual framework for a theory of library management, suggesting a working hypothesis that could perhaps be
expanded and tested in future research. Meanwhile, it at least offers an overview of library management itself.

In the model, the library is presented as an organic system,
composed of many interdependent subsystems. The model's rationale is based on an ancient dialogue between Parmenidas' denial
of change and Heraclitus' argument for an ever-changing process.
We have attempted to combine the static library structure along
with its dynamic functions into one model. The desirable, the
actual, and the constantly modified concepts of library system
were interrelated so as to suggest that this integrative process expresses the essence of conceptual management of information.

3. The Management of Libraries as Professional Organizations

Miriam A. Drake

In his address to the American Library Association in 1975, Peter Drucker discussed the basic changes in librarianship which are coming about as a result of the shift away from "book worship" to the provision of information service.[1]

The discussion which follows assumes that libraries exist primarily to provide information services. The proposition advanced is that libraries, especially large libraries, are *not* providing effective information services to consumers because the goals and attitudes of librarians are in conflict with the goals of libraries as organizations. The focus here is on the roles of professionals and managers in service organizations, in general—to demonstrate that libraries and librarians share these problems with other organizations, serving the needs of a defined clientele. The role of library management and its responsibility for changing organizational goals of libraries are considered.

The change in the mission of librarianship has significant implications for the library professional, the library administrator, and the managers of organizations employing librarians. There are great differences emotionally, intellectually, and professionally between the concept of warehouse maintenance and that of information provision. The warehouse function involves sentimental attachment to books rather than the active intellectual commitment needed to provide effective information service.

A survey of the library literature reveals a consistent and

Reprinted from *Special Libraries* 68:181–86 (May-June 1977).

long-term concern with professionalism and what it means. Generally, the approach has been prosaic and provincial. The material fails to give any insight into the relationship of the library profession to other professions or to the larger organizations of which libraries are but one part. Little attention has been given to the view of the library as a service organization or to the function of management in the context of a service organization.

Librarians have a double need to understand management in the context of professional service organizations. First, in libraries which focus their objectives on information provision, the main working assets are library and information professionals. Contrast this with the traditional library in which the main assets are books and journals. Second, most libraries are part of and are funded by larger professional organizations, both not-for-profit and profit making. The emphasis here will be on the not-for-profit organization.

Librarians as Professionals

Wilensky states: "A profession is based on technical or systematic knowledge of a specific field which is acquired by its members through a prescribed course of training."[2] The profession determines both the content and standards of this training through its accrediting agency. In general, after the training period, professionals enter the marketplace to sell their time, training, and experience. They do not produce a product, they sell a service to those who do not possess this special knowledge. Customers and clients, whether associated with a hospital, law firm, or library, are buying knowledge they cannot supply for themselves. In library situations, the purchase decision may be based on choice or may be motivated by necessity. In medicine or welfare the decision, most often, is based on necessity.

Librarians differ from professionals in other fields in two significant respects—training and internship. Doctors, lawyers, and accountants go through a lengthy training period, often a formal internship or apprenticeship, and must pass formal examinations before they are admitted to practice. The librarian undergoes a very brief formal training period, no formal internship, and does not need to pass examinations before being allowed to practice. The librarian's internship begins when he or she takes the first job. Professional status for the librarian is not obtained when the degree is handed out or the exam is passed, as in law or medicine, but is earned over a period of time on the job.

Libraries as Professional Organizations

Anthony and Herzlinger write that professional service organizations are characterized by the dominance of professionals, lesser role of the marketplace, multiple objectives, politics, vague measures of output, and inadequate management controls.[3] To the client or the parent organization they may appear to be self-serving, expensive, and bureaucratic. Librarians often see these negative characteristics in their parent organizations but rarely perceive them in the library. Widespread budget cuts by parent institutions, whether corporations, universities, or municipalities, are clear evidence that libraries are viewed as expensive and nonessential relative to other services.

The unimportance attached to libraries is due, in part, to ineffective and unresponsive performance which has resulted from the dominance of traditional library professionals who view the library as an end in itself. Their goals are centered on books, journals, and the niceties of cataloging, not on the people being served. The user is often viewed as an ignorant patron who needs enlightenment rather than as a client who comes to the library for service.

Unfortunately, the brevity and content of training for librarianship reinforce this view. The new librarian leaves school with a missionary attitude toward service but has not been given sufficient training and experience necessary for competent and effective information work in real organizations. In addition, the new librarian approaches his/her first job with the attitude that client-oriented services are neither suitable nor feasible in large libraries, but can be performed only in small special libraries. Two significant articles have challenged this view: Bundy and Wasserman in 1968[4] and McAnnally and Downs in 1973.[5]

Doralyn Hickey has summarized the problem: "The special library model of client-centered information services is regularly envied but at the same time eschewed by the staff of other types of libraries who understand this model to be applicable only to small compact libraries."[6]

The formulation of client-centered objectives in large or small libraries is not a simple matter because most libraries serve two constituencies—funders and consumers. Obtaining the resources necessary to plan and implement customer service programs is contingent upon satisfying the needs of funders who may or may not be aware that the library user is a consumer rather than a supporting patron. The problem is exacerbated by funder demands for accountability and organization effectiveness which have no solid framework or context. These demands by funders often create outrage in the minds of professionals in all fields who believe that their goals, values, and activities should not be questioned.

Librarians working in large institutions no longer have a complete monopoly in information provision. They are operating in an environment which is growing increasingly competitive. In many areas library clientele have a choice; they may use a library which is institutionally based or they may purchase services from the growing number of private firms which are offering information services on a fee basis. These profit-making enterprises are providing valuable services for which busy physicians, professors, business persons, and others are willing to pay directly. Persons purchasing these services receive the information they seek, usually at a reasonable cost considering the time it would take for these individuals to be educated to find the information themselves. Kotler points out: "To the extent that consumers are able to choose among sellers, they will give their greatest support and loyalty to the seller who gives them the most satisfaction. Therefore the seller must strive to help consumers solve their real problems in a better way than competitors."[7] Currently, many libraries are unable to compete effectively because their goals are not centered on the "real problems" of consumers.

Profession vs. Organization

The professional, the organization, the market, and the relationships among them are important factors in analyzing current library management problems. Organizations have lives, values, and purposes of their own which may or may not be in congruence with the values and objectives of the professionals who work in organizations. Durbin and Springall believe ". . . the professional's training, intellectual inclination, and emotional composition tend to make him seek finite solutions to all questions. He categorically rejects compromise, as being unprofessional and therefore unsatisfactory. The organizational man, on the other hand, is constantly forced to utilize the techniques of compromise. . . ."[8] Bucher and Stelling make the same point: ". . . the career of the professional, both within and without the organization, depends on his ability to control his working conditions, whereas in other organizations one's career may depend on how well he can accept and work within the conditions set by the organization."[9] The problem as it relates to librarianship has been stated by Bundy and Wasserman: "As is equally true of professionals who practice in formal organizations, librarians are faced with conflicts inherent in the incongruence between professional commitments on the one hand, and employee requirements on the other."[10]

The differences between organizational and professional goals and values produce major conflict in organizations, especially those which consist of a number of professional groupings. For example, in universities and teaching hospitals the disparate values, attitudes, and operating modes often create insurmountable barriers to the achievement of the organization's objectives and produce continuing friction between librarians, teachers, doctors, and management.

In many libraries, the lack of interest in the life of the organization is reflected in the inability of the librarians to relate to the parent organization's goals, preoccupation with internal politics, and inability to adapt or change. At library conferences, one hears many discussions about patrons and service; however, librarians rarely discuss the specifics of service in terms of the consumer. The same situation, no doubt, exists at medical and legal conferences where procedures are discussed endlessly with little regard to satisfying the real needs of patients and clients. Happily, there are exceptions in the library field, ranging from public libraries which have instituted consumer information services to the corporate library which produces a variety of information products and research services for the corporate staff.

The Role of Management

The role of managers in not-for-profit service organizations is growing increasingly complex as professionals demand a greater voice in decision-making, funders ask for more specific accountability, and clients complain about officious and unresponsive service. Managers are accused of being rigid and dictatorial on the one hand and ineffective on the other. The squeeze on library management is coming from three sides: institutional management, clients, and library staff. University, government, corporate, and other institutional managements are demanding that the library justify itself by providing benefits in excess of cost.

Librarians, in pleading for more participative management, often are seeking greater freedom to pursue their professional ideals while clinging to the safe operating modes of the past. The traditional library ideal, as contrasted with the special model, generally does not satisfy the information needs of parent organizations or of library users. Similar situations occur in hospitals and law offices when the last person to be considered in operations or planning is the patient or client.

Given the conflict between professionals and the organization, the most difficult problem for management in Drucker's words, ". . . is how to imbue the staff with a sense of mission that over-arches individual professional goals—to integrate them into an institution in which their professional goals are secondary."[11] Achievement of this integration is likely to be a painful process for both management and library professionals; however, it is essential if libraries are to become effective service organizations. Goal congruence necessitates the abandonment of tradition, encouragement of innovation, and a commitment by the people working in the organization to change their behavior and attitudes.

The responsibility for providing direction and leadership in any organization is the major task of managers. Library managers, especially those who feel frustrated and insecure because of internal pressures, need to be made aware that they are responsible for leadership. Their failure to give direction and take up the challenge of customer-centered services exacerbates the severity of the pressures. It appears that in many libraries the managerial mode is to cope on a day-to-day basis without contemplating the library's purpose, future, or accomplishments. The major excuse offered by some library managers is that library performance and output cannot be measured; therefore, management cannot set goals and measure their achievement. Given the library professional's lack of motivation to change and the inertia of management, it is unlikely that significant change in most libraries will occur until managers realize that they are responsible for the outcome of professionals' work in terms of organizational goals focused on satisfied customers.

The Manager's Burden

In order to fully assume this responsibility, managers need to free themselves of the daily routines and concentrate on appropriate questions and outcomes. They must define the library's goals and provide direction to library professionals and staff to achieve those goals. It should not be inferred that a dictatorial management style is being advocated. On the contrary, if professionals and managers are to achieve a meaningful existence for the library, librarians need to be integrated into the decision-making process.

They should be made accountable for daily operating decisions which affect the achievement of the library's goals. In addition, they should be active contributors to the formulation of short- and long-range plans. This type of participation can actively involve the staff in the life of the library while preserving the responsibilities of management.

The change to customer-centered services in libraries carries both burdens and risks for management. The major burden is management control which necessitates monitoring the system to see that resources are obtained and used effectively to achieve the library's goals. Management also has the burden of evaluating the performance of librarians and rewarding those persons who contribute positively to the organization as well as those who contribute to the library profession.

Change in any area of life involves risk and uncertainty. An innovative service concept, which looked exciting on paper, may fail in practice. Professionals in all fields very likely will resist any change in an organization which threatens their autonomy and security. McAnnally and Downs, in their study of university library directors, observed, "It may seem strange that the Director should be under attack from his own staff, or fail to receive badly needed support in relations with the administration and faculty, but it is so in many cases."[12]

Conclusions

The survival of large libraries in their present form is very much in doubt. Few organizations can outlast protracted conflicts between funders, managers, staff, and clientele. The manager of a large library, who is barely coping with current conditions, must plan and implement changes which will provide a purposeful existence for the library as an organization.

The "special library model" in which the objectives of the library are focused on the information needs of specific constituencies or clients, provides a framework for change. If applied carefully in large libraries, the special library model could produce satisfied customers, interested funders, and a challenging work environment for library professionals.

The successful implementation of the model is contingent upon three main elements—managerial commitment, leadership, and the integration of library professionals into the organization. Managerial commitment is the most essential factor in effecting

change. If the manager does not truly believe that change is necessary and is not dedicated to a sustained effort to implement client-
centered services in the library, the activities initiated by management become perfunctory and produce greater frustration.

Library management must demonstrate its leadership by sharing authority with library professionals and working with them in
merging their professional goals into the library's organizational
goals. In addition, management must support its professionals by
allocating its scarce resources to facilitate the achievement of library goals.

The current frustration experienced by library professionals,
clients, managers, and funders can be replaced by satisfaction.
The large library can be changed but first it must focus its mission
on people and give up the warehouse.

4. Administration: Which Way— Traditional Practice or Modern Theory?

Charles Martell

Where communication is perception, information is logic. As such, information
is purely formal and has no meaning. It is impersonal rather than personal.[1]

When the book was preeminent and unchallenged, the function of the library in society was relatively clear. Events unfolded
rather slowly and the library profession was allowed the luxury
of adapting gradually. As an organization, the library conformed
to the traditional mold. It was, in essence, machinelike. "A properly designed administrative machine has correctly assigned positions and levels of authority and definite rules exist for ensuring

Reprinted from *College & Research Libraries* 33:104–12 (Mar. 1972).

the correctness."[2] This mechanistic approach tended to ignore differences between individual and organizational goals.

The book is no longer preeminent nor unchallenged. Technological developments have helped to create an environment wherein "acceleration, diversity and novelty" are the rule, and gradual adaptation has become inadequate as a generalized response to change. As Lipetz suggests, the entire fabric of traditional library practices and procedures borders on the state of chaos.[3]

Outmoded procedures are but one small part of a far more general, far more complex malaise, i.e., the library's apparent inability to respond to the demands of an external reality. The library is not unique. Technological and societal developments have placed many organizations in a similar position.

For years studies in the management and behavioral sciences have dealt with the problem of rapid change and its effect on the viability of organizations. "The accelerative thrust forces time into a new perspective in our lives. It compels us to make and break our relationships with the environment at a faster and faster tempo."[4] Both individuals and organizations are caught in this seemingly endless spiral.

An administrator who can successfully integrate the often conflicting demands of employer and employee within a responsive organizational structure has come a long way toward insuring the survival of that institution, whether it be in business, government, or education. However, there are many elements inherent in traditional management practice which militate against such responsiveness. In the following discussion, traditional practice and theory will be contrasted with certain aspects of modern management and behavioral theories; however, modern theories are frequently unsuccessful in practice because they are largely incompatible with traditional forms of organization and managerial styles. Awareness of this dichotomy should help the administrator gain a new perspective into the opportunities and shortcomings existing in his own organization and in his own leadership style.

This article will focus on three specific areas: (1) leadership; (2) group processes; and (3) organizational structure.

Leadership

Traditional managerial philosophy bases leadership on the principles of control, direction, and planning. The organization itself is structured to facilitate this arrangement. Within this structure, the manager manipulates his employee by administering rewards and punishments in a systematic way. According to McGregor (see list of suggested readings which follows this article) natural human tendencies are considered antithetical to regular work requirements or, at best, are merely ignored. Managerial tasks are constructed so as to counteract those internal forces which are not directly supportive of the goals of the organization.[5]

Throughout the twentieth century, management theory has incorporated certain findings derived from the behavioral sciences. The current emphasis upon the individual as a social being rather than as an isolated phenomenon has refined management theory; the once prominent view that saw man as a mechanical entity has changed. Management practice, however, has failed to keep in step with these developments. When defined within the context of table 1, management practice is primarily "custodial" in nature. While most research today is being conducted at the "supportive" and "collegial" levels, managers have progressed only slightly from the "custodial" toward the "supportive" area. A manager with an affinity toward a supportive style would frequently find himself handicapped by practical organizational constraints. Unfortunately, some of these so-called practical constraints result from

TABLE 1. Four Models of Organizational Behavior

	Autocratic	Custodial	Supportive	Collegial
Depends on:	Power	Economic resources	Leadership	Mutual contributions
Managerial orientation:	Authority	Material rewards	Support	Integration & teamwork
Employee orientation:	Obedience	Security	Performance	Responsibility
Employee psychological result:	Personal dependency	Organizational dependency	Participation	Self-discipline
Employee needs met:	Subsistence	Maintenance	High-order	Self-realization
Performance result:	Minimum	Passive cooperation	Awakened drives	Enthusiasm
Morale measure:	Compliance	Satisfaction	Motivation	Commitment to task & team

Adapted from Keith Davis, *Human Relations of Work: The Dynamics of Organizational Behavior* (3rd ed.; New York: McGraw-Hill, 1967), p.480. Used with permission of McGraw-Hill Book Company.

managerial perceptions poorly attuned to contemporary environmental and societal developments.

The popularity of labels is not restricted to the area of management practice. They have also been used to characterize a particular manager's style of leadership. McGregor lists three categories of managerial styles: "hard, soft, and firm but fair." These
categories are directly related to the Blake Managerial Grid, which
is based on a manager's perception of his own style. The Grid
theory suggests that there are two major variables affecting management style: (1) concern for production, and (2) concern for
people. Concern for production and people are the two coordinates
on the Managerial Grid. As each coordinate ranges in intensity
from 1 to 9, it is possible to have eighty-one different managerial
styles. For example, the team theory of management (maximum
concern for production and people) would be (9,9) on the Grid.

Managerial styles are frequently unsuccessful because they
ignore the significance of intrinsic rewards and punishments. Intrinsic rewards are "inherent in the activity itself: the reward is
the achievement of the goal. Intrinsic rewards cannot be directly
controlled externally, although characteristics of the environment
can enhance or limit the individual's opportunities to obtain them.
Thus, achievements of knowledge or skill, of autonomy, of self-
respect, of solutions to problems, are examples."[6] No one style of
leadership is appropriate to all situations, extrinsic or intrinsic
reward systems notwithstanding. Each manager is unique and this
will always be reflected in his style. Nevertheless, rapid change
creates conditions in which the manager will have a greater likelihood of success if he uses an "optimizing" rather than a "controlling" leadership style.[7]

How, then, can managers change their style of leadership?

I have come to believe that the presentation of facts and theories, utilizing
conventional intellectual methods of training and education, may often be ineffective when the subject matter involved is related to the perceptions of
managers with respect to their own ideas and to the nature of man. The most
fruitful methods are those which utilize direct experience of a not too threatening kind, a safe environment for the open examination of issues, opportunities to test new behaviors, and positive reinforcement of such changes as
do occur.[8]

Summary

In traditional management theory, an administrator exercises
his leadership role by means of control and direction whereby important psychological needs of the employee are ignored. This

often results in a mechanistic form of organization. Thus, leadership is ill equipped to cope with rapid change, since it must rely on prearranged signals rather than on the adaptive ability of the employee. Concern for production is the primary concern of the administrator in a mechanistic organization. Contemporary management and behavioral theories treat the organization as a biological entity. Administrators using an optimizing leadership style are more attuned to modern theory, which both accepts and seeks to encourage employee motivation.

Group Processes

The tempo of contemporary existence is forcing management to consider ways of involving the employee in the attainment of organizational goals. Slater and Bennis state in their article entitled "Democracy Is Inevitable" that "democracy becomes a functional necessity whenever a social system is competing for survival under conditions of chronic change," but that for "adaptability to change conditions, for rapid acceptance of a new idea, for flexibility in dealing with novel problems" and for "generally high morale and loyalty, the more egalitarian or decentralized type seems to work better."[9] Coordination of individual and organizational goals is one important step in the creation of an "egalitarian" organization. The mechanistic approach to management is ill suited for the task since it assumes that all but a few workers are unmotivated. Seen from this point of view, the principle of involvement is farcical. Argyris believes that "the old forms are going to be more effective for the routine, noninnovative activity that requires little, if any, internal commitment by the participant."[10]

The problem of unmotivated workers is based on a misconception which is common to most managers:

How do you motivate people? . . . You don't. Man is by nature motivated. He is an organic system, not a mechanical one. . . . This is the sense in which the behavioral scientist distinguishes between an organic and a purely mechanical theory of nature.[11]

Involvement will tend to release motivational forces inhibited by traditional management practice. It is only after the employee recognizes that his actions will lead to a degree of self-fulfillment that he will feel a sense of commitment toward the achievement of organizational goals. There is every reason to believe that this will have a positive effect on performance (see figure 1).

Participation in the decisions which affect his work situation

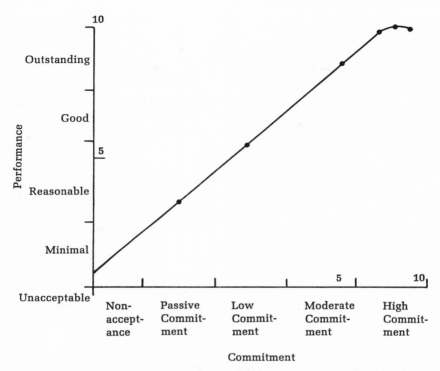

From *The Professional Manager* by Douglas McGregor. Ed. by Caroline McGregor and Warren G. Bennis (New York: McGraw-Hill, 1967). Fig. 3, p.128. Used with permission of McGraw-Hill Book Company.

FIGURE 1. Relation of commitment to performance

is one means of obtaining individual commitment. Peter Drucker in his comments about the communication process and its traditional influence on motivation shows why participation is a prerequisite for commitment:

> For centuries we have attempted communication downward. This, however, cannot work, no matter how hard and how intelligently we try. It cannot work, first because it focuses on what we want to say. It assumes in other words that the utterer communicates. But we know that all he does is utter. Communication is the act of the recipient . . . all one can communicate downward are commands, that is, prearranged signals. One cannot communicate downward anything connected with understanding let alone motivation.[12] The start of communications in organizations must be to get the intended recipient himself to try to communicate.[13]

Group processes through dynamic interaction have the potential to bring the individual employee into the communication process. In spite of overwhelming evidence to support the notion of group participation, however, difficulties are frequently encountered in actual work day situations.

Interpersonal Barriers to Effective Group Participation

Behavioral scientists romp through management councils. Extemporizing on modern techniques for involving the individual in the accomplishment of organizational goals, they have created considerable interest among many administrators who feel that their organizations have shown themselves incapable of adequately anticipating the form of future markets, the effects of technology, and the specialized interests of the community served by that organization. However, administrators implementing programs suggested by the behavioral scientists often find themselves thoroughly frustrated by the results. Participatory management, T-groups, D-groups, and a host of other laboratory-approved techniques have usually failed to meet management's subjective criteria for effectiveness. A number of recent studies have explained these failures primarily in terms of interpersonal barriers, and organizational structure.

At the upper levels the formal design tends to require executives who need to manage an intended rational world, to direct, control, reward and penalize others, and to suppress their own and others emotionality. Executives with these needs and skills tend to be ineffective in creating and maintaining effective interpersonal relationships; they fear emotionality and are almost completely unaware of ways to obtain employee commitment that is internal and genuine. This results in upper level systems that have more conformity, mistrust, antagonism, defensiveness and closedness than individuality, trust, concern and openness.[14]

In the group process there must be some balance between emotionality and the demand for effective participation. Unfortunately, many individuals exhibit little patience with emotionality. This is especially true of administrators who are accountable for group productivity. Groups which do not immediately conform to expectations are categorized as unsuccessful and relegated to the administrators' mental dumpheap, or in rare instances disbanded. A great deal of time and patience is necessary on all sides before a group can even begin to exhibit the first signs of true productivity. Openness and trust cannot be secured overnight.

Summary

Social conditions are forcing administrators to consider ways to involve the employee in the attainment of organizational goals.

Group participation is one technique that is frequently used. Unfortunately, administrators participating in these groups are usually conditioned to a mechanistic style whereby openness, trust, and emotionality are suppressed. The absence of these qualities causes group participation to be no more than tolerably effective. Democratic styles of organization which recognize and seek to encourage employee motivation are inevitable, in spite of the fact that most organizations still adhere to more traditional forms.

Organizational Structure

Organizations are created for the purpose of exploiting a perceived need. People are grouped into various formal patterns or relationships in order to provide the most effective ordering of resources. According to traditional organization theory, this is best achieved: when workers are closely supervised, when workers and/or their superiors report to and take directions from one and only one person, and when those individuals with authority are held accountable for their actions and decisions. Such a structure lends support to a managerial philosophy which views the worker as unmotivated and mechanical.

The traditional structure is best suited to those organizations in which it is possible for the top administrator to be effectively knowledgeable about most aspects of his industry, where markets are relatively stable, and where the impact of technology is inconsequential. Frequent communication between different levels in such organizations is not essential, since it is assumed that change occurs slowly and habitual patterns of response are well ingrained.

During the 1950s, behavioral scientists offered management a systematic body of research findings which many felt would cure the ills affecting most organizations. Group participation would, if applied correctly, encourage employee involvement, motivation, and commitment. This in turn would enable individuals to cope with a rapidly changing organizational environment, and hopefully would stimulate more creativity and innovation. When group participation methods faltered, numerous studies were undertaken to determine why. The study of organizational structure and design has provided some useful insights.

What the behavioral scientists overlooked was the complex nature of an organization's internal environment. Many administrators initiating participatory management functioned within settings or structures which were inherently authoritarian. The organization was mechanistic, and it supported similar attitudes among its administrators. Accordingly, when participatory management was undertaken, the primary emphasis was still on changing technology rather than on individual needs. Besides leading to many failures, this subjugation of human considerations to those of the organization demonstrated a continuing misconception of man's nature.

The external environment has finally pushed itself right into the boardrooms. Management has been witnessing wholesale disenchantment with the traditional structure of its institutions. Consequently, the study of organizational structure and design has become a popular pastime. Unique structures have been developed to answer specific problems. Likert's "linking pin" structure, the "Matrix" concept, and the "ad hoc-racy" or transitional task group are the best known. They feature free flowing systems of communication and more effective utilization of specialized knowledge. Unfortunately, they all share one basic weakness: relative inflexibility. They are merely limited types of response to a particular set of circumstances.

Lawrence and Lorsch in *Organization and Environment* present a situational approach to organizational design called the "contingency" theory of organization.[15] "Their general point is that there is no 'one best way' to organize, but that different companies in different industries require different kinds of organization structures at different times."[16]

The process of designing an organizational structure appropriate to a particular situation is extremely difficult. The number of variables to be examined, coupled with the complexity of the unit, precludes the creation of a "best way" structure. Three important variables to consider are: external environment, internal environment, and interaction between the two. On the surface this listing appears somewhat ludicrous. Yet how can one ever hope to reduce the size of these variables to manageable proportions? Obviously, one cannot cope with their full dimensions. The favored approach is to attempt an isolation of the most important factors. The state of the national economy certainly has an observable influence on the budgetary constraints of many organizations. Technology alone can have a distinct impact on the structure of viable institutions. Leadership styles can be determined, and clearcut suppositions based on these styles enumerated.

Since the variables affecting an organization are in constant flux, many planners are trying to create individualized, adaptive structures. Some are even ignoring formal charts—a radical event to say the least. The degree of flux is a crucial element in planning for change. Some industries are relatively static. Others are in a state of dynamic growth. It is important to recognize the vital factors. An industry is often static merely because perception of its potential has been inhibited. The railroad is a classic example of an industry which failed to develop as a viable medium of transportation because it chose to ignore the potential for expansion into other areas of transportation. An organization must be able to release the creative energies of its personnel. A sick, static industry, unable to free itself from outmoded practices, stifles the very energies which can lead to revitalization.

Studies in the design and structure of organizations have yet to make a significant impact on managerial practice. This is due in part to the traditional gap between practice and theory. More important is the magnitude of change required for an organization to restructure itself. Every function, division, and human relationship is affected. For this reason, widespread restructuring is unusual. It is more common to find administrators fiddling with their formal, organizational charts. To many, minimizing loss appears safer than maximizing profit.

Management is not riding a calm sea. As affirmed earlier, several developments are underway which seriously threaten traditional institutions. The aura of rapid change and acceleration has stimulated an entire bevy of prophets. The "knowledge worker" introduces difficulties of another kind. ". . . Knowledge has become the central 'factor of production' in an advanced developed economy . . . to make knowledge productive will bring about changes in job structure, careers and organizations as drastic as those which resulted in the factory from the application of Scientific Management to manual operations."[17] Employees classified as knowledge workers are likely to be influenced by technical competence "rather than on the vagaries of personal whim or prerogatives of power."[18] Inevitably this will lead to a direct confrontation with traditional structural approaches. A letter written in 1750 by the Earl of Chesterfield for his son contained a truth which lasted more than two hundred years: "Knowledge may give weight, but accomplishments give lustre, and many more people see than weigh." If knowledge has indeed become the central factor of production, however, then those who neglect to revise the Earl's sentiment will gain little wisdom and less lustre.

Summary

Knowledge as a central factor of production creates difficulties for the typical mechanistic organization. It is possible that technical competence based on knowledge will become more valued and respected than personal power and authority. Where effective group participation is hampered by organizational structure, changes in that structure will be called for. Anticipatory measures may become a matter of survival. Administrators must try to obtain a clear perception of their industry in order to develop organizational goals and time orientations appropriate to their environment. New approaches to organizational structure stress the need for adaptability and flexibility.

Conclusions?

There are none. One should not tidy up perceptions. Hopefully they remain amorphous, and competently so. And yet . . . a few months ago I read an article in *Newsweek*, "New Architecture: Building for Man" by Douglas Davis. It gave me a new awareness: a mental connector between the substance of this discussion and the field of architecture . . . and further. Perceptions of structure, whether of organizations, buildings, or people, must be perceptions of life. Idealistic? But of course!

"Behind the new architecture is no one design concept or social ideology but the basic idea that structures must be part of the social organism that includes people and what they do as individuals, families and communities. . . . The new architects see that promise in the beauty of flexible forms that inspire, enhance and adjust to the changing energies of human life."[19]

Suggested Readings

Argyris, Chris. "Today's Problems with Tomorrow's Organization." *Journal of Management Studies* 31–55 (Feb. 1967).
   Interpersonal barriers to effective management.
Bennis, Warren G., ed. *American Bureaucracy.* New York: Aldine Publishing, 1970.
   Innovation, change, and need for new patterns of organization.
Drucker, Peter. *Age of Discontinuity.* New York: Harper & Row, 1969.
   A new age, new organizations—essential.
Lawrence, Paul R., and Jay W. Lorsch. *Organization and Environment: Managing Differentiation and Integration.* Homewood, Ill.: Richard D. Irwin, Inc., 1967.
   A comparative study of several organizations—get your feet wet.
McGregor, Douglas. *The Professional Manager.* New York: McGraw-Hill, 1967.
   Finely balanced presentation—a must.

Mockler, Robert J. "Situational Theory of Management." *Harvard Business Review* 146–55 (May–June 1971).
   Generalized update of latest developments.
"What's New?—In Personnel Theory and Practice." Reported by the 1970 ASPA Professional Information Committee, *Personnel Administrator* 9–16 (Jan.–Feb. 1971).
   Discusses shift in values—useful bibliography.

Additional Readings

The thousands of books and articles that address either the topic of management in general or some specific part of the management process present an often confusing array of choices to a would-be reader of management literature. An important starting point in any examination of this literature should be Koontz's "The Management Theory Jungle Revisited" (*Academy of Management Review*, April 1980), in which a systematic framework for the classification of management theory as represented in the literature is offered; a much briefer examination of management literature is provided by Kipp's "Management Literature for Librarians" (*Library Journal*, 15 January 1972).

In attempting to formulate a systematic understanding of management, several questions should be addressed. What is management—is it an art, a science, a technology, or some combination of these? Can a general model of management be constructed? Is management as a concept applicable to all kinds of organizations? In *An Introduction to Management* (Wiley, 1978), Litterer discusses management as a social necessity, noting that in his view, it is indeed a "third culture"—the connection between the sciences and the humanities that revolves around action to accomplish goals. Magee, on the other hand, views management as a technology, or "art in the application of scientific knowledge."[1] In "Management: An Evolving Technology" (*Human Systems Management* 1, 1980) this author suggests that both the art and science sides of management are gradually being refined as the management process is carried out. Taking a generalist approach, Harrison

("Towards a General Model of Management," *Journal of General Management*, Winter 1979/1980) conceptualizes a possible model of management that delineates the relationship of key elements in the management of formal organizations to environmental, management process, performance, and organizational constraints. Especially useful to this book of readings is Harrison's illustration of the relationship of the management process to the other elements in the overall management model.

Since this collection of readings is concerned with library management, it is necessary to concentrate a review of additional management literature first on the larger, nonprofit organizational setting, and then on general examinations of library management. An appropriate beginning for a review of management applications in a particular setting can be found in Fottler's "Is Management Really Generic?" (*Academy of Management Review*, January 1981). This article forms a background for Drucker's essay on "Performance in the Service Institution" (*Management: Tasks, Responsibilities, Practices*, Harper & Row, 1974) and Anthony's "Can the Nonprofit Organization Be Well Managed?" (in Borst and Montana, *Managing Nonprofit Organizations*, AMACOM, 1977). In this and a later article written for libraries ("Managing the Public Service Institution," *College and Research Libraries*, January 1976), Drucker explores the nature of the "service" institution, and elaborates on why many service organizations do not perform; likewise, Anthony's essay identifies a number of reasons for the lack of good management in nonprofit organizations, including absence of a profit measure and competition, tradition, and weak governing boards. Other views of nonprofit management are included in Borst and Montana's *Managing Nonprofit Organizations* (AMACOM, 1977) and Zaltman's *Management Principles for Nonprofit Agencies and Organizations* (AMACOM, 1979).

In the library setting, several books provide an overview of management, including Rizzo's *Management for Librarians: Fundamentals and Issues* (Greenwood, 1980), Evans's *Management Techniques for Librarians* (Academic Press, 1976), and Stueart and Eastlick's second edition of *Library Management* (Libraries Unlimited, 1981). A brief review of management issues and selected readings for the past decade is offered in *Library Management in the 1970s: Summary of Issues and Selected Bibliography* (Association of Research Libraries, 1977). Several essay collections also contribute to this general overview, including *Current Concepts in Library Management* (Libraries Unlimited, 1979), Shimmon's *A Reader In Library Management* (Linnet Books, 1976), *Advances* in *Library Administration and Organization* (JAI Press, 1982), *Library Management Without Bias* (JAI Press, 1981), *Library Management in Review* (Special Libraries Association, 1981), and the volumes of *Studies in Library Management* (Shoe String Press). Gardner's examination of managerial processes and systems in "Current Concepts of Management" (*Current Concepts in Library Management*, Libraries Unlimited, 1979) is of particular note, as is volume 6 of the *Studies in Library Management* which highlights the evolution of library management during the last two decades. *Library Leadership: Visualizing the Future* (Oryx Press, 1982) offers twelve original predictions of trends for the future, showing how these trends may affect all types of libraries and what kind of leadership is needed to manage change.

Management in each of the major types of libraries is also covered separately by numerous works. These include Altman's *Local Public Library Administration* (ALA, 1980), Rochell's *Wheeler and Goldhor's Practical Administration of Public Libraries* (Harper & Row, 1981), Jenkins's *Management of a Public Library* (JAI Press, 1980), Rogers and Weber's *University Library Administration* (Wilson, 1971), Lyle's *The Administration of the College Library* (Wilson, 1974), Allen and Allen's *Organization and Administration of the Learning Resources Center in the Community College* (Shoe String Press, 1973), Strable's *Special Libraries: A Guide for Management* (SLA, 1975), Prostanto and Prostanto's *The School Library Media Center* (Libraries Unlimited, 1977), and Hicks and Tillin's *Managing Multimedia Libraries* (Bowker, 1977). While these are only a few of the works available that specifically relate to library management, they do provide overviews of the various functions of management in particular types of libraries.

A number of articles also explore the general nature of management in the library setting. In an informal address, Baldwin identifies and explores the functions of management ("Managerial Competence and Librarians," *PLA Bulletin*, January 1971). Heinritz incorporates a general management theory into the library framework in "Modern Scientific Management in the Academic Library" (*Journal of Academic Librarianship*, July 1975). Waller reviews the functions of management and links improper library management practices to managerial anxieties ("Libraries, Managers, and People," *Special Libraries*, September 1975). And Ochs presents an integrated view of modern management theory as it applies to the library setting in "A Holistic View of Modern Management Theory" (*Southeastern Librarian*, Fall 1976).

The role of the manager in the library management process

can also be examined through the literature. Mintzberg ("The Manager's Job," *Harvard Business Review*, July–August 1975) offers a unique view of the manager's job as a set of roles that form an integrated whole; DeGennaro supports this view as being a realistic assessment of the library manager's job ("Library Administration and New Management Systems," *Library Journal*, 15 December 1978). In two other *Library Journal* articles, Smith ("Do Libraries Need Managers?" 1 February 1969) and McClure ("Library Managers: Can They Manage? Will They Lead?" 15 November 1980) explore additional dimensions of the manager's role in the library. Edwards examines the professional-managerial dichotomy that influences the practice of management in the library setting ("Management of Libraries and the Professional Functions of Librarians," *Library Quarterly*, April 1975).

Finally, in examining the process of management in libraries, it is important to look toward the future. Although Odiorne's "A Management Style for the Eighties" (*University of Michigan Business Review*, March 1978) is directed at the leadership of organizations, many of the ten major elements highlighted as being especially significant relate to other facets of the management process. In the library context, Galvin suggests critical issues that must be recognized and resolved if the library management process is to retain its vitality ("Beyond Survival; Library Management for the Future," *Library Journal*, 15 September 1976).

Decision-Making and Planning

    Decision-making and planning are becoming an increasingly important part of the library management process. Attention to both of these management functions as they concern specific services and activities has long been a part of the library setting. But the complex and often turbulent internal and external library environment (as described in chapters 1 and 4), and the increasing financial problems that libraries face, make management decisions more difficult than in the past. The library's planning of long-range directions is becoming an increasingly important vehicle for reducing uncertainty and coping with the "inherent ambiguity" of management itself.[1] Planning, of course, cannot solve all of the library's problems, for we "can only plan for the surprises we know about;"[2] but planning can provide a framework within which the library can operate and decisions can be made under both short- and long-term conditions.

    The relationship between decision-making and planning is an interdependent one. In this sense, planning may be viewed as a special type of decision-making, in that "planning is clearly a decision-making process; but, equally clearly, not all decision-making is planning."[3] Decision-making takes place during many other library activities aside from the planning function; at the same time, planning is dependent upon decisions made during these times.

The readings in this chapter reflect both the growing importance of decision-making and planning in the library setting, and the interdependence of these two management functions. The readings cover both general and specific topics related to the design, development, and implementation of decision-making and planning processes in the library environment. Three selections have particular relevance to decision-making as it applies to library management. Because both decision-making and planning are process oriented, Drucker's classic article outlining the necessary elements in making an effective decision has been included. His emphasis on a structured, sequential process that includes problem classification and definition, identification of boundary conditions, and provisions for action and feedback is as relevant to the planning process as it is to decision-making. Following this discussion of process, Taylor's article identifies psychological variables that impede decision-making and planning, and Prentice provides an illustration of problem-solving in the context of library financial management.

Initiating and implementing of planning and decision-making processes is often difficult in organizations. In his article, which succinctly summarizes the literature on this topic, Taylor examines the psychological barriers to planning, including perceptual processes, cognitive ability, motivation, and values. In a more library-specific examination, Davis identifies self-initiated barriers to planning in the library setting, and suggests a strategy for implementing and improving the planning of change in the library. His analysis of "stakeholder management" is particularly useful for readers who wish to develop new ways of identifying major influences on the library's direction. Finally, because financial problems are so critical in libraries, an essay on economic decision-making has been chosen to illustrate the application of the decision-making and planning processes in libraries.

5. The Effective Decision

Peter F. Drucker

The effective decision results from a systematic process, with clearly defined elements, that is handled in a distinct sequence of steps.

Effective executives do not make a great many decisions. They concentrate on what is important. They try to make the few important decisions on the highest level of conceptual understanding. They try to find the constants in a situation, to think through what is strategic and generic rather than to "solve problems." They are, therefore, not overly impressed by speed in decision-making; rather, they consider virtuosity in manipulating a great many variables a symptom of sloppy thinking. They want to know what the decision is all about and what the underlying realities are which it has to satisfy. They want impact rather than technique. And they want to be sound rather than clever.

Effective executives know when a decision has to be based on principle and when it should be made pragmatically, on the merits of the case. They know the trickiest decision is that between the right and the wrong compromise, and they have learned to tell one from the other. They know that the most time-consuming step in the process is not making the decision but putting it into effect. Unless a decision has "degenerated into work," it is not a decision; it is at best a good intention. This means that, while the effective decision itself is based on the highest level of conceptual understanding, the action commitment should be as close as possible to the capacities of the people who have to carry it out. Above all, effective executives know that decision-making has its own systematic process and its own clearly defined elements.

Sequential Steps

The elements do not by themselves "make" the decisions. Indeed, every decision is a risk-taking judgment. But unless these elements are the stepping-stones of the executive's decision process, he will not arrive at a right, and certainly not at an effective, decision. Therefore, in this article I shall describe the sequence of steps involved in the decision-making process. There are six such steps:

1. *The classification of the problem.* Is it generic? Is it exceptional and unique? Or is it the first manifestation of a new genus for which a rule has yet to be developed?
2. *The definition of the problem.* What are we dealing with?
3. *The specifications which the answer to the problem must satisfy.* What are the "boundary conditions"?
4. *The decision as to what is "right," rather than what is acceptable, in order to meet the boundary conditions.* What will fully satisfy the specifications *before* attention is given to the compromises, adaptations, and concessions needed to make the decision acceptable?
5. *The building into the decision of the action to carry it out.* What does the action commitment have to be? Who has to know about it?
6. *The feedback which tests the validity and effectiveness of the decision against the actual course of events.* How is the decision being carried out? Are the assumptions on which it is based appropriate or obsolete?

Let us take a look at each of these individual elements.

The Classification

The effective decision maker asks: Is this a symptom of a fundamental disorder or a stray event? The generic always has to be answered through a rule, a principle. But the truly exceptional event can only be handled as such and as it comes.

Strictly speaking, the executive might distinguish among four, rather than between two, different types of occurrences.

First, there is the truly generic event, of which the individual occurrence is only a symptom. Most of the "problems" that come up in the course of the executive's work are of this nature. Inventory decisions in a business, for instance, are not "decisions." They are adaptations. The problem is generic. This is even more likely to be true of occurrences within manufacturing organizations. For example:

A product control and engineering group will typically handle many hundreds of problems in the course of a month. Yet, whenever these are analyzed, the great majority prove to be just symptoms—and manifestations—of underlying basic situations. The individual process control engineer or production engineer who works in one part of the plant usually cannot see this. He might have a few problems each month with the couplings in the pipes that carry steam or hot liquids, and that's all.

Only when the total workload of the group over several months is analyzed does the generic problem appear. Then it is seen that temperatures or pressures have become too great for the existing equipment and that the couplings holding the various lines together need to be redesigned for greater loads. Until this analysis is done, process control will spend a tremendous amount of time fixing leaks without ever getting control of the situation.

The second type of occurrence is the problem which, while a unique event for the individual institution, is actually generic. Consider:

The company that receives an offer to merge from another, larger one, will never receive such an offer again if it accepts. This is a nonrecurrent situation as far as the individual company, its board of directors, and its management are concerned. But it is, of course, a generic situation which occurs all the time. Thinking through whether to accept or to reject the offer requires some general rules. For these, however, the executive has to look to the experience of others.

Next there is the truly exceptional event that the executive must distinguish. To illustrate:

The huge power failure that plunged into darkness the whole of Northeastern North America from the St. Lawrence to Washington in November 1965 was, according to first explanations, a truly exceptional situation. So was the thalidomide tragedy which led to the birth of so many deformed babies in the early 1960s. The probability of either of these events occurring, we were told, was one in ten million or one in a hundred million, and concatenations of these events were as unlikely ever to recur again as it is unlikely, for instance, for the chair on which I sit to disintegrate into its constituent atoms.

Truly unique events are rare, however. Whenever one appears, the decision maker has to ask: Is this a true exception or only the first manifestation of a new genus? And this—the early manifestation of a new generic problem—is the fourth and last category of events with which the decision process deals. Thus:

We know now that both the Northeastern power failure and the thalidomide tragedy were only the first occurrences of what, under conditions of modern power technology or of modern pharmacology, are likely to become fairly frequent occurrences unless generic solutions are found.

All events but the truly unique require a generic solution. They require a rule, a policy, or a principle. Once the right principle has been developed, all manifestations of the same generic situation can be handled pragmatically—that is, by adaptation of the rule to the concrete circumstances of the case. Truly unique events, however, must be treated individually. The executive cannot develop rules for the exceptional.

The effective decision maker spends time determining with which of the four different types of the above situations he is dealing. He knows that he will make the wrong decision if he classifies the situation incorrectly.

By far the most common mistake of the decision maker is to treat a generic situation as if it were a series of unique events— that is, to be pragmatic when lacking the generic understanding and principle. The inevitable result is frustration and futility. This was clearly shown, I think, by the failure of most of the policies, both domestic and foreign, of the Kennedy Administration. Consider:

For all the brilliance of its members, the administration achieved fundamentally only one success, and that was in the Cuban missile crisis. Otherwise, it achieved practically nothing. The main reason was surely what its members called "pragmatism"—namely, the administration's refusal to develop rules and principles, and its insistence on treating everything "on its merits." Yet it was clear to everyone, including the members of the administration, that the basic assumptions on which its policies rested—the valid assumptions of the immediate postwar years—had become increasingly unrealistic in international, as well as in domestic, affairs in the 1960s.

Equally common is the mistake of treating a new event as if it were just another example of the old problem to which, therefore, the old rules should be applied:

This was the error that snowballed the local power failure on the New York–Ontario border into the great Northeastern blackout. The power engineers, especially in New York City, applied the right rule for a normal overload. Yet their own instruments had signaled that something quite extraordinary was going on which called for exceptional, rather than standard, countermeasures.

By contrast, the one great triumph of President Kennedy in the Cuban missile crisis rested on acceptance of the challenge to think through an extraordinary, exceptional occurrence. As soon as he accepted this, his own tremendous resources of intelligence and courage effectively came into play.

The Definition

Once a problem has been classified as generic or unique, it is usually fairly easy to define. "What is this all about?" "What is pertinent here?" "What is the key to this situation?" Questions such as these are familiar. But only the truly effective decision makers are aware that the danger in this step is not the wrong definition, it is the plausible but incomplete one. For example:

The American automobile industry held to a plausible but incomplete definition of the problem of automotive safety. It was this lack of awareness—far more than any reluctance to spend money on safety engineering—that eventually, in 1966, brought the industry under sudden and sharp congressional attack for its unsafe cars and then left the industry totally bewildered by the attack. It simply is not true that the industry has paid scant attention to safety.

On the contrary, it has worked hard at safer highway engineering and at driver training, believing these to be the major areas for concern. That accidents are caused by unsafe roads and unsafe drivers is plausible enough. Indeed, all other agencies concerned with automotive safety, from the highway police to the high schools, picked the same targets for their campaigns. These campaigns have produced results. The number of accidents on highways built for safety has been greatly lessened. Similarly, safety-trained drivers have been involved in far fewer accidents.

But although the ratio of accidents per thousand cars or per thousand miles driven has been going down, the total number of accidents and the severity of them have kept creeping up. It should therefore have become clear long ago that something would have to be done about the small but significant probability that accidents will occur despite safety laws and safety training.

This means that future safety campaigns will have to be supplemented by engineering to make accidents themselves less dangerous. Whereas cars have been engineered to be safe when used correctly, they will also have to be engineered for safety when used incorrectly.

There is only one safeguard against becoming the prisoner of an incomplete definition: check it again and again against *all* the observable facts, and throw out a definition the moment it fails to encompass any of them.

The effective decision maker always tests for signs that something is atypical or something unusual is happening. He always asks: Does the definition explain the observed events, and does it explain all of them? He always writes out what the definition is expected to make happen—for instance, make automobile accidents disappear—and then tests regularly to see if this really happens. Finally, he goes back and thinks the problem through again whenever he sees something atypical, when he finds phenomena his explanation does not really explain, or when the course of events deviates, even in details, from his expectations.

These are in essence the rules Hippocrates laid down for medical diagnosis well over 2,000 years ago. They are the rules for scientific observation first formulated by Aristotle and then reaffirmed by Galileo 300 years ago. These, in other words, are old, well-known, time-tested rules, which an executive can learn and apply systematically.

The Specifications

The next major element in the decision process is defining clear specifications as to what the decision has to accomplish. What are the objectives the decision has to reach? What are the minimum goals it has to attain? What are the conditions it has to satisfy? In science these are known as "boundary conditions." A decision, to be effective, needs to satisfy the boundary conditions. Consider:

"Can our needs be satisfied," Alfred P. Sloan, Jr. presumably asked himself when he took command of General Motors in 1922, "by removing the autonomy of our division heads?" His answer was clearly in the negative. The boundary conditions of his problem demanded strength and responsibility in the chief operating positions. This was needed as much as unity and control at the center. Everyone before Sloan had seen the problem as one of personalities—to be solved through a struggle for power from which one man would emerge victorious. The boundary conditions, Sloan realized, demanded a solution to a constitutional problem—to be solved through a new structure: decentralization which balanced local autonomy of operations with central control of direction and policy.

A decision that does not satisfy the boundary conditions is worse than one which wrongly defines the problem. It is all but impossible to salvage the decision that starts with the right premises but stops short of the right conclusions. Furthermore, clear thinking about the boundary conditions is needed to know when a decision has to be abandoned. The most common cause of failure in a decision lies not in its being wrong initially. Rather, it is a subsequent shift in the goals—the specifications—which makes the prior right decision suddenly inappropriate. And unless the decision maker has kept the boundary conditions clear, so as to make possible the immediate replacement of the outflanked decision with a new and appropriate policy, he may not even notice that things have changed. For example:

Franklin D. Roosevelt was bitterly attacked for his switch from conservative candidate in 1932 to radical President in 1933. But it wasn't Roosevelt who changed. The sudden economic collapse which occurred between the summer of 1932 and the spring of 1933 changed the specifications. A policy appropriate to the goal of national economic recovery—which a conservative economic policy might have been—was no longer appropriate when, with the Bank Holiday, the goal had to become political and social cohesion. When the boundary conditions changed, Roosevelt immediately substituted a political objective (reform) for his former economic one (recovery).

Above all, clear thinking about the boundary conditions is needed to identify the most dangerous of all possible decisions: the one in which the specifications that have to be satisfied are essentially incompatible. In other words, this is the decision that might—just might—work if nothing whatever goes wrong. A classic case is President Kennedy's Bay of Pigs decision:

One specification was clearly Castro's overthrow. The other was to make it appear that the invasion was a "spontaneous" uprising of the Cubans. But these two specifications would have been compatible with each other only if an immediate island-wide uprising against Castro would have completely paralyzed the Cuban army. And while this was not impossible, it clearly was not probable in such a tightly controlled police state.

Decisions of this sort are usually called "gambles." But actually they arise from something much less rational than a gamble— namely, a hope against hope that two (or more) clearly incompatible specifications can be fulfilled simultaneously. This is hoping for a miracle; and the trouble with miracles is not that they happen so rarely, but that they are, alas, singularly unreliable.

Everyone can make the wrong decision. In fact, everyone will sometimes make a wrong decision. But no executive needs to make a decision which, on the face of it, seems to make sense but, in reality, falls short of satisfying the boundary conditions.

The Decision

The effective executive has to start out with what is "right" rather than what is acceptable precisely because he always has to compromise in the end. But if he does not know what will satisfy the boundary conditions, the decision maker cannot distinguish between the right compromise and the wrong compromise—and may end up by making the wrong compromise. Consider:

I was taught this when I started in 1944 on my first big consulting assignment. It was a study of the management structure and policies of General Motors Corporation. Alfred P. Sloan, Jr., who was then chairman and chief executive officer of the company, called me to his office at the start of my assignment and said: "I shall not tell you what to study, what to write, or what conclusions to come to. This is your task. My only instruction to you is to put down what you think is right as you see it. Don't you worry about our reaction. Don't you worry about whether we will like this or dislike that. And don't you, above all, concern yourself with the compromises that might be needed to make your conclusions acceptable. There is not one executive in this company who does not know how to make every single conceivable compromise without any help from you. But he can't make the *right* compromise unless you first tell him what right is."

The effective executive knows that there are two different kinds of compromise. One is expressed in the old proverb: "Half a loaf is better than no bread." The other, in the story of the Judgment of Solomon, is clearly based on the realization that "half a baby is worse than no baby at all." In the first instance, the boundary conditions are still being satisfied. The purpose of bread is to provide food, and half a loaf is still food. Half a baby, however, does not satisfy the boundary conditions. For half a baby is not half of a living and growing child.

It is a waste of time to worry about what will be acceptable and what the decision maker should or should not say so as not to evoke resistance. (The things one worries about seldom happen, while objections and difficulties no one thought about may suddenly turn out to be almost insurmountable obstacles.) In other words, the decision maker gains nothing by starting out with the question: "What is acceptable?" For in the process of answering it, he usually gives away the important things and loses any chance to come up with an effective—let alone the right—answer.

The Action

Converting the decision into action is the fifth major element in the decision process. While thinking through the boundary conditions is the most difficult step in decision-making, converting the decision into effective action is usually the most time-consuming one. Yet a decision will not become effective unless the action commitments have been built into it from the start. In fact, no decision has been made unless carrying it out in specific steps has become someone's work assignment and responsibility. Until then, it is only a good intention.

The flaw in so many policy statements, especially those of business, is that they contain no action commitment—to carry them out is no one's specific work and responsibility. Small wonder then that the people in the organization tend to view such statements cynically, if not as declarations of what top management is really *not* going to do.

Converting a decision into action requires answering several distinct questions: Who has to know of this decision? What action has to be taken? Who is to take it? What does the action have to be so that the people who have to do it *can* do it? The first and the last of these questions are too often overlooked—with dire results. A story that has become a legend among operations researchers illustrates the importance of the question, "Who has to know?":

A major manufacturer of industrial equipment decided several years ago to discontinue one of its models that had for years been standard equipment on a line of machine tools, many of which were still in use. It was, therefore, decided to sell the model to present owners of the old equipment for another three years as a replacement, and then to stop making and selling it. Orders for this particular model had been going down for a good many years. But they shot up immediately as customers reordered against the day when the model would no longer be available. No one had, however, asked, "Who needs to know of this decision?"

Consequently, nobody informed the purchasing clerk who was in charge of buying the parts from which the model itself was being assembled. His instructions were to buy parts in a given ratio to current sales—and the instructions remained unchanged.

Thus, when the time came to discontinue further production of the model, the company had in its warehouse enough parts for another 8 to 10 years of production, parts that had to be written off at a considerable loss.

The action must also be appropriate to the capacities of the people who have to carry it out. Thus:

A large U.S. chemical company found itself, in recent years, with fairly large amounts of blocked currency in two West African countries. To protect this money, top management decided to invest it locally in businesses which (1) would contribute to the local economy, (2) would not require imports from abroad, and (3) would if successful be the kind that could be sold to local investors if and when currency remittances became possible again. To establish these businesses, the company developed a simple chemical process to preserve a tropical fruit—a staple crop in both countries—which, up until then, had suffered serious spoilage in transit to its Western markets.

The business was a success in both countries. But in one country the local manager set the business up in such a manner that it required highly skilled and technically trained management of a kind not easily available in West Africa. In the other country the local manager thought through the capacities of the people who would eventually have to run the business. Consequently, he worked hard at making both the process and the business simple, and at staffing his operation from the start with local nationals right up to the top management level.

A few years later it became possible again to transfer currency from these two countries. But, though the business flourished, no buyer could be found for it in the first country. No one available locally had the necessary managerial and technical skills to run it, and so the business had to be liquidated at a loss. In the other country so many local entrepreneurs were eager to buy the business that the company repatriated its original investment with a substantial profit.

The chemical process and the business built on it were essentially the same in both places. But in the first country no one had asked: "What kind of people do we have available to make this decision effective? And what can they do?" As a result, the decision itself became frustrated.

This action commitment becomes doubly important when people have to change their behavior, habits, or attitudes if a decision is to become effective. Here, the executive must make sure not only that the responsibility for the action is clearly assigned, but that the people assigned are capable of carrying it out. Thus the decision maker has to make sure that the measurements, the standards for accomplishment, and the incentives of those charged with the action responsibility are changed simultaneously. Otherwise, the organization people will get caught in a paralyzing internal emotional conflict. Consider these two examples:

When Theodore Vail was president of the Bell Telephone System 60 years ago, he decided that the business of the Bell System was service. This decision explains in large part why the United States (and Canada) has today an investor-owned, rather than a nationalized, telephone system. Yet this policy statement might have remained a dead letter if Vail had not at the same time designed yardsticks of service performance and introduced these as a means to measure, and ultimately to reward, managerial performance. The Bell managers of that time were used to being measured by the profitability (or at least by the cost) of their units. The new yardsticks resulted in the rapid acceptance of the new objectives.

In sharp contrast is the recent failure of a brilliant chairman and chief executive to make effective a new organization structure and new objectives in an old, large, and proud U.S. company. Everyone agreed that the changes were needed. The company, after many years as leader of its industry, showed definite signs of aging. In many markets newer, smaller, and more aggressive competitors were outflanking it. But contrary to the action required to gain acceptance for the new ideas, the chairman—in order to placate the opposition—promoted prominent spokesmen of the old school into the most visible and highest salaried positions—in particular into three new executive vice presidencies. This meant only one thing to the people in the company: "They don't really mean it." If the greatest rewards are given for behavior contrary to that which the new course of action requires, then everyone will conclude that this is what the people at the top really want and are going to reward.

Only the most effective executive can do what Vail did—build the execution of his decision into the decision itself. But every executive can think through what action commitments a specific decision requires, what work assignments follow from it, and what people are available to carry it out.

The Feedback

Finally, information monitoring and reporting have to be built into the decision to provide continuous testing, against actual events, of the expectations that underlie the decisions. Decisions are made by men. Men are fallible; at best, their works do not last long. Even the best decision has a high probability of being wrong. Even the most effective one eventually becomes obsolete.

This surely needs no documentation. And every executive always builds organized feedback—reports, figures, studies—into his decision to monitor and report on it. Yet far too many decisions fail to achieve their anticipated results, or indeed ever to become effective, despite all these feedback reports. Just as the view from the Matterhorn cannot be visualized by studying a map of Switzerland (one abstraction), a decision cannot be fully and accurately evaluated by studying a report. That is because reports are of necessity abstractions.

Effective decision makers know this and follow a rule which the military developed long ago. The commander who makes a decision does not depend on reports to see how it is being carried out. He—or one of his aides—goes and looks. The reason is not that effective decision makers (or effective commanders) distrust their subordinates. Rather, the reason is that they learned the hard way to distrust abstract "communications."

With the coming of the computer this feedback element will become even more important, for the decision maker will in all likelihood be even further removed from the scene of action. Unless he accepts, as a matter of course, that he had better go out and look at the scene of action, he will be increasingly divorced from reality. All a computer can handle is abstractions. And abstractions can be relied on only if they are constantly checked against concrete results. Otherwise, they are certain to mislead.

To go and look is also the best, if not the only way, for an executive to test whether the assumptions on which his decision has been made are still valid or whether they are becoming obsolete and need to be thought through again. And the executive always has to expect the assumptions to become obsolete sooner or later. Reality never stands still very long.

Failure to go out and look is the typical reason for persisting in a course of action long after it has ceased to be appropriate or even rational. This is true for business decisions as well as for governmental policies. It explains in large measure the failure of Stalin's cold war policy in Europe, but also the inability of the United States to adjust its policies to the realities of a Europe restored to prosperity and economic growth, and the failure of the British to accept, until too late, the reality of the European Common Market. Moreover, in any business I know, failure to go out and look at customers and markets, at competitors and their products, is also a major reason for poor, ineffectual, and wrong decisions.

The decision maker needs organized information for feedback. He needs reports and figures. But unless he builds his feedback around direct exposure to reality—unless he disciplines himself to go out and look—he condemns himself to a sterile dogmatism.

Concluding Note

Decision-making is only one of the tasks of an executive. It usually takes but a small fraction of his time. But to make the important decisions is the *specific* executive task. Only an executive makes such decisions.

An *effective* executive makes these decisions as a systematic process with clearly defined elements and in a distinct sequence of steps. Indeed, to be expected (by virtue of position or knowledge) to make decisions that have significant and positive impact on the entire organization, its performance, and its results characterizes the effective executive.

6. Psychological Aspects of Planning

Ronald N. Taylor

Concern for the essential rationality of the planning process is of obvious importance in prescribing planning models. Although psychological variables figure prominently in many of the planning processes discussed in the literature (e.g., user's goals, communication, resistance to change and complexity of computation), only a few published studies have empirically investigated the impact of psychological variables on planning.[1] It seems useful at the present state of development of planning models to review what is known about the psychological variables that appear most likely to influence their effective implementation.

First, two definitions are in order. "Psychological variables" reflect behavioural predispositions of the various parties to the planning process (e.g., the scientist and users of the model—including both top management and others involved in carrying out the planning). Examples of such variables are functional fixedness, cognitive ability, motivational level and values of these individuals and groups. By "implementation" we refer to Ackoff's definition: ". . . design of decision-making procedures and a way of organizing them so that the plan can be carried out."[2] This perspective seems reasonable in that it does not isolate implementation as a stage that occurs late in the planning process; rather implementation also includes all the activities that lead up to the final stages of planning. Starr reinforced this position by pointing out that ". . . implementation procedures cannot be divorced from those of model building (problem solving and decision-making)."[3]

Following the lead of Starr, we subsume planning under problem solving and decision-making—a perspective we employ in an

Reprinted from *Long Range Planning* 9:66–74 (Apr. 1976).
Some of the ideas expressed in this paper were first discussed by the author at the TIMS XXII International Conference, Kyoto, Japan, July, 1975.

effort to draw insights for implementing planning models from the burgeoning literature on the role of psychological variables in problem solving and decision-making. Ackoff has also emphasized the relationship between decision-making and planning: "Planning is clearly a decision-making process; but equally clearly, not all decision-making is planning."[4] Hence, planning is a special type of decision-making and presents challenges in application of findings from studies of decision-making. Planning decisions possess the features of: (1) being performed in advance of the planned actions, (2) involving a system of decisions, and (3) causing things to be done (e.g. motivating).[5]

These defining characteristics of planning decisions provide a focus for relating the psychological literature on decision-making to planning. Our discussion of psychological variables that are likely to influence the effective implementation of planning models is structured around these characteristics. The list of psychological variables of the various parties to planning that may influence its implementation is potentially a very long one, yet most of the empirical and theoretical studies have focused on only a few decision-maker attributes. Taylor and Dunnette[6] empirically investigated the relative impact of a number of psychological variables on performance of 79 industrial managers in a simulated decision task. It was found that, although many psychological variables were involved in decision-making, only a few emerged as key variables in terms of their influence on performance in decision-making.

Review of the Role of Key Psychological Variables in Implementation of Planning Models

It is evident that the influence of psychological variables comes from several sources representing each of the parties involved in planning (scientist, manager, employees). Thus far, most emphasis has been placed on the correspondence between scientists and top management in cognitive styles. But individuals throughout the organizational hierarchy are involved in carrying out plans and should be included in our discussion. Much of the literature we interpret here is concerned with psychological processes that occur within organizations between managers and subordinates.

Unfortunately, the current state of development in the behavioural sciences does not permit prescription of normative strategies to fully capitalize on our knowledge of these psychological variables.[7] We are still at the stage of attempting to describe and understand the ways in which these variables influence the implementation of planning models. Key psychological variables that appear to underlie four aspects of planning model implementation are the focus of our discussion. These aspects are: (1) resistance to planning activities and the resulting plans, (2) motivating the attainment of performance against planning goals, (3) cognitive limitations of planners, and (4) blocks to innovative planning.

Resistance to Planning Activities and Plans

A tendency for those involved in planning implementation to resist both the planning activities and the resulting plans has been well documented.[8] For example, Ewing stated: "Probably the most universal difficulty arises from people's *fears of planned change.* As indicated earlier, almost all ambitious plans are intended to produce new patterns of thought and action in the organization. However, as has been said innumerable times, people resist change —or, more accurately, they resist *being* changed by other people, e.g., planners."[9] Reasons for such resistance can be quite varied; ranging from fear of change, threat of being manipulated, conflicting interests, constrained freedom of choice in work activities, failure to see the value of planning, to increased workload due to planning activities. However, even the best designed plans will fail if those who must carry them out refuse to do so. Resistance can take the form of either open hostility or covert sabotage of the planning effort.

Resistance has generally been dealt with by educating those who implement plans concerning the values of planning, by properly introducing the planning system, and by rewarding organizational members for their planning activities (either financially or otherwise). In addition, writers[10] have recognized that involvement of those who carry out plans in the initial design of the planning system is valuable both in improving the quality of planning decisions and in assuring the acceptance (and implementation) of the resulting planning decisions. A few quotes may demonstrate the attention given to this point. Steiner mentioned: "Long-range planning is a new and significant communications system. It permits people to participate in the decision-making process. People are more adaptable to change because they participate in making the change."[11] Mockler has explained this more fully: "A survey of how large companies manage overall organization change showed that a participative (as well as phased) approach was used in all the successful changes studied. Unlike the authoritative approach (where higher management dictates the solution) or the delegated approach (where lower level managers develop piecemeal solutions), the participative or shared approach allows both direction from higher management and some measure of decision-making by those affected by the change."[12] He admonishes, however, that: "The participative approach can create problems, however, if too many people are involved and if considerable time and effort are devoted to solving minor problems. Care must be taken, therefore, to limit use of the participative approach to those situations where the complexities warrant it."[13]

Relatively little is known about the manner in which users contribute to planning decisions (the decision processes involved in the participative meetings, content, interactions among group members, quality of the decision, etc.). Limited evidence indicates that the effectiveness of participation of subordinates in managerial decisions depends on the nature of the decision and the subordinates involved.[14] The desirability of having participated and the manner in which information is collected from subordinates for use in management decisions (or the degree to which subordinates are actually involved in the decision process) seem to depend on such factors as the extent to which subordinates accept organizational goals, the quality of the decision necessary, and the degree of acceptance necessary. Maier,[15] for example, has differentiated between problems which are quality-dominant and those which are acceptance-dominant. If the problem is one for which quality is much more important than acceptance, then a nonparticipative decision seems appropriate. If, however, acceptance of the decision is more important than quality, then a group decision seems desirable. Decisions that require both high quality and high acceptance are best handled by combined procedures.

Vroom and Vroom and Yetton consider these factors and present a procedure by which decision urgency, resources of subordinates and need for acceptance of the decision, are analysed through a "participation tree," to yield strategies that guide the manager in the degree to which he should consult with his subordinates and in the form the interaction should assume. The model, basically, prescribes participation (e.g., group decisions) when: (1) there is time to involve subordinates, (2) subordinates can contribute to the quality of the decision (have relevant information, etc.), (3) acceptance of the resulting decision by subordinates is essential for it to be successfully implemented, and (4) subordinates can be trusted to act in the best interests of the organiza-tion.[16] This model suggests that most planning situations represent decisions in which considerable participation of, in this context, users and other organizational members is advisable. This ap-proach tends to remove distinctions between planners and imple-menters and should facilitate the coordination of the various stages of planning.

Since the participative approach to planning would encourage group decision-making, it is appropriate to examine the influence of groups on decision processes. Risk-taking propensity of decision makers has emerged as a key psychological variable in group deci-sion-making. Knowing whether groups or individuals have greater risk-taking propensity may be helpful in determining appropriate situations for using planning groups and appropriate interpreta-tions to be placed on group decisions. Although early management literature suggested that groups tend to make less risky decisions than do individuals, within the past decade a number of experi-ments have indicated that groups make riskier decisions than do individuals.[17]

Many of the experiments have used the choice dilemma prob-lems in which individuals are asked to provide a minimum ac-ceptable probability for a hypothetical choice situation. Then the individuals are formed into groups which discuss the problem until a consensus is reached. The groups typically recommend a proba-bility higher than the average of the individual recommendations, implying a shift toward risk. There is some disagreement in ex-plaining this shift,[18] yet the implications for implementation of planning seem clear. Planning groups would be expected to tend toward riskier decisions than would individuals. This tendency should be anticipated and, hopefully, controlled.

Motivation for Improved Performance against Plans

Acceptance of planning recommendations generated by in-volving those who must carry out the plans in the design of the planning system is closely linked to another key psychological variable. Goal setting tends to motivate performance, and self-set goals tend to be more highly motivating than are goals set by others. As Steiner stated: "The more people in organizations par-ticipate in the objective-setting process, the greater is their moti-vation to achieve them."[19] This is the basis of the Management by Objectives (MBO) programme in which subordinates are asked to set their own work goals in conjunction with their superiors. This consideration of values of all those involved in planning appears central to effective implementation of planning decisions. Radosevich commented: "If plans are to guide the behaviour of all members in the firm, the values and needs of all participants, not just top management, should be accommodated to the greatest extent possible."[20] This appears wise, since planning also imparts values and objectives to members of the organization. Cleland reflects this view in stating: "The identification and dissemination of strategic values and objectives is a major responsibility of managers; the other management functions (organizing, motivating, control) depend ultimately on effective planning."[21] Wherever possible, implementation of plans can be facilitated by building in values and objectives which are shared by those who must carry them out.

Goal setting can influence performance through operation of the psychological variable of aspiration level. Essentially, the aspiration level represents a threshold that the decision maker tries to attain[22] and, according to some theorists, aspiration level represents the only vehicle for incorporating preferences into the decision.[23] Three conditions that affect aspiration level in decision tasks—prior experiences of success or failure, setting specific goals, and receiving knowledge of results—have been extensively researched. Although these conditions may prove effective in a strategy for modifying the aspiration level of a decision maker, the major efforts to empirically investigate the impact of aspiration level on decision-making have dealt with bargaining situations and are difficult to relate to planning decisions.

Helson's "hypothesis of par" states that individuals set a standard of excellence for themselves which is usually below their capabilities and that they try to meet, but not exceed, this standard. It is important that standards be set at an optimal level. Standards that are set too high lead to frustration since the decision maker continually fails to achieve them; aspiration levels that are set too low either do not serve as effective motivators of performance or do not provide appropriate standards for problem identification, since they can be readily achieved. Stedry[24] examines the implications of aspiration levels for setting tight vs. loose budgets and Ansoff discusses the uses of aspiration level in corporate strategy decisions (e.g., setting goals such as achieving an increase of 20 percent in earnings per share).[25]

The generally accepted conclusion from studies of prior success or failure and subsequent aspiration level is that successful performance leads to an increase in standards, while failure decreases standards set for future tasks.[26] While failure does not automatically lead to decreases in aspiration level or performance, the higher the ratio of success to failure the more stable the performance. Bourne interpreted this finding as failure tending to reduce the individual's expectancy of success, leading to less effort being expended or to less appropriate attempts at solution (e.g., looking for overly complex solutions).[27]

Many experiments also have found that level of aspiration can be modified by arranging the task to suggest that high level of performance is expected (e.g., self-fullfilling prophecy). Mace, for example, improved performance in an aiming task simply by adding more concentric rings within the established periphery, thus making what once appeared to be good performance look mediocre.[28] Experimenters have also varied aspiration level by manipulating instructions to indicate that good scores have been obtained by others. Similarly, auctioneers are well aware of the effect of obtaining high prices on items sold early on raising the prices at which subsequent items are sold.

Much of the incentive which motivates the activities of a decision maker comes from the consequences of his own actions. Research has shown that decision makers tend to set more realistic standards and have a stronger motivation to resolve the problems they face when they are provided with knowledge of results concerning their performance relative to either their own previous performance or to the performance of others.[29] It seems clear that motivation to implement plans effectively can be enhanced by providing augmented feedback (i.e., from sources external to the individual). Augmented feedback in implementation of plans can take the form of dissemination of information regarding accuracy of planning forecasts, performance against planning goals, etc., and involves communication of the results of evaluation.

The effect of setting *specific* goals on motivation to resolve a problem has also been investigated and serves as the basis for the widely used management by objectives programmes (MBO). It is generally accepted that specific goals serve to motivate individuals with low task motivation to perform at higher levels. Bryan and Locke,[30] for example, found that groups with specific goals were able to match the performance of initially more highly motivated groups who were told merely to "do your best." Bruckman and Campbell provide additional findings concerning conditions affecting aspiration level which may suggest to readers other strategies for motivating improved performance against plans.[31]

Cognitive Limitations in Implementing Planning Models

Systems of planning decisions[32] represent considerable complexity to challenge the cognitive ability of individuals involved in planning. March and Simon[33] have suggested that human cognitive inability to deal with complexity in decision-making leads to "bounded rationality." According to the theory of behavioural decision-making proposed by these writers, human decision makers act rationally only within the boundaries of their perception of the problem—and these boundaries generally have been found to be quite narrow when compared to the scope of complexity typifying most organizational problems. In theories of administrative decision-making, it is this notion of bounded rationality that commonly serves as the basis for explaining departures from nationality (e.g., use of other than a maximizing mode).

Frequently the restrictions of bounded rationality can be attributed to cognitive strain—a breakdown of the decision maker's cognitive processes which occurs when the informational demands of the decision problem exceed his information processing capacity.[34] That cognitive strain is a chronic condition of administrative decision-making in governmental policy, military tactics, business, and natural resource management[35] has been demonstrated in both laboratory research and organizational studies. Psychological variables of decision makers influence the levels of cognitive strain they experience in that they underlie ability to organize and evaluate information. Psychological variables which have been found to relate to information search and organization are short-term memory, category width, general mental ability, pattern seeking and cognitive style. The research relating each of these decision-maker attributes to cognitive strain is reviewed briefly below.

In the area of short-term memory, Miller[36] found that humans were capable of retaining only about seven chunks of information in short-term memory. That ability to recall information in a continuous short-term memory task tends to decline as storage load is increased has been well-documented.[37] To explain the influence of short-term memory on information storage capacity, Posner[38] has proposed that a decision maker rarely stores a pure representation of information; rather he is an active information handler who applies his knowledge of the nature of the information to reduce his memory load. This form of manipulating information tends to reduce cognitive strain. A chess master, for example, can apparently store complex configurations of pieces on the board in his short-term memory as easily as a less-expert chess player stores the position of a single piece.

Short-term memory is generally acknowledged to be a central aspect of general mental ability and the latter characteristic of decision makers has received some research attention. Generally, decision makers having a high level of intelligence have been considered better able to cope with heavy information-processing loads, yet research into this issue has already led to quite mixed results.[39] In a study of managers, however, Taylor and Dunnette[40] observed that more intelligent managers were able to handle information much more efficiently and to diagnose information value much more accurately than were less intelligent managers. On the basis of such evidence, it seems reasonable to conclude that a more intelligent decision maker, by virtue of his increased information-processing capacity, acts within broader bounds of rationality.

One of the more pervasive tendencies in human behaviour is the search for meaning in stimulus patterns. Because humans have a limited ability to process information, they typically use a few broad concepts to classify information, even when such broad categorization suppresses important information.[41] Individuals do, however, differ markedly in the width of categories they tend to use.[42] Narrow categorizers, utilizing a greater number of categories, obtain more precise information, but they also impose greater strain on their ability to process information than do broader categorizers. Attempts to categorize information to deal with large information loads and to reduce cognitive strain can lead to perceptual biases. For example, people tend to classify information even when it has no pattern (is random). Using randomly generated sequences of binary digits, Feldman[43] reported that even people who knew they were dealing with a random process still insisted that they found patterns. Likewise, some gamblers insist that sequences occur in spins of a roulette wheel and the particular tendency to expect alternation (i.e., to think that black is more likely if a sequence of reds has just appeared) is labelled the "gambler's fallacy."

One psychological variable which has received some empirical study in the context of implementation of planning systems is cognitive style. Research into this variable has dealt with the correspondence between scientists and managers in cognitive style and the resulting implications for acceptance of recommendations.[44] Witkin and his associates, in developing the measure of cognitive style, distinguished between field-dependent and field-independent subjects on the basis of their ability to differentiate an object from its context.[45] In the form of this test which has been used most widely in studies of decision-making, the subject is asked to identify a simple figure which has been embedded in a complex design. It has been demonstrated that the style of perceptual functioning identified in these tests manifests itself in intellectual activity involving symbolic functioning.[46] Thus, cognitive style refers to a self-consistent way of functioning that an individual exhibits across perceptual and intellectual activities. As Witkin described this variable: "At one extreme is the tendency for experience to be global; the organization of a field as a whole dictates the way in which its parts are experienced. At the other extreme the tendency is for experience to be delineated and structured; parts of a field are experienced as discrete and the field as a whole is structured."[47] Hence, subjects can be classified as having a propensity to be either high analytic (field-independent) or low analytic (field-dependent).

Huysman[48] investigated the impact of cognitive style differences between management scientists and managers on the managerial implementation of recommendations. He distinguished between analytic and heuristic ways of reasoning in a computer-simulated business game similar to that used by Churchman and Ratoosh.[49] The experimental task required subjects to accept and use an operations research proposal. Some analytic and some heuristic subjects were exposed to an explicit operations research argument aimed at gaining the subjects' explicit understanding. Here, the management scientist's proposal presented formulas within the main body of the report to support the research findings. The second treatment was called an integral approach and subjects were given a report with essentially the same arguments presented in the explicit approach, but no formulas were included in the main body of the report. No significant differences were found between the acceptance behaviour of analytic and heuristic subjects. However, he did find that a significantly lower degree of actual use of the techniques was advocated by the heuristic subjects who received the explicit treatment condition. This study indicated that the implementation of management science recommendations is constrained, at least in part, by the cognitive style of the adopting manager.

Doktor and Hamilton[50] examined the effects of cognitive style in the implementation process through an experimental study of the influence of cognitive style and the style of written reports on the acceptance of management science recommendations. Graduate students and practising managers participated in parallel experimental trials and it was found that differences in acceptance rates were due not only to differences in cognitive style, but also to differences in the subject populations.

Strategies for coping with cognitive variables in implementing planning systems can range from simply being aware of their existence, to training individuals to overcome their limiting characteristics, and to selecting and assigning individuals on the basis of their cognitive abilities. On the other hand, the nature of the planning process can be modified to reduce cognitive demands by sharing the activities more broadly or by adopting simpler models. As a shield from cognitive strain in planning decisions, decision makers may adopt approaches to planning that reduce cognitive strain by permitting the problems to be formulated in a more simplistic manner. Among these approaches are the planning modes of satisficing, optimizing and adaptivizing which have been described by Ackoff.[51] These approaches will be discussed below as methods for incorporating psychological variables into planning systems.

Blocks to Innovative Planning

Planning, as a future-oriented decision-making, represents considerable ill-structuredness. Innovative planning typically involves ill-structuredness related to the development of creative solutions to problems. Development of a new fuel for powering automobiles when faced with depleted supplies of petroleum is an example of a creative decision problem.

The major psychological variable likely to inhibit creative problem solving is functional fixedness. Functional fixedness occurs to inhibit transfer of a response from an ordinary use to an unusual use.[52] The common laboratory setting for studying this phenomenon is the candle problem in which it has been found that using a box to support candles is easier to solve if the box is empty.[53] Hence, it has considerable interest for the development of "originality" in generation of decision alternatives. Much of the research on functional fixedness has concerned the impact of various attributes of the decision problem (e.g., labelling the box or other features of the problem) or hints in reducing the extent of functional fixedness. In an accounting application, Ijiri, Jaedicke and Knight[54] discussed methods for dealing with functional fixedness as accountants attempted to adjust to a change in accounting methods.

In solving creative problems, strategies are required for closing constraints regarding decision alternatives (e.g., names for a new product, rapid transit concepts, etc.). Maltzman[55] has presented a technique for prompting original behaviour by training subjects in unusual uses for an object to reduce the extent of functional fixedness.[56] Presenting a stimulus repeatedly and requiring the subject to give a different set of associations for each presentation has been shown to increase originality of responses on a subsequent free association test and on listing uses for objects.[57]

Creative problems require the generation of original alternatives by reducing functional fixedness, albeit, they must also be creative alternatives. To be creative, they must be courses of action which, in addition to being original (statistically improbable or infrequent), are also relevant and practical. Brainstorming and synectics are two techniques for assisting the decision maker in adopting problem-solving sets conducive to generating creative decision alternatives which appear promising for use in innovative planning.

Brainstorming, advanced by Osborn,[58] is an attempt to use group participation effectively in generating creative decision alternatives. In this strategy a group works together to develop a list of alternative solutions to a problem. To reduce the limiting effect of response sets inhibiting free expression, produced by the presence of other group members, the group works under three rules: (1) ideas are freely expressed without consideration of quality, (2) group members are encouraged to modify and combine previously stated ideas, and (3) a moratorium is placed on the evaluation of ideas until all ideas have been stated. In the synectics approach,[59] a carefully selected and trained group led by an experienced leader views the problem situation until they discover an innovative solution. To overcome perceptual blocks, the procedure forces participants to depart from the usual ways of thinking. To free participants from problem-solving sets involved in looking at the commonplace in a commonplace way, the procedure requires them to play the role of some element in the problem (e.g., a broken machine). In addition, they are asked to develop direct, symbolic and fantasy analogies representing features of the problem. The synectics approach has been used in a number of organizations, but systematic evaluation of its effectiveness is still needed. No formal study has determined whether, in fact, synectics is more effective than brainstorming, nor would it seem to be a fruitful line of research. Selecting promising features of each technique, investigating their effectiveness for innovative planning, and combining them into an eclectic creative planning procedure would provide a stronger basis for recommending strategies for overcoming blocks to innovative planning.

Toward Incorporating Psychological Variables into Planning Models

In this paper we have explored some of the psychological variables which appear influential for implementation of planning models. Much of the literature reviewed here is drawn from the decision-making studies performed by behavioural scientists and, in as far as possible, the research was interpreted to apply to planning decisions. Relatively little of the research into the influence of psychological variables was performed within the context of planning decisions, yet this appears to be a fertile field for additional research.

The influence of psychological variables can be seen in the points of view noted by Ackoff[60] as dominant in the field of planning—satisficing, optimizing and adaptivizing. We shall briefly discuss these points of view and the role of psychological variables they imply, plus one additional point of view which seems relevant to implementing planning models. This is the incrementalizing choice mode developed by Lindblom.[61]

Optimizing is, theoretically, one of the soundest approaches to planning. Unfortunately, the complexity of planning systems forces the optimizer to ignore goals that cannot be quantified and to neglect the organizational structure in his planning efforts. As Ackoff stated: "At present the best that can be done is to optimize either complex structures relative to very simple problems or simple structures relative to complex problems. As yet we cannot optimize complex structures relative to complex problems. For example, we can determine how to divide responsibility for inventories between the purchasing and selling functions in such a relatively simple organization as a department store. But the optimal division of this responsibility for finished goods inventory in a complex vertically integrated process (as in an oil company) is beyond our current capabilities."[62]

The concept of a satisficing decision-making has been suggested by Simon[63] as one strategy for overcoming bounded rationality. In a satisficing mode, the decision maker sets up a feasible aspiration level, then searches for solutions until he finds one that achieves this level. As soon as a satisficing solution is found, he terminates his search and selects that alternative. Studies have found that satisficing is commonly used, for example, by trust investment officers and department store buyers.[64] In satisficing, planners seek to maximize feasibility, but this is seldom defined. He does so by making few departures from current policies and practices, by specifying only moderate increases in resource requirements and by making few changes in the organization structure.[65] The approach would tend to reduce resistance to plans, since it involves few departures from what is familiar to organizational members and is quite conservative. It also would tend to reduce cognitive demands placed upon those involved in planning decisions, but it must be kept in mind that it only reduces the planners' *perception* of complexity, not the actual problem complexity.

Incrementalizing is an approach described by Lindblom[66] which relates quite closely to satisficing. In this strategy, a decision maker makes successive limited comparisons between existing programmes or conditions and alternative courses of action. Few objectives are considered, and the alternatives are generally ones that are familiar to the decision maker or that he can generate by local search. Potentially important outcomes, values and alternative solutions are neglected and agreement among decision makers is sought instead of high goal attainment. Lindblom has labelled this approach "muddling through" and it forms the basis for the more formal strategy of disjointed incrementalism as proposed by Braybrooke and Lindblom.[67] Although the strategy has been suggested as a guide for decision-making in complex environments (e.g., making social policy decisions), it has been used primarily as a descriptive model of how decisions are made in such contexts. Its ability to deal with complexity and conflict among those involved in planning seems appropriate for planning decisions and its recognition that planning decisions are frequently group decisions is in keeping with the approach suggested by our discussion of psychological variables. That is, planning approaches must recognize the increasing tendency for those who carry out plans to be involved in the design of planning systems.

Ackoff and Weick[68] have discussed a strategy in which the decision maker ignores uncertainty while building up an adaptive capacity. Rather than devoting resources to planning decisions, the resources are used to establish a capacity to respond quickly when action needs to be taken, no matter what the future situation may be. For example, when using an adaptivizing mode, you do not attempt to predict your competitor's prices and then choose an action, but rather you build up a flexible system and monitor his price movements so that you will be able to respond quickly when actions need to be taken. Such an approach to planning fails to capitalize on the motivational features of planning, yet it may be appropriate under certain conditions. As Ackoff has pointed out: "It involves motivating participants in the system to act in a way that is compatible with the interests of the organization as a whole, and it does this by providing incentives that make individual and organizational objectives more compatible."[69]

Although none of the planning modes discussed above effectively incorporate the role of planning variables for improved implementation of planning systems, each contains features that are useful in certain planning contexts. Future research into the influence of psychological variables on implementation of planning models could very profitably focus on prescribing programmes to operationalize planning modes for empirical study, and investigating conditions suitable for effective use of each approach to planning.

7. Libraries at the Turning Point: Issues in Proactive Planning

Peter Davis

Introduction

Library administrators are some of the unhappiest people we know. Ten years of austerity, and the pressures of plucking reasonable administrative solutions out of an unreasonable, hopelessly complex and muddled environment, have taken their toll. Ten years of fighting losing battles with publishers, of being "nickle and dimed" to death by faculty committees, of being denigrated as the scions of new technological indignities, and of being the nursemaids to a profession in the throes of a wrenching transition have been too much to bear. Able administrators are leaving the profession at a time when they are most needed. Librarians are unhappy; but why aren't they hopping mad?

In this paper we will examine an approach to planned change in the research library which falls somewhere between an expression of unhappiness and of indignity. We will look at the perceived barriers to self-initiated planning, which aims to redefine the future of the library and its relationship with its environment. We will then propose elements of a strategy which we feel meet the library's need, and offer a better chance for progress in this area. Much of the discussion below is unqualified for intended effect. Thus we talk about "librarians doing this or that." We know that not *all* in fact do. Our intent in generalizing in this way is simply to capture what we perceive as the tenor of the times. We try to

Reprinted from *Journal of Library Administration* 1:11–24 (Summer 1980).

build up a picture which is then used to derive specific recommendations for change.

This paper is written from the perspective of corporate planners whose primary professional interest in the process of planned change is in the private sector. After two years of effort to apply these ideas on planning in the library context, we are impressed (at the risk of overgeneralization) by (1) how desperate things seem and (2) the paucity of effort to do anything about it. We have asked ourselves many times why librarians are not involved in a more vigorous bootstrap operation, designed to pull themselves out of the mire. What we have in mind is as simple in theory as it is obviously difficult in practice—strategic planning, the setting of long-term goals, a strategic effort to redefine the relationship between the library and its environment, and a systematic implementation program.

Planning and Problem Solving

Ackoff has defined four approaches to problem solving.[1] These are:

1. The inactive approach
2. The reactive approach
3. The preactive approach
4. The proactive approach.

The inactivist sticks his head in the sand. The reactivist fights fires. The preactivist is a little more forward-looking. He predicts and prepares. His approach is to adapt to the real and anticipated contingencies in the environment in the best way possible. The proactivist takes the bull by the horns. He makes up his mind that he too has a stake and a say in the future, and that by taking the right kind of action with the right kind of support, he can begin to create a future that makes more sense for himself, and for those he serves.

In a turbulent and threatening environment, an inactive approach is suicidal. Reactivism and preactivism are coping strategies generally leading to short-term success, but the risks of long-term debilitation. Proactivism emphasizes mastery of the relationship between the institution and its environment, and codetermination of future outcomes. Proactivism offers short-term headaches, at the risk of strategic blunders, but the chance in the longer run to learn, and to grow, despite the obstacles.

The question we ask is: Why after so many years of trial, tribulation and coping is there not more of a spirit of proactivism abroad in the library community? As a constructive sequel we might question: What can be done to stimulate proactive management? And to be more practical: What are the strategies of proactivism in this field? We will address these issues.

Why Coping?

The evidence is that most library managers are, at best, coping under adversity. Some are going under, but most are keeping their heads above water. This state of affairs is damaging because the prognosis is for more coping . . . at least until the 1990s. Work is no longer fun. There is little chance to be creative; the strictly maintenance aspects of the job are all-consuming.

Whatever innovation is taking place is happening in protected pockets of activity. New ideas, concepts, and procedures are emerging not from library management but from network people, from commercial services, from government projects, and so on. The library manager, far from initiating innovation, spends most of his time either worrying what to do with it, or buffering his institution from its undesirable and unintended consequences. The major problem with on-line services, for example, is not how to create a wholly new kind of interface between the user and the service environment, but how to: (1) prevent such services from excessively disturbing the present service environment (e.g., by emphasizing the difference between the capability of such services to generate secondary information and the capability of the library to support the corresponding primary sources); (2) explain that charges for use do not violate the public utility concept of the library; and (3) keep associated costs under control. Innovation spreads exclusively from the outside-in with all the attendant problems of adaptation. There is little, if any, counterflow from the inside-out, which would provide truly grounded innovation.

There are several reasons for this state of affairs.

1. *Tradition.* The library has historically been a passive institution deriving from its tradition of service. As far as the key constituency (i.e., faculty) is concerned, almost anything goes, although there has been a rather delicate move of late to become more assertive, particularly on faculty abuse of borrowing privileges.

2. *Professionalism.* Most librarians find their rewards and

recognition either in their profession and from their peers outside their own organization, or from their affiliation with a prestigious institution (Ivy League universities, NASA, IBM, etc.). The job has little internal recognition value, but is instrumental for the rewards it brings in a broader arena. The relationship between the professional librarian and his library is in sharp contrast with that of the archetypal corporate man and his corporation (see, for example, *Business Week* (1979) on Texas Instruments).[2] Obviously, being too much wrapped up in the organization is as pathological as being too much focused out of it. However, unless greater organizationally related rewards are developed, not enough energy can be mobilized in the service of the organization. Equally, in a problem-bound setting, too much energy is devoted to swapping war stories, and too little to productive problem solving.

3. *Lack of support.* University administrations are chronically incapable of facilitating a proactive approach from the research library. Administrators have either been unwilling or unable to diagnose the nature of the predicament of the library. More often than not they have set themselves up in a "win-lose" bargaining situation with library managers and have lost sight of the possibility of constructive solutions.

4. *Politics.* To bolster themselves in terms of scarcity, library managers have played an astute political game, building constituencies among the more powerful members of the university community. Those who have neglected to do so have more often than not perished in the fray. Unfortunately, many of the survivors have become prisoners of their alliances. Of great concern is that those involved are often disinterested or antagonistic toward innovation. Having staked a reputation on so-and-so's ability to pull the library through, they don't want to see too many changes taken which might imperil their hard-won victories.

5. *The carpet-baggers.* Most institutions in trouble can call on outside experts to help out. In the opinion of many library administrators, most of the economists, statisticians, operations researchers, and planners are carpet-baggers of the classic mode. They get in, sniff around, collect some data, and leave as quickly as possible. This bolsters the impression that there are no answers to the problems of the library—or at least if there are, they cannot be communicated to the library manager.

6. *Poor slack management.* Most managers have learned that organizational slack (in the form of discretionary resources) is essential for healthy organizational development; not so the library manager. Over the bad years, library managers have not learned

how to draw the line, and have allowed their slack to drop to practically zero. They have always felt that they could in a pinch give up the nonessentials, and have hence designed a straight-jacket for themselves.

7. *Lack of strategic thinking.* In the placid world of traditional librarianship, strategic thinking was an unnecessary and indeed alien idea connoting conniving in its worse extreme. The library was meant to be carried wherever the satisfaction of user needs took it. In the turbulent, resource scarce environment of contemporary librarianship, strategic thinking becomes indispensable. However, most librarians are simply not practiced in strategic thinking, which requires a shift in mind set. A mind which is used to thinking forward from action to consequences, must begin to focus on "backwards analysis" from desirable future outcomes to immediate requirements. Capability to think strategically needs to be developed in most managers; unfortunately, it seldom is.

What Can Be Done?

There is a famous Will Rogers story about planning. During World War I, the United States Navy went to Will Rogers with a question: "Mr. Rogers, what are we going to do about the German submarine problem?" "Simple," replied Rogers, "drain the oceans!" Several weeks later, after extensive analysis, the Navy came back. "Mr. Rogers, how are we going to drain the oceans?" Rogers' reply was immediate: "Please, gentlemen, don't bother me with tactical questions, I deal only with the strategic issues."

Moral: there are no simple answers.

The problem of the modern library is not a money problem. The problem is how to develop a strategic capability in the library itself to facilitate organizational effectiveness, meaningfulness, and vitality in a complex world. Many librarians have said to us that to talk of strategic capability development in the library context is to whistle into the wind. However, the topic must be put in context. A better sense must be developed of the concept of strategic capability, and what it implies for the library. There are a number of component issues which we will briefly address.

1. *Strategic participation.* Strategic participation involves, as we might expect, the participation of those who work in the library in the determination of its future direction. Librarians are not used to this kind of thing. Many find it threatening, and it is indeed an issue which is clouded by the complexity of role relationships

found in the modern research library. However, strategic participation is beginning to play an important role in organizational change efforts for several good reasons. It develops a better sense of organization and of commitment to a future direction. It enables everyone involved to better see their role in future developments. It serves as a useful vehicle for job enrichment, gives people a sense of involvement, and makes their work more meaningful. It also allows "collective intelligence" to be brought to bear on problem solving.

Business planners distinguish several levels and types of participation in corporate affairs. These are shown in table 1 with some familiar illustrations.

There has been extensive experimentation in American industry with operational and financial participation, at both the tactical and strategic levels. Participation in development or planning activities is an idea which is just beginning to catch on.[3] However, there is a good deal more experience with this kind of participation in Europe. In the library, we are just beginning to see tactical, operational participation through the introduction of sociotechnical ideas on work management.[4] While financial participation will not be a relevant approach so long as the library operates as a public utility, there are still a great many more opportunities for participatory approaches that have not been tried. The concept and methods will have to develop more fully for the library. Whether the exercise starts with those with a greater stake in the library's future (e.g., full time and professional staff), or whether everyone is involved from the start, is a design question which cannot yet be answered. However, the intent would be that, in one way or another, those who work in the library would be encouraged to participate in the development of its long-term goals, as well as the derivation and implementation of the steps required to achieve those goals. We would see experimentation in this area as a vitally important means for institution building.

TABLE 1. Levels and Types of Participation

		Application		
		operations	financial	development
Level	tactical	autonomous work groups	gainsharing	job bidding teams
	strategic	job design facility design	stock options	strategic planning teams

2. Stakeholder management. The concept of stakeholder management was introduced into the planning literature by Ansoff.[5] He argued that as organizations become more and more dependent on each other for effective performance, the focus of planned change must shift from individual solutions of individual problems, to joint solutions of joint problems. The traditional approach to corporate planning has focused on *shareholder* management, i.e., management in the interests of those who own the corporation. With the growth of interdependence, the emphasis shifts to *stake*-holder management, i.e., those who have a stake in the corporation but do not necessarily own it. All shareholders are stakeholders but not all stakeholders are shareholders. A typical stakeholder for the corporation, and for the library, is shown in figure 1.

Stakeholder planning emphasizes strategic participation of those groups who have an important stake in the institution, and who are willing to search for jointly advantageous solutions to problems. It may not be easy to elicit cooperation since many stakeholders are involved in "win-lose" battles with the institution (e.g., labor unions and management, publishers and librarians). However, the approach is a constructive one and often pays off handsomely. For example, recent work establishing community labor-management committees with the explicit intent of searching for cooperative "win-win" solutions to labor-management issues, has proven successful in the creation of new jobs and the reduction of unemployment in the community.[6]

Librarians don't practice stakeholder planning. They meet with the various stakeholders in different arenas, mostly off their own turf. They do not pull the various groups together with a request for them to participate in a design of future alternatives for the library. There are various reasons for this including: (1) a belief that there *are no* implementable alternatives beyond "muddling through," (2) a fear of loss of control, i.e., that someone will come up with a scatterbrained idea which the librarian will be stuck with, and (3) an unwillingness to disturb existing political processes. Stakeholder planning requires considerable skill in the management of the process, and a willingness to take risks.

3. Strategic confidence. A willingness to take risks can only arise out of confidence in the process, in the ability of someone to manage the process, and a good sense of what ought to be done when complexities arise. If any institution is to undertake a strategic change effort, it has to know where it wants to go, and how it is going to get there. A great many institutions don't know what they want, including most corporations, and certainly most librar-

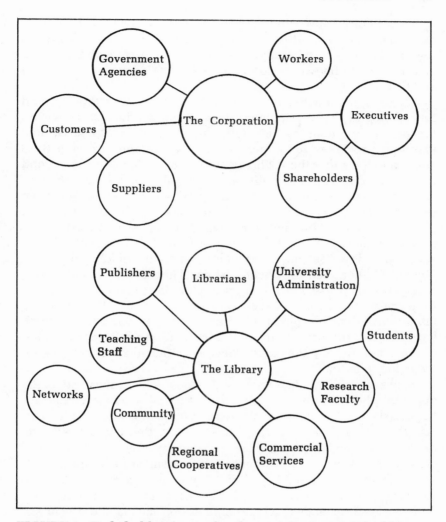

FIGURE 1. Stakeholder groups for the corporation and the library

ies. As a consequence there is no cathexis: there is no spark to ignite excitement when alternatives are discussed. We have seen this time and time again, working with corporations, when management examines diversification options. A list of options is produced—and nothing happens. Then another list is made up—still nothing. A third list appears—still nothing, and so on. The data may show any number of desirable alternatives but members of the organization cannot get excited about any of them. They don't know what they want.

They don't know what they want either because: (1) they have never been asked what they want, and/or (2) they would consider the whole process whereby they would set organizational goals and proceed to take steps to implement them as rather outlandish and bizarre.

Developing a sense of organizational mission is the first and crucial step in the development of strategic confidence. However, the process of defining this mission requires careful attention. Planning processes force people to define ambitious objectives when they fear that the achievement of these objectives is beyond their control (because of political, technical, social, or psychological constraints). This fairly rapidly produces a dissociation from the planning process, and leaves that process an empty ritual. On the other hand, planning efforts which emphasize the setting of parochial goals produce trivial and parochial results. The trick in such cases is to set up a dynamic tension in which people are pushed further than they want to go. They are then led into a reality testing phase, in which they explore the path between where they are now, and where they want to go. Eventually the determination of feasible paths and goal setting become increasingly harmonious processes, with each part facilitating the formulation of the other. Slowly the exercise becomes meaningful and a genuine guide to action.

Sarason,[7] in the "Creation of Settings," has investigated the opposite phenomenon in which the focus is on goals which are hopelessly out of reach. Watzlawik, Weakland, and Frisch[8] call this the utopia syndrome. In a curious way, the utopia syndrome becomes an avoidance mechanism whereby the setting of unattainable goals becomes a defense mechanism protecting the individual from doing anything at all. The emphasis of the planning exercise, in these cases, is to bring the goals to a reasonable motivational level through constant emphasis on means and resources.

With strategic confidence there is a willingness to explore the relationship between the desirable and the feasible, while insisting that the relationship be maintained and be understandable. There is also a sense of being able to control runaway effects in which goal setting drifts into an ethereal realm or in which people dig in their heels and close their minds in the interests of practicality. With strategic confidence, "flip-flop" effects are avoided. In reaction to blue sky proposals, some have a tendency to become excessively practical and incrementalist in their thinking, and vice versa.

The development of strategic confidence facilitates a process and a climate in which members of the organization are able to participate in the setting of organizational goals and can appreciate the relationship between goals and means. They also can understand how means are to be implemented and see their role in the implementation process.

4. *Strategic facilitation.* Strategic confidence building, strategic participation, goal setting, and stakeholder planning are not processes which can be entered into easily or casually. Implementation requires a conviction and determination, particularly among library management. It also requires facilitation. There are three aspects to facilitation which make it essential to utilize third party professional planners for the purpose. The first aspect is legitimization. Strategic planning has to be legitimized as a process, particularly in terms of the need for, and expected value of, the approach.

The second aspect involves framing and reframing. The situation of the library has to be placed in a context which facilitates the search for positive solutions. Relationships and processes which are framed in nonproductive ways have to be reframed. Thus, user needs have to be segmented and placed in a historical context. Management style has to be located in a space of alternative options (perhaps utilizing labels such as interactive, reactive, preactive, proactive). The political process has to be explicated. In this way, library stakeholders have to begin to see the situation of the library in a new light—a light which allows them to envisage productive alternatives. Such reframing provides the necessary stimulus to involvement in the planning process. It most often requires the good offices of a third party to be successful.

The third role of a facilitator is to protect individuals who are encouraged to take risks as part of the planning process. Participation can only be nurtured if people feel free to think and express their feelings and desires. Individuals must be protected from ridicule or victimization, and importantly in the library context, from a fear of personal loss of role and relevance in a redefined future. An outsider who is not involved in internal alliances can perform this role most effectively.

5. *Organizational strategy.* "Then would you read a sustaining book such as would help and comfort a Wedged Bear in Great Tightness."[9]

Correct treatment of organizational strategy can have a tremendous liberating effect on the very capability to conceive and act on alternative futures. Incorrect treatment can very rapidly stultify initiatives. Organizational effects on morale and capability are subtle and hard to pin down. The need for careful thought and consideration in this area is therefore quite critical. It is our feeling that the modern library is trapped by the way it organizes itself. The setting of strategic goals which take for granted that libraries will continue to organize themselves in the future as they have in the past is unlikely to be particularly productive. The formulation of futures which allow for major modifications in organizational form may stimulate many new initiatives. While we cannot provide any definitive guidelines for reorganization, we can show how analysis might proceed and indicate some preliminary conclusions.

In the past, the library has been buffered from the need to make strategic organizational decisions. It has effectively controlled the expression of demands by its various stakeholders. Traditionally, so long as the needs of certain key faculty members were met, the librarian could proceed in relative tranquility. The library has also had the resources necessary to insulate itself from many of the more difficult and consequential decisions. Despite recent cutbacks there are still quite a number of research libraries which do not make major decisions on the allocation of book acquisitions budgets.

However, we have entered another era. For most libraries the buffer has gone. The library is closely "engaged" with its environment and must adapt itself to it. The days in which a library could move into the future riding on past traditions, buffered by a cushion of slack resources, are over. This commonly perceived fact has major implications for the activities which are carried out and the resource allocation decisions which are made. It also impacts greatly on the way the library ought to be organized.

Once the buffer is dissipated, organizational strategy comes to the fore. The way in which the organization establishes an interface with its environment is a key issue for effective organizational design. If the environment is relatively stable and homogeneous, transactions across the boundary can be regulated through rules and procedures. Thus, a user with a well formulated request falling into an established body of knowledge, can successfully complete the library transaction by simply following the clearly defined search and location procedures. Exceptions are handled separately in a rule-governed structure. Failure to locate a reference would be handled by one group of exception-managing specialists (reference librarians); failure to find the material on the stacks would be handled by another specialist group (the circulation desk), etc.

Clearly, however, as the environment of user needs becomes less stable, more heterogeneous, and less predictable, such a system is prone to breakdown and failure. Eventually the number of exceptions begins to far exceed the number of routine transactions. The appropriate response under such circumstances is to segment the environment into clusters which are as homogeneous as possible, and to assign an organizational unit to specifically manage the boundary spanning role for each cluster. In an extreme case, this unit acts as an interface between the user and the library on every single transaction. This is current practice with on-line services. A user is met by a librarian who understands the relevant set of on-line systems. The librarian explains and interprets the system for the user, helps to formulate the research question as precisely as possible, and conducts the search in a companion mode. Obviously this is expensive. Intermediate steps to improve boundary spanning in order of increasing cost include:

1. Improvement and enrichment of the rules and procedures governing access, with allowance for more contingencies
2. Training of the users in the application of these rules and procedures (i.e., library instruction)
3. The development of computer software systems which will interact with the user and facilitate access.

Most libraries rely primarily on rule-governed access. Only a few have well developed boundary spanning activity. Most libraries cluster the user environments according to traditional disciplines. However, as boundary spanning becomes a more critical function, it becomes as important to cluster according to the level and type of boundary spanning required. This was recognized in a recent Arthur D. Little study[10] which proposed that the user environment be clustered in Era I (disciplinary), Era II (mission oriented), and Era III (problem oriented) research needs. Such a classification better captures differences in the complexity, uncertainty, and heterogeneity of the user transaction, and hence is more relevant to the design of boundary spanning activity.

The loss of stability, predictability, and simplicity in the user (output) environment is mirrored in the service (input) environment. At one time management of input activity meant applying certain priority rules to a list of proposed book and journal purchases. Now materials acquisition is an art in and of itself. Often costs are so high that materials must be obtained through sharing or swapping arrangements. Copies may be purchased from the

British Lending Library. The OATS service may be used. Network services will be frequently required. On-line bibliographic services are becoming as important a source of information as the card catalogue. There has been an impressive proliferation of services, hence a corresponding growth in the heterogeneity of this service environment. Together with heterogeneity there has been a corresponding growth in uncertainty in dealing with this environment. For example, the chance of conducting an on-line search which results in the location of the needed document is not all that great.

Again, heterogeneity and uncertainty promote environmental clustering and the development of specialized boundary spanning roles. Thus, the library begins to require OCLC specialists, various on-line specialists, full time people devoted to resource sharing schemes, expert purchasing agents, and so on.

But this is not the end of the story. Input and output specialist groups arise in order to deal with environmental complexity and uncertainty. The next question is: How are the various input groups and output groups coordinated so that the library functions effectively as a unit? How do you insure that references cropping up repeatedly in on-line searches appear in the acquisitions list? How can a reference librarian know about, and effectively utilize, network based interlibrary loan services? It is important to realize that in simpler times with plenty of slack resources these coordination problems could be handled informally, allowing staff to take time to follow through on individual cases, and through the development of a pooled interdependence. With the growth of scope and complexity, such issues must be addressed through organizational strategy.

There are several possible strategies to adopt. The right one would depend on the particular organizational capabilities and contingencies. The general strategic problem has been discussed by Thompson:

[The] proposition is that boundary-spanning components facing heterogeneous and dynamic environments have serious adaptive problems; if they are, in addition, reciprocally interdependent with a technical core which itself is complex, the resulting set of constraints and contingencies exceeds the organization's capacity to adapt and coordinate. By identifying several separable domains and organizing its technical-core and boundary-spanning components in clusters around each domain, the organization attains a realistic bounded rationality.[11]

Put more simply, the organization *divisionalizes*, in much the same way that, say, General Electric divisionalizes. Key domains in the output environment are identified and the organization mobilizes its input and output boundary spanning activity, its technology, and its people around these domains. The divisions work semi-autonomously, their activities being coordinated by a central management activity.

Traditional disciplinary groupings won't work for clustering purposes since they do not provide a focus for common types of technology and boundary spanning activity. In an earlier paper[12] we have suggested an alternative breakdown into five subunits. These would be:

1. *The Contemporary Information Subunit*—which would eventually become a coordinated full text and secondary information system similar to that described in the SCATT Report (1976) and by Wilfred Lancaster.[13]
2. *The Information Fellows Subunit*—which would be rather similar to the Congressional Research Service except that the members of this unit would also perform a direct "information brokering" role as described by Boss.[14]
3. *The Library Core*—which would continue to meet the homogeneous well defined Era I demands providing discipline oriented collections, classroom materials, reserve sections, etc.
4. *The Collections* (Historical Legacy)—which would preserve and foster intellectual tradition through the establishment of collections designed to represent the history of thought in a few chosen areas. Collections would be representative, not exhaustive. They would be maintained under high security to prevent degredation.
5. *The Missions Subunits*—which would provide service to specific mission oriented units (e.g., energy research) and would be similar in structure to a corporate R & D library.

Each unit would be broadly responsible for its own funding, internal management, staff recruitment, and development. A central management unit would coordinate, facilitate, help to maintain a balance between the different units, and allocate certain capital development funds.

Divisionalization is one approach which seems to make sense knowing what we know about organizational response to complex environments. There are undoubtedly other approaches. Any approach would place new demands on the librarian. However, changes in organization of the kind indicated might well reveal a great many hidden constraints in the current mode of operation and hence prove an invaluable stimulus to effective planning.

Postscript

We have attempted in this paper to spell out some of the issues which we feel need to be addressed if the modern research library is to proactively plan its future. We realize that to discuss these issues is to skim the surface. Hopefully, however, we have been able to give a flavor of what we feel ought to be done.

We have provided a few ideas, but no answers. But that is not our job. Answers have to come out of the library, and out of the stakeholder groups who so rigidly support and constrain it. We fully realize that the library is a highly constrained institution which is heavily dependent on others to shape its future. But a lack of activity on these grounds will insure a continued dependence with no guarantee that reasonable alternatives will emerge. Just think of the potential for good, and for disaster, embodied in the current rampant explosion of information technology. Whatever the outcome of this may be for others, it will almost certainly not work out well for the library, unless the library takes a more active stance to guide its development, regulation, and application

The Mantua Community Planners in Philadelphia have a slogan: "Plan or be planned for." Librarians could well take this to heart, as the research library enters its second decade of austerity.

8. Economic Analysis

Ann E. Prentice

A General Overview of Financial Problem Solving

Without scarcity there is no need to choose and without discretion there is no possibility of choice.[1]

Economic analysis is the process of decision-making within a financial context. It is the process of collecting relevant information, identifying alternatives, and selecting the optimum decision(s). From this process the best course of action can be selected in terms of what you wish to accomplish (desired objective) and the way(s) in which you wish to go about it. There are always at least two ways in which to perform a function even if one of those two ways is not to perform it. The process of economic analysis enables one to clarify the problem, identify variables, and proceed to determine the alternative ways to solve a problem and to identify means of evaluating the success of the choice made to perform that function.

Eight clearly defined steps in this process have been identified by economists and planners. The first of these is to *define the problem*—the real problem. The most severe general problem facing libraries and related institutions presently is the lack of increase in funding, but is that the problem or a symptom of a larger problem? The political constraints on the level of library funding are many and derive less from a desire to "get the library" than from overall financial pressure, the relative decline in tax revenue, and priorities set by governing bodies at the local and state level which typically are not those of the library. Social factors of the

Reprinted from *Strategies for Survival: Library Financial Management Today*, Library Journal Special Report #7, 1978. Published by R. R. Bowker Co. (a Xerox company). © 1978 by Xerox Corporation.

environment, legal factors, and factors of supply and demand both within and outside the institution can impact the problem and cloud the issue. This process is similar to the process of research, wherein the first and most important task is to define the problem and as in the process of research the real problem may not be what was initially supposed.

Let us take the issue of the feasibility of adding bibliographic database services to the reference services of a public library. There is mixed reaction on the part of some of the staff as to the need for such a service and there is a need to study the request and determine whether or not to pursue it.

What are the political factors involved?

Who in local government agencies might utilize this service?

Would increased service to local government and business enhance the standing of the library in terms of its overall service and budget?

Would such a service appear too costly for a specific community and thus be detrimental to the library?

What are the legal implications?

Who would be able to use such a service? Community residents only?

Would the service be for a fee or would it be provided free of charge?

Is such a service too sophisticated for the actual need?

Could a good reference librarian with sufficient time provide an adequate level of information using existing resources?

Would the database serve only the most sophisticated need and user?

Can the library afford to provide an expensive service to a limited group?

Will it affect the level of service provided the rest of the community?

What competition exists for such services?

Are there other institutions that under contract would provide similar service?

Is a database service necessary at all?

What databases could local government agencies access from state, federal, or local government groups?

Are there areas—perhaps transportation, education, or health services that are covered adequately by other services?

What really different or unique function would the library perform

by contracting for such service(s) to be provided through the library?
Who will supply the database service?
Which of the commercial database suppliers would be most appropriate?
Is there a profile of library size, potential number of users, type of use that would identify the optimum user?

The emphasis of the questions is economic. That term broadly defined encompasses social, political, and other factors as well.

It is at this initial stage of analysis when questions should be asked and problems identified that the widest possible planning input should be sought.

Reference librarians, library administration, local government representatives, potential users of the service, current users of the service from other sources, database contractors, and all others with an interest in the service plus those whose participation in the planning process is sought for political or other purposes should be included. The success of a program must be measured in political terms as well as in financial terms. It is usually more economical in the long run to do this type of planning early than to develop a program with alternatives and try to promote it later.

The second step in financial analysis is *state the objective to be studied.* In our example, let us say that the objective is to provide enhanced reference services to specialized clientele through the provision of access to bibliographic databases. This objective is based on the background study made in step one. For our purposes we have identified an enhanced level of reference service to a specific clientele by means of a particular service. The decisions which are most political and require broad based input have already been made. The objective, once examined in political terms, is then to be evaluated in terms of the institution within which the service is to be conducted. Does the objective coincide with the mission and function of the parent organization?

In regular reexamination of the mission and function of the library, the chief administrator and trustees may have identified specific programs to carry out the mission and function. The provision of enhanced service would most probably be within that mission. The limiting of such a service to a specific clientele would be contrary to the mission of a tax-supported institution freely available to all who reside within the community, or who support the library in some other way such as through contract or nonresident fees. The objective might then need to be revised to conform to the mission by making the service available to all and then explore means of assuring that the service be used when it is proper to do so, given certain reference circumstances.

Once the objective has been clarified to meet internal requirements, it is to be defined according to the specific need(s) it will fill. This again goes back to the questions raised in problem definition—what reference services not now performed can be performed? What new services to existing and new clientele will be possible? How will this broaden the base of library users?

The objective is stated and enlarged upon when alternatives and a means for evaluating them are established. In what way will we determine if contracting for a database service is the best approach, given a specific reference service and resources and a present and potential clientele?

Such criteria for evaluating the alternatives could include: number of reference questions answered and not answered using existing in-house resources; number of reference questions requiring that an outside reference resource be queried; number of clients satisfied with amount and specificity of materials available in-house; and amount of time spent by reference librarians in responding to each reference question.

Are there certain types of questions that take more time than others?

What characteristics do they have—by subject? By recency of material?

Is a particular clientele unserved or dissatisfied with service?

Can the aforementioned data indicate the extent to which existing services are adequate?

Does there appear to be a pattern of adequacy/inadequacy at some point?

Would additional reference staff solve the problem?

What if several libraries contracted for service as a group and shared costs?

Would a database service solve the problem?

Would additional hard-copy reference tools solve the problem?

The third step in economic analysis is to *determine viable alternatives* to meeting the objective set forth in the previous step. The alternative of doing nothing exists and its implications should be explored. As complete a list as possible of viable alternatives should be developed. For each alternative the pro and con arguments are to be identified. If the alternative were for several libraries to contract for service as a group, the analysis sheet might look like the following:

Pro	Con
less start-up cost than contracting alone	legal problems of contract development among several libraries
promote co-op among libraries in area	overuse by one or more libraries
only one library would require special space	someone might not pay bills
only one library would require special staff	slowness of service if you have to go to another institution

How many arguments both pro and con are realistic? Do any overlap? How many are subjective and how many are objective? Are the arguments measurable in terms of speed of service, level of librarian satisfaction, level of client satisfaction?

For each alternative, similar pros and cons are to be asked and are to be evaluated according to whether or not they overlap, are subjective or objective, and whether or not they are measurable.

Having identified and outlined the viable alternatives the fourth step in the process is to *collect data where possible to determine more information on the alternatives.* Again, using the above alternative as an example, identify the sources of information necessary to understand each pro and each con statement. For the pro statements, what is the actual cost of a co-op contract among a number of libraries? Does this vary by size of library, by type of library (public, academic, special)? How many libraries constitute an optimum number for cooperative contracting? Are there specific rates for a certain number of libraries?

What would the internal costs be of space to house the terminal, security of the terminal, salary for the appropriately skilled reference librarian to operate the terminal? How would this cost be shared? Nonquantitative data as well as quantitative would be used to define whether or not such a joint service would promote cooperation among libraries.

What is the current climate of co-op? Does it vary by type of library? What co-op efforts now exist? What is the attitude of the parent bodies toward co-op by libraries? Looking at the possible negative arguments, again the quantitative and nonquantitative data are to be assembled and assessed.

If there might be legal problems in co-op contracting, what are they? Do they derive from state law? Are they institutional regulations? Can these problems be solved? At what cost? What type of contractual arrangement would alternately be feasible?

What about the potential problem of monitoring use? How would this be done to assure fair use of the service by contracting libraries? What cost is involved in developing and supporting the administrative structure?

Is there a point at which the co-op venture would include more libraries than could be served? What would be the cut off point? What speed of service is acceptable to contracting libraries? Same day? One or two days?

What problems would occur in delivery of search reports to member institutions? Would off-line printouts be delivered directly by owners? What about the quick, specific search requiring immediate feedback? What interaction at the terminal between client and reference librarian is possible? How much is needed? What if one of the member libraries does not meet its contractual responsibilities? Who must pay for this?

Information is collected and identified as to whether or not it is quantifiable or nonquantifiable. Although a wide range of sources and several individuals will be asked to respond to specific questions or provide specific materials, the task of assembling and assimilating the material is that of the analyst.

At the next and fifth step, the *actual costing of each alternative* begins. Depending upon existing data, the type of questions to be answered and a variety of other factors, the most appropriate method for determining cost is identified.

In addition to the cost of contracting for the service, there are the costs of personnel to operate the terminal and these include salary plus benefits for all time spent by any staff member in operating the terminal and in interfacing with the public in its use. Any postal or phone time that might result from transmitting information requested from the contracting institution to member institutions is included, as is time spent in supervising such activities. As database searching is a relatively new searching skill, training time in terminal use will be required.

Once the personnel costs have been identified, it is possible to compare the cost of database searching to the cost of manual searching. In terms of personnel costs for search time, is needed information retrieved fast enough to equalize cost? Is speed a factor in client satisfaction? Is the client satisfied with the amount of information retrieved manually? Is the volume of use, the cost per search, the client level of satisfaction such that the library should contract separately for service or would a cooperative arrangement suffice?

Other costs also must be added into the total cost package: maintenance of that part of the building devoted to housing the terminal and its operator. This includes cleaning, insurance, heating, and cooling. Administrative overhead and other general costs must be figured in as well.

What about the cost impact of the service on the total organization? Will the additional cost of the terminal, training in its use, etc., deprive or weaken another aspect of the reference function? Will there be fewer funds to purchase books and journals? Will a new reference librarian be hired to provide service from the terminal or will an existing librarian receive instruction in its use? Will an additional service spread the overall reference service too thin?

Will other aspects of the library's budget be affected by the increased reference service? Will funds need to be taken from budgets of other departments to cover the new service? Is it possible to identify costs that are not relevant to the service? Are all of the costs that have been assigned to the new service actually attributable to the service?

For each option, the above cost estimating questions are to be asked and figures obtained per alternative. The sources of all cost data are to be identified and the accuracy of the figures checked.

Once sufficient cost data per option has been assembled, the benefits are to be determined. Although the cost to an institution of contracting separately for service may be high, the benefit to clients in terms of access to the terminal on site may be sufficient to support that option. Perhaps the possible delay in time in shared access to the database may not be a critical factor in planning. Perhaps the cost of the service is not justified by the potential number of clients using it and a reliance on traditional reference services, with the possibility of paying for an occasional search in another fashion, would suffice.

In determining benefits, are all tangible benefits included? What benefits would accrue from having an in-house terminal? Who would use it, staff or community clientele? Would there be a public relations benefit? Studies have indicated that in the case of several public libraries, when a terminal providing access to bibliographic databases was installed, a new clientele from the community began to use it: professional people from local government, planners, analysts, and community business people. These are individuals who would benefit from traditional services as well and might use them once they had exposure to library service through the use of databases. Are there other database services available locally so that the library contracting for one might develop a sharing effort with the library contracting for the other?

What *measuring criteria can be developed to determine benefits?* Can need for the service be predicted on the basis of type of reference question now asked? What percentage would be more easily answered if the appropriate database were available? Can anticipated volume of use of the service be determined? What is the nature of the anticipated user—researcher, government official, student, general interest user? Are priorities by type of user to be set? Is there an optimum level of use? If data from a library with a similar size and clientele is available, this could help in responding to the above questions. If a pilot project has been developed to test these questions locally, a better response to the questions of cost-benefit would be available.

Nonquantifiable criteria also are to be taken into account—user satisfaction with the service, attitude toward the service of staff, of funding agency and of users. Negative attitudes of "too costly" or "too complicated" may emerge and cause operational difficulties. New services usually include selling jobs on the part of those wishing to implement them.

A series of measures is to be devised for each option, including the "no change" option, so that planning data can be collected for whatever option is selected. The continuous evalution thus built into the program will provide a basis upon which to adjust the program as it operates. As a means of determining attitudinal, nonquantifiable benefits one should ask what changes are anticipated. For example, will there be a new spirit of cooperation among libraries or excitement on the part of the reference librarians about the service?

Only now, that all background information has been assembled, alternatives identified, costs estimated and a means of benefit determined, are alternatives to be compared and a decision made. The alternatives are presented, each with cost figures and each with benefits stated in comparable terms. All figures are calculated for the same time frame.

At this point, there may be one alternative that stands out as being more appropriate, more cost effective and of greater benefit than the others. If the data concerning each alternative have been collected and recorded without bias, there is now sufficient reason to select the outstanding alternative. If two or more alternatives appear viable, on what basis is one selected over the other? It is often at this point, for better or worse, that personal preference is the reason for selection.

A pilot study to determine to what extent a preferred alternative or alternatives would meet the objectives of the program is often implemented. Data can be collected to determine who would use the service, how real operational costs compare to estimated costs, and what benefits accrue. From the data collected in the pilot study, a decision based on data, analysis, and planning is possible, thus insuring to the extent possible that through sound planning the most responsible use of funding has been determined.

The economic analysis process just discussed is essentially that which supports the programming and planning budgeting system (PPBS) and zero-base budgeting (ZBB). The planning aspect of both these systems have been found by consulting firms such as Booz-Allen and Hamilton to be "more effective as a planning than as a budgeting tool."

Within the past year or two, academic libraries have begun the process of examining their methods of decision-making when allocating funds for collection development. They must respond to increased costs and steady state or reduced budgets. The reason for examining the process has been financial, but the long range result, and a beneficial one, has been that planners have conducted a financial analysis. They have identified library collection development objectives and how they relate to the research and educational objectives of the university.

"The analysis of a SPEC (Systems and Procedures Exchange Center) survey carried out in May 1977 indicates that many libraries are moving away from a traditional mode of incremental allocation toward a regular, comprehensive review of how the library distributes its resources, the criteria used in distributing materials' funds, and the decision-making process itself."[2]

In making allocations, the academic library assembles a range of information including the library's history, its organizational connections, the nature of the parent institution, faculty pressures, and external pressures. Until the academic institution is clear as to its purpose, it is difficult for the library to establish compatible objectives.

In contrast to the past practice of almost automatic increments to existing budget items, libraries now include data on use of materials, on academic objectives, existing collection strengths, and costs of materials. The need for planning information reinforces the communication network by emphasizing input to decision-making by many staff members, faculty, administration, and other users. Among public libraries, only some of the largest have made a careful study of their decision-making processes. The precedent has been set and some guidelines drawn. It is anticipated that more and more public library managers and trustees will review their decision-making processes and thus have a clearer understanding of what services the library provides and the costs of those services.

Methodologies

Obtaining adequate information for analysis requires a variety of methodologies. Some of these provide general information, while others are quite specific. The general methodologies include those that are concerned with ways to approach the future and how to manage change. Much of what has been written in this area deals with managing growth. The realities of the past three to five years have added the need to manage a steady or declining state.

Regardless of whether one approaches library management from the view of continued growth, from steady state, or from that of decline, the basic strategy is to be able to manage the changing situation. Despite much discussion on the subject, no valid scientific principles have been set forth. Managing change is a seat-of-the-pants operation.

The basic information necessary to understand the change process in information agencies include:

Organizational. How does the library function? What is the overall organization and what subsystems exist? The formal organization chart provides one response to these questions, but the informal structure of leadership and communication within the system may provide a different response. How does change or innovation occur within the organization? Is it by directive or by consensus?

Strategies that can be used to institute and support change. What are the leadership dynamics of the organization? How does the manager inject new ideas into the organization? What is the role of change agents? What effect does organizational politics have on change? Are there concerns by the union that change will affect job security, by the professional organization that lack of change will jeopardize job security in the future? What role does program evaluation have as a strategy for change?

Practical experience with the dynamics of change as they affect information services. What is the information explosion and how can one cope? What is the impact of technological means of storing and retrieving information? The thrust of this presentation is on the need to manage change resulting from a shrinking financial resource. How can the library manager provide optimum service while living on an austerity budget? What changes in the way library services have been performed traditionally must be made in order to function, indeed to survive in a climate of increased information to be processed but with reduced resources to do so?

In their review of managing change in educational organizations Baldridge and Deal[3] present a set of rules for change that apply equally well to the information professions:

A careful needs assessment must be undertaken prior to instituting change. Organizations are complex and the obvious problem may be only a symptom of a deeper problem. The staff may have their own perspectives of the problem, and their input should be added to whatever quantifiable data is available. There is rarely only one possible solution to a problem and the administrator, the staff member, or the consultant who sees only one possible solution may be part of the problem. The one solution advocate has probably not investigated the problem carefully and is responding to the obvious.

Proposed changes must be relevant to the history of the organization. Each organization has its own saga, its myth and belief system explaining why the organization exists and what its belief system is and providing justification for the time and energy needed to maintain it. The purpose of the saga is to unite those working for the organization. Particular academic institutions such as Bennington College, Harvard, or West Point have very strong sagas, while many of the newer institutions and many of the large public institutions have different and probably less complex sagas. The library of one of these institutions derives its saga from that of the overall institution. Public libraries have their sagas as well. For example, the New York Public Library, with its origins in 19th century philanthropy and its missions of research and uplift; and the Boston Public Library, the first tax supported library. Each public library derives a large measure of its organizational saga from its historical community, its founding members, and their view of a library's purpose. Successful changes are made as a continuation of the institutional saga, not against it.

Organizational change must take into account the environment. This includes, in addition to the institutional environment or governmental environment of the library, its suppliers of information in its many formats and its clientele's needs for information in its many and possibly other formats and the way in which services are performed, including new technical means of acquiring information and serving the clientele. The financial climate, national and local, also forms part of the environment.

Serious change must affect both the organizational structure and the attitude of the individual.

. . . to approach institutional change solely in individual terms involves an impressive and discouraging set of assumptions—assumptions which are too often left implicit. They include at very least, the assumption that the individual can be provided with new insight and knowledge; that these will provide some significant alteration in his motivational pattern; that these insights and motivations will be retained even when the individual leaves the protected situation in which they were learned and returns to his accustomed role in the organization; that he will be able to adapt his new knowledge to that real-life situation; that he will be able to persuade his co-workers and accept the changes in his behavior which he now desires; and that he will also be able to persuade them to make complementary changes in their own expectations and behavior.[4]

Change must be directed at factors that can be manipulated, such as the structure of the organization, the reward system, or the environmental relationships. A library is vulnerable to environmental influences. Because of a lack of political power, when compared to police and fire services, public library budgets are traditionally hit harder than other services in time of crisis. The New York Public Library 1973–77 is a case in point. The library's budget was cut up to 50 percent while other city departments were cut by 10 percent or 25 percent. Population shifts also affect library income. As urban residents move to the suburbs, the tax base is eroded and budgets suffer. Changes in the population's age and/or ethnic representation also require continuous response from the library or it finds itself serving the community of a previous decade.

The academic library is vulnerable in terms of declining enrollment. As full-time enrollment declines over the next decade or more, and as part-time enrollment increases, a different type of student and student need becomes evident to the academic librarian. The academic library that functioned well in an era of growth, of resident, full-time student bodies, now must adapt to an era of steady state or decline, and of part-time, highly diverse student bodies in addition to the present although smaller full-time student bodies.

Technological changes—in the procedures, processes and activities of an organization, are those most often changed. Technology is defined as processes and activities rather than narrowly as machinery. As the library's ways of doing things change, so will the implementing technology. As new ways of doing things are devised, new roles will be created—the OCLC terminal operator, the outreach librarian, the bibliographic skills instructor.

The change in organizational structure and in ways of doing things (technology) go together. New methods often do not fit into old structures. Intertwined in this is also individual attitude toward change, the willingness of an individual to adapt to new technologies and new responsibilities.

There are those who resist change, as it is upsetting to their routine and to their view of library service.

Change must be thus both politically and economically feasible. It is necessary to determine what internal political pressures and external political pressures exist. For example, if the change considered was to charge a few for extensive research services by a public library, a whole range of political pressures would appear: from the librarian who is committed to free access, from the administrator who is trying to find ways to provide augmented service and still balance the budget, from community action groups opposed to any charges, from the professional association and its views toward access, and from various other groups having definite ideas about the change and its impact.

Finally, the projected change must be effective in solving the problems that were diagnosed. If the proposed change does not solve the problem, of what value is it?

The emphasis of this presentation is on the financial aspects of change. Can you perform a service better for less? What is the least expensive, most effective way of performing a task? To prepare for change and to provide needed information to assist in economic analysis, the following methodologies are useful: Delphi analysis to provide a tentative view of the future, community analysis to determine existent clientele and level of service needs, budgeting techniques such as line item, program, performance, and zero base to set planning in financial terms, model building to project a program into the future, and depreciation analysis to determine the life of existing resources. These methodologies are representative rather than complete and serve to indicate approaches to acquiring input for economic analysis that in turn leads to financial decision-making.

Delphi Technique

Delphi technique is a method of structuring group communication so that the group as a whole will have input into decision-making. This method has been used in library studies[5] to gain from experts in the field some sense of the future direction of specific courses of action or developments. For example, the California voters' passage of Proposition 13 to reduce local taxes will have an effect on local library service. Views as to what the outcome will be are varied. Bringing the Delphi technique to bear on this problem, a panel of experts in the field of library funding could be selected and asked to provide their best guesses as to the impact of Proposition 13. The various responses would be compared. Those most often reported would be listed and returned to panel members for prioritization as to which effects would most likely occur. As a research method, this is a faulty procedure. There are too many variables and too little quantifiable data, but as a means of communication among concerned experts it is most useful. It is a way for many sides of a problem to be heard, for new solutions to be posed and evaluated by one's peers, and for ranking solutions in order of priority. Within an organization, the use of the Delphi method is a means for all those involved in carrying out a possible program to discuss it in the preformative stage. It is particularly useful in situations when human judgment is necessary, when there are several possible responses to a problem, and when it is important to have strong support for the decision made. This method takes time and should not be used for every decision that needs to be made, but when goals of the library are under discussion, long range plans are being developed, or when particularly serious problems occur such as a major cut in the budget, this method of input for communication and planning is useful.

Nominal Group Technique

Somewhat allied to this planning method is the nominal group technique. Here a small group or groups of people, having been given available background information and having been allowed time to digest it, then pose solutions to the problem under consideration. Each member of the group in turn presents a solution or recommendation until all persons have contributed and all possible approaches have been suggested. The group then discusses all approaches, establishing priorities for these approaches, and presents them as a basis for planning. The composition of groups is important: if groups are separated by their work role—clerical, professional, administrative—the objectives or solutions of that one group are limited. If each group is a mixture of the three, useful communication is more possible. These and other methods of planning and priority setting serve to lay the groundwork for the final decision when it is made. Opportunity for all staff members to respond, to ask questions, to propose alternatives has been afforded. New alternatives may emerge, new perspectives may be identified. Although the final decision is made by the library administrator, its acceptance and implementation is dependent to a large degree on the willingness of the staff to accept the decision.

Community Analysis

Community analysis is a means of identifying a library's market; the geographic, demographic, and economic information on the individuals who have the legal right to use a library's services. It is not solely a study of who uses the library's service; it also includes those who do not use the library. Information obtained is essential to the planning function, to the development of priorities, and to the justification for financial support.

Community analysis is a relatively new method in library planning, as it is based on the concept of access. As the concept of elitism in the library declines, the concept of access develops and it becomes important to know who your users are and who has not been reached by library services. Questions that can be answered by a demographic study of a public library include:

What is the age range of the community?
What percentage are children, adults, retired adults?
How will this change in the next decade?
Is the population mobile?
What segments are moving?
What is the economic health of the community?
What level of tax support does the library have?
What level can the library expect to gain?
How will these factors change over the next decade?
What is the educational level of the community?
What kinds of jobs do residents hold?
What levels of education are necessary for these jobs?
What other informational resources are available in the community and how do they interfere with the library?

A study of the library's users, that 10–25 percent of the population (as identified by Berelson) who use the library, will identify the characteristics of the library user and this in turn can be compared to the profile of the community.

The user can also be asked to indicate how he or she uses the library; what services are used and for what purpose. How adequate is the collection in various subject areas; is the reference service adequate? Are indexes, the card catalog, and other tools easy to use? What services are missing? What services should be added?

From the planning view of the academic librarian, community analyses are equally important. It is easier to define the academic community than the public library community. One also assumes that the academic community, because of its purpose, is information dependent, but the degree of dependence on the library can vary by type of academic institution, by subject specialization, and according to the attitudes held by faculty and students.

The community college serves a commuting population, many of whom are working toward a two-year technical degree. The four-year college attracts a different clientele: more apt to be resident, full time, and more dependent on academic library services than the two-year college student. The university as a research and teaching institution with a large graduate student component would, one would assume, be the most information dependent of all. These are assumptions and require testing by the individual institution.

Who are the users of the academic library?

What are the current demographics of the student body?

How many are full time, part time?

How many are undergraduate, graduate students?

With the projected decline in full-time students over the next decade, what kind of student population must be planned for?

What about the faculty? What are their teaching and research specialities? To what extent do they rely on library resources and services? How do they view the library in terms of its support function in teaching and research? When new teaching programs are contemplated, what communication takes place between teaching faculty and library resource developers?

What about other users of the academic library: the administration, the alumni, the local community, other libraries through interloan, and other networking systems?

As budget increases slow, allocation of funds to build library collections slow and competition for funds grows. The amount of information available to library staff concerning faculty attitudes toward the library, faculty use of the library and the degree of faculty input in collection and program development will be of considerable political value in decision-making.

The purpose of community analysis is to collect data on the community of users and of nonusers, to determine who is served and who is not served, to identify clienteles not being served, to identify programs that are needed, and to plan for library service in at least a partial client-centered fashion. Community analysis can be seen as a feedback and evaluation system for library service.

In addition to the planning function and data-gathering function of community analysis, it also serves a political function. In the initial data-gathering activities, the public librarian will need to approach county planners, local assessors, and keepers of various census data. This approach will develop ties that can be useful for the future. Planners may not have considered library services in their long range projections and municipal agencies may not have been aware of some of the library resources that complement their own.

Changes in the composition of the clientele requires planning for changes in program. As the birth rate goes down, all levels of information service are affected. What plans should be made for children's services if there will be fewer children? Does serving a smaller child population mean that a smaller part of the budget can be devoted to children's services? Or is the physical plant and resource base needed to support this service such that it cannot be conveniently reduced even if the number of users shrinks?

In the academic library, as the student body becomes more heterogeneous, what additional services must be provided? Can the part-time student survive under the same rules of access that hold for the full-time student? How much bibliographic instruction in traditional and new services do students require? Does this vary depending on whether the student arrives at college directly from a secondary school or is a returning student?

What new needs of the researcher have been prompted by the availability of bibliographic databases? What varied roles in meeting client needs are being expected of the academic librarian? Are priorities correct if all needs cannot be met? Who sets these priorities and on what basis? The primary loyalty of faculty and students is to their own department and discipline, not to the library.

Each community is varied in its members, in its structure and its rate of growth or cutting back. The environment: national and regional economic picture, national politics affecting education and information policies and their funding, the growth in the service provided (information base and technology), and the expectations of the user must be taken into account along with local demographics if a client-oriented service is to be planned.

(The administrator) must be able to assess the environment and either influence the direction of community attitudes toward education or make internal changes that permit the school to adapt to changed conceptions of teaching and learning.[6]

Zero-Base Budgeting, or ZBB, Technique

Development of the budget is also an important planning tool. The budget is the goals and objectives of the library's long range plan presented in dollar figures. The *line item budget* is based on the costs of the preceding year as adapted to the next year, taking into account increased costs and added services. Increases are based on the ingredients of library service rather than on the objectives of service. There is no requirement that the library's programs or objectives be reviewed when developing this budget form. The *program budget* focuses on the programs of a library; reference, circulation, children's services; it indicates the cost of each program in terms of personnel, books and materials, overhead, etc. This budget form does require an annual review of the library's objectives to assure that the programs being carried out further those objectives. Performance budgeting carrries that program one step further by including an evaluation factor so that levels of performance for work and resources expended can be determined. These budget forms and their application in planning are detailed elsewhere and will not be discussed in depth here.

The most recent budgeting, planning technique is *zero-base budgeting*, a product of the 1970s. As outlined by Peter Phyrr[7] the concept of zero-base budgeting is that all programs and expenditures are to be reevaluated annually from the view of "Is this program necessary at all." Zero-base budgeting was implemented at Texas Instruments in 1971 and was applied to the budget of the State of Georgia in 1973 by the then Governor Carter. It has since been applied to both profit and not-for-profit organizations and despite mixed reactions is likely to be around for awhile.

As outlined by Phyrr, there are two basic steps in zero-base budgeting. The first of these is to develop decision packages for each library activity. The decision package includes a description of program, its goals and objectives, total budgeted cost of the package broken down by classification of expenditure, a description of personnel needed to perform the activity and a time frame for completion of the activity. A basic package is prepared, and then additional items are included: more staff, more resources, etc., that would enhance the basic package and its objectives. In addition, the decision package includes a statement of benefits that will accrue if the package is implemented. It also includes alternatives to the recommended packages or aspects of the package. The second step, once the decision packages have been developed, is to rank them in order of priority. The development of decision packages and their ranking focuses on the purpose of the program and its dollar needs and not on the amount of annual increase needed to maintain a program.

Writing in the *Wall Street Journal* of April 27, 1977, Robert N. Anthony, Walker Professor of Management Control at the Harvard Business School, labelled zero-base budgeting a fraud. His criticisms: There are too many decision packages that take too long to be reviewed and ranked by importance. Ranking decision packages according to priority does not work as program priority is influenced by the amount of funds apt to be available and not the other way around. Politics can be played in the ordering of priorities of packages, thus negating the process. What would be of real value, stated Anthony, is a zero-base review where outside experts visit an agency and review its reason for being, its method of operation, and its costs. Because of the time and trauma involved in such an activity, once every five years is sufficient. Decision packages are the same as program elements in a program budget and measurable results are similar to management by objective. One could surmise that zero-base budgeting is old wine in a new bottle.

James Hayes, president of the American Management Association, carries zero-base budgeting back a step to zero-base thinking —evaluation of activities of the organization in terms of the extent to which they further the organizational objectives. Budget decisions begin only after the planning and thinking of the managerial staff has determined those programs that should be costed. It is this function of zero-base budgeting that is of particular importance in the early stages of planning fiscally responsive budgets. The actual development of packages and their prioritization becomes important when the overall objectives have been set and the general framework of programming established.

Model Building

The model provides an estimate of the effect of increasing costs and inceasing demand for service. It provides an estimate of rising costs and their effect on service, given the same variables that exist at the time the model is developed.

To develop a model for financial planning, data is collected on all library operations. Many libraries lack such data and therefore it must be developed. The direct labor costs of each operation are determined. If such data does not exist, the diary method of recording actual time required to perform a task is used. From this, standard times for each operation and thus standard costs can be derived. This information is still not as accurate as one would wish as it is dependent on the time a limited sample of workers take to complete a task in a specific way. It is difficult to generalize such information from institution to institution because of the different variables involved. "How we did it good in . . ." may provide ideas for change elsewhere, but the idea itself may be the only transferable aspect.

A mathematical study of trends of costs in libraries, such as costs of books and labor, found that because of present library technology, productivity has not increased in that there has been no significant development of labor saving techniques. "Therefore the cost of library operations can be expected to rise regardless of a lack of improvement of service or higher levels of activity because of increased labor costs and no improved methods of operation." Rising costs of labor and materials will continue to cause financial difficulties for libraries, particularly because of inefficient ways of performing tasks.

Diane D. Cole[8] in her dissertation developed a model for a library charging mechanism. The library she studied serves twenty institutions, through annual contracts with each institution. These are health-care libraries with varying needs, from back up services to extensive resource needs in certain subject areas, as well as support services in acquisitions and cataloging. A model was devised listing all direct and indirect services provided, the level of service (self-service, mediated service, and in-depth service), the amount of staff time, level, and cost per service. A variety of models were set up; for acquisition, for cataloging, and for interlibrary loan. Users were categorized by institution and type of user per institution. Demand was then estimated per user type reflecting each service and level of service. The study resulted in the identification of use patterns by different users; for example, medical professionals use the expensive services such as computer services and assisted reference service while students served themselves to the extent possible. From these models a fee schedule based on actual patterns of service was set up.

Models are also designed to respond to "what if" questions. What if book processing increases but additional staff is not available? How long will it take to get a title into the user's hands? What if the collection increases at the present rate? When will the library run out of space?

A model was devised of Stanford University's budget "based on estimates of long-run growth rates of income and expense, policies for increasing tuition and determining spending from the endowment, and alternative assumptions about the size of further extraordinary budget adjustments in the short-run. The objective of each simulation run was to determine how fast the budget would go out of balance, given a particular combination of the above factors."[9] The foregoing methodologies are approaches to acquiring inputs for analysis; the following represents a methodology to assess existing resources.

Depreciation Analysis

Institutions that are tax supported cannot depreciate equipment and physical plant in the same manner that is possible in a business situation. In both instances, however, equipment does depreciate and must be replaced on a planned schedule and buildings require maintenance.

In planning for any program alternative, the use of equipment is usually considered part of the overhead of the library unless the equipment is used specifically for a program. When planning for cost, however, some consideration must be given to the replacement of typewriters, desks, circulation systems, etc.

There are several ways of calculating depreciation. Depreciation takes into account the useful life of each asset; five years for a typewriter, six years for some circulation equipment, ten years for a desk. Useful life varies according to the physical environment in which the typewriter or the desk is used and the characteristics of its use. Will the typewriter be in constant use or will it be used only part of each day? How heavy is the circulation? Will equipment be used by people expert in its use or will it be used by several people with varying levels of skill?

At what point is the equipment too costly to repair? When does worn equipment slow output? When does new equipment with new design make existing equipment obsolescent? When maintaining old equipment is more costly, both in terms of servicing and loss of work due to down time, then replacement is needed. A depreciation method will estimate the rate of wear and forecast the replacement date. The most common method is to indicate a life span for the equipment and depreciate a percentage each year, e.g., 10 percent depreciation over a ten year period. A declining balance method places the greatest rate of depreciation in the first years and less thereafter. Automobiles are an example of the declining balance method in which depreciation the first year or two is high, then declines more slowly and finally levels off.

When including this in calculation of cost of services, depreciation cannot appear as an item in the budget. What can appear is a planned replacement program. For information purposes, the library manager keeps a list of equipment, data on when purchased, its present condition and project replacement, and then in each annual budget lists items of equipment for purchase. Although it is often equipment purchases that are cut when budgets must be pared, if the pool of equipment ages and is not systematically replaced, time may be lost in working with faulty equipment and the day will come when major investments in equipment will be necessary.

The largest resource of the library—books, periodicals, and other informational material—depreciate but in a different fashion. Use declines for materials as they become outdated. Paper deteriorates and bindings wear out. A planned program of maintenance of the collection is another item in the depreciation package. Quality of information and depreciation of the physical collection are two different factors, both of which need to be considered In a research library, all materials are kept as they have a function beyond their current informational value. In a small- to medium-sized public library, space is at a premium and the local collection is used largely for current interest and ready reference with research collections available elsewhere. Here the information can be said to depreciate in the sense that patrons use it less. For the smaller academic library the collection needs fall somewhere between the ready reference and the research function. A planned program of binding, replacement of newspapers and journals with microfilm, and restoration of materials of historical value are part of the depreciation analysis.

Statistical Data

Among the continuing difficulties for library managers is the lack of relevant statistical data collected internally for decision-making. The lack of standardization both among libraries and over time which would permit analysis of library clientele and operations is another. One response to this need by library managers for information to improve management and decision-making in their own libraries was made by the National Center for Higher

Education-Management Systems in its *Library Statistical Data Base.*[10]

The need for data ". . . that will provide foundations on which to base decisions on complex internal questions and that will allow librarians to be responsive to the information needs of their external constituents, . . ." prompted the NCHEMS to develop a project that would identify data items most needed for both internal decision-making and external reporting. A three-level model was set up with administrative services, user services, technical and collection services, instructional services and support services as the first level. Two succeeding levels are increasingly specific. For example, user services at the second and third levels are divided into:

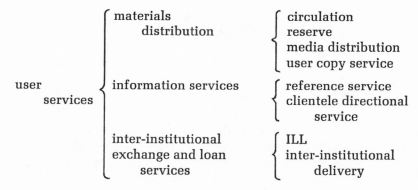

For each program a series of questions are asked: sources of library funding, amount received, and amount spent as well as questions related to human resources, facilities and space, clientele, outcomes of service, and level of performance and extent to which objectives are met. These then lead to a list of units of measure—financial, personnel, facility, activity, user, and performance—which can be used for planning. This study is an important step in the direction of developing a uniform recording and reporting system. Academic libraries have the LIBGIS format they can use for this purpose, but public library reporting, although uniform within a given state, is often not compatible with reporting from other states.

Other responses to the need for statistical data have been made: the development of methodologies to measure library service (Altman and DeProspro, Lipetz, Dainte and Gorman); compilation of statewide library statistics gathering forms; and the development of statistical programs as spin-offs of circulation control, automated systems, and manual systems.

The long-held myth that it is not possible to submit library and

information services to analysis is slowly giving way to an awareness that it is possible to develop quantitative data for many aspects of library service. The application of these data and financial
planning techniques to library services cannot help but provide
more cost effective and therefore more financially responsive decisions, provided that the nonquantifiable aspects of services are
taken into consideration as well.

Additional Readings

The expanding scope and size of the literature of decision-
making and planning reflects the greater importance placed on
these management functions in turbulent and uncertain times. Both
the qualitative and quantitative aspects of decision-making are
treated with increasingly greater depth in both business and public
administration and library science literature. Reflecting the increased need for uncertainty reduction in the management of organizations, the literature of planning has also increased dramatically over the past decade. Both long-range (or strategic) and
operational planning now receive wide coverage, as do the various
elements in the planning process.

Decision-Making

General Discussions

Many views of the decision-making process are available. Two
selections in this chapter have outlined this process, one in general
terms and the other in terms of library financial management. In
"Organizational Communication and the Decision Process," Lewis
provides another examination of the sequential steps in the decision-making process and highlights both the occasions for making
decisions and phenomena influencing decisions (*Organizational*

Communication, Grid Inc., 1975). Managerial decision-making is explored by Huber (*Managerial Decision Making*, Scott, Foresman, 1980), Vroom ("A New Look at Managerial Decision-Making" *Organizational Dynamics*, Spring 1973), Nutt ("Models for Decision-Making in Organizations and Some Contextual Variables which Stipulate Optimal Use," *Academy of Management Review*, April 1976), Summers and White ("Creativity and the Decision Process," *Academy of Management Review*, April 1976), and Ford ("Manage by Decisions, Not by Objectives," *Business Horizons*, February 1980). Argyris addresses the interpersonal nature of the decision process in "Interpersonal Barriers to Decision-Making" (*Harvard Business Review*, March-April 1966). In spite of the existence of the various decision-making models outlined above, some problems do not lend themselves well to these neatly structured processes. Ackoff has termed these "messy" problems[1]—complex combinations of problems that can neither be formulated nor solved apart from one another. Mitroff and Emshoff ("On Strategic Assumption-Making: A Dialectical Approach to Policy and Planning," *Academy of Management Review*, January 1979) identify a new methodology for dealing with these kinds of organizational problems. In outlining this methodology, they argue that conflict is an important organizational force, and in this case is central to the suggested methodology. Their discussion of assumption-making methodolgy and stakeholder analysis provides a thought-provoking view of the future of organizational problem solving as library problems become more and more complex.

In the library environment, Mason explores the complexities of decision-making in "Decisions! Decisions!" (*Journal of Academic Librarianship*, March 1975). Raffel suggests the utility of political analysis in library decision-making ("From Economic to Political Analysis of Library Decision-Making," *College and Research Libraries*, November 1974), and Sanderson suggests the need for more sophisticated and flexible decision-making methodology to cope with a rapidly changing and sometimes unexpectedly turbulent environment ("Coping with Turbulence," *Journal of Academic Librarianship*, September 1978).

Decision-Sharing

Input into and/or participation in planning and decision-making are critical topics to be considered in the library management process. Palmour outlines this kind of involvement in "Planning in

Public Libraries: Role of Citizens and Library Staff" (*Drexel Library Quarterly*, July 1977). Kaplan also contributes to the examination of involvement in decision-making in "On Decision-Sharing in Libraries: How Much Do We Know?" (*College and Research Libraries*, January 1977). Problems associated with group participation are outlined by Huseman, Lahiff and Hatfield ("Problems with Groups," in *Interpersonal Communication in Organizations*, Holbrook Press, 1976) and Von Bergen ("Groupthink: When Too Many Heads Spoil the Decision," *Management Review*, March 1978). Since there continues to be emphasis on group decision-making in libraries, it is important to consider whether groups reach more risky or more cautious decisions than do individuals, particularly library administrators. In the library environment, Eggleton explains and discusses "risky shift" and the applications of this theory to libraries ("Academic Libraries, Participative Management, and Risky Shift," *Journal of Academic Librarianship*, November 1979). Finally, if group decision-making is to work, what elements are necessary? Schmuck addresses this question in terms of leadership in "Developing Collaborative Decision-Making: The Importance of Trusting, Strong and Skillful Leaders" (*Educational Technology*, October 1972).

Information Gathering and Analysis

In *Information for Academic Library Decision-Making* (Greenwood Press, 1980), McClure suggests that if decision-making is defined as "that process whereby information is converted into action, then decision-making is largely concerned with the process of acquiring, controlling, and utilizing information to accomplish some objective."[2] There are a growing number of readings that suggest ways of gathering, analyzing, and using information for decision-making in the library setting. The following selections are identified merely as examples of the wide variety of materials available.

Information gathering as a part of the decision-making process is discussed by Brown ("Library Data, Statistics, and Information," *Special Libraries*, November 1980), Kunz ("Use of Data Gathering Instruments in Library Planning," *Library Trends*, January 1976), and Anders ("Statistical Information as a Basis for Cooperative Planning," *Library Trends*, October 1975). The development of information in a systematic way for library decision-making is discussed by Runyon in "Towards the Development of a Library

Management Information System" (*College & Research Libraries*, November 1981).

Other planning and decision-making aids are outlined by Webster ("Planning Aids for the University Library Director," ARL Occasional Papers #1, 1971), Martin ("User Studies and Library Planning," *Library Trends*, January 1976), Fish ("Community Analysis: A Planning Tool," *Bay State Librarian*, June 1978), and Coughlin, Taieb et al. (*Urban Analysis for Branch Library System Planning*, Greenwood Press, 1972). Approaches to the examination of future trends that will shape the library's environment are discussed by Fischer ("Delphi Method: A Description, Review, and Criticism," *Journal of Academic Librarianship*, May 1978), Drake ("Forecasting Academic Library Growth," *College and Research Libraries*, January 1976), and Kang and Rouse ("Approaches to Forecasting Demands for Library Network Services," *Journal of the American Society for Information Science*, July 1980). Quantitative methods useful in the decision-making process are described by Chen (*Quantitative Measurement and Dynamic Library Service*, Oryx Press, 1978), Dougherty and Heinritz (*Scientific Management of Library Operations*, 2nd ed., Scarecrow Press, 1982), Rowley and Rowley (*Operations Research: A Tool for Library Management*, ALA, 1981), Bommer ("Operations Research in Libraries: A Critical Assessment," *Journal of the American Society for Information Science*, May-June 1975), and Cook and Greco ("The Ugly Duckling Acknowledged: Experimental Design for Decision-Making," *Journal of Academic Librarianship*, March and May 1977). Analysis of library procedures and systems is discussed by Heinritz ("Analysis and Evaluation of Current Library Procedures," *Library Trends*, April 1973) and by Chapman (*Library Systems Analysis Guidelines*, Wiley, 1975), while cost analysis as a part of decision-making is outlined by White ("Cost Effectiveness and Cost-Benefit Determinations in Special Libraries," *Special Libraries*, April 1979) and Mitchell (*Functional Cost Analysis for Libraries: A Total System Approach*, JAI Press, 1977).

Planning

General Discussions

A number of reading selections provide a general overview of planning. Mockler offers a retrospective examination of planning literature that helps put the present literature into perspective ("Theory and Practice of Planning," *Harvard Business Review*,

March-April 1970). A comprehensive—although dated—treatment of planning as a part of the management process is provided by LeBreton and Henning's *Planning Theory* (Prentice-Hall, 1961). Steiner's *Top Management Planning* (Macmillan, 1969) focuses on the planning process from an executive perspective, emphasizing strategic rather than tactical planning. The nonprofit viewpoint is represented by Hardy's *Corporate Planning for Nonprofit Organizations* (Association Press, 1972).

Additional views that highlight particular aspects of planning as a management function include Ansoff's "The State of Practice in Planning Systems," (*Sloan Management Review*, Winter 1977), Stephens, Ezell and Kuntz's "Conceptualization of the Corporate Planning Process: A Micro and Macro View" (*Journal of General Management*, Spring 1980), Leontiades's "Perspectives on Planners and Planning" (*Business*, September-October 1980), Mintzberg's "Planning on the Left Side and Managing on the Right" (*Harvard Business Review*, July-August 1976), and Shank, Niblock, and Sandalls' "Balance 'Creativity' and 'Practicality' in Formal Planning" (*Harvard Business Review*, Jan.-Feb. 1973). While planning is an important part of the management process that benefits both organization and individual, there is still resistance to this management function. Tagiuri summarizes these forms of resistance and the counter-arguments that can be directed toward each objection to planning in "Planning: Desirable and Undesirable" (*Human Resource Management*, Spring 1980).

In the library setting, Kemper suggests a general and systematic framework in which planning may be examined ("Library Planning: The Challenge of Change," *Advances in Librarianship,* 1970). In a carefully constructed overview, McClure ("The Planning Process: Strategies for Action," *College and Research Libraries,* November 1978) provides a comprehensive outline of the planning process—the whys, the hows, the important questions to ask, and the overall view necessary to interpret this management process in the library environment. His article offers a vantage point from which to examine some of the most pressing issues in the planning process. Bell and Keusch ("Comprehensive Planning for Libraries," *Long Range Planning*, October 1976) present an overview of planning that combines both strategic and tactical elements, using examples from a health sciences library to demonstrate planning for a total library system. In addition, a special triple issue of the *Journal of Library Administration*, called "Planning for Library Services: A Guide to Utilizing Planning Methods for Library Management" (Summer/Fall/Winter 1981) provides a set of essays that cover almost all aspects of planning in the library setting

Several sources more specific to a type of library are also useful in examining the overall concept of planning in the library setting. *A Planning Process for Public Libraries* (Palmour et al., ALA, 1980) provides detailed direction for the design and implementation of planning in the public library setting; Lynch describes the background that resulted in the publication of this manual and suggests a rationale for any library's involvement in planning ("Public Library Planning: A New Approach," *Library Journal*, 15 May 1980). The library's place in institutionwide planning, the importance of developing an analytical planning model for the library's role in institutional planning, and the description of such a model are provided by Hubbard ("The Ecology of the Academic Library: Articulating Library Needs to the College Planning Process," ED 190 161, 1979). The development of an analytical framework for planning and decision-making in the large library environment is covered in depth by Hamberg et al. (*Library Planning and Decision-Making Systems*, MIT Press, 1974).

Strategic Planning

"Long-range" and "strategic" are terms used to refer to an overall level of planning that considers the future of the entire organization within its changing environment and determines the major objectives of the organization and the policies and strategies by which they will be achieved. Daniells has compiled a selected, annotated guide to recent literature on strategic planning in *Business Intelligence and Strategic Planning* (Baker Library, Graduate School of Business Administration, Harvard University, 1979). Ewing's *Long-Range Planning for Management* (3rd ed., Harper & Row, 1972) offers a number of selected essays that explore this level of planning from the managerial perspective. Steiner (*Strategic Planning*, Free Press, 1979), Lorange and Vancil (*Strategic Planning Systems*, Prentice-Hall, 1977; "How to Design a Strategic Planning System," *Harvard Business Review*, 1976), and Drucker ("Strategic Planning: The Entreprenurial Skill" in *Management: Tasks, Responsibilities, Practices*, Harper & Row, 1974) also address this important aspect of planning.

Newell offers a library approach to strategic planning in "Long-Range Planning for Library Managers" (*PNLA Quarterly*, October, 1966) as do Kennington ("Long Range Planning for Public Libraries," *Long Range Planning*, April 1977) and Dorff, who focuses on eight steps to determine *what* the library wants to do in the future and *how* it will accomplish this mission ("Librarian as Planner," *Catholic Library World*, July 1974). Several examples of long-range planning in individual library settings will be helpful to the reader who wishes to translate theory into practice. On the state level, Eberhart's "The Future of Long-Range Planning" (*Wisconsin Library Bulletin*, January 1973) illustrates the development of a comprehensive, long-range program of library services in Wisconsin; Fox's article on "Library Planning and Evaluation Institute: Helping State Libraries Write Effective Long-Term Programs" (*American Libraries*, May 1972) illustrates a methodology for providing support to the long-range planning process. Stone's "Long-Range Planning: An Interim Report on the Duke Experience" (*North Carolina Libraries*, Winter 1978) and McGrath's "Development of a Long-Range Strategic Plan for a University Library—the Cornell Experience" (Cornell University, 1973) also offer insights into the long-range planning process as it has been applied in individual libraries.

Understanding the environment within which the organization must operate is a crucial element in the strategic planning process. Preble's review of "Corporate Use of Environmental Scanning" (*University of Michigan Business Review*, September 1978) and House's "Environmental Analysis: Key to More Effective Dynamic Planning" (*Managerial Planning*, January-February 1977) delineate environmental analysis techniques that can be used to identify the external forces affecting organizational planning. The organization's environmental impact has been outlined by Lindsay and Rue's "Impact of the Organization Environment on the Long-Range Planning Process: A Contingency View" (*Academy of Management Journal*, September 1980).

Goals and Objectives

Determining overall goals and objectives for the organization and the policies and strategies by which they will be carried out is a crucial part of the long-range planning process; in fact, the entire process, as well as organizational control, rests on this element. In "Use or Value of Goals and Objectives Statements" (*Journal of Library Administration*, Fall 1980) Pings describes the need to search for goals and objectives in libraries as a "quest for certainty"[3] in a rapidly changing environment. Because libraries and other service organizations often orient their programs toward abstract ideas, they may be susceptible to "goal displacement" in which "means become substituted for claimed goals."[4] Libraries also encounter difficulties as a result of conflicting priorities and multiple goals. Burr ("Library Goals and Library Behavior," *Col-*

lege and Research Libraries, January 1975) elaborates on the idea of utility maximization as a response to multiple and conflicting goals. In outlining this approach, he also provides a description of the goal-setting process. In "Goal Determination," Haak identifies the differences between tangible and intangible goals and methods for using these principles in goal setting (*Library Journal,* 1 May 1971). Davis also focuses on "Goals" (*Illinois Libraries,* January 1975) as does Young, who describes the goal-setting process and the construction of written goals and objectives in the library setting ("Generating Library Goals and Objectives," *Illinois Libraries,* November 1974). In addition, Granger focuses on the development of a conceptual framework in goal setting that is useful for all kinds of organizations ("The Hierarchy of Objectives," *Harvard Business Review,* May-June 1964).

Several examples of goal setting in particular types of libraries are also useful to the reader, including "Setting Objectives for School Media Programs" (Adcock, *Illinois Libraries,* June 1978), "Review of the Formulation and Use of Objectives in Academic and Research Libraries" (*ARL Management Supplement,* January 1974), and "The Public Library Goals and Objectives Movement: Death Gasp or Renaissance?" (Bone, *Library Journal,* July 1975). Various descriptions of goal formulation and actual goals identified are provided for academic libraries in *SPEC Kit #58* (Association of Research Libraries, October 1979).

While not only a part of the planning process, the Management-by-Objectives (MBO) approach to management may be seen initially as an extension of the focus on goals and objectives. In this integrated management system, however, objectives are only one part of a total system, the others being plans, managerial direction and action, control (monitoring) and feedback.[5] A thorough explanation of MBO, its major elements, and its implementation in many service organizations is provided by McConkey's *MBO For Nonprofit Organizations* (AMACOM, 1975). Other particularly helpful reading selections from the business and public administration literature include Drucker's "What Results Should You Expect? A User's Guide to MBO" (*Public Administration Review,* January-February 1976), Odiorne's "How to Succeed in MBO Goal Setting" (*Personnel Journal,* August 1978), which provides twenty-seven steps that can be taken to avoid errors in applying MBO, and a second selection on goal setting that discusses the hierarchical and horizontal integration of goals throughout the organization (Salton, "The Focused Web—Goal Setting in the MBO Process," *Management Review,* January 1978). Levinson offers a critical assessment of MBO techniques that highlights possible pitfalls in the application of MBO ("Management by Whose Objectives?," *Harvard Business Review*, July-August 1970).

Several library-related reading selections also offer insights into MBO and its application in the library, including "Management by Objectives in the Library: Guidelines for Use" (Tansik, *Catholic Library World*, May 1979), "Management by Objectives: Organized Common Sense" (Deegan, *Illinois Libraries*, June 1978), and "Library Management by Objectives: The Humane Way" (Fields, *College and Research Libraries*, September 1974). More specific applications of MBO are addressed by Lewis ("Management by Objectives: Review, Applications, and Relationships with Job Satisfaction and Performance," *Journal of Academic Librarianship*, January 1980) and by Mancall and Barber ("Management by Objectives as a Process to Facilitate Supervision and Staff Development," *Drexel Library Quarterly*, July 1978). Ford offers a reexamination of the usefulness of MBO in "MBO: On Idea Whose Time Has Gone" (*Business Horizons*, December 1979); Michalko ("Management by Objectives and the Academic Library: A Critical Overview," *Library Quarterly*, July 1975), Dworak ("If Not MBO, Then What?" *Illinois Libraries*, June 1978), and Jones ("An Evaluation of the Use of MBO Procedures in a Library," *Special Libraries*, July 1975) offer critical examinations of MBO in the academic library setting.

The establishment of policies to support identified goals and strategies is vital to the success of the planning process. Steiner and Miner devote one chapter of *Management Policy and Strategy* (Macmillan, 1977) to the principles of strategic management and policy formulation applied to the nonprofit organization. Focusing on a highly useful nine-point problem-solving model of the policy process, Zand outlines methods of reviewing and improving policy formulation in large organizations ("Reviewing the Policy Process," *California Management Review*, Fall 1978). Tersine also defines policy making and its relationship to objectives, available resources, restraints and external influences ("Structure and Content of Policy Decisions," *Managerial Planning*, November-December 1978). Because some problems defy adaptation to standard organizational policies, Mitroff and Emshoff's suggestions for dealing with "messy" problems are particularly relevant ("On Strategic Assumption-Making: A Dialectical Approach to Policy and Planning," *Academy of Management Review*, January 1979). Two selections from the library literature offer insights into policy making—first, Kingseed's chapter "Guidelines for a Library Policy" in *The Library Trustee: A Practical Guidebook* (3rd ed., Bowker, 1978), and second, Townley et al. "Policy Negotiations: Simulation as a Tool in Long-Range Library Planning" (*Special Libraries,* March 1978).

Tactical Planning

Operational, or "tactical," planning involves the "determination of the specific processes by which the strategic plans are implemented and will include such activities as medium range programming, short-term budgets, and detailed functional plans."[6] Bryson's "Using Maxims in Library Administration, Planning, and Research" (*Minnesota Libraries,* Winter 1977–78) briefly illustrates a planning process model for making program changes in the library. Goldberg's *A Systems Approach to Library Program Development* (Scarecrow Press, 1976) and the June 1978 issue of *Illinois Libraries,* "Participatory Program Planning and Management for Libraries," provide helpful insights into tactical planning. Kingsbury suggests an incremental approach to the process ("Plan by Increments," *Library Journal,* 1 February 1972), and Pekar offers guidelines for implementation of planning ("Planning: A Guide to Implementation," *Managerial Planning,* July-August 1980).

Specific examples of library planning are especially useful in helping to delineate the process of tactical planning. Leisner's *Systematic Process for Planning Media Programs* (ALA, 1976) and "The Development of a Planning Process for Media Programs" (*School Media Quarterly,* Summer 1973), Winstead and Tucker's practical "trip-planning" outline of the process in an academic environment ("Management Planning: One Library's Approach," *Illinois Libraries,* June 1978), Kaser's "Planning in University Libraries: Context and Processes" (*Southeastern Librarian,* Winter 1971), Birula's "Planning a Branch Library" (*Special Libraries,* June 1980), Gell's "Cooperative Planning in Action: The Washington Experiment" (*Special Libraries,* July 1976), and Lorenzi's "The Art of Planning for Library Personnel" (*Bulletin of the Medical Library Association,* April 1976) are but a few examples of applications of the planning process in a type of library or within a library function.

At the operational level, control processes become an integral part of planning, particularly in terms of budgeting. This integration is suggested in three articles—"Operational Planning: The Integration of Programming and Budgeting," by Camillus and Grant (*Academy of Management Review,* April 1980), by Reimnitz's

"Testing a Planning and Control Model in Nonprofit Organizations" (*Academy of Management Journal*, March 1972), and in the library environment by Sellers ("Basic Planning and Budgeting Concepts for Special Libraries," *Special Libraries*, February 1973).

Implementation

Implementation of a planning program is often the most difficult part of the planning process. As Taylor and Davis have suggested in the reading selections in this chapter, many barriers stand in the way of implementation. The human factors that often present such barriers are discussed by Reichman and Levy ("Psychological Restraints on Effective Planning," *Management Review*, October 1975) as well as by Lenz and Lyles ("Tackling the Human Problems in Planning," *Long Range Planning*, April 1981). A discussion of the implementation process is provided by Pekar in "Planning: A Guide to Implementation" (*Managerial Planning*, July-August 1980), while Farmer and Hess outline "A Proposed Change Strategy for Organizational Management Planning Programs" (*Illinois Libraries*, June 1978), which represents only one of the many discussions of planned change to be found in the literature.

Control

The control process is one of "attempting to maintain conformity between actual and desired results."[1] The major elements of this process include: setting standards and determining means of measurement, observing and checking performance, evaluating this performance, and taking corrective action if required. Here "performance" may refer to *any* part of the organization that is supposed to contribute to its effectiveness—individuals, work units, services—as well as the organization as a whole. All of the elements in the process are equally important and interdependent; together, they should form a dynamic, ongoing process essential to keeping the library moving toward organizational effectiveness. Control may be preventive or remedial—through the control process, possible chances for poor performance to develop may be prevented through consistent observation and feedback; remedial action may also be taken if errors develop.

Judging from the literature, control is perhaps the most difficult part of the management process to relate to the library setting. In selection 1, Newman and Wallender suggest that the hard-to-measure, sometimes ambiguous, and often multiple objectives of not-for-profit enterprises limit their ability to establish an impersonal and predictable feedback system. Also, like other service organizations, libraries have a "lack of a tradition of constructive control."[2] They tend instead to rely on control over inputs and volume of activity, with little reward offered for meeting control standards.

There is little in the literature that provides a general overview of control as it applies to libraries. Much is fragmented into discussions of budgeting or the need for standards and measures of effectiveness in libraries. Few authors discuss feedback, corrective action, or the overall nature of "control" as a management function, yet nowhere is the need greater for these elements than in the library environment. Because of this fragmentation, Rizzo's essay on control is included to provide an overview of the entire process as it relates to the library. This broad perspective stresses the integral nature of control and builds on Newman and Wallender's brief discussion of the problems that not-for-profit organizations encounter with control. Also, Rizzo's analysis supports Drucker's view of the relationship of efficiency and effectiveness; i.e., "to control is to increase the probability that the organization will achieve effectiveness and do so efficiently. Control should be viewed as uncertainty reduction."[3]

Budgeting is an important form of control, and there are numerous discussions of the budgeting process, as well as of various approaches to budgeting, in the library literature. The Cherrington essay on budgeting, however, moves the reader beyond a simple process description toward an examination of the real intent of any control process—improvement of organizational effectiveness. The danger in any control process is that it may become merely an end in itself—so focused on process that no real outcomes are ever utilized. For example, in the case of employee performance appraisal, no improvement can take place unless managers make use of the *results* of the appraisal. As the Cherringtons suggest, control-related activities and the control process itself should be considered a management tool to be used for organizational improvement. Specific ways that budgeting can become not only a measure of cost control but an aid in the overall improvement and change of the organization in terms of planning and successful goal attainment are also identified. This selection reminds the reader that other organizational processes should be used in the same way—as a means to an end.

Standards of performance and criteria of effectiveness are central elements in the control process. Without them, the process loses focus, since there is nothing against which to measure actual performance to ascertain whether goals have been met. Du Mont explores the concept of effectiveness in libraries and deals with the problems of multiple and conflicting objectives which Newman and Wallender identify in selection 1. Rather than look for a single model of library effectiveness, it is suggested that a systems model be utilized to view effectiveness itself as a process. In this way, the library can move beyond the focus on measurement of inputs to a broader view of control.

9. Control

John R. Rizzo

It is best to view control from a broad perspective and to show sensitivity to its many characteristics and ramifications. Control has many facets. Failure to have a full grasp of its implications can result in lost opportunities and severe organizational problems. Too many managers have learned that ill-conceived control practices can result in the failure or even in the direct opposite of what was intended. Instead of improved performance and predictability, a poorly designed control process may, at best, have little effect. At worst, it can breed more problems than it solves, and these new problems can trigger implementation of additional controls. These, in turn, may serve to exacerbate an already troublesome situation. The escape from such a deteriorating cycle lies in full understanding of the control concept, with due consideration given to opportunities and pitfalls in achieving control.

Control Defined

To control is to help ensure that actions and results achieved are consonant with objectives, standards, and plans. To control is to increase the probability that the organization will achieve effectiveness and do so efficiently. Control should be viewed as uncertainty reduction, an important managerial role requirement.

Reprinted from *Management for Librarians: Fundamentals and Issues*, pp. 76–95, by John R. Rizzo and used with permission of the publisher, Greenwood Press, a division of Congressional Information Service, Inc., Westport, Connecticut.

Interpreting this definition in its broadest sense, virtually any behavior in an organization can be interpreted in control terms. For example, a clerk who is performing a job well is acting predictably and according to expectations. Control is invisible on the surface, but it is unquestionably operative. If the supervisor observes that clerk, makes an evaluation that the clerk is doing well, and chooses to leave well enough alone or to offer praise, control is also operative. If the clerk smells a wire burning and unplugs a machine before irreparable damage occurs, control has taken place because an undesirable outcome was prevented. The clerk anticipated an unacceptable and harmful consequence and acted to reduce the probability of its occurrence to zero. The clerk may also participate in a staff meeting that same day with peers and the supervisor. In that meeting, standards might be agreed upon, plans may be made, or objectives established. In doing so, the probability that desirable performance will occur is increased. In other words, some uncertainty is reduced, and improved control is achieved.

If control is viewed in these ways, it is not a process that is separable from other processes. That is, one does not do one's job and then control. One does not plan, organize, and then control. Unlike control, some other managerial processes can be conceptually and operationally separated or isolated. One can plan and later implement. It is possible to design an organization and later staff it. But control does not come before or after other events. It is an integral part of other functions and processes. Furthermore, these functions and processes need not be managerial. Control was relevant in the situation where the clerk was working independently, and this would hold true whether or not the supervisor were observing. In this way, control cannot be viewed solely as a managerial prerogative or overt action.

There are other serious implications to defining control broadly. Perhaps the most obvious is the fact that control opportunities and problems can arise in any organizational situation. Managers in particular are oriented toward improved control practices in virtually all phases of what they do. They are better prepared to anticipate control problems regardless of the situation they are currently dealing with. Another way of saying this is that uncertainty reduction issues legitimately enter into much of what managers do.

This discussion appears to raise the specter of overcontrol or poorly executed control practices. One might envision an organization in which concerns about control pervade and permeate everything and everyone. Widespread needs for predictability and supersensitivity to deviations would lay a paranoid blanket over the entire organization. But this is an unnecessary and a spurious implication of viewing control in its broad sense. To say that control is relevant in all organization situations is not to say that there will be too much of it or that it will automatically be poorly executed. Neither overcontrol nor poor control need occur as a consequence of seeing control opportunities and problems in all phases of organization life.

Another way to look at this is to say that control, like anything else, has quantitative and qualitative aspects. Quantitatively a manager can exercise too little, the right amount, or too much control. Qualitatively the manager can have too wide or too narrow a scope of control, use appropriate or inappropriate methods and measures, act too quickly or too slowly, or create conflict or cooperation in exercising control. Thus the goodness or badness of control processes lies in how much or in what ways it is executed. A broad perspective on control does not automatically produce either a good or bad result. It is what the manager does with that perspective that counts.

Many texts on management confine their definition of control to focus on the correction of deviations from expectations. In this narrower perspective, performance is observed and measured; then it is compared to some standard. If a sufficient magnitude of deviation is judged to exist, corrective action is taken. A wide variety of remedies for unwanted deviations is possible. One needs only to determine the cause of the deviation and eliminate it. This is usually easier said than done, but nevertheless, this is the essence of a narrow view of control. It is no wonder then that chapters on control appear near or at the end of a text when it is defined in this way. The practicing manager seemingly engages in planning and all other functions and processes, and once they are established and operative, he or she checks on how well things are going. Surely this is control. But it is only part of what control means. It is really "after the fact" or post-control. Use of this kind of control is both important and necessary, but it cannot exist alone, and if it is viewed only in this way, a great deal is lost to the manager. Post-control is also the area where human emotions and resistance are most apt to come into play. It is the most problematic area of control. Consequently focus or overemphasis on post-control multiples rather than eases the manager's problems. A broader perspective allows examination of precontrol and in-process control in addition to post-control.

Precontrol

In the practice of precontrol, attempts are made to make events more predictable and certain before those events actually take place. Precontrol occurs before the event. It is a visionary process in which managers anticipate future conditions in advance of actual implementation. It is quite appropriate to think of precontrol as a design process.

In many ways, precontrol is the preferred form of control because it can reduce the need for other forms of control, which can become quite expensive and are more likely to create human emotional strain. On the whole, employees are more likely to be attracted to processes we call precontrol, yet are apt to resist or feel stress when subjected to post-control techniques.

One form that precontrol can take is planning. When people participate in planning, they not only establish but have an opportunity to learn expectations for performance. Once objectives are formulated and translated into unit and individual assignments, the predictability of performance is significantly enhanced. This is particularly true when employees agree with and personally are committed to objectives. A tremendous and powerful level of control exists when someone strongly desires to achieve a clear objective that has the consensus and support of colleagues in the organization. This condition is not easily accomplished, but to the extent that it is, an ideal form of control has taken place. Unless conditions change significantly, there is great assurance that resources and efforts will be focused on accomplishment of the objective. Assuming an adequate level of competence on the part of the unit or employee responsible for the objective, effective performance is highly likely. Concerns about possible failure are reduced.

In reality, planning rarely produces perfect predictability. It never completely eliminates additional forms of control. But managers do not sufficiently take advantage of planning as control. In the pressures of the day, planning activities give way to other behaviors, partially because planning is a less than spontaneous or naturally occurring phenomenon. It is not something that most of us habitually do. While we verbally extol the values of planning, our behavior is not always consistent with what we profess. Managers must therefore come to believe more forcefully that planning is worthwhile and that it can serve as an important contribution to control.

Policies, another form of precontrol, are general guides to action. They may be written statements that reflect the values and be-liefs of the organization or unwritten but widely held opinions about matters of central concern to organization members. It is usually better to have policies in written form, especially when they ad-dress concerns that repeatedly arise or when serious problems could arise in their absence. Thus managers should periodically review policy statements. In this way, outdated policies can be eliminated or revised and new policies instituted to cover a critical concern.

Policies can range from general statements of philosophy to more specific guides, although they should not be so specific that they describe acceptable or unacceptable behavior in concrete terms. Such statements are reserved for those of procedure, rules, or standards. Nor should they be so general as to fail to serve as a guide to action. A university that says that its policy is to provide the best educational opportunity to a broad segment of the adult community has virtually no policy at all because the statement cannot serve as an effective guide to action. What is meant by "best"? How broad a segment is really feasible or desirable? Is no one from the adult community ever to be excluded? On the other hand, a university that says that its policy is to offer continuing education opportunities for credit and noncredit purposes to adults mid-career or seeking new careers has a clearer guide to action. Its policy directly suggests particular programs for a particular segment of society. But the policy is general; it is a form of com-mitment to action that dictates consideration of alternate forms of implementation. From such a policy, proposals and plans can be devised, and current activities can be evaluated.

Policies can cover a wide range of concerns. In a library, poli-cies can apply to employees as well as to clients or other segments of the community. One policy may define total hours of operation without specifying a schedule. Another might state that the library considers the preschool child a key client group. Policies can be prepared to guide circulation practices or the collection and acqui-sition processes. For example, it may be the library's policy not to offer textbooks or best-sellers for general circulation. Regarding its own employees, a number of policy statements are possible. A library may wish to make it policy to provide educational support to employees. It may develop a personnel policy manual to cover matters such as annual leave, sick leave, promotion, and termina-tion. It may need an additional policy to govern eligibility for finan-cial support and release time for attending professional society meetings.

The matters that policies can cover can become quite lengthy. As a result, a good deal of judgment is required in developing policy. A major criterion for exercising such judgment has to do with necessity. A good policy is a needed policy, which is one that helps employees to know what is expected or what is appropriate behavior, prevents problems that are not trivial or that are bound to recur, and helps employees to make decisions and solve recurring problems without having to seek clarification and approval repeatedly. A policy that helps little, prevents nothing, or addresses infrequent and trivial situations is unnecessary. The criterion of necessity is easily demonstrated if one considers a case of a request to attend a professional society convention. In the absence of policy, a manager cannot adequately decide on approval for time off or financial support. If the decision is made in the absence of policy, a number of dysfunctional consequences could ensue; cries of inequity are bound to arise. Permission to attend the meeting might be utilized as a reward for good performance, whereas a policy might make such attendance a right of employment rather than have it contingent on performance. Some managers might approve the request if the employee is an officer of the professional society but not for other reasons. Other managers would undoubtedly use other criteria. Diversity and arbitrariness take over where uniformity and consensus are possible.

Another criterion to judge policy has to do with whether it simplifies rather than unduly complicates the organization. Policies should not be overly complex, constraining, or burdensome and should not create more problems than they solve. They can easily do so when there are too many of them and when a significant proportion are unnecessary. They can complicate work life when one policy urges one kind of behavior while another prohibits it. Policies should not block desired consequences unless they prevent worse consequences or enhance clearly superior ones. For example, a policy for a university library that disallows acquisition of textbooks blocks access to needed material for students. The undesirability of this policy may be outweighed by other considerations, such as theft rate potential, rights and expectations of publishers and authors, and student disappointment when supplies cannot meet demand.

Good policy making can be viewed as an opportunity to take advantage of experience. Experience often tells what works and what does not, what appears worthwhile and what is not worthy of attention. This experience can be our own or that of others. We can take advantage of others' experience in preparing and evaluating policy in several ways. All we need to do is to put ourselves in contact with other similar organizations directly or through the use of consultants. From them we can learn about their policies. We avoid learning from experience by looking at what others have done. However, several critical cautions are in order here. One is that learning from our own personal experience has its distinct advantages. The learning is more lasting and understanding is deepened. Nevertheless it is sometimes best to take another's word for it. One need not test a poison by taking it so as to ensure a lasting and deep understanding. Learning from others should also be tempered by knowledge of their situation and how it compares to one's own. Few things, policies included, can be transplanted from one situation without revision or adaptation. Minimally one would scrutinize for applicability before introducing someone else's policy into one's own organization. Finally experience should always be viewed as a double-edged sword, whether it be one's own or someone else's. Experience allows us to avoid traps, reduce error, and add to efficiency. One edge of the blade cuts in our favor. The other edge cuts our finger or could cause more severe damage, for experience puts blinders on us. It focuses us more narrowly and inhibits creativity and seeing options that less experienced people might see. Experience and training have a potential to incapacitate us outside their confines and to limit our flexibility. This is a widely accepted tenet in problem solving, decision-making, and creativity theory.

Managers must exercise good judgment in the use of policy. It is an invaluable precontrol device that all too often is seriously underestimated. Of parallel importance is the requirement to review policy periodically. Managers should conduct an annual review individually, by unit, or by a review committee. It might also be useful to have an avenue by which employees can suggest new policy or revisions at any time. A committee that meets periodically or as needed can be used to handle policy problems or review policy-related suggestions.

Specific rules can also be written as extensions or interpretations of policies. Unlike policies, rules are more concrete in nature and narrower in scope. They describe and define certain practices and may apply to anyone reasonably expected to comply. Rules sometimes simply state a precise expectation, such as, "The circulation desk must be staffed by at least one person at all times the library is open to the public," or "Undergraduates requiring materials from the stacks must submit a written request on form S-2 to the circulation desk on the second floor." Some rules embody the rule and punishment for violaters in the same breath: "Any employee with three unexcused tardinesses will be suspended for one day without pay," or "Withdrawal privileges will be denied patrons with a third overdue notice until the overdue material is returned."

Much of what was said about policy can be said about rules. They must be judged for their necessity, their ability to simplify rather than complicate, and their capacity to be useful rather than dysfunctional. Rules, however, require some additional considerations, some of which lie in the relationship between policies and rules. First, the two must be consistent. Rules cannot require behavior that violates or is otherwise unreflective of policy. Also not all rules require that a policy exists to justify them. Conversely a policy may be sufficiently clear that rules would be redundant and pedantic and communicate an unwarranted level of concern.

Policies and rules are interrelated in another very important way: good policy statements reduce the need for rules proliferation. Here it is assumed that it is better not to have a rule if it can be avoided. Rules are distasteful to most of us, even though we might see a need for some. They are clearly more acceptable when they apply to others and make our own life easier. On the whole, however, if control can be achieved without a rule, that should be preferred. Good policy (not the amount of it) may help avoid rules, for rules often arise in the absence of policy. They crop up here and there to control this situation or that one. They often serve as substitutes for policy.

There is truth to the old saw, "Rules were meant to be broken." This may have several meanings. One obvious interpretation is that no rule can cover all circumstances for which it was meant to apply and that an occasion is always possible wherein the rule should be suspended. For example, it is not difficult to think of circumstances under which undergraduates are allowed access to library stacks or under which a user is allowed to withdraw materials even though overdue notices are outstanding. A more important interpretation of the necessity to break rules is a bit more subtle. One way to avoid having to break rules is to make the rule very detailed and specific such that it never can be broken because it defines the conditions so well. This would create at least two undesirable results: the rules would be longer and more complicated, and more rules would have to be written to cover the conditions excluded in the original rule. The end to such a process becomes unidentifiable. The process could go on interminably. It is much more reasonable to allow judgment and breaking of the rule.

Procedures are a fourth form that precontrol can take. On many occasions for a wide variety of tasks, we find that it is helpful and efficient to document a procedure and expect it to be followed. Procedures usually describe a step-by-step routine for dealing with a particular task or situation. For some procedures, departures or variations are tolerable, and for others strict adherence is considered essential. The latter would be true where it is critical that errors be avoided because they are judged in advance to be very costly. In their own way, procedures help ensure reliable performance and prevent undesirable consequences. Procedures also contribute to efficiency. They can save time and eliminate wasted effort and thus reduce the cost of labor and even materials. Procedures are particularly useful for efficiency objectives when the procedure is repeatedly utilized by several workers. When many people do the same job over and over again, the opportunity for savings using an efficient procedure is significant.

Well-documented procedures can be very useful for training purposes. Many organizations develop procedural manuals that not only summarize a procedure but give workers full explanations and rationales for each step. These manuals have the effect of reducing the amount of time a new worker takes to achieve acceptable performance and can reduce the costs of training. They also can reduce the difficulties and tensions associated with interpersonal dynamics that arise when a trainer or supervisor has to observe the trainee. With these kinds of interactions reduced, the trainee can learn on a more independent basis.

In some ways, plans, policies, rules, and procedures can operate as standards of performance. In these cases, the standard refers essentially to compliance. People are characterized as performing well if they follow plans and procedures while staying within the confines of policies and rules. But such compliance standards are aimed at means, not at ends. The most important and critical standards apply and pertain to outcomes or results. Thus in the performance arena, standards apply to units of productivity, to objectives, and to their qualitative and quantitative components. Any time that an organization can arrive at a performance standard and feel comfortable that it is a reasonable and important expectation, the standard should be communicated clearly to job incumbents. Standards should reflect what the organization expects. Therefore standards of performance should never be arbitrary, nor should they be established or changed without the most serious management attention.

Standards can apply to virtually any effectiveness or efficiency criteria. They may be stated in terms of units of productivity, costs per unit of productivity, circulation or other user behavior indexes, turnover, satisfaction, or any other measures reflective of the result areas. Standards that grow out of professional organization publications may also be utilized. The library field publishes standards for collections, expenditures, and many other factors that could be adopted or adapted by any library that feels they are appropriate. All that is required in establishing standards is that the managers of a particular library decide which standards they wish to use for their own organization. These then need to be examined, put into practice, and tested for their validity in the particular situation. Standards from professional societies or from other organizations must never be accepted and implemented uncritically. Rather they should be treated as suggestions, as a starting place, as a source of ideas. The rest of the difficult task of developing and applying standards locally should be the responsibility of a particular management team. In the process of reviewing and setting standards, it would be ill advised to assume that employees will automatically accept them. Standards are very important to workers, who typically resent and resist standards that are externally imposed or changed. It is unfortunate but true that managers cannot easily change performance standards. Recall that outcomes or results cannot be directly manipulated. In order to change performance, managers must work on antecedents to that performance. Reconsideration or establishment of standards frequently involves a direct focus on outcomes. Hence the manager who is dealing with standards is in volatile territory and should expect resistance and even aggression under some conditions. Standards should be taken very seriously, and participative approaches to their implementation or change are strongly indicated. Participation is not without its own risks, but it can help overcome resistance and prevent disastrous and regretful consequences.

When managers create an organization or reorganize, they are also engaging in precontrol. A well-designed organization provides a great deal of predictability and certainty. When managers create jobs and job descriptions, departmentalize, delegate, establish reporting patterns, coordinate, and the like, they do so with an aim toward preventing chaos and bringing order to the organization. The same holds true when they select and place individuals in positions—an important decision for organizing that eliminates problems or that eliminates the need for additional controls. One form of organization creates one set of problems, and another form generates a somewhat different set of problems. Management in general, and control in particular, lies in addressing the problems that inevitably arise from a given form of organization.

Budgeting is both a planning and a control device. Regarding its precontrol potential, what has been said about planning applies when the budget is an integral part of the planning process. The budget can be used to communicate expectations, especially when dollars are allocated to given programs or performance areas. The budget is also a set of constraints and as such acts to control. One simple way to prevent certain behavior is to deny an allocation to pay for it or to limit the allocation and define the ways in which it may be spent. Organizational units, based on their plans, are given funds specifically earmarked for prearranged purposes. This is a powerful form of control.

In-Process Control

In-process control has its core meaning in the notion of anticipation. It occurs after plans, budgets, standards, and so forth are set. It depends on knowledge and acceptance of an expectation. The way it works is that as individuals engage in activities, they anticipate or predict the effects of those activities. Predictions are made whether and to what extent those activities will result in what is desirable. If people anticipate a sufficient deviation, they can take action to avoid it by correcting their behavior. They also can correct some other conditions to prevent an unwanted deviation. For example, they might adjust a machine control, warn another employee, or freeze expenditures. Many other actions might be taken, so long as they are viewed as preventing an anticipated problem that it is deemed to be worth avoiding. The key component is the ability to predict the impact of what is now occurring upon some relevant future outcome. It further depends on an ability to evaluate the desirability of that outcome in order to decide on whether or how to impose a preventative correction.

In-process control can also apply to conditions other than those where individual perceptions operate on a moment-to-moment basis. For example, inventory control systems have in-process control properties. When supplies diminish, a point is reached where it becomes necessary to reorder to avoid running out of them. Manual or computer-operated counts and calculations are devised so that reorders take place at optimal times and in appropriate quantities. The optimum is established to avoid being out of stock and to minimize costs. Some refer to in-process control as "feedforward control": activity feeds forward information to the result that has not yet occurred, and that information is used as a basis of correction decision.[1]

In-process control requires both knowledge and attentiveness. One needs to know the desired result and have a notion of the magnitude of deviation that would warrant corrective interventions. One needs also to know the relationship between current activities and given outcomes—in other words, what is causing or will cause what. The ability to see patterns and combinations is helpful. Attentiveness and vigilance are required, for without them information is lost and the ability to predict is seriously diminished.

An understanding of in-process control points dramatically to the importance of employees' understanding and acceptance of objectives and standards. If they are uninformed or do not care, their motivation to be attentive and prevent problems is weak. Either little will be observed or what is observed will not trigger a prediction. When organization conditions are poor, some employees will predict problems and simply let them happen. This could be their way of telling managers they are dissatisfied, and it is an easy way to do so. All that is required is to do nothing. This type of passive aggression is not easy to reverse. One first needs to know what is disturbing employees and eliminate that as a cause of apathy or aggression. The employee dissatisfaction may have its roots in nonacceptance of standards or plans or in some other unrelated issue, such as pay inequities.

In-process control is facilitated when employees meet with each other or with their superiors or subordinates to discuss work in progress. In these meetings, current performance can be compared to expectations. Many conditions can be evaluated in terms of their potential effect on standards and objectives. Documented incidents can be used as a basis for improving existing conditions so as to help ensure performance and prevent future problems. These day-to-day discussions are invaluable for keeping an organization on track. They should be scheduled periodically or held as needed. Such discussions should never be delayed or reserved for annual performance appraisal interviews where people are more concerned about their individual status. Progress review discussions permit more of a focus on mutual attack on problems when they are occurring or before they occur.

When in-process control is working well, it is a desirable form of control. Employees are interested in results and motivated to see that they are achieved. They have a personal vested interest in accomplishment. They show attentiveness to what is happening around them and often interact in a cooperative and helpful way. They may even enjoy looking for conditions that could lead to problems and are reinforced by acts of prevention. They have incentives to raise control problems in progress review meetings. This kind of a situation is near the ideal. What managers need to do to sustain it when it is occurring is to be open to and encouraging of expression. When employees see problems, they must be heard rather than suppressed or characterized as negative or pessimistic. Employees learn very quickly to withdraw when superiors react defensively or otherwise ignore their suggestions especially perhaps when those suggestions are aimed at preventing unnecessary problems.

Post-Control

Because precontrol and in-process control are apt to be imperfect, post-control is necessary. Unexpected events can arise, and inappropriate execution is always possible. Post-control acts upon deviations after they have occurred. Sometimes the result can be corrected only for the future, not for the present. This would be the case when one discovers that some parts have to be thrown out, a report page retyped, or a book replaced because of a failure of the system to perform adequately. Steps can be taken to lower the probability that those events will occur in the future, but one must pay the price of the error in the present.

Post-control requires measurement of events, comparison of the event with some standard or expectation, judgmental decision whether deviation exists, and correction of the deviation if it is judged to warrant it (the deviation can be ignored if it is acceptable). Whereas in-process control involves monitoring activities with an anticipatory bent, post-control involves monitoring the results of performance. It is after the fact with regard to both means and ends.

If deviations are outside tolerable limits, the problem has already occurred. Preventative actions have failed. The organization is saddled with the unacceptable result and must live with its ramifications. It can only hope to prevent more of the same. Herein lies one of the reasons why post-control is the least desirable form of control. If errors that exceed tolerable limits have occurred, the psychology of success and failure enters the picture. The employees involved may feel that what has happened will reflect on them or their unit. They may be branded responsible for the error and will, at a minimum, speculate about how others will view their performance. They will have their own perceptions and feelings about what has befallen them and could wonder whether other relevant parties will share their perceptions. They are not always in a position to explain or clarify what went wrong and why it did. The psychology of success and failure thus has interpersonal implications. The critical interpersonal dimension in many instances is a vertical one concerning superior-subordinate relationships. Not only is there evaluation going on when errors are detected, but these evaluations pass between those in the hierarchical chain, and the dynamics can become complex. For example, does the supervisor feel the problem could have been prevented? Do subordinates agree? Will the subordinates blame their superior or top management for the failure? Will superiors see this as shirking responsibility? Will the immediate superior reveal the error to peers or to their own superior? Human emotions relating to self-esteem, blame, embarrassment, trust, competence, threat, defensiveness, and so forth could all bubble to the surface. These are difficult to deal with and highlight the conclusion that although post-control is necessary, it is problematic and the least desirable form of control.

There is no easy solution to the emotional and interpersonal tensions of post-control. One way to mitigate its effects is to treat errors as learning experiences. This is based on the principle that people learn by doing and they learn the most from mistakes. In educational settings, some trainers systematically force mistakes because they show what is to be learned and they provide a strong incentive to do well. A blame-oriented climate can be devastating to the learner and to an organization. Once I was a consultant to a firm where when something went wrong, there was an unspoken and predictable process to locate the culprit. Once he or she was identified, subtle pressures were applied that often led to resignations because the employee saw little future with the company. The firm also had high expectations for outstanding performance, yet its performance standards were rarely made explicit. The emotional stress, even on very competent employees, reached severe proportions. One local minister was counseling a large number of his congregation on problems that grew out of job-induced tensions. In such an organization, employees develop ingenious techniques for hiding or rationalizing errors. Some of them simply hide themselves and trade anonymity for visibility. Had standards been arrived at through improved management practices and had the blame orientation been less severe, many of these unfortunate conditions would have abated.

Still, errors are errors, and organizations have a right to expect that not too many occur. Even if errors are treated as learning experiences, there is probably a limit to how many can be tolerated by any one employee. An effective manager applies a long-term perspective and evaluates performance patterns over time. Hence if an employee makes an error, the supervisor will be more sensitive to its recurrence or to the number of errors that have accumulated. Along the way, the errors will be treated as learning experiences, but the employee will be told that correction is expected. If poor performance continues in the face of support, help, and clear expectations for improvement, administrative action can be taken. The employee can be transferred or dismissed. But such a strategy is hardly a severe blame orientation and is apt to be viewed as fair and even lenient by other employees. Many employees expect help in preventing and dealing with errors; they do not expect to get away with everything. But they also know that a quickly instituted blame orientation is both unfair and hardly deals with the cause of the problem. Heavy-handed blaming is punishment against symptoms; it is not constructive or preventative feedback.

Let us examine some specific post-control techniques recognizing their potential for arousing tension. Each of the following techniques can be simultaneously applied as an in-process or anticipatory control device. To do so, one need only take action before a deviation that would require correction occurs.

Any document that contains objectives, standards, deadlines, or other potential measures of performance can be utilized as a post-control device. The measured performance can be compared to what is stated in the document, and decisions made about corrective action. An excellent example exists when one uses Gantt charts or PERT networks, visual techniques that provide good monitoring devices because they communicate a good deal of information that is useful for control purposes. Some managers use the original planning device to record progress, anticipate problems, or identify actual deviations. In some cases, these documents can contain corrective suggestions or methods to handle problems when they arise.

Budgets serve as a post-control device as well. One way to do this is to have managers report expenditures on a regular basis or as they occur. These expenditures are subtracted from appropriate accounts or budget lines, and the manager is kept informed of the balance. Overspending is easily identified. It can also be seen whether certain expenditures were given appropriate approval before payment is executed. Checks can be made to see whether expenditures fall within other limits, such as when departments are allowed only a certain amount of overtime hours.

Whenever there is sufficient experience with a situation or

piece of equipment, procedures can be written to help diagnose a problem that might arise. These procedures are often called trouble-shooting manuals. Sometimes they describe symptoms of the problem followed by the appropriate action to alleviate the symptoms by correcting its cause. Other devices present a sequenced set of questions to follow, which should lead the reader to corrective action. These questions are often in the form of a graphic diagram with boxes and arrows that systematically lead one through the diagnostic process. Sequenced questions are frequently of an if-then nature. The troubleshooter searches for the answer to the question and if the answer is yes, proceeds to the next step. If the answer is no, a different instruction is given. Usually these devices are highly developed where equipment is involved. If the equipment is sufficiently complex, the troubleshooting manual may be useful only to highly trained technicians. Some may be used by equipment operators to handle a subset of the conditions that could arise. In a few instances, these tools have been developed to handle human situations as well. Mager and Pipe have an interesting schematic for diagnosing employee performance problems.[2] They start by asking the manager to describe the performance problem and then lead the manager through a series of diagnostic questions designed to find the cause. They offer remedies for different types of causes.

Often controls are implemented at a point in the organization located somewhere other than where the performance is occurring. If this is the case, information has to be transmitted from one place to another. This is a common occurrence in post-control. Typically higher-level managers or staff units require that information that reflects performance and progress be submitted on a regular basis. The budgeting example given earlier is a case in point. The information, whatever form it might take, is used as a basis for comparison with expectations. When sufficiently high deviations are detected, action is taken toward correction. This system appears straightforward enough, but actually it is far from simple to implement. It is complicated by human emotional issues, which arise whenever an external agent collects data on another person or unit. And, of course, the difficulties accelerate when the agent engages in evaluative and corrective actions.

Technical complexities also must be reckoned with. Most of these have to do with deciding on the exact nature of the information to be submitted and examined. It takes some sophistication to devise measures that reflect performance. It also is not a simple matter to design methods to record measurement information and to transmit it accurately and in a timely manner. When employees submit written reports, it is conceivable and often likely that there will be varied report formats, material that is omitted, data that are difficult to interpret, superfluous information, and so on. Management and staff groups must standardize reporting formats and be sure that those who report understand all reporting requirements. A competent and concentrated effort is required to prevent making the control process annoying and frustrating to those involved in it. Systems analysts who utilize computer-based information systems know these problems well. They face them when they have to devise reporting formats to ensure accurate and valid data. Without that, analyses of that data can border on meaningless. The term *GIGO* (which means "garbage in, garbage out") reflects what systems analysts know can happen.

There are many good reporting and information systems in use. Consulting firms have developed systems that can be purchased as a package or that can be adapted to a particular organization. The systems provide reporting forms, analytical modes, and printouts of data. Sometimes these systems are on-line, which means that managers can enter or call out data at any time from computer terminals in their offices. The most common control systems available apply to such relatively routine matters as payroll, inventory control, and financial and budgeting systems. In addition to these, libraries have been using computer-based circulation systems for control purposes. The information bank records materials checked in or out, prints overdue notices, and so forth. Even the method of entering data has been simplified with the introduction of bar codes, which are rapidly read with a light pen. The bar codes of the user and the material checked in or out of the library are entered when the transaction takes place. The computer program is designed to keep and analyze circulation data and identify and print any information deemed relevant for control purposes.

In many reporting systems, the information transmitted to a central source is sufficient to indicate only the possibility of a problem; one may not be able to discern what the problem is or what may have caused it. From data that indicates only a deviation, no corrective action can be taken until further questions are answered or additional data provided. In this case, which is quite common, the central control point in the organization must institute some form of inquiry process. This pattern of events sets a difficult and sensitive situation into motion. The unit or person that identified the deviation must initiate interaction with the unit or person from which the information came. The manner in which the initiation is made and the quality of the interaction between parties can affect the success or failure of a control system. The parties must work cooperatively toward joint resolution of a problem. There needs to be trust and mutual respect. This situation can also arise when the interaction is between superiors and their immediate subordinates, with no staff unit involved. The requirements for trust, cooperation, and mutual respect hold just as firmly. The objective is not only to check out and correct a deviation, for the goal is to protect and maintain a good control system. There is little point in probing a control problem in a manner that jeopardizes control for the future. If the interaction between parties deteriorates to one of mistrust, tension, and conflict, much is lost. It can lead to a situation in which employees have incentives to withhold and distort information in the future. Control systems, like other managerial concerns, benefit from some reasonable level of participation when they are designed and reviewed. Participatory styles require time and skill, but if they can yield more widespread acceptance of a control system, the effort could well be worth it.

Another form of post-control is the audit, an appraisal of an organization or some element of it. It may be done on a regular basis, or only when management feels that the organization needs one. An audit can examine any aspect of an organization. One of the most common audits looks at budgeting and financial operations; one might wish to conduct an audit of manpower and personnel requirements, operations and work flow, materials and equipment, or products and services.[3]

An audit may be conducted by a single individual, but usually there is an audit team, which can vary in size from two to a rather large group. The size depends on the magnitude of the audit and the speed with which it must be completed. The auditors can be members of a staff unit in the organization, a representative committee of employees, or an external consulting firm. Some prefer outsiders when they can afford them because they often bring high competence and experience. They are also more apt to be objective and free from the organization reward system. Internal teams are more likely to be subject to biases, political forces, and other intraorganization pressures, but frequently they do a thorough and competent job. It is probably best, however, to use outsiders when objectivity and independence are critical to the success of the audit. It is also wise not to subject inside personnel to undue pressures and strains when the audit is conducted on a particularly sensitive issue.

Audits should be conducted on a regular basis or when they

arise out of consensus that they are needed. Under both of these conditions, the audit has a good chance of being successful. Regular audits come to be expected and have a lower surprise element. With regularity comes opportunity to improve them in various ways. Audits that arise from consensus have the benefit of greater acceptance and help achieve cooperative behavior. Employees are less defensive when they see the need for an audit and anticipate benefits from it. Contrast these conditions to those in which an audit is conducted on an irregular or unannounced basis and does not have the benefit of a shared need for it. In this case, it almost always is viewed with suspicion or any of several other negative reactions.

Audits have many potential problems. At the human emotional level, they can cause a variety of reactions. At the technical level, they must be valid, timely, accurate, and otherwise sound. Unlike reporting systems, audits do not blend into the everyday life of the organization. A commitment to an audit leads employees to expect a distinguishable intervention that is apart from the more routine events in their work experience. Audits require the same or even more care than other control processes.

We have seen how control systems depend on data collection and interpretation, coupled with judgments about corrective action. In this sense, an element of inspection is truly present. Taking this one step further, an organization can formalize the inspection function and have staff positions titled "inspector." Libraries are unlikely to have such positions, or at a minimum are unlikely to use the particular job title. Inspectors are most often found in manufacturing organizations, where their major responsibility is to oversee the quality of products, work flows, and procedures. Sometimes they are housed in a quality control or production control department. They experience all of the manifestations of other control structures.

Additional Thoughts on Control

Despite the necessity of post-control, it is less preferable than precontrol or in-process control. It is better for managers to devote their time to giving direction to an organization rather than watching over its operation. The managerial job will be more enjoyable and productive if the manager decides on objectives and designs an organization for achievement rather than monitoring incessantly. The former activities are much less affected by dimensions of trust, suspicion, blame, fairness, and so on. The solution is not to eliminate post-control but to reduce its dominance and approach it with sensitivity and respect for its volatile nature. Above all, control should be viewed as a means to success, not an end. Managers with control problems that require repeated post-control intervention must wonder whether control is dominating them. They must look more to planning and in-process control as the way out of an uncomfortable and exhausting condition. If they do anything to improve post-control processes, they must move to make them more valid, timely, and acceptable. The notion of acceptability here has strong connotations. Problems should be solved and controls instituted at a point closest to where they are needed. The employees at the location where control is needed are the ones who should react and make corrections. The use of external or high-level interventions should be kept at a minimum. It does not take much ingenuity to see how acceptance of a standard and for the need to control facilitates the ability to follow the principle.

There is no necessary relationship between the amount of control and organizational success. In fact there may be a curvilinear relationship between the amount of control and success. Too little control and too much control are more apt to cause ineffectiveness and inefficiency. There is probably an optimum point where moderate amounts of control are correlated with the best results; however, there is probably a linear relationship between the type or quality of control and success. The more sophisticated and higher quality the design of the control process, the more it should contribute to effectiveness and efficiency. There should be no logical limit to improving the quality of control processes.

Managers must have some general way to decide on the appropriateness of their control activities. One solution lies in giving attention to the consequences of an error. The principle would be that if the consequences of an error are tolerable and if the error is not apt to be repeated, formal control procedures should not be instituted. Let the error occur, and let learning take place. The cost and other problems that arise out of a onetime relatively inconsequential error are far outweighed by the benefits of avoiding overcontrol.

In order to control behavior or anything else that takes place in the organization, feedback is necessary. The information used to evaluate becomes the source of feedback. When an external agent is the source, we have a situation of mediated feedback. The agent must be skilled at it and know how to make such feedback timely, concrete, helpful, impersonal, nonthreatening, constructive, and so forth. Another way is to use cue feedback, which eliminates the external agent. Cue feedback is possible when the employee engages in self-evaluative and self-corrective behavior. Knowledge of standards is necessary. Sometimes dials, counters, or other instrumentation can be used. These devices can convey information, such as number or quality of units produced, directly to the employee. Reports that go directly to the employee also can be a source of cue feedback. When feedback information is impersonal in nature, it eliminates the need for the interpersonal skills that are required in mediated feedback. The recipient need know only what the standard is, what constitutes a sufficient deviation, and how to correct or get help to do so. Herein lies the power of planning, standards setting, and so on, and the power of acceptance. With these, cue feedback can and should substitute for mediated feedback.

Inherent in a control process is the capacity to destroy its own purposes. This fact is inescapable, and from it emanates the mandate to respect its power to do so. Many management theorists and organizational sociologists have recognized the self-destructive cycle, which begins with the need for certainty and reliable performance. This generates policies, rules, and supervisory practices to help ensure the desired result. These tend to make power relationships visible and cause uncomfortable and dysfunctional tensions. Instead of excellent performance, the net result is minimal acceptable performance, which arises out of fear, apathy, or retaliation and disturbs those concerned about that performance. They react with more rules, and power relationships are made even more visible. The result reinforces more minimal performance, and the cycle repeats. This potential, to the extent it is inevitable, means that managers must approach control with respect and with an eye to preventing its deleterious effects. The self-destructive cycle lies in waiting to frustrate the naive manager.[4]

Control is not a set of techniques and tools; it is a human condition, an attitude. It grows out of desire, not method. Ultimately it is a volitional system, not a technical or unemotional matter. To the extent that this is true, it is likely that opportunities for effective control rest with commitments and in feelings and beliefs that lead people to want to work in a successful organization. As a motivational state, control is most effectively achieved through planning and goal formulation.

Additional Readings

Anthony, R. N., and John Dearden. *Management Control Systems*. 3rd
. ed. Homewood, Ill.: Irwin, 1976.

————, and Regina Herzlinger. *Management Control in Non-Profit Organizations*. Homewood, Ill.: Irwin, 1975.

Bonini, C. P.; R. K. Jaedicke; and H. M. Wagner, eds. *Management Controls: New Directions in Basic Research*. New York: McGraw-Hill, 1964.

Bower, J. L. "Planning and Control: Bottom Up or Top Down?" *Journal of General Management* 1:20–31 (Spring 1974).

Cammann, Cortlandt, and David Nadler. "Fit Control Systems to Your Managerial Style." *Harvard Business Review* 54:65–72 (Jan.-Feb. 1976).

Davies, C., and A. Francis. "The Many Dimensions of Performance Measurement." *Organizational Dynamics* 3:51–65 (Winter 1975).

Dawson, R. I., and D. P. Carew. "Why Do Control Systems Fall Apart?" *Personnel* 46:8–16 (May-June 1969).

Eilon, Samuel. *Management Control*. London: Macmillan, 1971.

Emery, James. *Organizational Planning and Control Systems: Theory and Technology*. New York: Macmillan, 1969.

Gannon, M. J. "Behavioral Monitoring Systems in Complex Organizations." *Academy of Management Review* 2:667–71 (Oct. 1977).

Giglioni, G. B., and A. G. Bedeian. "Conspectus of Management Control Theory." *Academy of Management Journal* 17:292–305 (June 1974).

Hage, Jerald. *Communications and Organization Control*. New York: Wiley, 1974.

Herzlinger, Regina. "Why Data in Nonprofit Organizations Fail." *Harvard Business Review* 55:81–86 (Jan.-Feb. 1977).

Hofstede, Geert. "The Poverty of Management Control Philosophy." *Academy of Management Review* 3:450–61 (July 1978).

Jackson, J. H., and S. W. Adams. "The Life Cycle of Rules." *Academy of Management Review* 4:269–73 (April 1979).

Jasinski, F. J. "Use and Misuse of Efficiency Controls." *Harvard Business Review* 34:105–12 (July-Aug. 1956).

Koontz, Harold, and Robert Bradspies. "Managing through Feedforward Control." *Business Horizons* 15:25–36 (June 1972).

Lawler, E. E., and John Rhode. *Information and Control in Organizations*. Pacific Palisades, Calif.: Goodyear, 1976.

Lindberg, R. A. "Operations Auditing." *Management Review* 58:2–9 (Dec. 1969).

Livingstone, J. L., and Joshua Ronen. "Motivation and Management Control Systems." *Decision Sciences* 6:360–75 (April 1975).

Lorange, Peter, and M. S. Morton. "A Framework for Management Control Systems." *Sloan Management Review* 16:41–56 (Fall 1974).

Macchiaverna, Paul. *Internal Auditing.* New York: Conference Board, 1978.

Machin, J. L. "Measuring the Effectiveness of an Organization's Management Control Systems." *Management Decisions* 11:260–79 (Winter 1973).

————, and L. S. Wilson. "Closing the Gap between Planning and Control." *Long Range Planning* 12:16–32 (Feb. 1979).

Newman, W. H. *Constructive Control: Design and Use of Control Systems.* Englewood Cliffs, N.J.: Prentice-Hall, 1975.

Ouchi, William, and Mary Ann Maguire. "Organizational Control: Two Functions." *Administrative Science Quarterly* 20:559–69 (Dec. 1975).

Patz, A. L., and A. J. Rowe. *Management Control and Decision Systems: Text, Cases, and Readings.* New York: Wiley, 1977.

Reimann, B. C., and A. L. Negandhi. "Strategies of Administrative Control and Organizational Effectiveness." *Human Relations* 28:475–86 (July 1975).

Sayles, Leonard. "The Many Dimensions of Control." *Organizational Dynamics* 1:21–31 (Summer 1972).

Shillinglaw, Gordon. *Cost Accounting: Analysis and Control.* 3rd ed. Homewood, Ill.: Irwin-Dorsey, 1972.

Sihler, W. H. "Toward Better Management Control Systems." *California Management Review* 14:33–39 (Winter 1971).

Stedry, Andrew. *Budget Control and Cost Behavior.* Englewood Cliffs, N.J.: Prentice-Hall, 1965.

Stroud, B. L. "Common Fallacies in Monitoring and Control." *Managerial Planning* 23:18–21 (July-Aug. 1974).

Tannenbaum, Arnold. *Control in Organizations.* New York: McGraw-Hill, 1968.

Vancil, R. F. "What Kind of Management Control Do You Need?" *Harvard Business Review* 51:75–86 (Mar.-April 1973).

Vardaman, G. T., and C. C. Halterman. *Management Control through Communication.* New York: Wiley, 1968.

Woodward, Joan. *Industrial Organization: Behavior and Control.* London: Oxford Univ. Pr., 1970.

10. The Role of Budgeting in Organizational Improvement

David J. Cherrington and J. Owen Cherrington

Several processes of organization development (OD) have been proposed recently to help organizations avoid "organizational dry rot," i.e., rigidity, conflict, and/or disintegration.[1] These renewal processes are designed to achieve greater coordination, flexibility and adaptability; to regain vitality, creativity and innovation; and to encourage individual commitment, motivation and development.

Organizational development attempts to initiate these renewal processes through well-designed interventions.[2] OD interventions have been defined as a set of structured activities in which selected organization members engage in tasks where the goals are directly or indirectly related to organization improvement.

The development and implementation of the budget usually has not been considered as an organization development intervention nor is it contained in the lists of popular OD interventions. Nevertheless, what we are suggesting here is that the preparation of the budget, if it is done right, is a meaningful, relevant, and critical organizational intervention. Our central point is that the effectiveness of an organization can be increased if the preparation and use of the budget follows some elementary, but important rules.

One of the important characteristics of organization development which distinguishes it from the earlier sensitivity training or

Reprinted from *University of Michigan Business Review* 27:12–15 (July 1975).

T-group training is the focus of organizational development on "real" problems. This focus of OD is a significant advantage over traditional sensitivity training. The problems facing organization members are real, not hypothetical; the problems which members are rewarded for solving are real problems, not hypothetical problems; and the problems central to the needs of organization members are real, not hypothetical.

Several organizational development interventions, however, do not have direct transfer of training to the work situation. Team-building interventions, for example, generally remove the individual from the immediate organizational problems and ask the work team to focus on specific tasks which may not be directly related to their real work. Occasionally, it is desirable to focus on abstract hypothetical problems or tasks, especially when there are excessive conflicts and emotional feelings related to the real task. However, real problems are usually preferred because there is greater transfer of learning.

Transfer of Learning

The problems of transfer of learning become greater as the specific activity of an OD intervention becomes further removed from the real problem of the work environment. The process of entropy is an additional problem confronting OD interventions. Entropy is the gradual wearing down, disintegration or negation of the beneficial effects of the OD intervention.[3] After an OD intervention is instituted, the effects of the intervention gradually decline unless there is some revitalizing process or negative entropy which reinstates the effect of the intervention.

The great advantage in using budgeting as an OD intervention is that budgeting is a critical activity which all large organizations perform. It is also an activity which is critically important to the effectiveness of each organization. Unfortunately, however, the preparation and implementation of the budget is frequently done with little regard for its potential benefit as an OD intervention. Usually, the controller has the major responsibility for the budget. In some organizations the preparation of the budget is handled entirely by the upper levels of management, while the performance standards are imposed upon individuals at the operating level. In other instances, the employees at lower levels in the organization are asked to submit a budget of their production or their needed materials, then these estimates and requests for materials are significantly changed by higher levels of management. Such practices usually have resulted in numerous "budgeting games" where estimates are submitted without respect to actual levels of production anticipated by the worker. In some instances, the budget is at best a useless and meaningless document, and at worst it is a monumental irritant which polarizes workers against management. Consequently, many dysfunctional consequences of budgeting have been identified and discussed in accounting literature.

Budgeting and Effective Organization

There are, however, several very good reasons why organizations use budgeting. The three major purposes for having a budget are planning, coordinating and controlling enterprise activity to achieve its goals. In some organizations the budget serves as a major instrument for planning the activities of that organization. In such instances, the several subsidiaries within the organization coordinate their activities by having a written document such as the budget to guide their activities. The budget can also be used to control the activities by identifying the areas of concern when the activities are not going according to the predetermined plan. What we are suggesting here is that budgeting can also be used as an OD intervention to improve the quality of the decision-making, to achieve greater creativity and innovation, and to establish conditions which encourage individual commitment, motivation and development.

To use budgeting advantageously within an organization, there are several simple but essential rules centered around (1) the development of a budget and (2) the implementation of a budget.

The procedure used to develop a budget is probably as important as how the budget is used after it is prepared. In fact, the process by which it is prepared may sometimes be more important than the content of the budget.

Rule 1. Provide adequate preplanning so that everyone is working on the same assumptions, targeted goals and agenda. Make sure everyone understands the limitations and constraints of their participation and the bounds of their decision-making. Most organizations have some idea of the level of activity which they expect to achieve within the coming year, and this information ought to be communicated to those individuals participating in the development of the budget. Most short-range, middle-range and long-range goals for an organization are determined by upper levels of management. When an individual is deciding what his level of activity is going to be in the coming year, he needs to know how his activity should fit into the large picture determined by top levels of management. It is useless for the individual to believe that he has full opportunity to determine his performance when, in fact, he does not have full opportunity because of upper-level administrative decisions. Consequently, the individual should be told, prior to the time he establishes his budget, how his activity will fit into the entire organization and what constraints will be placed upon him and his activities by upper-level administrative decisions.

Rule 2. Allow and encourage participation in the budgeting process at each level within the organization. Structure the activity of developing the budget so the relevant people are there. The relevant people are those who are responsible for implementing the budget and who will be rewarded according to its accomplishments. There are generally three benefits to those firms which allow employees to participate in the budgeting process. First, when the employees participate in establishing and developing a budget, they tend to accept it as their own plan of action. The belief that an individual will be more receptive and more favorably disposed to a procedure if it contains his ideas is common to several theories of management and organizational behavior.[4] Participation in the budgeting process has been found in some studies to increase the probability of its acceptance.[5] Second, participation in developing the budget tends to increase morale among employees and toward management. The evidence in the literature seems to suggest that participation improves morale.[6] Active participation in the budgeting process seems to be desired by employees and makes them feel more a part of the activities, less dominated by a superior, more independent, and thus improves the employee's attitude towards his job. Third, increased productivity may, but will not necessarily result from participation. Prior research has been contradictory on this point. It has been argued by some that participation exerts an impact on productivity chiefly because of its effect on group cohesiveness.[7] However, several studies have shown there is no direct relationship between group cohesiveness and productivity, but that the relationship is mediated by the norms of the work group.[8] If the group goals are consistent with the goals of the organization, then increased group cohesiveness usually leads to increased productivity. However, if the group norms are counterproductive or inconsistent with the organization, then increased group cohesiveness most likely reduces productivity.

Rule 3. Structure the climate of the preparation of the budget so individuals are more "relaxed" rather than anxious or defensive. The proper structuring of the climate requires that each individual has the freedom and authority to influence and accept his own performance level and then assume the responsibility for accomplishing it. This activity should be structured so it is (1) problem-oriented or opportunity-oriented, and (2) oriented to the problems and opportunities of the participant. The company should avoid using the participation in budgeting as an opportunity to reopen old wounds and past failures. Instead, it should use past experiences of success and failure simply as information from which they could learn.

Rule 4. Structure the preperation of the budget so there is a reasonably high probability of successful goal attainment. Challenging but attainable goals, once achieved, produce feelings of success, confidence, and satisfaction. This, in turn, raises aspiration levels and feelings of self and group worth.[9] The budget can still be difficult and challenging, but it should be attainable. If the group fails to accomplish the goal, the reasons for this should be clear so they can be avoided in the future. A careful distinction should be made between the controllable factors for which the individual should be responsible and the uncontrollable factors influencing the budget for which the individual should not be responsible.

If the proper procedure for developing a budget has been followed, the difficulties of implementing the budget are minimized. Proper implementation of the budget requires adherence to the following elementary rules:

Rule 5. Establish rewards and reward contingencies that will lead to achieving the organizational goals. Too often, the budgeting process does not provide sufficient rewards to induce workers to accomplish departmental objectives. The only reward many employees receive is $4.50 per hour for each hour of work. The contingency for receiving $4.50 per hour is that the individual be at his assigned work area doing a job. He is paid for his time, not his performance. Such a reward and reward contingency often induces mediocre performance but does not induce compliance with the budgeted objectives.

The type of rewards and reward contingencies that are appropriate depend on the type of firm and its operating procedures. In organizations where there are significant costs resulting from over- or underestimation, such as the perishable goods industry, an individual should be rewarded according to how close he comes to producing according to his budget. However, when the costs of overproduction are not so great, such as in the steel industry, an individual's rewards should not be tied so closely to the costs of overproduction.

A system of rewards and reward contingencies reduces or eliminates several of the dysfunctional aspects of budgeting. One of the dysfunctional aspects, observed by Argyris, was that budgets are used as a pressure device that tends to unite employees against management.[10] That is not too surprising, since budgets are sometimes intentionally used to pressure employees to higher productivity. Rather than criticizing them for uniting against management, we perhaps should commend employees for being so perceptive. While varying degrees of pressure can be exerted by budgets, this pressure is not necessarily good or bad. It has been demonstrated, for example, that high budget pressure can increase performance without reducing employee satisfaction, but only when the subjects are rewarded accordingly.[11] Therefore, it would seem to be fair play to ask for extraordinary performance from employees only if appropriate rewards are provided. If appropriate rewards are not provided, the likely result will be substandard performance and dissatisfied employees.

Other dysfunctional aspects of budgeting observed by Argyris were: (1) reward structures provide success to the finance staff by making factory personnel appear as failures, and (2) emphasis on the departmental level to achieve the budget creates a department-centered enterprise.[12] These problems are created by an inadequate system of rewards and reward contingencies. When the success of the finance staff is at the expense of the production personnel or when one department can maximize its rewards at the expense of another department, there quite clearly is a need to rearrange the reward contingencies. If two departments are interdependent, then their reward contingencies ought to be tied together to the extent that cooperation is induced. On the other hand, if they are independent, their reward contingencies should not be tied together since such a situation leads to a loss of control and noncontingent rewards.

A system of appropriate rewards and reward contingencies will help assure the accomplishment of enterprise objectives while reducing the dysfunctional consequences of the budgeting process.

Rule 6. The organization should focus on the use of positive rewards for achieving the budget rather than negative reinforcement. Feelings of success or failure largely determine an employee's attitude towards the budget and determine in a large measure the level of performance to which he will aspire in the future. It has been suggested that an individual's level of aspiration is a goal that, when barely achieved, has associated with it subjective feelings of success, and when not achieved, subjective feelings of failure.[13] Success generally leads to an increase in the levels of aspiration and failure to a decrease.

Rule 7. Provide rapid feedback on the performance of each work team and/or individual. This necessitates the use of reports and reporting procedures that are understandable to the workers and supervisors at the department level so they can analyze their results and take corrective action on their own initiative.

We suggest that the focus of implementing a budget should not be on punishing workers or supervisors for significant variations from the budget, but on rewarding those responsible for the smooth-running phases of the operations. More emphasis should be placed on (1) identifying appropriate goals, (2) praising and rewarding workers when they meet their budget, and (3) designing reports which are understandable to both supervisors and workers and which enable them to analyze their own results and take corrective action.

11. A Conceptual Basis for Library Effectiveness

Rosemary Ruhig Du Mont

Most library analysts agree that achieving effectiveness is a basic responsibility of library management. However, there is a notable lack of agreement on what the concept of effectiveness means.

One major group sees library effectiveness as the achievement of goals.[1] A second major group measures effectiveness by the efficient use of resources in optimizing performance.[2] A third major

Reprinted from *College & Research Libraries* 41:103–111 (March 1980).

group defines effectiveness in terms of the personnel within the library and the satisfaction that they obtain from their jobs.[3] A fourth major group equates effectiveness with user satisfaction.[4]

In short, while there is general consent that all libraries should attempt to be effective, the criteria for appraisement remain unclear.

In light of the variety of ways in which administrators and researchers perceive library effectiveness, it should also be noted that there is equal disagreement over the best strategy for becoming effective.

One significant reason for this lack of agreement stems from the narrow focus that many people apply to the effectiveness construct. As already noted, many define effectiveness in terms of a single criterion (user satisfaction or optimal efficiency, for example). But it is difficult to conceive of a library that would survive for long if it pursued user satisfaction to the exclusion of employee needs or if it concentrated on efficiency to the exclusion of user satisfaction. Libraries as organizations typically pursue multiple (and often conflicting) objectives; and these objectives tend to differ from library to library according to the nature of the community within which the library operates and the nature of the services it is supposed to offer.

A second reason for the absence of concurrence on the nature of effectiveness arises from the vagueness of the concept. One might assume that it is relatively easy to identify the various criteria for judging effectiveness. As a matter of fact, such criteria tend to be difficult to establish; in reality they depend largely on who is formulating the criteria, for what reason, and within what specific frame of reference.

In a recent paper, Du Mont and Du Mont categorized relevant facets of effectiveness identified by researchers that could serve as useful evaluating criteria.[5] They synthesized four major approaches to assessing library effectiveness (figure 1 summarizes these approaches).

As figure 1 reveals, most major criteria of library effectiveness considered by researchers are related to library input, e.g., staff, money, materials, or services. There is only limited consideration of output, i.e., the effect of library service on its public.

Problems in Assessment

The lack of agreement on the significance of various techniques poses a serious problem both for library administrators and

1. Primary emphasis on physical input (number of staff, amount of money, etc.)

   As perceived by agents in the environment (accrediting agencies, funding agencies, etc.) who determine how much financial support the library does need to be viable

   As perceived by agents in the environment (professional library associations) who are interested both in what the library does need as stated in established standards, and what it could use as stated in established goals

2. Primary emphasis on the organizational dynamics of the library (the relationship between the library staff and the formal library organization)

   As perceived by individual staff, including subjective characterizations of needed library input for staff development

   As perceived by the library, including subjective characterizations of needed staff input for library development

3. Primary emphasis on library input (materials and services) as they are perceived by patrons

   Including characterizations made by patrons of how well the library is equipped to serve them

   Including characterizations made by the library describing how well the user is being supplied with materials and services

4. Primary emphasis on library input (materials and services) as they affect elements within the society as a whole

   As perceived by the library as an organization which wishes to serve that society

   Source: Rosemary Ruhig Du Mont and Paul F. Du Mont, "Measuring Library Effectiveness: A Review and an Assessment," in Michael Harris, ed., *Advances in Librarianship* 9:129 (New York: Academic Press, 1979).

FIGURE 1. Major approaches to viewing library effectiveness

for analysts of the library as an organization; it makes it difficult, if not impossible, to evaluate a library's success or failure adequately. This inability to concur on meaningful criteria to be used across the library spectrum results, in part, from ignoring a number of problems that must be solved before one can arrive at more meaningful approaches to assessing library effectiveness. These problems are delineated in the following questions.[6]

   1. *Is there any such thing as library effectiveness?* The very abstractness of much of the discussion that goes on in the name of library effectiveness can lead one to the conclusion that the con-

cept of effectiveness has little applicability to the actual working library. Those who believe that effectiveness is a viable concept need an explicit definition of the effective library.

2. *How stable—consistently valid—are the assessment criteria?* The Du Mont and Du Mont study pointed out that a time horizon is a significant component in assessment.[7] Perceptions of library effectiveness will vary over time. For example, in the short run the effective library may be one that is able to supply the current library patron with the materials he or she demands. Over time, however, if the library continues to fulfill only the demands of library patrons and makes no attempt to also fulfill unverbalized needs, the library may be considered to be ineffective.

Clearly, most criteria of library effectiveness do not represent permanent indications of library success. In fact, it is the changing nature of many effectiveness criteria that has led some library investigators to suggest that adaptability or flexibility represents a key variable in any model of effectiveness.[8]

3. *Which time perspective is most appropriate in assessment?* A major problem for a library administrator is to decide how best to allocate available resources between short-range and long-term purposes so that both receive sufficient support. In terms of assessment of resource allocation, the question becomes one of determining which time perspective to take in judging effectiveness.

It must be noted that what is effective in the short run may not be appropriate over the long term. For example, if day-to-day activities (a short-range approach) consume so much of a library's resources that little is left over for planning for the future, the library's outmoded services and materials may threaten its very survival.

4. *Are the assessment criteria related positively to each other?* Most approaches to assessing library effectiveness rely on a series of relatively discrete criteria (for example, workload indicators, physical standards, job satisfaction, etc.). However, it is difficult to judge the effectiveness of libraries using a number of these criteria simultaneously, because many of the criteria compete with one another.

Consider, for instance, a library that uses efficiency and user satisfaction as two of its criteria for effectiveness. The standard of efficiency can cause the library to purchase only high-demand materials and to rely on a centralized purchasing and storage facility for the remaining items. Such an effort can lead to reduced user satisfaction, as many items demanded will not be available on the library shelves when the user wants them.

On the other hand, it is possible to increase user satisfaction by yielding to every user demand for increased library materials in the local library, but at the price of greatly reduced efficiency. Thus while the use of multiple evaluation criteria adds breadth to any assessment attempt, it also adds complexity to the assessment process.

5. *How useful are the assessment criteria?* This question relates to the measurement of library effectiveness. Do the various criteria used to measure the effectiveness of library performance actually do so?

In point of fact, libraries tend to measure performance in terms of "proxy measures" easily quantifiable outputs such as circulation, that are assumed to say something about the effectiveness of library operations. Such measures obviously have their limitations, the most basic one being the lack of relevance between the "proxy" and the effectiveness of the program or process the "proxy" supposedly represents.

6. *How do effectiveness criteria help us understand library dynamics? How useful is the effectiveness construct? What purposes are served by the process of evaluating effectiveness? Does it provide insight into the dynamics of library operations? Does it help in the making of predictions for the future of the library?* Unless a model of library effectiveness facilitates a better understanding of library structure, processes, and behavior, it has little value for library analysts.

7. *At which level should effectiveness be assessed?* Library administrators face the problem of the level at which to assess effectiveness. Logic might suggest evaluating effectiveness on a librarywide basis. Such an approach may seem overwhelming, however, due to the complexity of the library as an organization.

For example, an examination of various processes within the library is likely to show that certain units are most successful or effective than others. The existence of such differences complicates any attempts to draw firm conclusions of the effectiveness of a given library. Yet, if understanding of the library as an organization is to be increased, models of effectivness must be developed that enable library practitioners, to the greatest extent possible, to identify the nature of the relationships between the individual processes and the behavior of the library as a whole.

Even a cursory examination of the problems posed by these questions reveals the complexity of the subject. If library administrators are to be able to reduce their dependence on simplistic measuring techniques for evaluating effectiveness, a framework must be provided for analysis that integrates the various elements within and without the library, allowing the library to be viewed as the sum of its parts.

What Is Library Effectiveness?

If the notion is accepted that libraries are unique and pursue divergent goals reflective of their own unique environment, then one must move away from a general conceptual definition of library effectiveness toward a more operational one. Thus it appears to be useful to develop a contingency approach and to define library effectiveness in terms of each library's level of ability in responding to its own unique situational and environmental constraints. Viewed from this perspective, effectiveness is perceived through the examination of *process* rather than the end result.

Such a view requires elaboration. In essence, the contingency approach stresses that contingent factors such as type of clientele or size of book stock have some direct influences on levels of success.

There may be, for example, economies available to those purchasing multiple copies for a large library system that are not available to its smaller counterpart. "It is assumed that a set of structured administrative arrangements consciously adapted to the tasks that are to be done, to the scale of the total operation, to its overall complexity, and to the pressures of change being encountered will themselves act to promote a higher level of effectiveness than will a structure ill-suited to those contingencies."[9]

The important point is that there are usually conflicting demands inherent in attempts to secure an effective match between a library's internal contingencies and the contingencies it faces in the environment, and each demand has its own potential measures of effectiveness. The contingency approach makes it possible to identify simultaneously many managerial and organizational factors that are related to library effectiveness.[10]

Inherent in such a view is the notion that effectiveness can best be perceived by viewing the library as a system. Systems theory suggests that understanding the library can come only through integrating knowledge about it from a variety of sources; i.e., structure, knowledge, techniques, equipment, facilities, users, personnel, etc., are all inextricably linked and to consider one means to consider them all. Additionally, any library, in judging its effectiveness, must consider the library/environment interface. Finally, a time horizon must be considered in examining the effectiveness of any given library.

A Model and Supporting Propositions for Conceptualizing Library Effectiveness

The systems model that is proposed in figure 2 emphasizes three major aspects:

1. the notion that achieving library effectiveness is a dynamic on-going process;
2. the perception that inputs and outputs are likely to change over time;
3. the outlook that individual human behavior (both within and out of the library) affects perception of library success or failure.

These aspects are different in each library and reflect the notion that it is unlikely that any single definition of effectiveness will be applicable to more than one individual library. Comparisons across libraries could be made with respect to one contingent factor (clientele, collection, etc.). However, it is unlikely that the systems models of libraries developed through use of the model presented here will be comparable.

How then does the use of this model aid in the investigating of effectiveness? The model provides a practical (but complicated) set of guideposts for assessing various elements of an individual library's effectiveness.

Ways of viewing individual elements within the model and propositions supporting these views follow:

The first element is the individual library employee.

Proposition 1: Libraries that adopt forms of administrative structure consistent with the expectation and perceived needs of

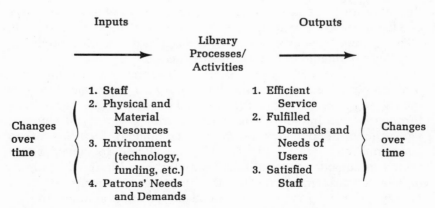

FIGURE 2. A systems model of library effectiveness

their personnel will tend to achieve higher levels of performance and be judged by their personnel as more effective.

This proposition is a cornerstone of the behavioral study of organizations.[11] Library researchers in this area argue for structures and styles of management that secure a higher degree of commitment to the library from employees by more adequately meeting their expectations and needs.[12]

However, some qualification is in order. Not only do these perceived needs change over time, but it is also clear that different types of people do not have the same needs on their jobs. Thus one might look to research on the differing psychological needs of professional librarians and paraprofessionals, or the changing needs of new professionals who remain long on the job as ways of dealing with this element.

The second element is the library itself.

Proposition 2: Libraries' ability to adapt to, buffer, or level environmental change is inversely related to their dependence upon instinct, habit, or tradition. Libraries able to learn and to perform according to changing contingencies in the environment will tend to achieve higher levels of performance, i.e., be more effective.

The influence of the environment on organizations has been considered by a number of writers.[13] Library/environment interface has been mentioned in this paper.[14]

This proposition expresses the fundamental argument for proving utility that has become a dominant cry among librarians. In order to do so, obtaining adequate resources (financial support as well as the more intangible emotional support) from the environment becomes the logical short-term goal. Libraries that obtain such support are more likely to grow and adapt over the intermediate range of time and survive over the long haul. Detailed research on the survival instincts of libraries is yet forthcoming. What does happen to libraries over time? How do they change and respond to diversity? What does being a more successful library mean over the short range as well as the long term?

The third element is the individual library user.

Proposition 3: Libraries able to supply timely, relevant, and accessible service to all users will be considered more effective than those that do not.

Effort must be made to match conceptions of service to the needs and tastes of the particular user in question. Most librarians, when dealing with service to patrons, consider only the demands made by present-day users of libraries. Unverbalized needs of those users and the whole range of needs and demands of non-users are generally not considered. Great care must be taken to consider all these categories of demands and needs in dealing with the concept of the effective library, not only as they relate to general concepts of library performance, but also as they relate to specific responses to individual users and potential users over time.

The fourth element is the society at large.

Proposition 4: In order to adapt to the changing external environment, one strategy for the library is to develop a systematic mechanism by which to measure the preferences of various groups for library services and the relative strengths of these groups to affect library welfare. This information can be incorporated into its decision-making strategies in such a manner that it maximizes social satisfaction against social expectations, sustains incentives for its funding agency to continue its support, and mobilizes its resources efficiently so that its traditional constituent groups, for example, employees and present patrons, are satisfied with its performance.

In supporting this proposition over a period of time, the library can actively seek to measure different groups' support for its actions and also the behaviors of those groups as they affect the library. Such behaviors may range from no action, verbal support, letter writing to potential funding agencies, and the like, to actual library use. The library may seek to investigate the relations between a group's appraisals of the library's behavior and the group's actual use of the library. Perhaps, also, some measure of a group's attitude toward the library can be related to its evaluation of the library's actions.

The study of attitudes is useful because of its relevance to creating within the library an improved understanding of the ways in which the library's behavior affects reactions within the environment.

To date, there have not been many serious attempts to study group attitudes toward library use.[15] The problems inherent in conducting such studies are great. That does not mean that an approach that is capable of analyzing the priorities of individuals, groups, or larger collections of groups should not be attempted. There is such a need to rank competing action alternatives of libraries; and to do so, the consideration of different group preferences over time is a necessity.

Implications for Library Management

Four propositions have been discussed, reflecting some of the components that make up the dimensions of library effectiveness.

Although most library researchers at present select only one of the components in an examination of effectiveness, it is concluded that consideration of the process by which these components interrelate is needed to create an overall framework for the judging of library effectiveness.

The idea of a model of library effectiveness, emphasizing some kind of specific end results, is rejected. The question posed may be: "What results should we look for in assessing the effectiveness of any given library?" The answer is that the question itself is inappropriate. There is no general model of library effectiveness categorizing specific outcomes appropriate to all libraries. To study the effectiveness of a given library, one needs to establish a unique model reflecting the uniqueness of that library. This can be done by using the framework illustrated in figure 2.

Let us assume we want to assess the effectiveness of a university library empirically. First, the identification of relevant inputs takes place. For example, the relevant user needs being served by the library have to be recognized. Recognition can be based on such criteria as (1) suitability of the user need, (2) the criticalness of serving that need, and (3) the degree to which a user group has formally organized to have its needs served.

We also need to identify the appropriate level of analysis of library processes. Let's assume, for example, that the distribution of new information to the users identified is a relevant process for the effective library. Do we measure the *library's* ability to distribute information, or do we examine the process in individual *units* of the library?

The resolution of the question comes from examining the activities of a number of public service departments in the library over time. The conclusion is reached that information distribution in various departments is different over time; thus the study of the effectiveness of this process can be made only on the department level. Output is also measured on a department level, not on a librarywide basis. The effectiveness of information distribution by the library as a whole is judged through the integrating of results from these individual levels.

The above illustration of the use of the systems model is brief because of space limitations. The basic point is that the model is not a picture of the effective library. Rather, it is a kind of outline for the administrator to complete. The appropriate inputs need to be identified, the significant processes and the levels at which they aggregate must be determined, and the appropriate outputs for these levels must be established.

The propositions stated in support of the model can aid in

filling in this outline. The first draws attention to the desirability of a committed staff that participates in the setting of library goals. It supports the general position of research on motivation and reward by indicating that the performance of libraries is enhanced when personnel are granted a sizable personal stake in its development.

The thrust of the second proposition is that the structure of the library is likely to influence its performance. Problems have to be worked out in the context of each library's own circumstances. Much examination needs to be done before deciding on the form of the library that is most appropriate.

First, the nature of present and future contingencies must be assessed. In other words, just what kind of institution is the library, what does it want to be in terms of scope of clientele, size, type of service, and so on?

Second, what are the organizational requirements imposed by relevant contingencies? For example, a large library will have particular problems of communication and coordination. What alternative organizational designs might satisfy these requirements?

Third, if different contingencies pose the dilemma of conflicting requirements, what policies could be formulated to modify the contingencies themselves? Some libraries, for example, that seek to broaden their scope of services or that seek to combine a successful new service with economies of a large scale, such as centralized technical processing, are finding that they can circumvent the size contingency by setting up small, internally flexible experimental service units or similar libraries within a library.

The important point is that there are usually several ways of securing an effective match between a library's internal organization and the contingencies it faces. This fact tends to be overlooked by those who share the present-day concern about the bureaucratization of libraries. A bureaucracy can be operated in different ways, depending upon its own unique circumstances. There are in most library situations various possibilities for increasing effectiveness, no matter what kind of contingencies are faced.

The third proposition emphasizes the fact that much more knowledge is needed on the nature of individual patron needs so that adequate systems can be designed that will satisfy those needs.

The fourth proposition points out the need for more political acumen on the part of librarians, an attribute necessary in the identification of the groups most likely to support various kinds of library service, so that libraries can survive over the long term.

Most libraries exist in a constantly fluctuating environment in which threats to survival and growth are relatively commonplace. Within such environments, library administrators must try to identify and use the various inputs at their disposal constructively in an effort to achieve outputs that meet up to the expectations of all those concerned with library performance. The process by which they do so, or fail to do so, is at the heart of the concept of library effectiveness.

Conclusion

In the previous discussion, a review of various approaches to perceiving library effectiveness has been made. Little homogeneity exists among the various approaches. This lack of consensus, in turn, results from the existence of at least seven problems inherent in the consideration of the concept of library effectiveness. In an effort to overcome these problems, a systems model of library effectiveness has been proposed.

The model described differs from previous models. Instead of specifying the criteria for effectiveness (for example, under what conditions is a library effective?), this model focuses on the *process* of being effective (for example, how are expectations satisfied at a given time for a given person to judge the library as effective?). It is argued that the actual criteria for evaluation vary depending on the particular expectations of the particular person (or group) in question.

It is stressed that the use of a systems model allows for the explicit recognition of the ways in which various organizational factors blend together to facilitate or inhibit activities concerned with library effectiveness. This perspective forces library administrators to use a more comprehensive approach in an examination of library performance, facilitating a broader vision of the nature of the effectiveness problem and on its possible solutions.

A general conclusion to be drawn from this discussion relates to the concept of effectiveness as a continuous process rather than an end result. Library responsiveness to expectations is an unceasing task. In view of the changing nature of inputs, administrators have a continuing responsibility to recognize changes in the environment, to restructure available resources, to modify technologies, to develop employees, and so forth, in order to best employ the resources of the library to fulfill expectations that are themselves constantly changing.

Additional Readings

Fewer additional readings about the control function as it pertains to the library are available than for most of the other functions of management. First, much of the business literature that relates to control is not oriented toward the nonprofit organization. Second, managerial control as a topic of discussion is a fairly recent addition to library literature. Aspects of control such as standards, performance measurement, and budgeting are often discussed, but control in the overall sense, the "process by which managers assure that resources are obtained and used effectively and efficiently in the accomplishment of an organization's objectives,"[1] is rarely examined. Third, "control" is often a misunderstood term, "taken to mean only regulation, domination or restraint," when in fact its real purpose is to "coordinate, balance and monitor the successful fulfillment"[2] of the library's basic plans.

As Rizzo's essay (selection 9) suggests, there are many approaches to control. This theme is further examined by Sayles in "The Many Dimensions of Control" (*Organizational Dynamics* Summer 1972). Anthony and Herzlinger's *Management Control in Nonprofit Organizations* (Irwin, 1975) is one of the few books relating to nonprofit management that approaches the control process from a broad perspective. These authors combine an examination of accounting in the nonprofit setting with a focus on organization theory and organizational behavior as it relates to control—a highly useful approach for readers who wish to broaden their perspective on control in the library environment. On a smaller scale but with a similarly broad perspective, Flamholtz presents a framework for looking at "Organizational Control Systems as a Managerial Tool" (*California Management Review*, Winter 1979). Using three case studies in manufacturing, real estate and professional accounting, Flamholtz illustrates the elements, design, and evaluation of effective control systems. Continuing the discussion of effectiveness in control, Odiorne identifies and explores the tendency to become so involved in a system that a view of the input-output relationship in control is lost ("Some Comments on Input-Output Relations in Nonprofit Bureaucracies," *Management of Nonprofit Organizations,* Lexington Books, 1975).

Goals and Standards

Goals are an inextricable part of the control process. Before measurement and evaluation can take place, goals must be determined or the outcome of the control process may be meaningless. If, for example, a library evaluates its effectiveness in meeting the needs of its users and ignores the unmet needs of nonusers, can the outcome of this process yield a true statement of effectiveness? All too often in the library environment, measurement is made of what *is* without asking the fundamental question, "what should be?" and the library literature reflects this direction. Readers who wish to develop a clear picture of *all* of the dimensions of control should therefore review the literature relating to the goal-setting process in libraries as discussed in chapter 2 Additional Readings.

Standards or criteria for performance are necessary to a workable control process. In *Recurring Library Issues: A Reader* (Scarecrow Press, 1979) a number of authors address the issue of library standards. Knightly summarizes some of the major approaches to the types of criteria used in overall library performance evaluation and suggests guidelines for future criteria selection ("Overcoming the Criterion Problem in the Evaluation of Library Performance," *Special Libraries,* April 1979). The issue of "effectiveness" as a criterion in the control process is addressed by White ("Library Effectiveness—An Elusive Target," *American Libraries,* December 1980), by Steers ("When Is an Organization Effective? A Process Approach to Understanding Effectiveness," *Organizational Dynamics,* August 1976), and by Connolly, Conlon, and Deutsch ("Organizational Effectiveness: A Multiple-Constituency Approach," *Academy of Management Review* 1980, no. 2). Chweh's "User Criteria for Evaluation of Library Service" (*Journal of Library Administration,* Spring 1981) presents an enlightening study of criteria for a "good" library as determined by service recipients. In-depth views of a wide variety of aspects of library effectiveness are also offered in the compilation of papers presented at the 1980 American Library Association preconference on library effectiveness (*Library Effectiveness: A State of the Art,* ALA, 1982).

Measurement and Evaluation

Actual measurement and evaluation of outcomes is an important part of the control process; these aspects of control have been discussed at great length in the library literature. Lancaster's *The Measurement and Evaluation of Library Services* (Information Resources Press, 1977) provides a broad perspective on these important aspects of control, while Fancher et al. offer more concrete examples of measurement and evaluation applications (*Measuring the Quality of Library Services: A Handbook*, Scarecrow Press, 1974). DeProspo et al. (*Performance Measures for Public Libraries*, ALA, 1973) suggest approaches to measurement that should be informative for all types of libraries. The entire *Library Trends* issue of January 1974 is devoted to evaluation as well, and *Library Journal's Special Report #7, Strategies for Survival: Library Financial Management Today* (*Library Journal*, Bowker, 1978) devotes a chapter to "Evaluation of Services." Additional selections such as Zweizig's "Measuring Library Use" (*Drexel Library Quarterly*, July 1977), Katzer's "The Evaluation of Libraries: Considerations from a Research Perspective" (*Drexel Library Quarterly*, July 1977), DuMont and DuMont's "Measuring Library Effectiveness: A Review and an Assessment" (*Advances in Librarianship*, 1979) and DeProspo and Altman's "Library Measurement, A Management Tool" (*Library Journal*, 15 December 1973) all contribute to a better understanding of the measurement/evaluation problem.

Specific library settings are also described in terms of evaluation. Such examples include Bommer, Chorba, and Grattidge's outline of a model of performance assessment for academic libraries ("Performance Assessment Model for Academic Libraries," *Journal of the American Society for Information Science*, March 1979), Kantor's "The Library as an Information Utility in the University Context: Evaluation and Measurement of Service" (*Journal of the American Society for Information Science*, March-April 1976), and Lowrey and Case's discussion of school media services in "Measuring Program Effectiveness" (*Drexel Library Quarterly*, July 1978). The public library is a focus of special concern, as reflected in selections such as Howard and Howard's "Measuring Public Library Performance" (*Library Journal*, 1 February 1981), Wood et al.'s "Measurement of Service at a Public Library" (*Public Library Quarterly*, Summer 1980), and Campbell's "Methods of Evaluation of Public Library Systems" (*Public Library Quarterly*, Summer 1980). Special library applications are identified in "Measuring Library Effectiveness: A Prelude to Change" (Murphy, *Special Li-*

braries, January 1979) and "One Measure of a Library's Contribution" (Kates, *Special Libraries*, August 1974).

Financial Control

In many organizations, a "management control system is built around a financial structure."[3] Thus the budget, a central element in the financial structure, can be viewed as a control device and the budgeting process as part of the overall control process of an organization. "Budgeting" as a topic is covered by numerous selections in the library literature, although the control aspect of budgeting is often overlooked. Martin's *Budgetary Control in Academic Libraries* (JAI Press, 1978) presents the entire budgeting process in the context of control. The chapters on "What Is a Budget" and "The Purpose of Budgetary Control" are particularly useful as preliminary reading about the role of budgeting as a means of control. Lee's *Library Budgeting: Critical Challenges for the Future* (Pierian Press, 1977) offers a collection of essays that deal with current approaches to library budgeting and the effects of trends on budgets. Additional readings on budgeting are available in Shields and Burke's *Budgeting for Accountability in Libraries* (Scarecrow Press, 1974).

The budget process from a public library perspective is presented by Gelfand ("Budget Preparation and Presentation," *American Libraries*, May 1972) and by Prentice ("Budgeting," chapter 9 in *Public Library Finance*, ALA, 1977); the special library viewpoint is represented by Koenig ("Budgets and Budgeting," *Special Libraries*, July-August 1977) and Randall ("Budgeting for Libraries," *Special Libraries*, January 1976). School media centers are represented by Drott's "Budgeting for School Media Centers" (*Drexel Library Quarterly*, July 1978). Operations audits can also serve in the same manner as the budget, as demonstrated by Herzog ("Operational Audit," *Journal of Systems Management*, October 1977) and Dayton ("Operations Auditing Answers Questions beyond the Scope of Financial Reports," *Management Controls*, September-October 1977). As noted in chapter 4, organizational review and analysis is also a form of control, as are review practices in *any* of the functional areas of the management process.

Integration of Planning and Control

The integration of planning and control is important to the outcomes of both, for "planning makes the rules, control enforces them."[4] Both Machin ("Closing the Gap between Planning and Control," *Long Range Planning*, 1979) and Bower ("Planning and Control: Bottom Up or Top Down?" *Journal of General Management*, Spring 1974) examine facets of this relationship. Reimnitz provides an application in the nonprofit setting by testing the efficiency of administrators in three educational service organizations ("Testing a Planning and Control Model in Nonprofit Organizations," *Academy of Management Journal*, March 1972) and Friedman offers additional evidence in "Control, Management, and Planning: An Empirical Examination" (*Public Administration Review*, November-December 1975). In this context, performance measurement is examined by Budde in *Measuring Performance in Human Service Systems: Planning, Organizing, and Control* (AMACOM, 1979).

Corrective Action

The "corrective action" phase of the control process is seldom discussed in library literature; yet, in times of financial exigency, increasing library productivity and reducing costs must become a part of the control process. Some approaches to productivity are outlined in "Identifying and Managing the Basics of Individual Productivity" (Kreitner, *Arizona Business*, May 1976), "Improve Productivity with Task Teams" (Shepherd, *Training*, April 1980), and "Quality Circles: A Tool for the 80s" (Yager, *Training and Development Journal*, August 1980). In the library environment, Samuelson suggests means of productivity improvement that can be applied in many library situations ("Improving Public Library Productivity," *Library Journal*, 1 February 1981). *Managing Costs and Services in College Libraries* (Council for the Advancement of Small Colleges, 1979) also provides a means of enhancing productivity, and Brown's *Cutting Library Costs: Increasing Productivity and Raising Revenues* (Scarecrow Press, 1979) offers specific means for accomplishing increased productivity in any size library. Organization development, as outlined in chapter 4, may also be seen as a form of "corrective action" in the overall sense, and additional readings are suggested in that chapter that identify ways of making changes that will enhance the library as an organization.

Organizing

The library management process would not be viable without an organizational framework. Conceptualizing this framework, designing an appropriate structure, and maintaining the organization (which may include possible restructuring) as a responsive entity is often termed the "organizing" part of the management process.

Organizing may be defined as "the process by which the structure and allocation of jobs is determined."[1] This process requires a consideration of structure and design, of environmental impact, and of the forces that affect organizational change. Within the organizing process, and within the organization itself, many opportunities for conflict exist. Lack of understanding or disagreement about the organization's mission as developed through the planning process, the implementation of that mission through specific tasks, and the roles of particular individuals in the organization are all potential areas of conflict. In the library setting, it is especially important to consider the effects of technology on design and structure, and the potential conflicts inherent in the nature of the "professional" organization as Drake has outlined in selection 3.

The readings in this chapter will help to pose essential questions for those who wish to understand the library as an organization. Such questions include: What is an organization? How is an organization designed? What are appropriate structures for organizations in the future? Is the bureaucratic model the most useful for the library? How can organizations be structured to meet future requirements? and How can libraries, most of which are bureaucratic in nature, be encouraged to develop and respond to change?

Before design begins, it is essential that a conceptualization of the organization and its environment be developed. The readings in chapter 1, as well as selection 7, identify and delineate the environment within which the library as an organization must exist. Using this framework, the reader can then examine the design process that may be utilized to shape or reshape an organizational structure. McCaskey presents a carefully outlined description of this process. Pointing out the close interrelationship between all parts of the organization, this author poses important questions that must be answered in approaching an organizational design problem, and suggests research and theory that can be used as guidelines. A more specific examination of *job* (as opposed to organization) redesign is also offered in selection 19 as a counterpart to McCaskey's overview.

There are numerous pressures on libraries to alter their traditionally bureaucratic nature and hierarchical structure. Networks and other cooperative arrangements, funded fixed-term service projects, or internal library development programs related to technological changes may present different kinds of organizational requirements and suggest new relationships for both work units and individuals. There is continuing pressure to adopt a more collegial approach to structure to ease the professional-bureaucratic tension that often exists in the "professional" organization. Thus libaries are embarking on new ventures and facing challenges which may make structural alteration desirable. Sayles suggests that the matrix structure represents a workable alternative in both the profit-making and nonprofit environment. Often thought of as being useful largely in the high technology/temporary project setting, matrix management represents a possible way for many other organizations to cope with an inherent organizational conflict—the need for specialization versus coordination. This matrix structure allows a level of adaptability and flexibility that may lend itself more and more to the constantly changing set of organizational and service requirements in the library setting.

As McCaskey has illustrated, however, no organizational structure can be perfect and all organizational design is thus a series of complex trade-offs. Sayles identifies such trade-offs in the matrix organization, particularly in terms of authority and responsibility; still, the matrix provides a possible alternative for libraries of the future when their responses to changing demands can no longer be accommodated by traditional structures.

The first two selections in this chapter point to the ideal organization as an organic system capable of responding to change and becoming self-renewing. They provide the reader with important ideas about future directions for the library organization in terms of flexibility, openness, and careful analysis of structural alternatives. Because most libraries tend to be bureaucratic in nature, however, it is particularly important to examine ways in which such organizations can develop and change. Schein and Greiner present a further look at the movement toward organizational change by identifying ways that "organizational development" processes can become more adapted to bureaucratic organizations. "Organizational development" is often counted on as a way of affecting organizational change; these authors suggest that if this movement wishes to prosper, it must learn to meet the needs of bureaucracy. Specific ways in which such methods and processes can be adapted to a bureaucratic setting are the focal point of this reading. Although directed at "organizational development" practitioners, the lesson from this reading is clear for *all* managers —that the "one-best-way" approach to the development of organizations must be put aside in favor of a broad range of methods and techniques designed to enhance the organizing function within the process of management.

12. An Introduction to Organizational Design

Michael B. McCaskey

How does a manager choose among organizational design alternatives? How does he, for example, decide how precisely to define duties and roles? Should decision-making be centralized or decentralized? What type of people should he recruit to work on a particular task force? Organization design tries to identify the organizational structures and processes that appropriately "fit" the type of people in the organization and the type of task the organization faces.

Organizational design determines what the structures and processes of an organization will be. The features of an organization that can be designed include: division into sections and units, number of levels, location of decision-making authority, distribution of and access to information, physical layout of buildings, types of people recruited, what behaviors are rewarded, and so on. In the process of designing an organization, managers invent, develop, and analyze alternative forms for combining these elements. And the form must reflect the limits and capabilities of humans and the characteristics and nature of the task environment.[1]

Designing a human social organization is extremely complicated. An organization is a system of interrelated parts so that the design of one subsystem or of one procedure has ramifications for other parts of the system. Furthermore, the criteria by which a system design is to be evaluated (economic performance, survival capability, social responsibility, and the personal growth of organizational members) cannot be maximized simultaneously: the de-

© 1974 by the Regents of the University of California. Reprinted from *California Management Review* 17, no. 2:13–21 (1974) by permission of the Regents.

sign of a human social organization can never be perfect or final. In short, the design of organizatioinal arrangements is intended to devise a complex set of tradeoffs in a field of changing people, environment, and values.

Minor adjustments in organizational design are always being made during the life of an organization, but the times for major concentration on organizational design are:

Early in the life of an organization, most likely after the basic identity and strategy have been largely worked out
When significantly expanding or changing the organization's mission or
When reorganizing.

Who designs the organization, organizational units, and task forces? Since organizational design concerns the arrangement of people and the division of tasks, a designer or planner has to have some influence or control over these variables. This task is most often handled by middle-level managers and up. However, the charter to design could be broadened to give organizational members at all levels more of a say in organizational design matters.

Key Concepts and Questions

In approaching an organization design problem, some of the important questions to be answered are:

1. How uncertain is the task environment in which the organization operates?
2. In what ways should the organization be mechanistic and in what ways organic?
3. How should the subtasks be divided and how should the organization be differentiated? Should subsystems be organized by the *functions* people perform, by the *products* or services the company provides, or should some other form such as matrix organization be used?
4. What kind of people are (or can be recruited to become) members of the organization? Under what conditions do they work and learn best?
5. How are activities to be coordinated and integrated? What mechanisms will be used, involving what costs?

Research and theory provide some findings that can be used as design guidelines, and we turn to consider them now.

Mechanistic Patterns of Organizing. Tom Burns' and G. M. Stalker's 1961 study[2] of electronics firms and firms contemplating entering the electronics industry in Scotland and England contributed the important design principle of distinguishing between mechanistic and organic patterns of organizing.

Mechanistic organizational units are the traditional pyramidal pattern of organizing. In a mechanistic organizational unit, roles and procedures are precisely defined. Communication is channelized, and time spans and goal orientations are similar within the unit. The objective is to work toward machinelike efficiency. To that end the task is broken into parts that are joined together at the end of the work process. Authority, influence, and information are arranged by levels, each higher level having successively more authority, more influence, and more information. Decision-making is centralized at the top and it is the top levels that make appreciative judgments[3] to determine what is important in the environment. Top levels also determine the channels whereby the lower echelons will gather and process information.

Thus the social organization is designed as a likeness of a machine. People are conceived of as parts performing specific tasks. As employees leave, other parts can be slipped into their places. Someone at the top is the designer, defining what the parts will be and how they will all fit together.

Under what conditions is this pattern of organization appropriate? When the organizational unit is performing a task that is stable, well-defined, and likely to be programmable, or when members of the organization prefer well-defined situations, feel more secure when the day has a routine to it, and tend to want others to supply direction, the mechanistic pattern is applicable. Organization design findings show that, to the extent these conditions hold, a mechanistic form of organizing is more likely to result in high performance.

The mechanistic form is efficient and predictable. For people with a low tolerance for ambiguity it provides a stable and secure work setting. However, the mechanistic form is less flexible: once a direction and procedures have been set, it is hard to change them. Furthermore, mechanistic forms also entail the danger of stultifying their members with jobs that are too simple, with little responsibility, and no sense of worthwhile accomplishment.

Organic Patterns of Organizing. In contrast to mechanistic units, organic organizational units are based on a more biological metaphor for constructing social organizations. The objective in designing an organic unit is to leave the system maximally open to the environment in order to make the most of new opportunities. The demands of the task environment are ambiguously defined and changing, so people have multiple roles which are continually re-defined in interaction with others. All levels make appreciations and there are few predetermined information channels. Decision-making is more decentralized, with authority and influence flowing to the person who has the greatest expertise to deal with the problem at hand. An organic organizational unit is relatively hetero-geneous, containing a wider variety of time spans, goal orienta-tions, and ways of thinking. The boundaries between the system and the environment are deliberately permeable, and the environment exerts more influence over the activities of the system than is true for the mechanistic unit.

An organic form is useful in the face of an uncertain task or one that is not well enough understood to be programmed. The organic form is also appropriate for people who like the disorder of an ambiguous setting, for people who prefer variety, change, and adventure and who grow restless when they fall into the same routine day after day. The organic form is flexible and responds quickly to unexpected opportunities. However, the organic form is often wasteful of resources. Not having precisely defined author-ity, control, and information hierarchies, time can be wasted in search activities that duplicate the efforts of other members. Fur-thermore, the stress of uncertainty and the continual threat of power struggles can be exhausting.

Making the Choice. The choice of the most suitable form of organization is *contingent* upon the task and the people involved. There is no one form of organization that will work best in all situ-ations, in all cultures, with every type of person. Organization de-sign scholars using a contingency theory approach emphasize the need to specify the particular conditions under which a given form is most appropriate.

Note, too, that the same organizational unit can change its position on the organic/mechanistic continuum over time. The unit might start out being very mechanistically organized. But as the environment or staff change, the unit might move toward the or-ganic end of the continuum. In fact, if the unit does not change its structures and processes to meet changed conditions, it is likely to suffer lower performance.

Even more important, one organization is likely to contain both organic units and mechanistic units at the same time. Burns and Stalker[4] characterized whole organizations as mechanistic or organic; but Paul Lawrence and Jay Lorsch[5] found that these descriptions more accurately described units of an organization. They researched and elaborated on a major contribution to organization design in the concepts of differentiation and integration (D&I).

Differentiation

Differentiation, the creation or emergence of differences in the organization, can take place in several ways:

Vertically—into levels
Horizontally—into sections, departments, divisions, and so on
Division of labor—into occupational roles
Patterns of thinking—differences between units in members' goals, time, and interpersonal orientations.

By differentiating, the organization gains the advantages of both economies of scale and people becoming experts in particular areas like production, accounting, contracting, and so on.

Lawrence and Lorsch found horizontal differentiation and the differentiation of patterns of thinking to be the most important types of differentiation for organizational design. The organization segments the environment into parts so that organizational units interact with different subenvironments. While marketing interacts with the media, ad agencies, legal departments, competitors' advertising, and the other elements that make up the marketing subenvironment, production is dealing with the machines, labor market, scheduling, cost consciousness, and safety regulations that pertain to their subenvironment. Furthermore, the structure and setting for each unit must supply the appropriate training and support for different job demands. Scientists, for example, need a milieu that will supply specialized information as well as support in projects that may take years to complete.

An important question in organization design, therefore, is how differentiated should the organization be? How should the environment be segmented and what activities should be grouped together? To what extent should the units differ in structures and procedures, types of people, and patterns of thinking?

Research indicates that business organizations in newer and more uncertain industries, like aerospace and electronics, need to be more highly differentiated because they face a greater range of subenvironments. As James Thompson[6] argues, organizations try to shield their technical core from the uncertainties of the environment. The subenvironment of the core technology unit, then, will be relatively stable and call for more mechanistic patterns of organizing. The units having uncertain subenvironments (often the R&D subenvironment) will need to be more organically organized. Looking at the organization as a whole, the differences between the units will be significant because the range of unit organizational patterns extends from the mechanistic end to the organic end of the continuum.

Conversely, research indicates that organizations in older, more established and more certain industries need to be less differentiated. They face a narrow range of subenvironments near the certainty end of the spectrum, and will probably pursue the efficiency given by more mechanistic patterns of organizing. An organization in a relatively stable and certain environment benefits from having uniform rules and procedures, vocabulary, and patterns of thinking throughout the organization. The problem of integration for these organizations, therefore, is less demanding.

Integration

At the same time the organization is differentiated to work more effectively on tasks, some activities of organizational units must be coordinated and brought together, or integrated. The manager/designer must resist differentiating the organization too radically—the greater the differences between the units, the harder it is for them to coordinate activities with each other. If all the units have similar goals, values, and time horizons, messages and meanings are more likely to be clear. But when an organization is highly differentiated, people have to spend more effort translating and appreciating the frameworks of people in different units. Most people habitually think in their own terms and it takes increased effort to move into another's frame of reference. The chances for misunderstandings increase in a highly differentiated organization.

The greater the differentiation, the heavier the burden on information processing and upon decision-making in the organization. This shows up in the array of techniques for coordinating the activities of a firm:

1. The use of rules and procedures along with the hierarchy of authority
2. If two units are crucial and have trouble integrating, the appointment of a liaison[7]
3. The building of a new unit into the work flow to serve as an integrating department.

This list of coordinating mechanisms shows progressively more elaborate ways to achieve integration. With greater differentiation, an organization has to spend more effort integrating and use the more expensive devices.

So in addition to asking how much the organization should differentiate to meet environment and people requirements, another question must simultaneously be raised. How much differentiation, at what cost, can the organization successfully integrate? How should people be grouped to provide the best working conditions for individuals *and* to secure the most advantageous work flow for the whole organization? A manager/designer works for the best practical answer to these questions. Many times he may decide to stop short of differentiating to perfectly meet task environment demands because his staff would find it too great a strain or because it would be too costly. Research findings show that in uncertain environments, the most successful organizations are the most highly differentiated *and* the most integrated. The difficult design decision of how to differentiate and how to integrate is often framed as the choice between product or functional organization,[8] or some newer form like a matrix organization.[9]

The Research Studies

Table 1 summarizes a selection of research findings important for organization design theory. The studies were conducted mainly, although not entirely, with business firms. A wide range of methodolgies has been used including historical study methods, an intensive case study of one division, a questionnaire survey of managers in different organizations, surveying and interviewing the top managers of all the business organizations in a given geographical area, and so on. All of the studies support a contingency approach to organizational design. Researchers found that explaining their data required them to specify the conditions upon which the use of a particular organization form was contingent.

In spite of different methods and vocabularies, certain patterns and continuities run through the findings. The design principle of distinguishing between mechanistic and organic forms is supported by the studies. Peter Blau's and Richard Schoenherr's[10] findings based on all instances (53) of one type of government agency lends support to the Lawrence and Lorsch[11] findings based on a selected sample of ten business firms. Both studies found that environmental diversity is related to greater differentiation in the organization. Blau and Schoenherr[12]found that differentiation raises

TABLE 1. Empirical Research Findings on Organizational Design

Researchers	Types of Organizations Studied	Selected Findings
Burns and Stalker (1961)	20 firms in U.K. including a rayon manufacturer, an engineering firm, several companies in electronics and others contemplating entry into electronics.	"Mechanistic" management system suited to an enterprise operating under relatively stable conditions; "organic" required for conditions of change.
Chandler (1962)	Historical studies of DuPont, General Motors, Standard Oil of New Jersey, and Sears Roebuck, supplemented by brief reviews of over 70 other large American business companies.	By trial and error a new structural form (decentralized, multidivisional form) developed to fit changed environmental conditions.
Woodward (1965)	100 English manufacturing firms.	Patterns in management practice associated with how complex and how predictable production technology is.
Lawrence and Lorsch (1967)	10 U.S. companies in plastics, consumer food, and standardized container industries.	1. High performing organizations are differentiated to meet environmental demands; diverse and uncertain environments require greater differentiation of the organization. 2. Differentiation and integration are antagonistic states; the more differentiated an organization is, the more elaborate the integrative devices must be. 3. Additional support for above findings.
Galbraith (1970)	Case study of the Boeing Aircraft Division.	Structural changes to deal with greater task environment uncertainty related to the need to process more information.
Blau and Schoenherr (1971)	The 53 state employment security offices in the U.S.A. and territories.	1. Increasing size generates structural differentiation in organizations along various dimensions at decelerating rates. 2. Structural differentiation in organizations raises requirements for managerial manpower.

(continued)

TABLE 1. (Continued)

Researchers	Types of Organizations Studied	Selected Findings
		3. Horizontal, vertical, and occupational differentiation are positively related to environmental diversity.
Duncan (1971)	22 decision-making units in 3 manufacturing organizations and in 3 R&D organizations.	Structural profile used to make nonroutine decisions differs from that used to make routine decisions; suggests the same unit uses different organizing patterns over time.
Morse and Young (1973)	235 managers from 8 business organizations.	Individuals working on certain tasks preferred controlling authority relations and had a low tolerance for ambiguity; individuals working on uncertain tasks sought independence and autonomy and were high in tolerance for ambiguity.

the requirements for managerial manpower, and this is similar to Lawrence and Lorsch's[13] finding that greater differentiation requires more elaborate integrative devices. Furthermore, Jay Galbraith's[14] research provides something of an explanatory picture. His findings suggest that the need for more managerial manpower and more elaborate integrative mechanisms is related to the need for the organization to process more information.

Robert Duncan's[15] findings that an organizational unit appears to change its structure over time simply reinforces managers' feelings that organization charts are often incorrect and out-of-date. This is a promising area of research for developing a more accurate picture of how and when changes in organization structure occur.

As the studies indicate, substantial progress has been made. However, some important questions remain to be answered.

Work Yet to Be Done

Our knowledge of organizational design is still growing. Some of the important subjects which need further research are:

1. We need a better understanding of the *dynamics* of an or-

ganization developing a good fit to its environment and its members. The processes that span organization and environment, such as planning and selecting, recruiting and socializing new members, need to be researched. In addition to learning more about the enduring structural patterns, we also need to learn about the ways in which organization and environment adjust to one another.

2. We must consider the assertion of power in the interaction of organizations and their environments. How do organizations seek to make the environment more favorable to their operations? How does the environment coerce or influence the organization to meet its demands? What are the consequences of one element gaining sizeable amounts of control over the other? We need to learn about the processes which mediate this contest for control and influence.

3. Up until now researchers have mainly relied upon the criterion of economic performance to assess good fit. Clearly, using economic criteria alone is too limited. How can we judge goodness of fit in terms of people outcomes? Moreover, what about the people who are content to follow orders from the organization? Some argue that we cannot be normative on this value question. If a person is satisfied to be passive and dependent on the job, who can insist that he take more control over his own work life? My view is that a democracy can hardly afford a work system which mainly trains people to be docile, to follow orders, and above all to be loyal to the organization. But others emphasize that many prefer following orders, and this is where the issue is joined.

4. A related issue is the possible conflict between efficiency and human needs. Some elements of organization design concern social engineering to devise the most efficient organization to accomplish a task. Other elements of organization design are concerned with the full growth and development of individuals. It is too optimistic to assume that efficiently designed organizations will always or even usually be conducive to human intercourse. Mammoth operations built to meet economies of scale considerations teach us that efficiently engineered operations can be inhumane. If we had better noneconomic measures of outcomes, maybe we could more accurately assess the design tradeoffs. As it stands now, much of organization design emphasizes an engineering approach, neglecting human growth aspects. Another challenge: How can we design organizations to meet both people and engineering concerns?

5. We also need to learn more about how facilities design supports or detracts from the intent of an organization design. How

does the physical layout influence the pattern of social interaction? How does the visual display of information affect decision-making? At what distance for what types of activities does physical separation of people or units greatly strain the organization's ability to integrate? How can facilities be designed so that physical spaces can be rearranged to fit changes in organizing patterns? Robert Propst,[16] Fritz Steele,[17] and Thomas Allen[18] have begun work on some of these questions.

Summary

A convenient guideline for reviewing what we know about designing organizations is the continuum from mechanistic to organic patterns of organizing. Most suited to stable, certain environments and a staff that prefers stability, the mechanistic form is the traditional hierarchical pyramid that is controlled from the top and programs activities tightly. Most suited to an unstable, uncertain environment and people tolerant of ambiguity, the organic pattern of organizing is more collegial and stresses flexibility in rules, decision-making authority, procedures, and so on. Of course, there are more than these two types of organizing patterns. They should be considered the ends of a continuum of types of organizing patterns.

An organization is likely to contain both organically and mechanistically organized units. How widely the units should range on the mechanistic/organic continuum is part of the question of differentiation. How great should the differences be between units in terms of structures, types of people, and patterns of thinking? Overall, organizations in mature and stable industries contain units that face more or less well-defined and certain subenvironments. Therefore, to meet environmental demands, the units should generally be more mechanistically organized and the organization as a whole will be less differentiated.

On the other hand, organizations in dynamic new industries must have some units organically organized to deal with an uncertain subenvironment. At the same time it should devise more mechanistic units (for example, production and accounting) to face more stable subenvironments. To cover that range of subenvironments, the manager/organization designer creates or allows to develop greater differences between the units. In addition, the organization tends to create more job roles (occupational differentiation) and more levels (vertical differentiation) in response to environmental diversity. The organization, therefore, becames more highly differentiated.

The opposite tendency from differentiation is the need to integrate, to coordinate the activities of different parts of the organization. The greater the differentiation, the harder it is to integrate. The choice of a particular integrating mechanism, such as a liaison in addition to rules, signals the manager/designer's decision to expend a certain amount of effort to coordinate activities. Concurrent with designing the extent of differentiation in an organization, a manager must consider what effort at what cost will be needed to integrate those differences. The greater the differentiation, the more elaborate and costly are the mechanisms needed for integration.

Organizational design choices are tradeoffs between good fit to the task environment and people characteristics, to monetary and human costs, and to short-term and long-term consequences. Such a design is never perfect or complete. Organizational design seeks to build knowledge about and provide guidelines for designing more efficient and more human organizations.

13. Matrix Management: The Structure with a Future

Leonard R. Sayles

Every organization faces two problems: first, how to specialize (creating a division of labor); and second, how to integrate the specialized parts to create a whole product or service. Of the two, specialization—breaking the whole into parts—is easier. To make everything come out consistent and complementary—a coordination problem—is more difficult. Alas, most managers believe the opposite.

In recent years, management philosophies on organizing to achieve coordination have alternated between two extremes. In the 1950s, the rush to decentralize put managers in charge of their own businesses, while in the 1960s many of the same corporations recentralized to gain better control and realize economies of scale. In the process, they recognized that they could not artificially create autonomous units when the major segments of their businesses were highly interdependent. It is unfortunate that such companies, which alternate almost in cycles between "flat" and "tall" structures, fail to recognize a third alternative that avoids many of the inherent problems of the more popular structural forms.

Reprinted from *Organizational Dynamics* 4:2–17 (Autumn 1976). © 1976 by Leonard Sayles.

This article is adapted from material to be incorporated in a forthcoming book tentatively titled *Leadership in Complex Organizations*. The author is indebted to the Faculty Research Fund of the Graduate School of Business, Columbia University, for supporting this research. Professor Michael Tushman made a number of helpful criticisms of an earlier draft.

We are referring to matrix structure that allows for the coexistence of a good deal of decentralization and centralization. In many ways, product/project systems coordinators are like the heads of decentralized units in that they make all the critical trade-offs relevant to running an independent activity. At the same time they draw upon centralized resources that not only provide high levels of technical proficiency, but also facilitate cost control and economies of scale.

There are obvious reasons for neglect of the matrix alternative. One is the basic misconception that the usefulness of matrix structures is limited to R&D environments or projects with a predetermined life span. The other is the correct assumption that matrix management is not consistent with the traditionally accepted and comfortable "principles" of good organization and good management. This, we maintain, is a point in favor of matrix management—because the managerial qualities required by matrix management are precisely what is required of all managers functioning in today's complex managerial environment. There are just too many connections and interdependencies among all line and staff executives—involving diagonal, dotted, and other "informal" lines of control, communication, and cooperation—to accommodate the comfortable simplicity of the traditional hierarchy, be it flat or tall.

This article spells out various applications and types of matrix structures in the belief that many organizations have already adopted some form of matrix structure without the name. We begin by emphasizing that modern organizations require new structural forms because they must cope with more uncertainty than can be handled by classic hierarchical techniques—clear plans, detailed job descriptions, unambiguous orders, and so on.

Lateral Relations

Modern organization theory stresses placing more responsibility on individual line managers to improve their own patterns of coordination without hierarchical intervention. Sometimes this is accomplished through administrative techniques that focus efforts on changing the perceptions, goals, awareness, and loyalties of managers, and sometimes through more structural devices. Think, for example, of the management training programs that stress "one-big-company" philosophy or the over-arching "goals we all share" motif and give the manager some awareness of how each department contributes to the whole. Consider too the OD movement, much of which represents sophisticated methods of encouraging managers to understand why the other manager may appear to be uncooperative or hostile, how their own behavior may contribute to the conflict, and how to improve relationships and acquire the necessary cooperation.

There is an interesting historical footnote here. As students of organization came to recognize that modern bureaucracy—the introduction of rational methods to the organization of work—was not truly depersonalized (as sociologist Max Weber had implied) because there were still "human" problems, they concentrated their attention on the problems of authority. In a heroic misinterpretation of the famed Hawthorne studies, the human relationists concentrated their attention on improving the relationship of boss to subordinate through leadership training.

Only recently have their successors in organizational behavior shifted attention to the problems of lateral relations and the attendant problems of coordination and integration. Perhaps the reason for OD's rapid growth is that observant managers recognize that the most crucial problems of the organization revolve around improving cooperation and coordination between departments, managers, and subsystems. Although OD has recently encompassed a broader range of interventions, it was originally a set of techniques for improving interpersonal relations, utilized by the personnel staff or outside consultants to facilitate intergroup communication and lateral cooperation. By contrast, matrix management induces these same effects through the use of organization structure. Conflict management, beginning with confrontation between specialists' standards and overall system needs, emerges from the very design of the matrix. No change agent is necessary to encourage feedback and the resolution of conflicts in goals and values.

Operationalizing Uncertainty

Many students of organizations believe that modern organizations face more uncertainty than can be handled by traditional hierarchical methods or by the usual patchwork of improved lateral relationships; they argue the need for a very different style of organization—one in which integration or coordination receives as much weight as specialization. The key word is *uncertainty*. Let's see what we mean by it.

1. The frequency of exceptional cases—those requiring non-

standardized solutions based on human deliberations and/or involving unusual technical difficulty—is too great for the general manager and his aides to handle. Further, the occurrence of these problems—most of which upset the workflow—is unpredictable in both time and quantity. Problem solving therefore becomes the responsibility of on-the-scene experts and requires lateral interactions.

2. Many of these decisions require the simultaneous accommodation to diverse and legitimately conflicting interests and points of view, a process that can be resolved only by ongoing deliberations.

3. Implicit in the above is the need to recognize inherent contradictions in any effort to optimize toward one objective or one set of constraints. There is no "production function" by which a centralized executive or planning body can arrive at optimal solutions through rational decision-making techniques. (We have argued previously that as the number of legitimate interests and constraints proliferate, the only mechanism by which decisions can be reached is through a kind of negotiating/haggling/trading-off.) Many years ago Walter Lippmann noted the similar characteristics in U.S. history that ensured democratic political processes because no autocrat could simultaneously serve all the conflicting interests.

4. Unforeseen and unforeseeable problems arising from inherent instabilities in the technology or environment will destroy the integrity of any master plan for designing jobs, task specifications, and dollar and time allowances. Where the number of operative factors is large and they are mutually interdependent, as is frequently the case, even slight changes in any one will have profound effects on the total system.

An analogy to illustrate the point is the modern automobile, which consists of literally tens of thousands of interacting parts. Even minor technical defects—in design or quality, say, of a single bolt—can injure the total system, and advance testing and calculations can't predict *all* the in-service interrelationships. Thus the horrendous recalls of new vehicles.

In effect, these uncertainties require us to design a dynamic organization structure that can absorb and be quickly responsive to unanticipated changes in job definitions and allocations—a structure that will encourage rapid and continuous trade-offs throughout the total system, not merely on a one-to-one sequential basis. This, in fact, is the strength of the matrix structure. Readjustment, preferably in the form of simultaneous modifica-

tion and accommodation, is required—and both the encouragement and the management of this reciprocity can best take place
in a structure specifically designed to facilitate this type of exchange: the matrix.

The Customary View of Matrix Organization

Matrix organization, as an "advanced" concept of organization structure, typically is associated with complex technologies,
particularly in the aerospace industry. It is also generally assumed
that matrix management represents a relatively homogeneous
style of organizing work and therefore requires a single type of
management, what's usually designated as project management.
Actually, though, in looking at both contemporary government
and contemporary business, we find that the matrix may be becoming the dominant form of structure, a finding with profound
implications for modern management.

Let's look at the simplest definition of this form of structure,
and then we'll be able to observe how it is spreading to a variety
of settings beyond the high technology-temporary project case
with which it is commonly identified.

In the simplest terms, matrix management represents the effort, organizationally speaking, to "have your cake and eat it, too."
Traditionally, top management has alternated between organizing
work on the basis of functional specialization and structuring it
according to completed tasks, products, or service delivery. See
figure 1 for some obvious examples.

Although, in theory, employees have one boss in a "product"
or "functional" organization, in the usual view of matrix management they have two bosses. While this would be anathema to
most of the founders of adminstrative science—to whom unity of
command was essential—the resulting contradictions (between
authorities) are justified because of the extraordinary requirements of the new technologies.

Functional Units	Product/Service Units
Marketing	Men's toiletries division
Probation department	Criminal justice system
Pathology laboratory	Surgical patient care
Telecommunications	Spacecraft development
Stagehands	Opera production
Operations research	MBA degree program

FIGURE 1. Two traditional bases for organizing work

In the best-known application of matrix management—R&D projects—we found the following set of characteristics:

Top management could not plan in advance all the contributions of the various functional specialities. Unforeseeable technical difficulties would require different tasks, time allowances, or specifications from those anticipated.

While the projects involved sophisticated professional tasks requiring highly trained members of a given functional specialty to understand and undertake them, how and when these skills were to be employed depended upon an overall understanding of the projects' goals. Further, the way in which each functional task was performed would impact the problems faced by the other groups involved.

Thus a manager who would be responsible for the total effort was necessary as well as managers who would focus on the technical excellence of the parts involved. Because it was impossible to anticipate from the outset how parts would fit together, the organization needed *both* functional *and* project managers.

Further, it would be uneconomical to permanently assign tasks because in the R&D environment new projects come and go.

There is a similar kind of matrix organization built around the temporary project in a development-oriented organization. The key terms are *temporary* and *development-oriented*. The latter suggests a world in which change is a constant, a world in which fixed policies, rules, and group norms are destructive because each project is different—involving different problems, different people, different requirements. It is for this reason that some writers, notably Warren Bennis and Philip Slater in *The Temporary Society*, have argued that these are the organizations of the dynamic future, constantly in flux—a structure that forms and disbands depending on the unique needs of the moment or some special product or project.

In reality, matrix management is not so new or unusual. It frequently evolves in response to the inherent conflict that, Victor Thompson argues, haunts every modern organization: the needs of specialization versus the needs of coordination. Matrix organization is introduced to cope with these conflicts because management assumes they will occur too frequently to be handled by up-the-line appeals to some higher-level boss whose jurisdiction spans the contending groups. Moreover, the existence of matrix management assumes that an omniscient upper-level manager can't make an optimizing decision—he doesn't know enough. The project manager must act as a decision broker—working problems through the experts who in their respective fields know more than he does. But no expert, whatever his or her role in the functional organization, can have the final say because other needs of the project—to produce a useful overall result, to be on time and within costs, and to meet some external performance standards (created by customer or other external demand)—lie outside his or her province of expertise.

Kinds of Matrix Organizations

The basic structural principle of the matrix organization is that resource usage be controlled and/or directed by two opposing sets of managers. There is no law of nature, however, to discourage three sets of managers. As we have noted, most comments have assumed that matrix management was a relatively homogeneous organization form and largely limited to temporary R&D projects. (To be sure, the engineering management literature rather consistently notes that the proportion of required resources directly but temporarily controlled by the project manager—as distinct from the functional manager—could vary from almost zero to 100 percent.) The realities are another story. The differences in structural form among organizations justifiably called "matrix" may be almost as great as the differences between matrix and nonmatrix structures.

Our own field research plus a review of the literature suggest that there are at least five distinguishable styles of matrix management. Each is suited to a different environment and requires quite distinctive skills on the part of the various participating managers. Many of the intramanagement conflicts we observed resulted from failure of the organizations to make explicit—or even be aware of—the particular structural forms they had evolved. Managers could not understand why their authority and influence were different from what they had anticipated or were accustomed to. Another loss stemmed from problems that went unresolved because of the aforementioned stereotype that matrix management is commonly confined to an R&D-style structure.

The term "matrix," of course, reflects the opposed sets of managers, arrayed in matrix form. In its most usual form, each matrix involves a set of systems managers sharing or contending for resources controlled by a set of functional managers. (Since terminology differs broadly in this context, we will indicate the usual variations: By "systems manager," we mean what is often called a product, project, or service-delivery manager; by "functional manager," we mean managers who control specialized services, disciplines, or professional or technical activities.)

Table 1 summarizes the characteristics of the five types of

TABLE 1. Types of Matrix Structure

Type of Matrix	Systems Manager's Roles	Functional Manager's Role
1. Dispersed systems	(Example: court adminis-trator) To advise To audit To act as liaison	To direct workflow segments
2. Product manage-ment	(Example: consumer-goods brand manager) To stabilize To advise To audit To act as liaison	To direct workflow segments
3. Bipolar manage-ment	(Example: state conservation department head) To direct workflow segments To stabilize To audit	To direct workflow segments To stabilize To audit
4. Develop-ment projects	(Example: R&D project chief) To direct workflow	To stabilize To audit To advise To provide services
5. Internal consult-ing ser-vices	(Example: management science department head) To direct workflow	To exercise institutional management To advise (on career planning)

matrix organization we have observed and gives examples. It is designed to show a continuum from the less systems-oriented structures on the top to the more systems-oriented structures on the bottom. In addition, we have sought to explicitly define the managerial tasks of both systems and functional managers in each of the five types. The task or role elements specified for each are those that grew out of our earlier research on managerial behavior patterns.

Basic Elements in Administrative Roles

In this earlier research, we observed differing distributions of seven basic elements, or responsibilities, in administrative roles:

1. To manage workflow (to have operating responsibility).
2. To stabilize (to be responsible for approving certain technical decisions before implementation).
3. To audit (to be responsible for evaluating performance or decision effectiveness after completion of workflows).
4. To advise (to be responsible for providing technical assistance when and if requested).
5. To provide services (to be responsible for providing centralized support functions).
6. To act as liaison (to be responsible for acting as an intermediary between managerial or organizational elements).
7. To exercise institutional management (to be responsible for personnel and equipment housing and support).

Five Styles of Matrix Management

Now let us look at what the five matrix types are like, following the continuum in table 1 from the less systems-oriented structures to the more systems-oriented ones. Included in each are explicit managerial descriptions that serve to distinguish among the types. First, we'll look at the "dispersed systems" matrix.

Dispersed Systems Matrix

In most organizations, the problems that produced their original form of structure change or elaborate over time. Management usually adopts one of two strategies to cope with the new situation. Either it creates a new department, agency, or unit (say, for environmental affairs)—only to discover that the problem manages to seep out into the jurisdictions of other departments—or, alternatively, it seeks to create new hierarchies that have to be very "tall" if they are going to comprehend all elements of the problem. One example of the latter would be the superdepartments—such as human resources—created by John Lindsay and imposed on top of the existing organizational structure of New York City's municipal government when he was mayor. Both strategies complicate administration by cluttering up the environment with excessive numbers of new organizational units and adding extended, unwieldy reporting relationships in unworkable monolithic structures.

There are other approaches, however. Under the impetus of Chief Justice Warren Burger, for example, local, state, and federal courts have begun to employ "court administrators." Their job is to tie together the diverse and organizationally dispersed elements that make up the criminal justice system—not only the courts themselves, but law enforcement, prosecution, defense, probation, jury selection, correctional institutions, and so on. They don't manage these units—in fact, many of them are part of the executive, not the judicial, branch of government—but they seek to persuade each unit to modify its customary work procedures in a manner consistent with the needs of the total system.

To take another example, area managers in multinational companies—concerned with the company's viability in a given country or region with distinctive economic, social, and political constraints—seek to get various product and functional managers to modify their decisions in the interests of the company's growth in that area.

Consider how this worked in such a company that was deciding to build a new facility in what we'll call country Z. From the point of view of manufacturing, the new facility should have been a mass-production facility large enough to serve the entire Asian market and ensure economies of scale. But product management wanted a separate facility for their most technical products to ensure good engineering. In the interest of maintaining their "charter" to operate in country Z, the area manager got both to modify their plans and agree to place a smaller, high-technology plant in Z—which was insisting that it did not want to be simply a cheap labor contractor.

Recent studies of the technology change/diffusion field suggest that most new technologies are adopted only when a number of different organizations, all part of the larger system impacted by the innovation, are coordinated. Thus an effort to introduce a new fabric-cleaning technology would have to deal simultaneously with textile producers, clothing manufacturers, cleaning-supply distributors, commercial laundries and cleansers, and various regulatory agencies.

This is similar to Felix Rohatyn's role in seeking to resolve the stalemate likely whenever New York City municipal unions, banks, government agencies, and industrial firms all wait for one of the others to make concessions to save the city from default.

Focal-Point Integrators

Another kind of manager who works in a dispersed systems environment serves as an entry point to one or more organizations for an "outsider" client who has neither the clout nor the know-how to arrange for the relevant services. Typically, the client takes the initiative. Some examples:

1. NASA appointed a special manager for each foreign spacecraft team that would act as a point of contact to the diverse NASA groups necessary to launch and control outside, non-NASA hardware.

2. Social service agencies are finding that efforts to divide up family needs among a number of specialists are disastrous—that it is much more effective to have a single social worker responsible for the family, a social worker who can, in turn, make arrangements for the family to deal with other organizations: medical, political, welfare, and so on.

3. Naïve citizens seeking government aid in undertaking home construction, purchase, or remodeling in depressed areas usually find it impossible to learn to cope with the variety of agencies and regulations involved even though they qualify for the various kinds of aid. A focal office to make contacts facilitates the functioning of the programs designed to encourage reconstruction in ghetto areas.

The unique characteristics of the dispersed systems manager is that he or she seeks to integrate the activities of organizational units whose major goals and loyalties are not normally consistent with the goals of the overall system.

Managers of Special Projects Introducing Change

Obviously, almost any innovation to be implemented by simultaneous adjustments of a number of operating departments requires the use of a systems-type manager. As our own previous studies have shown, the major impediment to implementation is the shock and disruption to the ongoing routines necessary to achieve reasonable efficiency. Each impacted department finds countless unanticipated costs of adaptation. A sponsor-facilitator exerting encouragement and pressure is essential if the innovation is not to flounder because one department or another finds it easier to slip back to its more comfortable and successful past routines. Further, the facilitator often acts as a broker to resolve stalemates—where one department can't cope with the innovation because another department isn't adjusting and refuses to make concessions until still a third department modifies its procedures. And the third group, in turn, is likely to be dependent on some concession from the first group. Such circularity and inter-dependence require the energetic intervention of an independent "honest broker" who both wants the innovation to succeed and can identify and help resolve these inevitable stalemates.

Both in government and in business we see an increasing need for people who can influence the decisions of widely diversified groups with disparate objectives—influence them toward consistency with some otherwise elusive and easily ignored goals. The integrator-advocate-conscience is usually not in a position to make the relevant decisions himself because critical elements are controlled by autonomous organizations reluctant to make the required decisions themselves And each of these is loath to fulfill the requisite for one or more of the following reasons:

1. The goal involved appears to be less immediate, relevant, or powerful than other goals and internal constraints.
2. They believe that other units in the system have more to gain than they have.
3. They are wary of making costly concessions when these might well be nullified by a more intractable unit.
4. They may not believe or trust the information suggesting that their present behavior is injuring the larger goal or that a change will facilitate its accomplishment.

Thus a persuasive, energetic matrix manager who functions as a trusted source of information often can obtain marginal concessions from the key units of a dispersed system. This is the way that John Dunlop was reported to have functioned in seeking to obtain productivity improvements during the Nixon administration. Dunlop recognized that productivity was the result of a number of interdependent decisions, none of which would be made if they all weren't made. In his efforts to reduce the cost of food, for example, he sought to find ways of getting farmers, truckers, middlemen, warehouses, railroads, warehouse processors, and supermarkets to simultaneously change the way they handled food. Some of the "new ways" tried were standard-size pallets for loading and unloading, and changes in ICC rail and truck regulations.

Product Management

Although we have used a rather specific term, product management, as a category of matrix management, this particular matrix style is often utilized without any formal designation as such in a wide variety of settings. The most common is consumer sundries—soaps, dentifrices, and the like—but small-appliance and other manufacturers that constantly introduce new products utilizing a common set of marketing and production facilities fall into the same category. Product managers are systems managers who have obtained a measure of organizational power that they use to pressure the basic operating divisions to seek a goal that might otherwise go neglected. For example, a product manager will endeavor to persuade manufacturing—and packaging and advertising as well—to tailor its normal activities to meet the special overall needs of his particular product. To permit such managers to do this, top management usually gives them certain stabilization powers: They may have to approve functional budgets or plans for new facilities, work schedules, or final specifications. Let's look at an example.

Ellen Fisher is a product manager responsible for the introduction of new soap products. She works through several functional departments, including market research, the development laboratory's production, and sales. In designing the new product, market research usually conducts a test of consumer reactions. In this case, the market research head, Hank Fellers, wants to run the standard field test on the new brand in two preselected cities. Ellen is opposed to this because it would delay the product introduction date of September 1; if that date can be met, sales has promised to obtain a major chain-store customer (using a house-brand label) whose existing contract for this type of soap is about to expire.

At the same time, manufacturing is resisting a commitment to fill this large order by the date sales established because "new-product introductions have to be carefully meshed in our schedule with other products our facilities are producing. We aren't set up to produce overnight one huge order like that after development has okayed the new specifications. It's a three-month, not a three-week, job you're asking us to do."

Ellen's job is to negotiate with market research and manufacturing. This means assessing how important their technical criteria are, which ones are modifiable and, overall, what is best for the new product's introduction. A huge, first-time order from an important customer has to be weighed against possible manufacturing delays that could injure other parts of the new product's introduction. Increased validity of more extensive field testing has to be weighed against time and cost factors and the delays already incurred because of development problems. Another factor is that this soap is very similar to one for which complete test results are available. Of course, these alternatives are not merely weighed in Ellen's head, they are debated in meetings involving her and representatives of all four functional groups. Her goal is to balance off the legitimate objections of manufacturing and sales as she perceives them against her need to get the new product off to a flying start. If manufacturing is pressed too far to meet the big order, subsequent delays could hold up the general introduction of the new product. On the other hand, Ellen wants to avoid indecision or a stalemate. If sales or manufacturing proves too obstinate, Ellen can always invoke her stabilization power—but such power must be used sparingly to avoid impairing her future relations with sales and/or manufacturing. And there's always the chance that, pressed too far, sales and manufacturing would go over Ellen's head and appeal to top management.

Bipolar Management

Balance is the distinctive feature of the bipolar style of matrix management. Both systems and functional managers control workflows, but they require each other's cooperation for approvals, sign-offs, and certain highly technical activities. An example may clarify the distinctive characteristics of this type of matrix management.

One state government recently reorganized its conservation department into co-equal management teams—some responsible for various functions and others responsible for geographic segments of the state. Thus there will be statewide forestry, fisheries, wildlife, pure water and air programs. In addition, there will be decentralized programs for Region 1 (comprising several counties), Region 2, and so on—that is, systems managers. The Region 1 manager will obtain staff from each of these centralized functional groupings, but the individual staff member will retain loyalty to the profession involved and see his or her long-run career plans in terms of that function. The regional manager will also be dependent on the functional manager for approving some of his activities that have to meet both local and regional needs and fit into statewide programs. Here's what one regional manager had to say:

I have two kinds of arguments. For example, the state-level wildlife head doesn't think we should let local interests create this additional wildlife refuge; it's the wrong location, he argues. And the wildlife staff I have resent my insistence that they become broader and be willing to perform tasks related to fish, forestry and so on. But I can't afford to have people who draw tight jurisdictional lines around their jobs and I want my staff to be sensitive to what the people in this area want.

At the same time, those functional heads need the regional managers to provide help in implementing their statewide annual programs. For these the regional manager becomes a check, usually through stabilization, on where, when, and how the statewide wildlife program is to be handled. Note: Both regional and functional managers are directing ongoing workflows with their counterparts providing certain resources and "approvals."

Deceptive Variants. Many of what at first appear to be a type of "development project" matrix organization (see below) are really bipolar. Instead of simply providing technical services and personnel—and some controls—systems managers in such organizations also have their own projects, some of which require cooperation from functional management.

In one computer company, for example, new computer hardware developments are coordinated through specialized departments—the memory department, for instance. However, the memory department also has its own projects, independent of any new computer effort. These are concerned with developing new memory components, advanced memory systems that might some day be used in a computer, and improvements in existing memory units. The "memory" managers seek out managers of new machine development to become their customers.

Mass-Market Retail Chains. Although never labeled as such, many of the big retail chains such as J. C. Penney are organized as matrices. They contain two sets of managers, with relatively equal power and somewhat opposed interests, who are supposed to negotiate their differences. The systems managers are the store- or regional-level executives, responsible for operating a diversified department store that is responsive to the consumer tastes of particular communities and areas. They are dependent for their merchandise on equivalent functional managers—divisional merchandise managers. The latter identify, specify, and purchase the major categories of merchandise the stores will carry—furniture, for example, or tires or women's fashion apparel. These two sets of managers have separate performance responsibilities, report up separate lines of authority, and see the world from separate perspectives— the former from a store in a particular place or geographic area, the latter from the perspective of the overall market.

Development Projects

This is probably the type of matrix management most students of organization conceive of in dealing with this subject. The functional manager heads up a group, but most of his or her personnel are employed on one or more projects directed by systems managers or their representatives. However, work may be performed in work areas controlled by functional managers under subsystem project managers who report to the head of the project. It is just as likely that employees are temporarily transferred out of the area to work under the immediate control of the systems manager.

In addition, to permit economies of scale, the functional manager also operates certain facilities that are shared by a number of development projects. Minor conflicts can occur over which project ought to have priority, just as conflicts occur over any scarce service resource.

The more important conflicts revolve around the auditing-stabilization roles of the functional manager. Thus the systems manager (as in the Ellen Fisher case) may want to take a shortcut or seek a number of modifications in the customary working standards. Depending on how top management has arranged the matrix, the systems manager may have to obtain approval from the functional manager before proceeding—what we call a stabilization pattern—or at least be subject to the functional manager's appraisal and evaluation. This pits the total workflow concerns of the systems manager against the technical standards set by the functional manager. When both are good managers, the result is constructive compromises and a wholesome exploration of when it is desirable to be unorthodox and bend rules or make exceptions to existing standards. Further, the employees involved in the project come to see that their professional outlook is only one of many professional outlooks represented in the interdisciplinary team supervised by the functional manager.

Internal Consulting Services

This kind of matrix characterizes organizations with a number of centralized service, support, and advisory functions that have to be integrated by product managers. The latter act in the capacity of general contractors—except that there is no project, since the product or service is continuously in production.

This provides the weakest role for the functional manager. Primarily, he or she controls a personnel inventory, usually consisting of skilled professionals awaiting assignment to special projects designated by systems managers. While the institutional or functional manager may occasionally provide technical advice, his or her primary role is one of assisting in the selection, assignment, and career development of this "warehoused" workforce.

Typical problems arise when a systems manager wants an individual professional to begin or continue on an assignment that the individual (or his or her manager) feels is inconsistent with his or her professional career development plan. In the words of one systems manager:

> I wanted to keep Jane Cohen on that computer facility development project. She does outstanding work and, in fact, she was probably qualifying herself to take over the new department. But she and her boss felt that she was getting too narrow and ought to work in other parts of the company. I tried to show her the possibilities and how difficult it would be to get someone else acquainted with all she had already learned. After a couple of weeks of going back and forth on the matter, the three of us agreed that she would stay on for another couple of months. If a management slot opened up during that period, she could decide whether to apply. Otherwise, she would be available for reassignment.

The functional manager in this kind of matrix is not very different from the head of a consulting firm and may occasionally render advisory assistance within his field of technical competence. Primarily, however, such managers function as personnel managers, matching people to assignments of relatively short duration.

Conclusion

Most traditional managers are accustomed to well-defined tasks, single goals or goals that are multiple but compatible, clear and well-guarded jurisdictions, and requisite authority flowing from fixed plans. Matrix management, by contrast, is concerned with managers whose authority is limited in comparison with their responsibility. Matrix management leads to overdefined jobs in which there are more requirements than can possibly be met and conflicting goals that make tradeoffs between them continually necessary.

What Happens to Authority and Responsibility

Most organizations seek to equate authority with responsibility. Every manager, from first-line supervisor to company president, wants to control the resources needed to achieve his or her predetermined goals. To be sure, modern organizations equivocate on this traditional principle of good management. They have "dotted line" staff who can wield power equal to that of line managers; outside service groups and vendors who have to be negotiated with rather than ordered about; and a welter of clients, regulators, and community pressure groups who constrain the manager's decision-making autonomy. But the ideal both for the manager and for the student of good management is still clear lines of authority backed by resources porportionate to responsibilities. The ideal is compromised, but not forsaken.

Many companies, in fact, tie themselves in semantic knots trying to figure out which of their key groups are "line" and which "staff." Since some versions of traditional management theory permit only one real line operation, the other departments by definition must be staff. This terminology contradicts the obvious power of the so-called staff to control critical resources and to be responsible for important corporate objectives.

By contrast, matrix management assumes that plans will have to change because of the inevitably unstable equilibrium in these highly interdependent systems. Given such uncertainty, unanticipated problems of even minor dimensions will lead to major dislocations as their impact is felt throughout the system. These impacts, in turn, require adaptive plans and a constant remaking of the consensus.

In opposition to decentralization that requires new organizations whenever new tasks or goals are conceived, matrix management stresses a tight organization economy. It reuses old organizations instead of creating new ones for new goals and problems. It forces organizations to keep changing themselves because of conflicting goals, values, and priorities and builds instability into the very structure of the organization.

Like our social and political world, matrix management introduces pluralism—multiple sources of authority—into economic organization. It recognizes the necessary and desirable role of both specialization and coordination. Decisions, it assumes, cannot be made by a well-programmed computer or small, expert planning groups—not because such approaches are undemocratic or unparticipative, but rather because sensible systems decisions, whenever there is a reasonable amount of technological uncertainty, require the active and continuous involvement of technically qualified, key functional managers.

For the sake of psychological security and professional development, and in order to give a loud enough organizational voice to technical excellence, specialists often need a functional home base. In the modern organization with its inevitable stress on technical excellence, we cannot expect product or systems groups to foster such standards. At the same time, most managerial controls—including the kind encouraged by MBO systems—are easy to "beat" by actions that improve unit performance at the expense of the larger organization or system.

The trade-offs between unit success through suboptimization of goals versus larger system interests can best be made in the context of the countervailing forces of matrix managment that encourage relevant confrontations over issues whose solutions can't be preplanned or solved by decision models.

The role of coordinating managers is to act as a catalyst—to force accommodation and flexibility, to compel attention to unanticipated and boundary problems, and to achieve a consensus by means of an organized give-and-take between the constituent elements and individuals. Underlying the very existence of matrix organizations is the presumption that most critical organizational decisions *cannot* be made by all-purpose generalists. Although many trends in modern management, like OD, assume that managers can attain a broad, systemwide perspective, our studies of both public and private organizations belie this. Professionalization and a relatively rigid and specialized method of analysis are likely to prevail.

Under such circumstances, the contribution of matrix management is to introduce structural imperatives that serve to maintain fluidity in the balance of power among the major subdivisions of the organization or system and discourage the formation of rigid, exclusionary norms and suboptimal, vested-interest goals. Tension, reasonable conflict, and forced negotiation can provide a healthy environment in the long run for both executive development and decision-making.

Matrix management purposely seeks to separate resources from managers responsible for goal attainment. But the rationale is *not*, "Since struggle and frustration build character, why do things the easy way when we can just as well build in challenge?" Instead, the growth of matrix-style organizations reflects the increasing recognition that it is impossible—and uneconomical—to allocate resources to one use. Organizational goals are, at once, multiple and conflicting and changing—and they need to reuse the same technical talent and technology for a multiplicity of end results.

Last, modern organizations have come to recognize that there is no accounting or operations model that will enable decision makers to balance a wide range of technical and human values in order to attain systems effectiveness. Rather, because of the quantity of interdependencies, a continuous process of brokerage is required between, on the one hand, highly trained professionals acting as advocates of each technical and business (or political) constraint and, on the other, a generalist advocate of the overall system's needs. The matrix forces decision-making to be a constant process of interchange and trade-off, not only between the overall system and its specialized components and interest groups, but also between and among the specialists in the interest groups themselves.

As such, the matrix is a far cry from the organizations most managers have read about and idealized. Clean lines of authority; unambiguous resource allocation to each problem or goal; clear boundaries separating jobs, divisions, organizations, and loyalties are all part of that simpler life that we need to forsake in a dynamic world of overlapping and contradictory interests and goals.

A Postscript

Where, then, should a matrix structure be used, as distinct from the usual centralized or decentralized organization? Answer: It is probably already very pervasive since most larger public and private organizations do intermix centralization and decentralization; some balance of power already exists between functions-oriented and systems-oriented managers. The symmetry of the organization with one boss for each subordinate, staff neatly separated from line, one goal or set of goals, and unity of the management team is a rarity except in very small or undifferentiated organizations.

Most complex organizations benefit from the sensible struggles and compromises between and among functional standards and systems standards. They also would benefit from more formal recognition of the new structures that have evolved, often without formal planning. You can have the game without the name, but names make it easier for all concerned to accept and understand what has taken place.

Selected Bibliography

A number of different researchers have noted the impact of the degree of uncertainty on organizational structure. While their definitions differ, their basic finding is the same—increasing amounts of uncertainty ought to lead management to develop organizational forms that permit, encourage, or require more lateral relationships. Below are the major contributors.

Chapple, Elliot, and Leonard Sayles. *The Measure of Management.* New York: Macmillan, 1961.

Galbraith, Jay. *Designing Complex Organizations.* Reading, Mass.: Addison-Wesley, 1974.

Lawrence, Paul, and Jay Lorsch. *Organization and Environment.* Boston: Graduate School of Business Administration, Harvard University, 1971.

Perrow, Charles. "A Framework for the Comparative Analysis of Organizations." *American Sociological Review* 32, no. 2: 194–208 (April 1967).

Thompson, Victor. *Modern Organizations.* New York: Alfred A. Knopf, 1961.

For two good reviews of our sparse knowledge of matrix organization see Jay Galbraith, ed., *Matrix Organizations: Organization Design for High Technology* (MIT Press, 1971) and Jay Galbraith, "Matrix Organization Designs: How to Combine Functional and Project Forms." *Business Horizons* 14, no. 1: 29–40 (February 1971).

14. Can Organization Development Be Fine Tuned to Bureaucracies?

Virginia E. Schein and Larry E. Greiner

Firmly embedded in most of the organization development (OD) literature—and its professional culture—is the basic ideology that organizations need to become more organic systems capable of responding to a rapidly changing environment. Fueling this belief have been the futurists, such as Alvin Toffler in his *Future Shock*, projecting an increase in environmental turbulence and calling for organizations to abandon rigid bureaucratic structures in favor of ad hoc arrangements to cope more effectively with changing events.

OD's action-emphasis similarly holds that bureaucratic organizations need to be "unfrozen" and moved toward an organic state characterized by a matrix structure (or at least by project teams) and by open communications, interdependence among groups, and expanded levels of trust, participation, joint problem solving, risk taking, and innovation within groups. Accordingly, the OD change agent employs a variety of organic-oriented techniques centered around team building, encounter sessions, survey feedback, third-party consultation, interface labs, and confrontation meetings.

Despite OD's preoccupation with organic practices, we contend in this article that the millennium of organic organizations is not on the horizon, which in turn causes us to question the relevance of the present OD movement for the great bulk of business and public organizations. The preponderance of evidence, by contrast, shows that bureaucratic structures are still the dominant organizational form, either for an entire firm or for product groups. Such organizations are characterized by pyramidal authority, downward communications, a workforce largely employed on "rational" functions, and the omnipresence of the specialization of labor. Recent surveys of OD activities in these organizations indicate that the new ideology has made few inroads, except in limited settings such as R&D units, experimental plants, occasional training courses, or special task groups.

Why haven't organic structures been more widely adopted? One explanation is that unenlightened managers and conservative business mentalities are simply resistant and slow to change because of past conditioning. Another explanation is that basic human nature is the villain. Warren Bennis offers support to this explanation with the observations that man tends to place self-interest above public interest, cannot tolerate ambiguity and frustration, and is more concerned with power and profit than with human warmth and love. His view as to the unworkability of truth and love is counter to his earlier writing that bureaucratic structures should be replaced by organic ones built on a foundation of openness and trust. Of special note is that Bennis revised his view after experiencing the realities and frustrations of being an administrator in two academic institutions.

The optimistic OD change agent, however, might still argue that these self-oriented attitudes and values will, if enough effort is applied, change eventually. The pessimist, though, might counter that mankind will always be self-serving, so OD will never be a major force.

An entirely different explanation, providing a way out of philosophical arguments about the nature of man, comes from the weight of emerging research by the structural-contingency theorists, most important of whom are Tom Burns, G. Stalker, Joan Woodward, Paul Lawrence, Jay Lorsch, and John Morse. Their trail of evidence leads to the general conclusion that a prime determinant of organizational effectiveness is an organization's fit between its structure and the demands of its environment and technology. Most significant here is the finding that mechanistic, bureaucratic structures are not only appropriate for relatively stable environments and routine technologies but that such structures are more conducive to high performance than organic-adaptive structures in similar environments.

Unknown is just how broad is the scope of stable environments and programmable technologies that are conducive to bureaucratic structures, but Charles Perrow concludes that "moderate routineness continues to characterize almost all large organizations . . . and most of the small ones, (hence) bureaucracy . . . will remain the dominant mode of organization." James Thompson takes another point of view suggesting that, even with turbulent environments, organizations need to buffer themselves with formal structures and procedures in order to avoid the chaos of succumbing to rapidly changing events.

The consensus among those who have addressed themselves to the issue seems to be that bureaucracies are the predominant form of structure, now and for the foreseeable future—in short, they are here to stay. Managers in these organizations may intuitively recognize the inappropriateness of the organic-adaptive structure to the demands of their routine technology. Hence managerial resistance to organic approaches in bureaucracies may not necessarily be based on their clinging to old values or needs for personal power but rather on their soundly based concern for organizational effectiveness.

The Challenge to OD

If we assume that bureaucratic structures will continue to be the dominant organizational form, what are some possible courses of action for organization development? First, it can continue to prescribe universalistic organic change approaches for all organizations. Advocating structural change, however, without considering the technological and environmental demands of the particular organization may only increase resistance to organization development within bureaucracies. More importantly, the use of current OD techniques in inappropriate situations can easily damage the credibility of OD as a whole.

A second route for organization development is to limit its change techniques to organizations whose complex technical and environmental demands are more congruent with organic structures. But given the high ratio of routine work to complex jobs, and the apparent continuation of such an imbalance, the growth and impact of OD would be severely restricted by this approach.

If organization development is to continue as a vital force for organizational improvement, it seems imperative that a third route be considered—that of expanding and differentiating applied OD to deal with the behavioral problems of *both* bureaucratic and organic structures. Without such an expanded focus, the field runs a serious risk of becoming a narrow and limited force for change and of being applied within a relatively few organizations.

This challenge to organization development to expand its focus and repertoire of approaches comes out of our belief that by returning to an original cornerstone of the OD movement—its focus on dealing with emergent behavioral problems in organizations—it can make a significant contribution to the functioning of traditional organizations. That the need for this expertise exists within bureaucracies is evidenced by examining the work of other behavioral science groups currently operating in bureaucratic settings.

Behavioral Sciences and Bureaucracies

Three major schools—industrial psychology, structural-contingency theory, and sociotechnical approaches—have all been well received by bureaucracies and acknowledged as having valuable contributions to make. This acceptance indicates that bureaucracies, as such, are not opposed to behavioral science. Nevertheless, a noticeable gap appears in their contributions as all three schools concentrate on *systems design* at the expense of addressing emergent behavioral problems in on-going worklife.

Long entrenched in bureaucracies, industrial psychologists have made major contributions in areas such as selection, manpower planning, and performance appraisal. Their basic assumption is that if the abilities of employees are assessed with sufficient care, future behavioral problems can be avoided.

The structural-contingency theorists, while stressing the necessity of maintaining bureaucratic structures, have not directly addressed behavioral process issues within bureaucratic structures. Like the industrial psychologists, they concentrate on formal design, seeking to find the appropriate structural apparatus to fit a given technology and environment. Organizational input is their concern. With regard to behavioral problems, their assumption, with some supporting research evidence, appears to be that individuals will be attracted to the organizational structure—organic or mechanistic—that meets their needs and will leave the organization that does not appear to fulfill them, thereby reducing the possibility of dysfunctional behavior occurring.

Job design has been one focus of the sociotechnical advocates—altering the technical input to tap the inherent motivational needs of workers. Applied efforts here have concentrated primarily on the experimental design of work arrangements at lower levels in manufacturing plants and within clerical processing functions. Again, the underlying premise is largely formalistic and impersonal, assuming that more challenging work settings and job requirements will automatically reduce or elminate problems on the job.

All three schools have addressed bureaucratic problems as formal planning issues, presuming that a correct blueprint of inputs (people, organization, and technology) will obviate behavioral problems at work. None recognizes that even with appropriate designs, significant behavioral problems can still arise, some of which may even be caused by the very solutions they recommend. For example, across the board enrichment of jobs for everyone in a work setting may produce dissatisfaction among those employees who prefer routine, nonchallenging jobs. Or the use of the same selection procedures or predictors of job success for all applicants may result in a homogeneous group of employees. At a later point in time, this same homogeneity may reduce the opportunities for divergent thinking and creativity commonly found among heterogeneous groups. It is this gap in design thinking that provides a significant opportunity for OD to apply its process skills in bureaucratic settings.

Contingency Theory for OD

For OD to enhance its effectiveness within bureaucratic structures, what is needed is a conceptual point of view. The absence of conceptual thinking has long plagued OD. Robert Kahn, after reviewing many definitions of the field, concludes that "organizational development is not a concept, but a convenient term for a variety of activities." Without a conceptual framework to direct the application of these activities, methodological and universalistic solutions have tended to predominate.

Our starting point for the development of a framework grows out of the work of the structural-contingency theorists. Just as the choice of a mechanistic versus organic organizational design is contingent upon environment and technology, so too is the appropriateness of an OD change strategy dependent on the uniqueness of each organizational context. Our proposed contingency theory for OD begins with the basic assumption that different structures develop inherent behavioral problems due to the ways in which their particular configuration conditions the behavior of people within them. The dysfunctional behavioral aspects of classical structures have long been noted by sociologists.

We extend this deterministic view further by drawing upon a medical analogy to hypothesize that behavioral diseases are a natural outgrowth of any given structure, regardless of how well designed it may be by systems planners (industrial psychologists, structural-contingency theorists, or sociotechnical consultants). Moreover, we believe these diseases can never be eradicated but only controlled by preventative OD care. Without such interventions, however, a disease may grow and seriously undermine organization effectivness.

Our contingency approach to OD further contends that behavioral diseases emanating from bureaucratic structures are uniquely different from those of organic structures; hence the treatments must be tailored to fit the disease. This contingency view explains why current OD practices both seem to be and are in fact more effective in organic situations. Inherent behavioral problems of matrix structures are typically those of interpersonal conflict, team formation, living with uncertainty, and coping with ambiguous authority relationships. OD techniques focusing on topics like team building, trust, interpersonal communication, assertiveness, innovation, and confrontation are highly relevant in a flowing matrix for enhancing intragroup and intergroup effectiveness.

On the other hand, bureaucratic organizations, with a hierarchical structure and a functionally based design, breed problems of a different kind and, therefore, require solution-oriented approaches of a quite different nature. Problems such as frustration due to limited promotional opportunities and vertically oriented career routes, alienation and boredom of lower-level employees, and inability to develop general managers are major issues that emanate directly from the nature of the structure. Attention to these emergent problems *within* the confines of the bureaucratic structure requires approaches quite different from those appropriate to organic structural problems.

The challenge to OD, in other words, is to develop new approaches designed to treat the diseases endemic to mechanistic structures. As a first step we propose a "fine tuning" approach as an effective means for OD to impact bureaucratic structures.

Fine Tuning Bureaucratic Structures

Fine tuning refers to a variety of OD interventions designed to sharpen the operations of an organization and free the system of dysfunctional behaviors. It draws on the best of OD—its strong humanistic concern and its knowledge of process—and applies these skills within the constraints of a bureaucratic structure. Two criteria are used simultaneously in the selection of an OD solution strategy: one, what actions will enhance the quality of working life of the employees and, two, what approach will not conflict with any existing structural requirements? It seeks to maximize people-oriented changes within the situations bounded by the environmental and technological realities of the organizations. By way of illustration, what follows is a discussion of four critical behavioral diseases we have observed as inherent to bureaucracies and some fine-tuning OD techniques for maximizing the utilization of human resources within these same bureaucratic structures.

Functional Myopia and Suboptimization

Functional managers and technicians tend to develop an allegiance to their particular function. Typically they have been "raised" over many years within that function and have acclimated themselves to its norms, sanctions, and language system. This approach is quite effective in developing and concentrating technical expertise on specific and relatively fixed tasks.

A dysfunctional consequence of this specialization, however, can be a myopic point of view toward the entire organization. Each function looks out for itself without appreciating or understanding the value of other functional entities. Behavioral problems such as interdepartmental conflict, lack of planning coordination, and inability to communicate due to knowledge gaps and different vocabularies are typical outcomes of functional myopia.

A variety of standard OD approaches can be used to reduce the negative impact of this form of suboptimizing behavior. Team building is especially relevant for the top-management group, which serves as a behavioral model for the rest of the organization. Only at this level do the functions, of necessity, come together; unnecessary conflict here will diffuse to lower levels, often with heightened intensity.

The chief executive of one large U.S. manufacturing firm recognized that conflict within his top group was creating divisiveness between functions; moreover, even his own behavior was contributing to it by his dealing constantly on a one-to-one basis with each functional head. As a result, he announced a new and simple policy of requiring the top group to meet twice weekly, to focus on operating problems on Thursday morning and on personnel decisions on Friday morning. His principal ground rule for the meetings was that the group should try to reach a consensus on most issues under discussion. One year later, consultant interviews with the CEO indicated that more "company oriented" decisions were being made; this impression was confirmed in interviews with various functional managers.

Another approach is to assist the top two or three layers of management from all functions to meet off-site for an annual participative planning and budgeting session. For example, TRW, Inc. takes its top corporate executives off-site at least once a year to debate and revise corporate plans in an atmosphere where open criticism is welcome. Consensus and commitment from these senior managers to overall plans and cost controls can minimize functional conflicts later on.

Alternatively, limited structural interventions designed to facilitate goal integration can also be helpful. For instance, a senior coordination group reporting to top management, full-time liaison roles assigned within each function, task forces to create action programs cutting across the organization, and a corporate profit sharing scheme for executives can do much to turn political infighting into cooperative problem solving.

Last, job rotation of high-potential managers can stimulate transfer of perspective and insights from one functional segment [to another. In one] petrochemical company, the senior management rotates high potential executives constantly through its major corporate staff groups. The organization planning group, for example, is made up primarily of line managers rotated from various functions, who spend one year in the group before moving on to other functions. The director of this group contends that the managers rotated not only contribute more realistic solutions than professional experts in planning, but also that they develop new perspectives to apply in their next assignments—including becoming more receptive clients for the organization planning group.

Vertical Lock-In and Incompetency

Promotion patterns in bureaucracies tend to reveal a close correlation between rank and seniority, with promotion ladders typically restricted to vertical movement within a single function. These practices lend certainty to career paths, promote loyalty, and facilitate the acquisition of tradition and specialized knowledge. Functional organizations would be chaotic and inefficient without these established career practices.

Nonetheless, such vertical "lock-in" has negative consequences for individual growth and organization decision-making. Limited promotional opportunities within functions can cause managerial frustration and boredom. Promotional decisions, when they occur, tend to be based more on tenure and being next in line, rather than on individual competence. Finally, technical knowledge can easily become more valued than managerial ability, causing a shortage of talented general managers who are sensitive to both people and broader company problems.

Numerous change approaches are available to OD practitioners that help in opening up career opportunities and making competency-based personnel decisions within bureaucracies. Assessment centers have proved effective in organizations such as AT&T and IBM in identifying managerial talent and providing more job-related information for promotion decisions. Job posting, as used at Polaroid, can publicize new openings to numerous employees who may wish to apply. Properly designed manpower information systems may assist in quickly revealing a range of candidates whose skills fit certain job requirements. Career counseling provides an outlet for managerial frustration, as well as making known aspirations ignored by insensitive superiors. Training programs designed in-house can impart general management skills and stimulate interpersonal sharing of cross-functional knowledge. These and similar programmatic change strategies are all possible within a bureaucracy without altering its basic functional makeup.

Many of these techniques have been brought together in a fascinating career program developed by a major U.S. corporation concerned with its lack of top-management talent. Senior management first developed a list of skills required to be an effective top manager in their company, surprising themselves in the process by producing such a long list. Then they analyzed the array of managerial jobs in the company to determine which jobs tended to develop which skills. Next, they assigned color-coded "job tickets" to jobs with similar skills, such as red tickets for all jobs that emphasize "basic accounting" skills, and blue tickets for all jobs that stress "staff consulting" skills, and so on through eight colors with different job-skill combinations. Last, a career program in which all managers aspiring to senior levels were expected to pick up the full range of tickets during their early career years was announced and explained. Each manager, however, was left relatively free to decide in consultation with his or her superiors, on the sequence in which he or she would acquire various job tickets. A manpower information system was also developed for top management to identify individual progress in acquiring job tickets, and special training programs were designed to provide "substitute" job tickets.

Top-Down Information Flow and Problem Insensitivity

The hierarchical and mechanistic nature of bureaucracies lends itself to top-down authority structures and routinization of task efforts. Plans and objectives are typically defined at the top, subdivided by function and directed downward. Moreover, routine technologies can be programmed in advance by specialists and results predicted based on historical performance. This clearly defined and stable structure serves to effectively allocate work, control costs, specify responsibilities, and convey acquired skills to lower-level employees. Too much autonomy or creativity in a bureaucracy would obviously interfere with the smooth functioning of the system.

However, an almost inevitable cost of this directive and deductive mode of operating is a lack of innovation and sensitivity to emergent problems and to suggestions from below. Top-management decision-making based on past experience, while also being insulated from lower levels, can paralyze or blind management from dealing effectively with nonroutine issues. Minor problems can grow into major crises before coming to top management's attention.

Organization development approaches need to provide new avenues for upward feedback of information and creative thought without significantly altering the everyday downward flow of operating decisions. A "shadow" structure can be introduced in which cross-functional teams meet periodically to assess organization practices and to recommend modifications directly to top management. Varying names have been given to this structural innovation: "reflective" by Larry Greiner, "collateral" by Dale Zand, and "parallel" by Howard Carlson at General Motors. Such a structure enhances the flexibility and problem-solving ability of the organization while maintaining and complementing the hierarchical organization.

The shadow-structure approach is being followed in a Swedish government agency that came under public attack for its ponderous bureaucracy. Six permanent teams that report directly to the director of the agency have been set up. Each group is assigned a critical agency activity to investigate and come up with recommendations in a written report. One group, for example, is examining the computer operations of the agency, while another is analyzing the agency's relationships with other government bureaus. Membership in each group represents a diagonal slice of the organization, ranging from clerical workers to senior managers. They are freed from their regular jobs for at least two days per month; membership is rotated every six months. Numerous changes have already been introduced as a direct result of the groups' reports, such as one in which the information system was revised to include fewer key indexes as well as a qualitative report from each supervisor on performance progress in his or her unit.

Another similar technique is the junior board composed of middle managers who meet every few months with senior executives. Off-site conferences, where rank is temporarily set aside, can also be held to identify major problems and discuss impending changes. Elements of both techniques have been combined in one intriguing exercise that a major plant of an aluminum company goes through once a year. First, the top-management group of eight meets for three days to lay out its key goals for the year and to develop a priority list of the major plant problems that need to be solved. Second, the key middle-management group is asked to perform the same exercise. At the end, the two groups meet for a week to hear their joint conclusions and to work out a common agenda based on small group meetings that intermingle senior with middle-level managers.

A corporate ombudsman can be established to hear employees' complaints and offer suggestions around blocked channels. Periodic personnel surveys can monitor trends and detect hidden problems. Based on employee attitude survey data indicating dissatisfaction with upward communication, one Canadian financial institution established a corporate ombudsman, who reports directly to the president. Among other activities, this person attempts to resolve employee difficulties by negotiating with their supervisors and managers and has the authority to take any unresolved issues directly to the president. A two-year follow-up of employee attitudes reported a marked increase in satisfaction with upward communication.

Managment by objectives (MBO) can be introduced to provide subordinates with a structured opportunity for melding their ideas with overall production goals. The same Canadian financial institution also successfully introduced MBO as far down as the junior-clerical level. Finally, younger high-potential managers can be assigned as temporary assistants to older top managers as a means, not only to enhance career development, but also to make middle-management views available to senior-management deliberations.

Routine Jobs and Dissatisfaction

Bureaucracies are born out of the need for economies of scale in production and distribution. There is a large fixed investment in plant and technology. Division of labor becomes the basic rationale for organization structure; efficiency is derived from labor specialization assigned to relatively finite and predetermined tasks sequenced along a production flow. Large numbers of unskilled and inexpensive workers are hired to perform simple and repetitive jobs, and labor is treated as a variable cost. When business turns sour, employees can be laid off; in prosperous times, new workers can be easily hired and trained. First-line supervision—assigning work, monitoring output, and ensuring discipline—becomes a critical management post.

Serious behavioral costs are paid for these necessary, but impersonal, economic and organizational logics. Boredom, absenteeism, and even physical deterioration are possible negative impacts of routine jobs. Supervisors feel caught in the middle between production pressures from above and resistance from workers below, and their response is often to overcontrol through tight rules and punishment-centered behavior. Workers thereupon respond with output restriction, grievances, and even sabotage.

A key role for organization development lies in relieving the negative impact of routine jobs. One well-known technique is job enrichment, in which work is redesigned to provide more complexity and autonomy without endangering efficiency. In fact, efficiency may be increased. The Volvo experiment in its Kalmar plant is a notable case in point. Through a complete redesign of the traditional assembly plant, jobs have been arranged so that they are to be performed by relatively autonomous working groups. Considerable freedom exists within groups to schedule production and assign jobs. While production levels have not increased significantly, the high absenteeism and turnover have been lowered dramatically in a plant whose initial costs were only 10 percent higher than in a plant designed along traditional lines. Less often acknowledged is the fact that there are many more jobs in bureaucracies where enrichment cannot occur due to fixed capital investment, the prescribed nature of technology, or limits in worker ability. What can be done under these restrictions? Variety can still be added through job rotation, where workers learn two or three jobs and alternate between them. Or job interest can be heightened by increasing the visibility of output, as one paper manufacturer found when it simply posted the output of work teams on comparable jobs across shifts, thereby increasing the competitive spirit. Another solution is to revise hiring practices to accommodate more people, such as part-time employees, who do not necessarily expect much from their work beyond a paycheck. Reduced boredom can also be achieved through increasing the employee's opportunity for personal growth off the job, made possible by work schedule variations—flexible working hours, four-day workweeks, flexible lunch periods, expanded vacation periods, and leaves of absence. All of these afford an employee some degree of freedom and opportunity for self-expression not achievable within the job itself.

OD can also be helpful in addressing the problem of alienation between supervisors and workers by considering alternative approaches to supervisory training. In one large insurance company, for example, a flexible-hours program became a vehicle that forced supervisors to place greater trust in employees. Varying work hours made it impossible for supervisors to monitor the work of all employees at all times, thereby causing supervisors to relax their vigilance and eventually recognize that most employees still performed effectively in their absence. Similarly, supervisory training in behavior modeling has proven quite effective. For example, in AT&T's Supervisory Relationship Training Program, supervisors learn how to cope with day-to-day employee problems, such as absenteeism, low productivity, and perceptions of discrimination by imitating or modeling the way an effective supervisor deals with these problems. In an experimental evaluation of the program, conducted by Joel Moses and R. Ritchie, there were significant differences between trained and untrained supervisors in their ability to cope with employee problems. Both trained and untrained supervisors were matched on relevant factors, such as experience and type of job, and both groups possessed equal theoretical or content knowledge in how to deal with such problems. Nonetheless, supervisors trained by the behavior modeling approach did far better in actually dealing with employee problems than those equipped with only theoretical knowledge.

Extrinsic rewards have also gained increased attention in stimulating employee-company goal congruence, such as team bonus schemes, the Scanlon Plan, salary in place of hourly wages, and employee stock ownership plans. OD skills will also be valuable in experiments to include union representatives in management decision-making, either through worker councils or board membership.

Reorienting OD

Some recent appraisals of OD have commented on its rigidity and narrowness of focus. Frank Friedlander and L. Dave Brown, in a major review of the field, call upon OD "to explore various technologies, different sorts of change agent-client relationships and alternative values currently emerging and to develop a framework to encompass this diversity."

Our contingency view of OD seeks to clarify what the current practice of OD is—and is not. It provides a directional framework, suggesting the differential utility of certain OD techniques, depending upon the structure of the organization. Much current OD is, in our opinion, far more suitable to organic matrix-type structures. Whether OD can be made relevant for bureaucratic structures is a critical issue the field faces today. We have attempted to show that a significant opportunity exists for OD to play a vital role in bureaucracies, and we have outlined an action focus for it to consider. But there is a big difference between accepting the challenge and actually implementing it. What steps might OD take to prepare itself?

1. *Adopt a more positive and accepting attitude toward bureaucratic organizations.* A "good guys-bad guys" revolutionary zeal still pervades much of OD—organic is good and bureaucracy is bad. Polarizing the issue, that is, humanism versus bureaucracy, may be energizing to the change agent's psyche, but whose objectives are being served? How much of the present OD emphasis on a few normative behaviors and on a limited range of techniques is merely a way of perpetuating and reaffirming the professional's personal value system? And to what extent does this polarization heighten organizational resistance and serve to strengthen the status quo? There is obviously room for humanism in mechanistic structures, but it cannot be achieved simply through encounter groups or an "organic revolution."

2. *Acquire a more thorough knowledge of bureaucratic operations.* Being open toward bureaucracies is not enough; to work effectively within them requires cognitive grounding in why they exist and how they operate. Knowing and being able to converse in terms of marketing, production, and finance is likely to be just as important as being proficient in process-consultation skills. Implementing effective OD programs in bureaucracies will require substantial managerial and worker inputs showing how technical and economic considerations have to be interwoven with proposed behavioral modifications. For instance, job enrichment may be appropriate when the technology is flexible, but job rotation may be necessary when the machinery is too costly to be altered.

3. *Adopt a more conceptual and realistic orientation for understanding bureaucratic behavior.* Conceptual advances derived from research and experience are critical for charting new directions in organization development. Much of the past intellectual effort in OD has been limited to research evaluation of OD outcomes and the design of new educational methods. Little has been

done at the conceptual level to identify new opportunities for OD or to put its existing methodology in perspective. Our central thrust, and it is only a beginning, is to offer a new conceptual roadmap for extending the impact of OD to bureaucratic organizations. A contingency link between structure and process has been made to show how pyramidal organizations breed certain behavioral diseases that inhibit both organizational and individual effectiveness. Answers to these problems are found, we believe, in making the existing structure work better, not in replacing it.

OD can build a significant research component by exploring further the behavioral processes and problems inherent in different structural arrangements. Is our concept of organization disease a useful one or merely an empty metaphor? What additional organizational diseases exist? How and why do they arise? What are their symptoms, functions, and dysfunctions?

For instance, political strife within bureaucracies may on the surface appear dysfunctional. On the other hand, winning a political battle, such as taking over another work group, may serve as a positive reinforcement to the victor and, within a stagnant promotional system, may be the only form of reward available. Or even if the fight is a standoff, it may serve to generate enthusiasm and excitement not forthcoming from the routine nature of everyday tasks. Attempts to eradicate these political behaviors without replacing them with alternative reward schemes and job excitement could be more dysfunctional than the political combat itself. And in structures that cannot be so changed, management of these behaviors may be a far more effective and realistic fine-tuning approach than elimination of the behaviors.

One European company has attempted a unique experiment that capitalizes on its political reality. Outside consultants analyzed the company's political structure, and produced a map of the firm's political system, including various power centers, their leaders, and a synopsis of the issues dividing and connecting the various centers. Then a new ad hoc structure was created wherein the various power leaders met as representatives in a council to debate publicly issues that had long been considered out of order, such as management's assumption that they could introduce major changes without consulting the union beforehand. The announced objective of the forum was to provide a setting in which all concerns would be aired. No promise was made that consensus solutions would be reached, but the hope, so far realized, was that a better and clearer understanding might emerge of the issues and of the realities of divisions within the firm.

Overall, then, what is needed is further research on the "hows" and "whys" of a variety of seemingly dysfunctional behaviors to develop innovative and realistic fine-tuning approaches. Political processes and their functional and dysfunctional aspects have long been ignored, as have the intricacies of boards of directors, compensation plans, and competitive practices in the marketplace, among others. By both understanding the realities of organizational life and placing these behaviors in a conceptual framework, OD can be far more effective within bureaucratic organizations.

4. *Develop a more versatile range of OD techniques that apply to bureaucracies.* Educationally based methodologies have been a strength of OD in organic situations, but our view holds that these same methods have limited utility for resolving behavioral problems in mechanistic organizations. Ad hoc interventions in bureaucracies are likely to produce only fleeting positive effects unless reinforced with more permanent structural and programmatic innovations that counteract continuing behavioral problems inherent to mechanistic structures. These structural devices, or fine-tuning mechanisms, include such previously mentioned techniques as coordination groups, job design, flex time, assessment centers, and so on. The OD consultant needs to be familiar with all these methods, as well as prepared to use them in combination to overcome the more powerful dysfunctions of bureaucracies. All of which implies that the effective OD practitioner in bureacracies will be, above all else, a diagnostician and generalist, concentrating on a broad range of behavioral processes, problems, and techniques, not a specialist wedded to one favorite technique.

The fate of OD? Fine-tuning approaches to organization development are neither glamorous, sexy, nor revolutionary. However, if bureaucracies, by reason of economics, technology, and even human behavior, continue to be the dominant organizational structure, then serious attention should be given to making OD more relevant to these organizations. The future growth and impact of OD may hinge on the acceptance or rejection of this challenge.

Selected Bibliography

The structural-contingency theorists' research and point of view can be found in T. Burns and G. M. Stalker's *The Management of Innovation* (Tavistock, 1961); Paul Lawrence and Jay Lorsch's *Organization and Environment* (Harvard University Press, 1967); and Joan Woodward's *Industrial Organization: Theory and Practice* (Oxford University Press, 1965).

Important research on and arguments for bureaucracies as the dominant organizational form are represented in Warren Bennis's "A Funny Thing Happened on the Way to the Future" (*American Psychologist,* July 1970, pp. 595–608); Charles Perrow's *Complex Organizations: A Critical Essay* (Scott, Foresman, 1972); James Thompson's *Organizations in Action* (McGraw-Hill, 1967); and Richard Walton's "The Diffusion of New Work Structures: Explaining Why Success Doesn't Work" (*Organizational Dynamics,* Winter 1975, pp. 3–22).

Research on and illustrations of fine-tuning approaches can be found in William Byham's "Assessment Centers for Spotting Future Managers" (*Harvard Business Review,* August 1970, pp. 150–67); Larry Greiner's "Evolution and Revolution as Organizations Grow" (*Harvard Business Review,* July-August 1972, pp. 137–46); Joel Moses and R. Ritchie's "A Behavioral Evaluation of a Behavior Modification Program" (*Personnel Psychology,* Autumn 1976, pp. 337–43); and Dale Zand's "Collateral Organization: A New Change Strategy" (*Journal of Applied Behavioral Sciences,* vol. 10, no. 1, 1974, pp. 63–89).

Cases illustrative of bureaucratic diseases include Higgins Equipment Company (FA–A 460B3); Twin City Trust (9-402-029); Lewis Equipment Company (6-408-005); and Superior Slate Quarry (6-471-071), all Case Clearing House, Harvard Business School, Boston, Mass.

Comprehensive reviews of organization development can be found in Frank Friedlander and L. D. Brown's "Organization Development" (*Annual Review of Psychology,* vol. 25, 1974) and Robert Kahn's "Organization Development: Some Problems and Proposals" (*Journal of Applied Behavioral Sciences,* vol. 10, no. 4, 1974, pp. 485–502).

Additional Readings

In many ways, "modern organization theory is a composite of theory on structure and function of organizations and theory on human behavior in them."[1] The literature related to the nature of organizations and the various elements of the organizing function is enormous. Here, too, the library literature provides numerous directions for the reader to explore, some of which are supplementary to the reading selections for this chapter, and some of which provide differing viewpoints. In large part, this library literature reflects a concern for the academic library environment, although other types of libraries are represented.

General Discussions

A number of readings discuss the general nature of organizations and organization theory. In the second chapter of *The Social Psychology of Organizations* (Wiley, 1978), Katz and Kahn address the question of organizational definition by using a theoretical model of the organization as an input-output system reactivated by energic return from output. By viewing organizations as "flagrantly open systems in that the input of energies and the conversion of output into further energic input consist of transactions between the organization and its environment,"[2] these authors further reinforce the relationship between organization and environment illustrated by the reading selections in this book. Scott ("The Systems Concept," in *Organization Theory: A Structural and Behavioral Analysis*, 1972) and Kast and Rosenzweig ("General Systems Theory: Applications for Organization and Management," *Academy of Management Journal*, December 1972) outline the systems concept as a means of analyzing complex organizations. Noting that systems concepts and contingency views do not provide a panacea for organizational problem-solving, Kast and Rosenzweig suggest nonetheless that these fundamental ideas "facilitate more thorough understanding of complex situations and increase the likelihood of appropriate action."[3] The stages of development of the organization as an entity, and the cultural characteristics that define individual organizations are outlined by Lippitt and Schmidt ("Crises in a Developing Organization," *Harvard Business Review*, November-December 1967), and Pettigrew ("On Studying Organizational Cultures," *Administrative Science Quarterly*, December 1979). While Deal and Kennedy's *Corporate Cultures* (Addison-Wesley, 1982) focuses on organizations in the business sector, their analysis of the relationship between organizational culture and organizational success is one library managers would do well to examine.

Central to the analysis and understanding of the library as an organization is the concept of organizational typology. Here the questions "how can organizations be differentiated?" and "what are the similarities that identify a particular *type* of organization?" must be answered. Carper and Snizek ("The Nature and Types of Organizational Taxonomies," *Academy of Management Review*, January 1980) and Mills and Margulies ("Toward a Core Typology of Service Organizations," *Academy of Management Review*, April 1980) provide the reader with a general view of some of these central questions and a broad perspective from which to examine the library as a type of organization. More specific to the library environment, Rayward examines libraries as formal organizations, providing a descriptive model of the library and speculating on appropriate bases for determining the successful attainment of organizational goals ("Libraries as Organizations," *College and Research Libraries*, July 1969). Swanson relates organizational theory to the management of libraries, concentrating on organization structure and function and the human behavior element in organizations. This author also raises important questions about the future role of libraries and their ability to become "multi-purpose, multiproduct entities"[4] ("Organizational Theory Related to Library Management," *Canadian Library Journal*, July 1973).

Organizational Design

As noted by Swanson in the introduction to this essay, organizational structure (and the design of that structure) is a critical element in organization theory and the management process. Organizational design refers to "the process of explicitly identifying and specifying the desired 'levels' of structural and technological variables"[5] (to maximize achievement of the organization's goals). Selection 12 has provided an overview of this design process. The essays in *Organizational Design: Theoretical Perspectives and Empirical Findings* (edited by Burack and Negandi, Kent State University Press, 1977) also examine the current state of the art of organizational design—the structuring of work activities, systems, and processes. Ranson, Hinings, and Greenwood offer another view of the organizational structuring process using several conceptual categories as a framework for discussion ("The Structuring of Organizational Structures," *Administrative Science Quarterly*, March 1980).

Decision-making is a critical element in selecting the optimum structure to fit the demands of the environment. This decision-making process, as well as specific steps that can be utilized to make a structure workable, are outlined in Duncan's "What Is the Right Organization Structure? Decision Tree Analysis Provides the Answer" (*Organizational Dynamics*, Winter 1979). Other perspectives on design are offered by Lorsch ("Organization Design: A Situational Perspective," *Organizational Dynamics*, Autumn 1977) and Pfeffer and Salancik ("Organization Design: The Case for a Coalitional Model of Organizations," *Organizational Dynamics*, Autumn 1977). Dalton et al. examine the very important relationship between structure and performance in "Organization Structure and Performance: A Critical Review" (*Academy of Management Review*, January 1980). Two examples of actual organizational review and redesign are offered by Huber, Ullman, and Leifer in the federal government setting ("Optimum Organization Design: An Analytic-Adoptive Approach," *Academy of Management Review*, October 1979) and by Dillon in the library environment ("Organizing the Academic Library for Instruction," *Journal of Academic Librarianship*, September 1975).

Structural Alternatives

Moving beyond a consideration of design as process, there are numerous structural choices available to the designer. This variety of structural alternatives is outlined by Drucker ("New Templates for Today's Organizations," *Harvard Business Review*, January-February 1974), Klein (*New Forms of Work Organization*, Cambridge University Press, 1980), Rice ("A Set of Organizational Models," *Human Resource Management*, Summer 1980) and Bryman ("Structures in Organization: A Reconsideration," *Journal of Occupational Psychology*, 1976). In the library environment, Haas suggests structural directions for the future in "Organizational Structures to Meet Future Bibliographic Requirements" (*Library Quarterly*, July 1977). In "Organizational Structure and the Academic Library" (*Illinois Libraries*, March 1974) Lynch reviews both prescriptive and descriptive approaches to the study of organizational design. In addition, she suggests questions to be answered and relationships to be identified by research in library organizational design. Howard's research provides a view of the effects of different structural variables on innovation ("Organizational Structure and Innovation in Academic Libraries," *College and Research Libraries*, September 1981). Kaser ("Modernizing the University Library Structure," *College and Research Libraries*, July 1970) and Moran ("Improving the Organizational Design of Academic Libraries," *Journal of Academic Librarianship*, July 1980) serve as examples of authors who look at possible structural changes in the library. Howard also offers an alternative view of structure in "The Orbital Organization" (*Library Journal*, 1 May 1970), and "Beyond Participative Management: The Orbital Organization as I See It" (*Focus on Indiana Libaries*, Summer 1973).

Organizing Professionals

In selection 3, Drake identifies the library as a "professional" organization and outlines critical management problems that arise as a result of this organizational setting. Schriesheim, Von Glinow, and Kerr suggest that "many difficulties arise from potential incompatibilities between professionals' characteristics and the bureaucratic structures and assignment of authority based on hierarchical position of most organizations."[6] These authors review potential problems inherent in many professional organizations and suggest the triple hierarchy as a means of alleviating professional-managerial conflicts ("Professionals in Bureaucracies: A Structural Alternative," *North-Holland/TIMS Studies in the Management Sciences*, 1977). Lebell also reviews the conflicts that arise in the management of professionals ("Managing Professionals: The Quiet Conflict," *Personnel Journal*, July 1980). In the library environment, Lynch presents a view of the library as a bureaucratic organization ("Libraries as Bureaucracies," *Library Trends*, Winter 1978). Finally, Toren identifies some possible positive relationships between hierarchical and professional authority useful to managers attempting to resolve this issue ("Bureaucracy and Professionalism: A Reconsideration of Weber's Thesis," *Academy of Management Review*, July 1976).

Trade-offs

All organizational design reflects a series of complex trade-offs between a number of variables. In suggesting that "Structure Is Not Organization" (*Business Horizons*, June 1980), Waterman, Peters, and Phillips note that "effective organizational change is really the relationship between structure, strategy, systems, style, skills, staff, and . . . superordinate goals."[7] Axford suggests some of these relationships in the library environment ("The Interrelationship of Structure, Governance, and Effective Resource Utilization in Libraries," *Library Trends*, April 1975). Library networks and other forms of cooperative arrangements present particular organizational problems in terms of these trade-offs. Dougherty ("Impact of Networking on Library Management," *College and Research Libraries*, January 1978), Minder ("Organizational Problems in Library Cooperation," *Library Journal*, 15 October 1970) and Parker ("Resource Sharing from the Inside Out: Reflections on the Organizational Nature of Library Cooperatives," *Library Resources and Technical Services*, Fall 1975) provide useful views of these relationships for the reader.

The impact of technology (i.e., physical devices used for library operations and service) on libraries must also be considered in examining the complex trade-offs to be made in structuring the organization. The technology *of* the organization (i.e., the "actions that an individual performs upon an object"[8]) also provides a basis for comparing and analyzing organizations, as outlined by Perrow ("A Framework for the Comparative Analysis of Organizations," *American Sociological Review*, April 1967). Reeves (*Librarians as Professionals: The Occupation's Impact on Library Work Arrangements*, Lexington, 1980), Shaughnessy ("Technology and Job Design in Libraries: A Sociotechnical Systems Approach," *Journal of Academic Librarianship*, November 1977) and Reimann and Inzerilli ("A Comparative Analysis of Empirical Research on Technology and Structure," *Journal of Management*, Fall 1979) provide views of these issues.

The Matrix Approach

In selection 13, the matrix organization was suggested as a structure of the future that may accommodate many of the variables identified above. Davis's *Matrix* (Addison-Wesley, 1977) examines modern matrix management from every angle, while Hill and White's *Matrix Organization and Project Management* (Division of Research, Graduate School of Business Administration, University of Michigan, 1979) offers selected readings on all aspects of matrix management. Middleton offers advice on "How to Set Up a Project Organization" (*Harvard Business Review*, March-April 1967), and Tytler provides reasons for adopting a matrix in "Making Matrix Management Work—And When and Why It's Worth the Effort" (*Training*, October 1978). Sager outlines a matrix approach for the public library that demonstrates the application of this structural alternative in a library environment ("Comfortable Pullman, Administrative Creativity on the Siding," *American Libraries*, June 1970).

Assessment and Analysis

Developing and maintaining the organization as a viable and responsive entity is a critical part of the organizing process. Important endeavors to be considered here include organizational assessment and analysis, the possible introduction of organizational change, and the specific role of organization development. Wildavsky's "The Self-Evaluating Organization" (*Public Administration Review*, September-October 1972) serves as an introduction to the assessment of organizations. Lawler, Nadler, and Camman's *Organizational Assessment* (Wiley, 1980) offers valuable insights into organizational effectiveness, methods of organizational analysis, and examinations of the quality of working life. Ghorpade's *Assessment of Organizational Effectiveness* (Goodyear, 1971) offers a collection of readings that identify theoretical considerations, methodology, and studies of effectiveness. Organizational effectiveness is also examined by Connolly, Conlon, and Deutsch, who suggest that an "organization's different constituencies will form different assessments of its effectiveness."[9]

In the library setting, assessment and analysis of the library *as an organization* are discussed in sources such as Samuels's "Assessing Organizational Climate in Public Libraries" (*Library Research*, 1979), Webster's "The Management Review and Analysis Program: An Assisted Self-Study to Secure Constructive Change in the Management of Research Libraries" (*College and Research Libraries*, March 1974),[10] and Morein's "Assisted Self-Study: A Tool for Improving Library Effectiveness" (*Catholic Library World*, May 1979). Since organizational analysis can in many ways be considered a part of the control function, readers should also refer to the "Additional Readings" section of chapter 3.

With the information generated through organizational assessment, as well as through the results of other management functions such as planning and control, organizational change may be required. "Organizational change is a term of many and varied meanings. At one extreme of a continuum, the term is used to refer to very basic changes in individual beliefs, values, and attitudes within an organization. At the other extreme, it has been applied in a holistic sense to total organizational shifts in objectives, policies, and general modes of operation."[11] A particular direction for change may be an effort "(1) planned, (2) organisationwide, and (3) managed from the top, to (4) increase organisational effectiveness and health through (5) planned interventions in the organisation's processes using behavioral science knowledge"[12]—in other words, "organization development," or "OD."

Hellriegel and Slocum suggest various change approaches in "Assessing Organizational Change Approaches: Toward a Comparative Typology" (*Group & Organization Studies*, March 1980). Sheldon also offers a view of organizational change in "Organizational Paradigms: A Theory of Organizational Change" (*Organizational Dynamics*, Winter 1980). In "An Interactive Approach to the Problem of Organizational Change" (*Human Resource Management*, Summer 1975), Shirley identifies the major organizational dimensions that may be considered for change or that may influence change (environmental, strategy, programs, structure, behavior, or technology), and the steps in the change process.

While change may be an organizational fact of life, there are numerous reasons why changes are resisted. Kotter and Schlesinger outline some of these reasons and ways of dealing with resistance, while also providing guidelines to various change approaches ("Choosing Strategies for Change," *Harvard Business Review*, March-April 1979). Francis and Woodcock (*People at Work, a Practical Guide to Organizational Change*, University Associates, 1975) and Cohen and Turney ("Introducing Organizational Change," *Civil Service Journal*, April-June 1979) also offer insights into the implementation of change. Student suggests that implementing change to increase productivity will be a crucial managerial task of the future, and that new change skills will be required ("Managing Change: A Psychologist's Perspective," *Business Horizons*, December 1978). Slocum and Hellriegel focus on the structural dimension as a means of change ("Using Organizational Designs to Cope with Change," *Business Horizons*, December 1979).

In the library environment, change is addressed in many ways. Berger suggests some of the important technological changes taking place in the library organization in "Managing Revolutions: Coping with Evolving Information Technologies" (*Special Libraries*, September 1980). Lee identifies influences on library change (*Emerging Trends in Library Organization: What Influences Change?* Pierian Press, 1979), while Drake suggests means of managing change and innovation in the academic library ("Managing Innovation in Academic Libraries," *College and Research Libraries*, November 1979). Farmer and Hess identify a "Proposed Change Strategy for Organizational Management Planning Programs" (*Illinois Libraries*, June 1978), and Bailey, Buckland, and Dagnese identify possible roles for the individual in the organizational change process in "Influencing Change: The Role of the Professional" (*Special Libraries*, April 1975).

Organization Development

The retention of organizational vitality may require the use of organizational development techniques and processes. An operational model of OD and description of various levels of change intervention is offered by Selfridge and Sokolik ("A Comprehensive View of Organization Development," *MSU Business Topics*, Winter 1975). Thorough coverage of all aspects of organization is also offered in Varney's *Organization Development for Managers* (Addison-Wesley, 1977) and Merry and Allerhand's *Developing Teams and Organizations* (Addison-Wesley, 1977). More specific aspects of organizational renewal and development are outlined by Steele and Jenks (*The Feel of the Work Place: Understanding and Improving Organizational Climate*, Addison-Wesley, 1977), Ouchi and Price ("Hierarchies, Clans, and Theory Z: A New Perspective in Organizational Development," *Organizational Dynamics*, Autumn 1978), Luke ("Training and Restructuring in Organizational Improvement," *Training and Development Journal*, November 1979), Lippitt and This ("Implementing the Organizational Renewal Process," *Training and Development Journal*, June 1979), and Scanlon ("Maintaining Organizational Effectiveness—A Prescription for Good Health," *Personnel Journal*, May 1980). "Organization Development in Library Management" is examined from a broad perspective in *Studies in Library Management* (vol. 4, Linnet Books, 1977) and by Johnson and Mann in *Organizational Development for Academic Libraries: An Evaluation of the Man-*

agement Review and Analysis Program (Greenwood Press, 1980). Musmann's "The Potential of Public Library Bureaucracy" (*Journal of Library Administration*, Spring 1981) presents ways of reducing bureaucratic repression and inefficiency in the public library setting. Finally, because a great deal of learning can result from the study of failure, Mirvin and Berg's *Failures in Organization Development and Change: Cases and Essays for Learning* (AMACOM, 1977) is perhaps the most valuable reading of all.

Communicating

Communicating is essential to the library organization. In fact, some communication theorists *define* organizations in terms of formal communication processes[1] and "complex, decision-related communication networks."[2] Without communication as a link, the other management functions could not exist, for they all depend upon the transmission of ideas, opinions, information, and directions.

The importance of communication in the management process is well documented. Even in 1938, Bernard noted in *The Functions of the Executive* that the first function of the executive is to "establish and maintain a system of communication."[3] Later empirical studies of managerial time allocation indicate that more than seventy percent of most managers' time is spent in communication activity. In the library setting, an analysis by Thomas and Ward estimated that library managers spend about eighty percent of their time in either direct or indirect communication in order to carry out the management process.[4]

What is meant by "communicating?" There are numerous ways to look at this aspect of the management process. For example, communication can be conceptualized by intent, by function, or by structure. In *Organizational Communications:*

The Essence of Effective Management, Lewis's definition seems particularly appropriate when considering communication in a management context: "the sharing of messages, ideas, or attitudes resulting in a degree of understanding between a sender (manager) and receiver (employee)."[5] Several elements in this definition are noteworthy—the individuals involved in communication and their interpersonal relationships, the nature of the information to be shared, and the purpose, structure, and climate of the organization. With all of these elements to be considered, it is understandable that communication problems and interpersonal and/or organizational conflicts can arise, particularly in a professional organization with increasingly specialized task functions.

The reading selections in this chapter have been chosen to provide insights into the communication function of the management process. They take the reader beyond an outline of the communication process to an examination of both individual and organizational perspectives on communication and the problems that arise in the communication process. In order to develop a framework for carrying out the communication function, it is necessary to understand potential communication obstacles in organizations. Huseman, Lahiff, and Wells use a phenomenon that occurs in natural systems to describe the identification of such obstacles. The nominal group method is offered by these authors as a process that can both identify and alleviate these so-called communication thermoclines.

Within organizations, communication and conflict are linked in many ways. While conflict is often viewed as a negative element in the management process, to some authorities, it is a "defining characteristic of organizational behavior,"[6] and a natural consequence of interaction and communication in organizations. Following this direction, some experts view the absence of any substantive conflict as a sign of an unhealthy or unresponsive organization. Derr approaches the question of conflict from this perspective and suggests three modes for managing serious disputes in organizations. In outlining feasible situations and possible consequences of using these three modes—bargaining, collaboration, and power—Derr emphasizes that none is appropriate for every situation and none can be used without consequence, another example of the trade offs in management. From this discussion, the reader should gain a clearer understanding of the role of communication in conflict management and resolution, and should be able to develop a situational approach to conflict management in the library setting.

In order to examine the communication function in the library setting, it is also necessary to understand *why* communication is important to the individual in the organization, and *what* role the individual plays in the organization. Using the work of three psychologists, Wilkinson develops a "psycho-organizational" theory of communication in the library setting that addresses these issues. He takes the communication process from the individual stages of development, through the establishment of work group communication patterns, to the organizational level. In this "psycho-organizational" framework, Wilkinson stresses that it is important to look at the "fit" between simple or complex objectives and individual behavior. It is also critical to understand the difference between the "professional act" and the "administrative act," the communication patterns that seem to fit each, and the way this fit affects libraries.

15. Communication Thermoclines: Toward a Process of Identification

Richard C. Huseman, James Lahiff, and Robert Wells

Work organizations are "contrived" social systems, and as such, they are uniquely different from and also similar to "natural" systems. In this article, we identify a phenomenon that occurs, with some frequency, in a natural system which has useful implications for understanding the phenomenon of upward and downward communication in man-made systems. What is more useful for the manager, however, is the description of a procedure which is useful in both identifying and alleviating this problem.

Reprinted from *Personnel Journal* 53:124–30, 135 (Feb. 1974). © 1974 by Personnel Journal. Reprinted with the permission of *Personnel Journal*, Costa Mesa, California. All rights reserved.

Katz and Kahn have clearly warned that there are dangers in comparing biological and man-made systems. They note:

Social structures are essentially contrived systems. They can come apart at the seams overnight, but they can also outlast by centuries the biological organisms which originally created them. The cement which holds them together is essentially psychological rather than biological. Social systems are anchored in the attitudes, perceptions, beliefs, motivations, habits, and expectations of human beings.[1]

With this warning in mind, we introduce the biological concepts of "stratification," and "thermoclines."

The Problem

During the summer, throughout this country and others, our system of lakes and ponds is severely affected by a process called "stratification." Essentially, the process is one where the water is divided into three distinct levels—an upper, middle and lower level. While stratification occurs to some extent in all lakes and ponds, it becomes critical when the middle level—the thermocline—experiences such a rapid drop in temperature within a few feet of water (e.g., sometimes a decrease of some $20°$ within three or four feet) that it prevents water from circulating and mixing between the upper, middle, and lower levels. The critical aspect of this phenomenon becomes obvious when one learns that "productivity," i.e., production of fish and plant life in the lower level, is a function of oxygen supply and light penetration. The thermocline, when severe, virtually eliminates the oxygen supply to the lower level by restricting water circulation and reducing plant growth which ordinarily replenishes the oxygen. Often, the oxygen supply is reduced to lethal levels and the fish either move up or die.

The illustration of the thermocline is not without a close and interesting parallel in modern organizations. Organizations can also experience stratification. When a thermocline develops in the organizational setting, it is communication rather than oxygen that is cut off from lower members in the organization. Extending the analogy, we find that while the bottom of lakes is usually rich in organic deposits, the lower levels of organizations are frequently rich with deposits such as young, energetic employees with fresh ideas and different approaches to old problems. Correspondingly, a lack of communication to lower levels in the organization can also be lethal, eventually resulting in turnover and other serious problems.

While this part of the analogy could be pursued in greater detail, the point has been adequately developed. Stratification and the thermocline are common in the natural system of lakes and ponds; likewise, the thermocline concept occurs in man-made systems such as organizations.[2] Buckley, Dewhirst and Read have all noted conditions in organizations that hamper communication. For purposes of illustration, let us look briefly at the areas of power, information sharing tendencies, psychological costs of information, superior's image, specialization, high status and job demotivation as conditions which are conducive to communication thermocline.

Power

In most organizations the possession of relevant information constitutes power. Upon relinquishing possession of the information by transmitting it to others, a person's power is reduced proportionately. Rather than suffer such a loss of power, individuals will often choose to retain sole possession of the information albeit at the expense of the organization. Such choices, if continued, will contribute to the thermocline. The refusal of the information-holder to transmit it to others prevents some from reaching their maximum effectiveness.

Recognizing the interrelationship between power and communication, some theoreticians have defined the former in terms of the latter. W. J. Buckley stated that power is "a specific mode of communication, a signal" and he considers the frame of reference of the subordinate to be the relevant one because it limits his "self-regarding" or independence. Such limitations symbolize the existence of a power relation.[3] In the organizational setting such limitation will continue as long as the information-holder retains possession of such information.

Information-Sharing Tendencies

After working in an organization over a period of time and growing familiar with the policies and practices, an individual formulates expectations about the readiness of his colleagues to respond to his requests for information. He grows to recognize the existence of a norm which governs the sharing of information. Research has shown that the use of interpersonal channels of communication will be directly related to the perceived strength of such information-sharing norms. Those who perceive strong sharing norms in the organization are much more likely to use the interpersonal channels to seek information than are those who perceive weak information-sharing norms. There were also indications in this study that some managers are more effective in creating an organizational climate that promotes strong information-sharing norms and thus greater use of the internal interpersonal channels.[4] It is in organizations in which the information-sharing norms are weak that this type of thermocline is most likely to develop.

Psychological Costs of Seeking Information

Another situation where a thermocline is likely to result is one in which one party considers the psychological cost involved in seeking information to be greater than he cares to "pay." When a person asks a co-worker for information, he may feel he is making a partial admission of that colleague's intellectual superiority. Should the colleague show reluctance or impatience, the cost to the other increases. After several psychologically costly experiences, the information seeker may either go elsewhere for the information or do without it.[5] If he chooses to go elsewhere, it could be to a source less qualified than his original choice and the worth of the information he receives may be less than it would have been otherwise. If he chooses to do without the information, he may find himself making decisions without adequate data.

Superior's Image

In many organizations there appears to be a natural hesitancy for a subordinate to discuss difficulties with his superior. W. Read found that this hesitancy increased as did the subordinate's desire for upward mobility. The amount of inaccuracy in upward communication was further influenced by the extent to which subordinates perceived their superior as having influence over their career and to the extent they trusted him not to hold disclosures against them in considering promotion. "The greater his perceived influence over their careers and the lower their trust in him, the more inaccurate their upward communication of difficulties."[6] With that combination present, conditions are ripe for a thermocline.

Specialization

One's area of specialization is often recognized as an impediment to communicating with laymen or with specialists from other areas. Too often specialists attempt to communicate with others as though they all shared the same specialty and hence the same sublanguage. Inability of the receiver to use the sender's sublanguage or failure to even recognize it as such often has humorous overtones, but always further complicates the entire communication process.

While the influence of specialization constitutes a real problem and is recognized as a major inhibitor of effective horizontal communication, there is another serious dimension to the dilemma. The specialization problem is magnified when the promotion of a specialist results in his reaching a position in which he is the immediate superior to persons representing a variety of areas of task specialization. In such cases a person is often much more receptive to interaction with those from his own special area. This natural proclivity may in turn produce a thermocline which will inhibit the transmission of information regarding the other more alien task areas.

Status

The reputation a person enjoys in an organization can also affect the climate of the organization and consequently the behavior of others in the organization. For example, the individual who acquires a reputation for inflexibility will, after a while, not be approached with suggestions. The higher status person, who uses the status of his office as a barrier by keeping co-workers constantly aware of it, significantly reduces the probability of his receiving certain kinds of messages.

Job Demotivation

When people feel that they do not "participate" actively in their jobs, they experience a type of communication thermocline that is best summed up in the phrase "I don't know. I just work here." This feeling is a result of not receiving enough information about one's job and feeling that one has little opportunity to present information that has any impact on decision-making in the organization. Stanley Peterfreund, a management consultant, identifies the problem as "jobs have been *demotivated*, so that while the . . . workers want a sense of self-development . . . they are made to feel unimportant . . . this is debilitating."[7]

While such job demotivation is usually associated with lower level jobs, that is not always the case. The investigation of a special task force of the Department of Health, Education, and Welfare revealed increasing dissatisfaction among "such traditionally privileged groups as the nation's four and one-half million middle managers." Management scientists contend that this discontent can be traced to the middle managers' perception that they lack influence on decision-making in the organization but still must implement company policy, even though they frequently have neither the authority nor the resources to do so effectively. In 1972 a Gallup Poll revealed that 57 percent of the total public felt "they could produce more each day if they tried," but the figure for businessmen and professionals was 70 percent.[8] One of the major causes of job demotivation is a general type of communication thermocline that causes workers to feel that they don't get enough information concerning their jobs and that they have little opportunity to contribute information at the decision-making level in the organization.

Identifying Communication Thermoclines

In addition to the communication thermoclines discussed above it should be stressed that individual organizations may have unique communication thermoclines. There is little concern, at this juncture, whether the "communication thermocline" occurs at one level or several; whether it is organizationally related (i.e., structure, specialization, authority, or hierarchy); or whether it is interpersonal in nature (i.e., climate, values, perceptions, motives, or attitudes). The major concern is how to identify and begin to alleviate communication thermoclines in individual settings.

A little attention to "identification" immediately points up some major differences between natural and contrived systems. The thermocline, in its natural setting, is easily identified by a rapid change in temperature within a few feet of water. A simple thermometer is an adequate and accurate method to identify the thermocline in its natural setting.

In an organizational setting, however, the communication thermocline is not nearly so easy to identify. In most cases, it can best be defined by those people who operate below it, but frequently the employees at lower levels are not provided the opportunity to identify the thermocline.[9]

Alleviating the thermocline is a much more simple process in natural systems than it seems to be in contrived systems. First, the thermocline, in contrived systems, does not necessarily occur at one point in time such as during the summer months in the natural system. Secondly, one cannot assume that the condition is "self-correcting" in organizations as it is in the natural environment with the changing of seasons. In organizations, the duration is likely to be longer and the consequences progressively more serious.

Finally, scientists have experimented with ways of breaking up the thermocline in lakes. One method involves a "bubble machine" which is lowered below the thermocline and supplies a continuous supply of oxygen to this level. This too can eventually break up the thermocline. A second method, only useful near dams, is to allow the flow of water to start from the fresh water on top rather than from the lower, more stagnant water. Up to this point, we have no dams in organizations and no one has developed a "bubble machine" which pumps communication to employees at lower levels in organizations.[10]

The Problem Identification Process

The communication problem identification process which follows is a process which some researchers refer to as the "nominal group procedure."[11] Employees from the organization are brought together in a group setting, but no verbal interaction is permitted—thus, the label "nominal group" is appropriate. The nominal group procedure involves three steps.

Stage 1: First, employees who are selected to participate meet in groups of six to nine. It is advantageous to include as many employees as possible from different levels in the total process.[12] Once assembled in a meeting room, the employees are requested not to speak to each other. Second, after the group has been seated around a table, each employee is requested to write on a prepared form what he sees as "personal communication obstacles." Ten minutes is usually sufficient time for this activity. In a second ten minute period, the employees are asked to list on another form what they see as "organizational communication obstacles." It is important that no conversation take place during these listing periods.

Stage 2: After the group has listed both personal and organizational communication obstacles, the consultant in charge of the group asks a group member to read one of his personal communication obstacles to the group. This item is then written with a large felt tip pen on a large paper pad which has been placed in front of the group. The consultant then proceeds around the group to receive one item from the next person in sequence and he numbers each item as he writes the problems on the large paper pad. This process is continued until each employee in the group has exhausted his list of items and all of the personal communication obstacles are listed on the large pad of paper in front of the group. When an item is put on the pad that other members have also listed, they are instructed not to repeat the item again and in this way each problem is listed only once on the master list of personal communication obstacles. This same process is then repeated for the organizational communication obstacles. The two lists of interpersonal and organizational communication obstacles are then taped to the wall in front of the group so that all group members can see them. At this point the two lists are carefully studied by the group to remove any items that overlap.

Stage 3: At this juncture in the nominal process, all individuals are asked to examine the lists of communication obstacles. They are asked to rank order, separately, the personal and organizational obstacles without consulting other members of the group. If the lists of obstacles are extremely long, the group members are asked simply to select the top five from each list. After the group members have voted privately on both lists, this information is collected and tabulated. All three stages of the nominal process can usually be completed in about one hour. When used in this way, the nominal group process serves as a method for identifying the major obstacles to communication and also allows for the establishment of priorities as to which are the most important. Since individuals rank these obstacles by secret ballot, there is some assurance that the high priority items are the most serious ones.

Rationale for the Problem Identification Process

Much of the recent experimental literature indicates that the nominal group is a more effective method for identifying the major dimensions of a problem than is the interacting group.[13] Our purpose here is only to briefly summarize the major reasons which support this point; a more complete analysis is presented elsewhere.[14]

Several factors explain the superiority of the nominal group approach. First, there is evidence that interacting groups inhibit the effectiveness of their members in generating the dimensions of the problem being discussed. Even when the group leader encourages the individuals to speak freely and share their ideas, the research suggests that most individuals only feel comfortable in sharing well-developed and well-thought-out ideas with the group.[15] This kind of reluctance may result in important dimensions of the problem never emerging in the group. The problem is intensified in newly formed groups where the members do not know each other well. Another part of this problem is that one or two strong members in the interacting group may dominate and keep other less powerful individuals from suggesting important dimensions of the problem. The nominal procedure does not permit verbal interaction, and the tendency for powerful individuals to control the group is minimized.

Second, sometimes interacting groups tend to start evaluating and elaborating on some of the early problem dimensions and as a result, some of the important dimensions of the problem area are never brought to the attention of the group. The nominal procedure, on the other hand, avoids evaluating and elaborating comments while the dimensions of the problem are being identified. This factor is supported by research on creative groups and identification of problem dimensions.[16]

Third, there is a tendency of interacting groups to focus on one particular train of thought and not attempt to identify all of the problem dimensions. Many individuals find it much easier to react to someone else's idea than to articulate their own. The nominal method, on the other hand, forces each individual to identify as many of the dimensions of the problem as he can. In this way, he is not permitted the luxury of simply reacting to dimensions generated by others in the group.

In addition, there seem to be at least two additional advantages to this method. Sirota and Wolfson recently noted that one of the major reasons for the failure of behavioral science techniques in industry is that they are adopted for the wrong reasons and applied to the wrong problems.[17] They state: "Companies confronted with employee discontent need to find out what the problems are before they set out to solve them."[18] The nominal group method could be superior to "survey methods" in identifying the communication problems to be addressed through training, policy and structural changes. Survey methods assume management "knows what to ask," and in this way, the problems are actually structured by management. These may not include the real communication ills. The nominal group method, on the other hand, allows participation by management as well as employees. In addition, a communication training program developed around the problems identified in the nominal group process is usually better received by the employees who had an input.

Finally, with respect to the superiority of the nominal group method, it is appropriate to consider the linkage between the "nature of the problem" and the "process for identifying and solving it." Recent studies of training methods and training objectives shed some light on this linkage. For example, if a transfer of information or an increase in knowledge is the stated objective of training, a lecture method with one person talking to many may be appropriate. However, if behavior change is the objective, a small group process which includes participants from several levels may be more appropriate. If a program has been designed to "increase participative management," its effectiveness may be hindered if the participants are "ordered" to attend the program.[19]

Given the nature of communication (i.e., it is a personal process, includes a variety of variables, is perception rather than logic, and is additive), the group process method is actually a part of the solution process. The "climate" of involvement and management's concern about communication, which is often generated by the group process itself, are conducive to creating a more open climate outside the group. The sharing of perceptions and shaping of expectations in the group process tend to carry over into the actual work environment, thereby enhancing the communication environment. A type of positive "Hawthorne Effect" is not an unusual product of the nominal group process.

In brief, we would submit that the concept, "communication thermocline," is a useful way to describe and think about communication obstacles in organizational settings. Since communication in organizations is best characterized as a "process" which moves through "structure," the thermocline concept has implications for both the cause and effect of communication obstacles.

The nominal group method for identifying communication obstacles enables one consultant to have personal contact with a large number of employees in an average work day. What's more, the very nature of the method (meeting face-to-face with small groups of employees) contains advantages over more traditional methods of identifying communication obstacles, and offers real potential to those practitioners interested in identifying communication thermoclines in organizations.

16. Managing Organizational Conflict: Collaboration, Bargaining, and Power Approaches

C. Brooklyn Derr

Conflicts are normal and natural consequences of human interaction in organizational settings. But they are also complex. Conflicts may occur for multiple reasons; for example: internal stress coming from the person and overlapping into the work place, incompatible expectations among workers and work groups, differences over task procedures, values, orientations, and desired outcomes, increasing interdependencies and work loads, and external pressures and crises.

As an illustration of this complexity, the author is well acquainted with a large urban school district in which serious conflicts occur between two associate superintendents. One party to the dispute appears to be experiencing intrapersonal stress as a result of a pending divorce and is often overly sensitive and angry.

© 1978 by the Regents of the University of California. Reprinted from California Management Review 21, no. 2:76–83 (Winter 1978) by permission of the Regents.

Superintendent A desires his colleague to deliver special reports to his division on a weekly basis, but Superintendent B claims that he cannot comply because of a work overload. One of these superintendents views all problems rationally-technically from a data systems point of view. The other is incensed and continually faults him for "not thinking humanistically about the needs of the kids." Moreover, pressure from the courts for forced busing have put an enormous burden on the superintendent in charge of planning and systems. He frequently arrives at 7:00 A.M. and leaves the office at 6:00 P.M. He works on the weekends. While he believes in long-range planning, he sees himself in a "reactive" mode. He resents his colleague's accusations that he could beat the problem if he were better organized.

This is an article for conflict managers who want to try a variety of methods to manage serious disputes which, like the one above, may have multiple and complex causes. A contingency approach to conflict management is suggested to provide managers with a conceptual framework for knowing what to do when.

This article . . . emphasizes the costs and feasibility issues of successful conflict management implementation; . . . this contingency approach stresses the realistic constraints and complexities that are important for practical and workable conflict management methods.

Three Conflict Management Modes

This article will focus on three major conflict management modes from which one can draw to formulate a situational theory. These are collaborations, bargaining, and power-play. Walton has already outlined the differences between collaboration and bargaining approaches.[1] Table 1 presents a modification of his ideas, with the addition of power-play, which serves to contrast the three conflict management approaches. Tabular schemes such as that in table 1 inevitably fail to account for overlaps. In reality, much of what is listed as collaboration also occurs in bargaining, and power-play also overlaps with bargaining. The table does serve to highlight basic differences, however.

None of these three conflict modes is appropriate for every contingency; neither is any one used without consequence. Following is a brief description of each mode with its possible cost, benefits, and requirements.

TABLE 1. Three Conflict Management Modes

Characteristic	Collaboration	Bargaining	Power-Play
Overall Objective	1. Seeking win-win position	1. Seeking compromise or win-lose position	1. Seeking win-lose
Strategic Objective	2. Emphasis on problem solving conflicts and using energy effectively	2. Emphasis on inducing and using conflicts for better bargaining	2. Emphasis on coping with and using conflicts to better one's power position
View of Man	3. Man is open, honest, trusting, collaborative	3. Man is united in the face of a common problem	3. Man acts primarily in his own self-interest
Type of Settlement	4. Psychological contracts	4. Legal contracts	4. Informal or unstated contracts
Individual's Relationship to Organization	5. Overall improvement orientation for the common good	5. Purposeful in pursuing goals of the group	5. Pure self-interest with a sense of limits
Efficiency/Effectiveness	6. Effective but inefficient use of conflict energy	6. Periodically ineffective and inefficient use of energy	6. Efficient but ineffective use of energy
Information Use	7. Information openly shared	7. Information strategically shared	7. Secrecy or distortion
Problem-Solving Mechanism	8. Joint problem solving	8. Trade-offs on positions to which there is apparent commitment	8. Unilateral, reciprocal manipulations to maximize self-interests
Power Relationship	9. Power parity	9. Struggle for parity	9. Power inequalities accepted
Parties' Support of Organizational Decisions	10. Voluntary (Internal commitment)	10. Voluntary support (Legal agreement)	10. Contractual support (Free to subvert)

Collaboration

Collaborative theory maintains that people should surface their differences (get them out in the open) and then work on the problems until they have attained mutually satisfactory solutions. The approach assumes that people will be motivated to expend the time and energy for such problem-solving activity. It tries to maximize the possible mutual gains of the parties in the dispute and views the conflict as a creative force pushing them to achieve an improved state of affairs to which both sides are fully committed. Information is openly and willingly exchanged.[2] When the parties stagnate because they are too close to the situation to perceive viable alternatives or are too protective of their own positions, a third-party consultant may be used to help clarify the problem, sharpen the issues, find commonalities, and, in general, help them to discover a win-win position.[3]

Essentially, the collaborationists argue that theirs is the most preferred strategy for the good of the enterprise because: (1) open and honest interaction promotes authentic interpersonal relations; (2) conflict is used as a creative force for innovation and improvement; (3) this process enhances feedback and information flow; and (4) the solving of disputes has a way of improving the climate of the organization so that there is more openness, trust, risk taking, and feelings of integrity.[4]

In my consulting experience, however, I have found that collaboration is not always useful or feasible. Collaboration seems best employed when there is a combination of factors that assures the method some reasonable degree of success. Four major conditions help to determine the practicality of the collaborative mode.

First, a moderately high degree of *required interdependence* is important to force parties to expend the time and energy necessary to work out their differences. Openly confronting the issues is hard work and not likely to occur unless there is a long-term stake in developing and preserving the relationship.

Second, seeking collaborative solutions to conflicts involves more than simply acting together in various roles to accomplish a task and reach an objective. It also requires feeling free enough to interact openly, including conflicting, in the collaborative relationship. A kind of *power parity* must exist which allows the parties to feel free to interact candidly and use all of their resources to further their beliefs and concerns (regardless of their superior-subordinate status).

Third, there must be potential for *mutual benefits* as a result of solving the specific dispute. The person or group in conflict should "feel" a need that leads to a desire to work on the issue. This is related to the two requisites cited above. But in addition to a compelling reason and feeling enough parity to be able to collaborate, the parties themselves must perceive some significant motivation concerning the issue at hand. Their motivation often depends on whether the mutual gains are self-evident.

When there is required interdependence, power parity, and a felt need provoking the will to engage in the process, then the fourth factor comes into play. It is the extent to which there is *organizational support* for such behavior. Considerable organizational resources are needed to effectively manage conflict using the collaborative strategy. Such a program often requires a commitment of time, money, and energy. For example, the organization (including top executives) should engage in a collaborative mode systemwide, so that the norms, rewards, and punishments of the enterprise will encourage such behavior. Most people are unaccustomed to open disagreement, especially with someone of higher organizational rank, and need assurance that such behavior will not draw reprisals.

To confront one another effectively and emerge having resolved a problem also requires numerous personal skills. Learning how to communicate effectively, how to synchronize the process, when and how to use a third party, how to engage in effective problem solving, and how to keep the tension level moderate for optimal results requires skills that can be taught but may not have already been learned. Indeed, many organizations would view such constructive openness as deviant. The enterprise should be sufficiently committed to fund training for building skills to manage conflicts via collaboration.

Thus, it has become apparent to me that the implementation of collaboration is often either infeasible (that is, the right conditions do not exist for it to work) or too costly to be justifiable. Accordingly, it becomes important to re-examine other alternative modes from the viewpoint of their benefits, costs, and feasibilities as they are related to the desired outcomes.

Power-Play

Collaborationists often view power-play as diametrically opposed to their own values and theory. Power-play, they say, will harm both the individual and the enterprise. They argue that it: (1) unleashes aggressive behaviors and hostile feelings between those involved in the power struggle, shutting off communication and interaction; (2) promotes vicious gossip, which in turn distorts the valid information needed to manage successfully; (3) drives needed information underground, where it is not used for feedback and learning from experience; (4) sometimes subverts the corporate mission through acts of sabotage and noncompliance; and (5) displaces goals because much of the energy employed in the power struggle is diverted from more productive purposes—in fact, winning the struggle can become a more important end than achieving an organizational goal.[5]

Much of the fear of power-play is connected with what Rapoport calls the "cataclysmic" view of conflict—that power struggles are necessarily unmanageable, irrational, and destructive. Although some escalated power struggles fit this description, Rapoport reminds us that the use of power strategies is often "strategic"— characterized by both rational self-interest and control.[6]

Four sets of considerations suggest that power-play is an appropriate method of conflict management in many situations. First, there is a view of individuals which says that *they act first and foremost in their own self-interest* and play an active power game to protect that interest. This view is increasing in popularity, reflected in the increased frequency of books on power in both the professional and popular literature.[7] Many people perceive that they can win more by competing than by collaborating. Or, they do not feel comfortable or skilled at problem solving, while they may feel particularly good, given their social experience, at power-play. Additionally, some individuals have primary outside-the-organization interests and do not want to be highly involved in or committed to their work; hence, it is not in their interest to get highly involved in collaborating.

Individuals typically play one or a combination of three different power games which strive for different types of power.

Authority is the power that is delegated by the organization to the holder of a certain position. Formal authority results in the ability to use rewards, punishments, and other organizational resources in order to impact on persons and to affect behavior. Much has been written about positional power or authority.[8]

Informal influence is normally defined as being able to affect behavior or gain compliance without holding a position of authority. Not everyone in authority has influence. Some persons have little or no authority but much influence. Some have influence far greater than that normally associated with their official role. It is possible to become influential in the enterprise without necessarily ascending the formal hierarchy.[9]

Autonomy. Unlike the other power intents described above, autonomy power derives from the need to be in control of oneself and to minimize unwanted influence by others. It is manifested in one's ability to resist formal authority (control) and informal influence (normative demands) and to have ample "space" to accomplish prescribed ends using unrestricted means. Highly trained professionals, for example, seek autonomy, are little supervised, and are accountable for the quality of their end products (such as a surgical operation, a scholarly book, an architectural plan).[10]

Individuals who strive for autonomy power may be very interested in building and protecting a piece of organizational territory. They try to become indispensable so they will be the experts, have the information, and hold unquestioned power. Autonomy-oriented persons may also have extraorganizational interests (such as a civic or religious organization) or parallel organizational interests (such as a professional association) and wish to remain "free" from organizational commitments or constraints in order to devote more time to those activities.

Power-play, it is hypothesized, will be the dominant conflict management strategy for those who seek autonomy. It has been pointed out elsewhere that it is unpolitical in organizations to appear uncooperative and "anti-system." One must appear to act in the best interest of the enterprise.[11] Those endeavors that are most self-interest-oriented, in which the interests of the worker and the organization are least congruent, require the most covert means. To be discovered as being aloof or free from the rules could cause a very negative, career-damaging impression. Autonomy is an unpopular intent in most organizations because marginality is discouraged and total commitment is rewarded. Power-play is a secretive mode that could work in the best interests of those whose covert objective is autonomy and whose desired impression is that of being committed. In contrast, collaboration requires the open sharing of personal intents and of preferred means for achieving them in the process of finding a mutually satisfactory solution.

A second set of arguments for power-play centers on the strategic reality that collaborating can increase one's vulnerability in competitive external environments. There are significant aspects of conflict of interest between firms which transact business directly or compete for resources, just as there are aspects of conflict of interest between managers within a firm over promotion and resources. Collaboration, and even bargaining, assumes the *exchange of information* necessary to resolve a problem. This information may apprise competitors of weaknesses and give them an unfair advantage. For example, disclosing strategic information (a key power-play resource) might provide another organization with data for increasing its efficiency, and therefore its competitive advantage.

Third, in some situations power-play strategies can contribute to the *joint welfare* of two adversary parties. Under conditions of routine and certainty, for example, the self-interests of the individual and the enterprise may be incompatible to a considerable degree. To maximize its objectives, the enterprise may tend to increase its efficiency through elaborate planning and control systems. The employees may likewise attempt to improve their working conditions through inclusive union contracts. In this way, power-play is the mechanism of flexibility used by both sides to cope within the confines of the rules (which are never so tightly delineated as to disallow some manipulation). Employees can use power-play to resist machinelike control; employers can use power-play to cope with union contracts during periods of uncertainty (such as rearranging work and calling for a common response to a crisis). Under this procedure, there exists a sort of dynamic equilibrium which works to the advantage of both within the rules. It is the dynamic interaction of finding compatible self-interests which is the substance of power-play conflict management. Such a mode allows multiple motives and various methods to eventually find a satisfactory equilibrium. Some activities are temporarily blocked as the power struggles are waged. Yet these are normally periods of realignment, reform and adjustment. In the long term, they may be effective ways to manage differences for the greatest number of persons and for the enterprise.

Fourth, power-play is often best suited to decide *ideological disputes*. When values or philosophies clash, the parties are usually intransigent in their conflicting positions. They refuse to problem solve or even negotiate. The only recourse is for one to try to win at the expense of the other, and although neither may emerge victorious, both may emerge saving some face and being "right" for having taken their stand.

Bargaining

While neither party may emerge completely satisfied and one party may be clearly dissatisfied under this mode, both will at least come to terms openly about how to best resolve the most immediate issues. Bargaining can be a more or less elaborate mode of conflict management depending on the situation (from interpersonal trading to collective negotiation). The important point is that, like collaboration, a common solution to a problem can be found. The actual act of trading and compromise highlights the assumed strength and influence of each party. In this process, the power position of each side is clearly defined in direct ratio to the information it reveals to the other, the concessions it makes, the punishment or penalties it can impose.

Bargaining, while remaining unique, contains elements that overlap with both collaboration and power.[12] It resembles the collaborative process because it is a systematic method which, in some of its forms, allows for collaboration between negotiators. Bargaining also contains many aspects of the strategic win-lose power struggles more typical in power-play. Figure 1 illustrates this point. Bargaining, therefore, can be viewed as a "connecting bridge" between the collaborative and power strategies of conflict management.

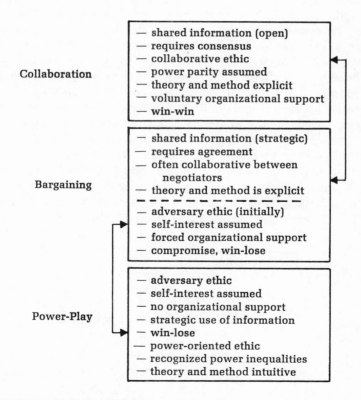

FIGURE 1. Relationship among strategies

Bargaining employs some of the methods, values and motivational forces used in each of the other modes. Bargaining is therefore a middle-ground orientation in which both power-players and collaborationists may feel somewhat comfortable. There is little hope that a power-player and a collaborationist could deal effectively with one another while using their own incongruent approaches. Bargaining can serve to neutralize the values of conflict managers so that they do not impose one set of assumptions (such as collaboration) on a very different situation (such as power-play). In the Organization Development movement, for example, many instances of failure have been reported where collaborative values and methods of dispute settlement were superimposed on power settings. It is proposed herein that bargaining would have better matched the intervention situation.

Bargaining might also be viewed as an intervention bridge to either elevate a stalemated power-play situation from a covert "lose-lose" condition to a situation in which both parties have at least made an explicit—albeit "hard" or "power-based"—agreement in their mutual interest. Or, using this bridge concept, it is a realistic alternative to fall back on when the conditions are not present for collaboration. Figure 2 illustrates this last point.

Those who favor the collaborative approach would argue that bargaining is of limited value because (1) it often creates new interpersonal-organizational conflicts by virtue of the win-lose strategies employed; (2) the commitments to resolutions adopted are formal (based on having to prove that an agreement has been violated) rather than intrinsic and are, therefore, often carried out only according to the letter of the law; and (3) no more than one, perhaps neither, of the parties emerges fully satisfied.

On the other hand, bargaining seems to work well in many situations. In addition to its middle-ground value, it is, for exam-

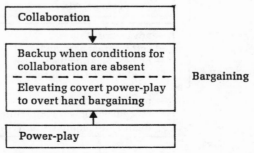

FIGURE 2. An intervention bridge

ple, a good way to establish *power parity* so that more collaboration can follow. Just getting into a trading position assumes some equality, as each side recognizes that the other has something of value to offer or withhold.

Additionally, scarce resources can often be bargained according to the strategies of important interest groups, whereas they are not easily distributed using the collaborative method. Bargaining trade-offs, where some win and some lose according to a criterion of importance, seem optimally suited *to deal with conditions of scarcity.*

Some persons or groups also feel skillful at and comfortable with bargaining. It fits their *personal style.* Finally, bargaining is somewhat *economical* in that parties meet only periodically to review the old contract and to recontract.

Conclusions

It is assumed that a wide variety of organizational conflicts will occur quite naturally. Many of them will promote creative tensions which lead to system improvement. Some will serve the interests of various parties and groups without disrupting the organization itself. Others will be of such import that they must be effectively managed.

This article attempts to make the point that there is no one best-way to manage organizational conflicts. The collaborative approach has been in vogue during the past few years but has proven inadequate on numerous occasions. This article has outlined three very different modes, one of which (power-play) is in sharp contrast with collaboration but optimal under some conditions.

In considering the use of these three modes, it is vital to separate our appreciation of organizational realities from the humanistic and sometimes utopian values that have affected the field. Conflict modes must be tailored to the actual motives, issues, and organizational circumstances of the conflict parties. Inappropriate application of collaboration or other modes by a conflict manager, however well intentioned, is apt to be ineffective at best—and destructive to one or both parties or to the organization at worst.

The following conclusions have been drawn:

Collaboration may be best employed when work relationships, which must be interdependent, would be substantially damaged by a given unresolved conflict, when the parties in conflict can openly confront their differences and state their preferences without fear of reprisal (there exists power parity in the relationship), when there is evident mutual interest in solving the dispute, and when the organization supports the open surfacing and working of disagreements.

Bargaining seems to work best to establish power parity (usually between competing people or groups), as a means of distributing scarce resources, and as a somewhat efficient option for achieving a formal agreement to a common dispute. Bargaining may also be the most effective way to manage a dispute between two parties who each use one of the two other modes (collaboration, power-play) and are, therefore, unable to reach a common solution due to the disparity between them. Bargaining is often a midway or "bridge" strategy.

Power-play, on the other hand, is an important way to cope with conflicts for the autonomous; advantages those who are most adept at this mode; is a means for achieving a dynamic balance of competing forces, and is often the only feasible way to resolve ideological disputes.

Of these three modes, there is perhaps the greatest need to know more about power-play. Very few empirical studies document the dynamics of power-play. One major problem has been to find an appropriate method for studying it. Since information is power and power is secretive, few will divulge their power game to researchers. Also, being "political" or "selfish" is usually a negative organizational image which requires covert rather than overt methods of power-play and an objective is to not be discovered and badly viewed. However, it is also very probable that the collaborative ethic in our field has discouraged research efforts on the uses of power-play in organizations, despite the fact that it appears to be the method most frequently used to resolve a number of kinds of differences. It is clear that more accurate descriptive theories of conflict management will require more extensive studies of the realities of power-play.

17. The Psycho-Organizational Approach to Staff Communication in Libraries

J. P. Wilkinson

The Need for a Psycho-Organizational Synthesis

It has become generally accepted that communication is an important element of organizational development. "Communication, the process of transmitting and receiving information, is so fundamental to the practice of management," I. L. Heckmann writes, "that without it an organization could not exist."[1] "The significance of an internal communications study for the library cannot be overstated," Millicent Abell echoes.[2] However, writing is one thing; practice in everyday performance is quite another.

Staff communication is an aspect of everyday activity which many librarians take for granted; they assume that their own particular communicative activities, and perhaps those within the library as a whole, are adequate and efficient. Staff communication, however, is not a secondary or derived aspect of management, but one that is central to organizational activity and is the basic process upon which other functions depend in their working and contributions to library goals.[3]

The problem is that librarianship has so failed to develop a stance in the social sciences that even our approach to a theoretical construct such as communication lacks any socio-psychological

Reprinted from *Journal of Academic Librarianship* 4:21–26 (Mar. 1978).

foundation. This is even true of Emery's excellent book quoted above. Because we do not understand just *why* communication is important to the individual in an organization, we are left without an objective basis for preferring one pattern of communication to another and hence for optimizing organizational structure in terms of basic communication.[4]

An organization is a communication network. Thus, it can be regarded in one sense as a synthesis of dialogues. Joe speaks to Harry, Harry communicates with Mabel, Mabel phones Bill, and Bill addresses a group of his staff. Whether the relationships are one on one or one on a group, they still involve individuals reacting with individuals to further or frustrate the organization's objectives.

Institutional sociology has many of its roots in psychological concepts. The discussion that follows postulates that the work of three preeminent modern psychologists, conjoined with one facet of current communications research and leavened with a pinch of management theory, can produce a perhaps novel "psycho-organizational" synthesis, which may be applied to improving the organizations of libraries relative to staff communication.

The Psychologists

The three psychologists are Lawrence Kohlberg, whose theories on cognitive development are familiar to those in education if not to librarians; the late Abraham Maslow; and the recently fashionable Thomas Harris, who is probably best known for his book *I'm O.K.—You're O.K.*, which popularized transactional analysis. To embark on our synthesis of psychological constructs, communication schemata, and management principles, it is necessary to present briefly some of the major relevant concepts of these three protagonists.

Basing his belief upon descriptive data obtained through repeated study of many populations, Lawrence Kohlberg teaches that all individuals progress through as many as six stages of moral development corresponding to six basic types of moral judgment.[5] These stages are defined not by particular opinion but by ways of thinking about moral matters as bases for choice.

The six stages are defined as follows:

1. Orientation to punishment and reward and to physical and material power

2. Hedonistic orientation with an instrumental view of human relations; beginning notions of reciprocity but with emphasis on exchange of favors ("You scratch my back and I'll scratch yours.")
3. "Good boy" orientation; seeking to maintain expectations and win approval of one's immediate group; morality defined by individualities or relationships
4. Orientation to authority, law and duty to maintain a fixed order, whether social or religious, which is assumed as a primary value
5. Social-contract orientation, with emphasis on equality and mutual obligation within a democratically established order; for example, the morality of the American Constitution
6. Morality of individual principles of conscience that have logical comprehensiveness and universality; highest value placed on human life, equality, and dignity.[6]

The relationship of Kohlberg's six stages to the five levels of need postulated by Abraham Maslow seems clear though it is nowhere explicit in the work of either man.

Maslow, like Kohlberg, bases his theory on observation.[7] He explains his evidence by suggesting an overlapping hierarchy of needs, starting with apparently homeostatic psychological needs and progressing through levels of security (safety), belonging (love), esteem, and self-actualization. Every "normal" individual possesses these needs. They are hierarchical in the sense that lower-order needs must be more or less satisfied before higher-level needs can become paramount. For the starving man, the need for food is dominant. Once immediate physiological needs are (partly) satisfied, the need to secure the physiological environment dominates. Once security is obtained to some degree, the need to belong to someone, some group, or something (fetishism?) must be met. To belong is not enough, however; once the belonging need is partly met, the need for (self)-esteem, derived from the esteem of others becomes pressing. Only when all these "lacks" have been obviated does a man become self-actualized (fulfilled) and mentally well enough to "be himself," free from the dysfunctional pressures of insecurity, isolation, and inadequacy.

Thus, for both Maslow and Kohlberg the "lower" levels of development (the development is both chronological and attitudinal) represent a preoccupation with the self: for Maslow, with self-protection; for Kohlberg, with favourable physical consequences and the exchange of favours. These levels are "usually occupied by children aged four to ten, a fact long known to sensitive observers of children";[8] but adults may easily freeze at or revert to "childlike" behaviour if lower level needs are not satisfied or if higher order needs remain unfulfilled.[9]

If the physiological (Maslow) or preconventional (Kohlberg) needs are in large part met, the individual can progress to the belonging and esteem needs (Maslow) and to the conventional level (Kohlberg). Again, there is a close match between the levels in the two models. "The second or conventional level also can be described as conformist, but that is perhaps too smug a term."[10] Smug or not, the term accurately describes a major consequence of Maslow's need to belong. It is certainly plausible to suggest that the belonging and esteem needs result in the perception of "the expectations and rules of the individual's family, group or nation . . . as valuable in its own right."[11]

Similarly, the "highest" of Maslow's levels of need—self-actualization—finds its close counterpart in the "highest" of Kohlberg's levels of cognitive development. Self-fulfillment, which represents for Maslow the achievement of a level of self-actualization, may perhaps be equated to an attunement to Ralph Emerson's "over-soul" and to an "orientation toward the decisions of conscience and toward self-chosen *ethical principles* appealing to logical comprehensiveness, universality, and consistency,"[12] which is how Kohlberg defines his Stage 6 consciousness.

The work of Thomas Harris, which is a development of the earlier theories of Eric Berne,[13] complements the concepts of Kohlberg and Maslow. Postulating the existence of three states of being in all of us—the parent, the child and the adult—Harris defines the parent as "a huge collection of recordings in the brain of unquestioned or imposed external events. . . . [They] are rigidly internalized as a voluminous set of data essential to the individual's survival in the setting of a group."[14] The parent state of being thus corresponds closely to Kohlberg's conventional level of development and to Maslow's needs for security and belonging.

The child state Harris defines as "the recording of *internal* events, the responses of the little person to what he sees and hears. . . . On the one hand he has the urges (genetic recordings) to empty his bowels ad lib, to explore, to know. . . ."[15] The child state, then, corresponds to Kohlberg's preconventional level of cognition and to Maslow's physiological needs and experiences.

The adult state is defined by Harris as consisting "of checking out old data, validating it or invalidating it (in terms of new data or experiences), and refiling it for future use. If this business goes on smoothly and there is a relative absence of conflict between what has been taught and what is real, the computer (i.e., the adult state) is free for important new business, *creativity*."[16] Thus the adult state approximates the creativity of Maslow's level of self-actualization and, in its freedom from the domination of more "childish" states of being, Kohlberg's Stages 5 and 6.

Men of the stature of Kohlberg, Maslow and Harris would, of course, recognize fully that their concepts are at best approximations of an absolute; but it does seem persuasive that, since all three schemata have basic features in common, there is a truth linking all the approximations that has not yet been fully defined. (To the synthesis could have been added the hygienic and motivational factors of Frederick Herzberg, the moral psychology of John Dewey, and the developmental stage approach of Jean Piaget.)

Implications for Communication in Organizations

It is clear, then, that when John speaks to Harry or Harry communicates with Mabel each individual initiates and responds to the communication from his or her own developmental stage. This is as true within an organization as it is outside it. If John, the chief librarian, speaks to Harry, the reference librarian, out of a need for self-esteem, using the parental mode ("You know, Harry, this has been discussed, and we have decided that the reference department *always* asks for too much money."), Harry can only respond in the child-to-parent mode ("Of course, John, whatever you say.") unless he wishes to cross the transaction. What this mode does to Harry's ego needs (which are just as strong as John's) can be readily appreciated. Harry, like all the other Harrys working for John, can only play the child with his "superiors" and play the parent with his "subordinates" or leave the organization.

Harry's communication matrix is, by extension, therefore, the matrix for the whole organization to which he belongs. The pattern "John ⟶ Harry ⟶ Mabel" becomes "top management ⟶ middle management ⟶ workers." If John, lacking the ability to self-actualize and to place the highest value upon human equality and dignity, establishes himself as the parent-figure at the hierarchical apex, then the organization he (consciously or unconsciously) creates will be a parent-child organization, lacking in all its parts the ability for sixth-level conceptualization or for the satisfaction of the belonging and esteem needs of its members. Just as individuals represent stages and levels of development, from "childish" needs for security and ego-centered reassurance to "adult" self-confidence, self-fulfillment, and untrammeled self-awareness, so too can organizations be represented in terms of the same stages. Similarly, just as many individuals fail to develop through the full growth range from "child" to "adult," so too may many organizations become frozen or static before they "grow up."[17]

Not all of us, of course, possess the innate ability to develop. Nor does every organization need "grown-ups." If the objectives of an organization are such that the tasks it requires are routine and undemanding, the organization needs employees who can self-actualize through routines and whose cognitive levels are at the rules-and-regulations stage. Such employees may well work best under "parental" supervision and within a communication pattern that reinforces a parentlike/childlike relationship.

Nor should we assume that "higher" levels such as those represented by self-actualization, adult-adult transactions, and fifth- and sixth-level cognition are necessarily concomitant only with "higher education" or "high intelligence quotients." Persons with "subnormal" intelligence may self-actualize if the challenges they face are appropriate to their levels of intelligence. Certainly communication transactions may be successful as long as both sender and receiver accept the nature of the transaction. (A parentlike sender can communicate quite adequately with a childlike receiver as long as both accept their own and the other's role.) Similarly, a person at the third level of cognitive development will get along perfectly well with another at the third level, although not with one at the first or fifth levels. Organizational breakdown will not occur, in other words, as long as the tasks and communication channels are matched to the psychological levels of the personnel involved.

This last point is particularly important. Not only is the "psycho-organization" that has been discussed of great interest to us; so is the communication structure involved. The type of communication structure that is dominant in an organization does much to determine not only the adequacy with which a task is performed but also the attitudes of those involved in performing it. Simple tasks appear to require one type of structure. By extension, that type of structure best suits lower-level psychological profiles. Complex tasks require a different type of structure. This structure may facilitate higher-level psychological development.

The Communication Researchers

Communication researchers such as Alex Bavelas, H. J. Leavitt, and M. E. Shaw have been attempting for some time to analyze the effects upon task accomplishment of different patterns of organized communication.[18] Their findings implicate, as we have noted, both the structure of the communication channels and the nature of the task to be accomplished. At the very considerable risk of oversimplifying the complex results of their studies, we may say they have identified four basic network patterns: the wheel, the chain, the circle, and the all-points ("star" or "each-to-all") patterns.[19]

In the wheel pattern, there is a hub-person; other members of the group are stationed where each spoke of the wheel joins the rim. This is considered the most structured and hierarchical pattern, for each member on the rim can communicate only with the hub and no one else. The members on the rim are equal to each other in terms of communication, but clearly are much more restricted than is the central or hub-person.

In the chain pattern, two or more members serve as end-persons, each communicating with one other person but not with each other, and the middle persons pass the information to a single "apex" who makes decisions and sends them back through the middle or relay persons to the end-persons. This is regarded as the next most structured pattern.

The circle, in which every member has equal communication opportunities since each can communicate with the group member to his left or right, is regarded as less structured than the wheel and chain. Each person can, in fact, become a decision-making centre, and the network becomes a circuit rather than a relay.

The all-points pattern places no communication restrictions on any member and may be thought of as the circle with all points joined. It is the least structured and least hierarchical of the four. (See figure 1.)

The writer has worked with library school students, using the two extreme patterns—the wheel and the all-points. His findings have substantiated those derived by Bavelas and Leavitt from the wheel and the circle.

The subjects' perceptions of their roles in the group (e.g., hub, peripheral, or equal) bring about specific behaviours, regardless of whether the implications of their roles are explained beforehand or not. Those in the most limited positions soon sense that they are, in fact, subordinates, serving only to pass on information and

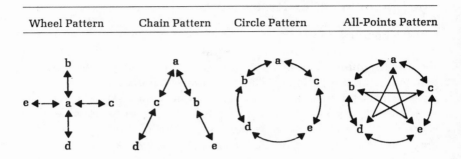

FIGURE 1. Patterns of communication

to wait passively for an answer. They evidence dissatisfaction with their roles and accept answers uncritically without attempting to correct errors. Errors are not caught as quickly in the wheel pattern, because only one person has all the information, and the others do not have enough information to correct errors. The all-points pattern uses more transactions than the wheel. Greater participation involves more meetings; but, although more errors are made in the all-points pattern than in the star, a greater percentage of those errors is corrected than in any other pattern. The position of leader rotates in the wheel, depending on the personalities and expertise evidenced at any given time. In the wheel, the leadership obviously is vested permanently in the hub. All-points members enjoy their roles more than members of the wheel; but perhaps surprisingly, all-points members feel less satisfied with their own performances than members of the wheel. All-points members, indeed, report a constant desire to improve their organization by stabilizing it.[20] The work by Bavelas (and the writer) involved a simple problem, but Marvin Shaw has set up an experiment that supports the hypothesis that the circle will require less time than the wheel to solve a relatively complex problem.[21]

Implications for Organizational Development

The implications of the above research for organizational development seem clear. The transition from the wheel or chain pattern to an organization hierarchy may be readily shown. Similarly, the transition from an all-points pattern to a collegial task group requires only the designation of one member of the group as the link (chairperson). The impact of the schemata of Maslow, Harris, and Kohlberg on communication patterns and therefore on organizational development also seems clear. For example, all-points communication based upon expertise depends on and can develop mutual esteem and self-confidence (self-actualization?). In contrast, the wheel pattern deprives peripheral members of satisfaction of belonging and, hence, of esteem. To a demonstrable degree, adultlike attitudes on the part of one communicator will attract adultlike responses, but the positional equality inherent in the all-points pattern renders such attitudes more probable than does the hub-centered wheel.

The Psycho-Organizational Fit

We may now conclude from the preceding discussion that simple, task-oriented objectives are compatible with the "low" end of Kohlberg's cognitive scale, with the parent-child interchange in Harris's transactions and with the lower levels of Maslow's need satisfaction. Complex objectives, requiring judgment and expertise, seem more compatible with the "higher" range of levels and interrelationships. This is not to say, be it carefully noted, that one type of objective is inherently better than the other. Each type has its place, and for each type there is an "ideal" (and desirable) pattern of behaviour. The purpose of psycho-organizational analysis is not to entertain value or moral judgments but to categorize the objectives and their ensuing tasks and to choose the appropriate behaviour patterns.

The proper "fit" between organizational objectives and behaviour patterns of relevant personnel is crucial to honest communication and participative management. No organization can develop much beyond the cognitive levels of its members. In the first place, as Kohlberg makes clear, effective communication itself tends to break down if either the sender (e.g., senior management) or the receiver (e.g., the worker) is more than one cognitive stage removed from the other. In the second place, as Maslow has noted, under "normal" circumstances an individual will not aspire to a need level higher than that which has not been sufficiently satisfied.

The chief librarian who would encourage self-actualization among his staff must, therefore, first remove any fears that free expression may result in demotion or that dissent may bring ostracism. Finally, as we have already noted, a good match between objectives and behaviour patterns is critical because "high" levels of behaviour can be as detrimental to an organization as "low" levels if the level and the task are mismatched. For example, an organization committed to routine tasks that attempts to staff itself with individuals possessing the highest education and intellect is asking for neuroses, frustration, and communication breakdown. On the other hand, the organization whose objectives demand highly complex judgments and decisions is unlikely to succeed utilizing "low level" (in the psychological sense) personnel.

Figure 2 is a graphic representation of the desirable fit between objectives and behaviour patterns. In the schemata, the distinction between objectives involving repetitive routines and those requiring judgment and initiative leads to both similarities and differences between the "ideal," "acceptable," and the "dysfunctional" elements. Many of the elements in each are the same, but the differences are important. In general, it may be said that task-oriented objectives can be met by lower levels of psychological development, although the "ideal" configuration for both task-oriented objectives and complex objectives remains virtually the same. Keeping in mind the distinction between education and intelligence on the one hand and basic psychological factors on the other, the

	Simple, Task-Oriented Objectives	Complex Objectives Requiring Judgment and Expertise
"Ideal" Pattern	Kohlberg's Stages 4 & 5 Harris's adult/adult Maslow's self-actualization all-points communication	Kohlberg's Stages 5 & 6 Harris's adult/adult Maslow's self-actualization all-points communication
Acceptable Pattern	Kohlberg's Stages 3 & 4 Harris's parent/child Maslow's belonging level chain communication	Kohlberg's Stages 4 & 5 Harris's adult/adult Maslow's esteem level all-points communication
Dysfunctional Pattern	Kohlberg's Stages 1 & 2 Harris's parent/adult Maslow's security level wheel communication	Kohlberg's Stages 2 & 3 Harris's parent/adult or parent/parent Maslow's belonging level wheel communication

FIGURE 2. Types of objectives and patterns of behaviour

most effective personnel in either case will be those individuals who are most free to communicate as self-fulfilled equals possessing a gestalt view of the relevant universe. However, the *acceptable* level of psychological development differs considerably for the two types of objectives, and the minimal dysfunctional pattern for the achieving of complex objectives is at a generally higher level than that for achieving routine objectives. It is not enough, in other words, for individuals who must make expert judgments and decide between complex alternatives to engage in parent/parent communication transactions or strive merely to "belong" to their organization; whereas, for task-oriented objectives, a parent/parent pattern, though less than acceptable, is not dysfunctional.

We increasingly have distinguished in this paper between "task-oriented objectives" and "objectives requiring judgment and expertise." An example of the former might be to maintain catalogue-card production at its present rate through the next three years. An example of the latter might be to coordinate the library's access tools with the information needs of a given clientele. The two types of objectives may be said to differ in the degree of "inspiration" they require, and "inspiration" is composed of approximately equal parts of self-actualized brainstorming, "adult" critique, and logical comprehensiveness. Task-oriented objectives also differ from judgment-based objectives. The former can be met within the confines of administrative authority, since the tasks can be codified within existing rules and regulations, and the approval of a superior is immediately applicable. Judgment-based objectives require professional authority, since their achievement depends not upon rules but upon the expertise and judgmental abilities of the individual concerned. Where there are both types of objectives, an organization normally subordinates the professional authority to the administrative and becomes a "semiprofessional organization."

The term "semiprofessional organization" has been used perhaps most notably by Amitai Etzioni in his classic study, *Modern Organizations.*[22] With this, we add the "pinch of management theory" promised at the beginning of this paper. By doing so, we hope to add the final stretch on the tour that has taken us from levels of cognition and transactional analysis through patterns of communication and types of objectives to Etzioni's concern for management structure.

Amitai Etzioni is no collegialist. He accepts the belief that administration "assumes a power hierarchy" but distinguishes between "the principle of control and coordination by superiors—

i.e., the principle of administrative authority" and the principle that accepts expertise as the justification for individual action within the organization.

> . . . The ultimate justification for a professional act is that it is, to the best of the professional's knowledge, the right act. He might consult his colleagues before he acts, but the decision is his. If he errs he will be defended by his peers. The ultimate justification of an administrative act, however, is that it is in line with the organization's rules and regulations, and that it has been approved—directly or indirectly—by a superior rank.[23]

Thus, Etzioni adds to our equation the concept of a professional act versus an administrative act. It would seem that his concept of a professional act corresponds closely to the pattern of behaviour that fits the complex objective and the all-points communication pattern. Conversely, the administrative act fits the routine objective and the wheel communication pattern.

Again, let it be stressed that neither pattern is inherently better than the other. Each has its place, but the places differ, *and the difference depends on the type of objectives specified for the organization.* Indeed, in context, the very meaning of the phrase "better organization" connotes optimized effectiveness in terms of objectives and the nullifying of dysfunctional operational elements.

Application to Libraries

How then to develop "better" libraries? If one accepts the schemata above as accurate, then their implications for libraries are considerable. Libraries, perhaps more than most organizations, have failed to define objectives and to match tasks to behaviour patterns.

Clearly (and tritely), libraries must first define their objectives vis-à-vis societal expectations. Secondly, the objectives as defined must be separated into those that generate repetitive routines and those that demand constant initiative and judgment. Assuming that there are objectives in each category, the schema for matching types of objectives to patterns of behaviour becomes applicable. Thus, on the basis of the indicated match, relevant personnel characteristics and organizational communication patterns are derived. Take, for example, the instance previously cited, in which a routine objective was to maintain catalogue-card production: A series of parent/child transactions, based upon a "benevolently despotic" wheel or chain pattern and catering to needs up to the "esteem" level, might appear to be the perimeters for the appropriate library organization. Such perimeters are based not upon value or moral judgments but upon an appropriate match. Insofar as persons with "subnormal" intelligence could self-actualize in the above organization while achieving institutional objectives, their being preferred over those with "higher" intelligence would be justified. The opposite would, of course, be true if the library's objective was seen to be judgmental and initiatory. In either case, the appropriate communication pattern would almost certainly have to be modified by the application of such a "linking" schema as Rensis Likert's supportive relationships[24] or Edward Howard's orbital organization[25] in order to accommodate different groups with different types of objectives within a single organization.

The modern library is clearly not a homogeneous organization, either in terms of its objectives, the demands it makes upon its personnel, or the mental sets it requires to achieve its goals. Why, therefore, attempt to impose a single authority structure, a single communication pattern, or a single personnel policy throughout a library? Why not instead let those parts of the library that develop complex objectives be organized along highly participative (if not collegial) lines involving an all-points communication pattern and striving towards adult/adult transactions based upon conceptions of individual "professional" conscience derived from logical comprehensiveness and universality? On the other hand, let those parts of the library that develop routine, task-oriented objectives requiring adherence to regulations and subordination to administrative authority be more structured, with chain communication regarded as acceptable, with Kohlberg's conventional stages regarded as entirely acceptable, and with conventional parent/child transactions not regarded as dysfunctional.

Above all, let those of us who are responsible for the development of libraries learn to recognize and apply the psychological principles underlying effective organizational structure so that we can select or foster the most appropriate communication patterns and personality characteristics for the objectives we expect to achieve.

Additional Readings

General Discussions

Communication serves as the linking function in the management process. Since, in many ways, the "business" of the library is communication, readers have a double need to understand this important management function. In-depth views of the various elements of communication, as it relates to the management process, are usually found in business and public administration literature, with literally hundreds of journal articles, books, and reports on managerial communication. Two of the most useful sources available for the reader interested in the process and problems of managerial communication are Huseman, Logue, and Freshley's *Readings in Interpersonal and Organizational Communication* (3rd ed., Holbrook Press, 1977) and Lewis's *Organizational Communication: The Essence of Effective Management* (Grid, 1975).

While a number of excellent sources are concerned with communication as a library function, few deal with the communication process as it relates to the *management of the library itself*. Emery's *Staff Communication in Libraries* (Linnet Books, 1975), Palmer and Cassata's *Reader in Library Communication* (Information Handling Services, 1976), which contains excellent selections on personal, small group, and organizational communication, and articles by Arthur and Fallis ("Communication: A Vital Link in Management," *Focus*, Summer 1973), Reid ("Staff Communication," *Catholic Library World*, October 1976), Emery ("Staff Communications: A Necessary Activity," *Library World*, December 1970), Carlson ("Communication Is Tougher Than You Think," *Catholic Library World*, March 1979), Kirby ("Staff Communication," *New Library World*, June 1978) and Durey ("Communication," in *Staff Management in University and College Libraries*, Pergamon Press, 1976) provide a general overview of communication in the library management setting. In addition, Euster's *Changing Patterns in Internal Communication in Large Academic Libraries* (Association of Research Libraries, Occasional Paper No. 6, 1981) analyzes the ways in which libraries have studied their communication needs and implemented changes as a result.

There are many models of the communication process. A number of these, however, have limited usefulness as a means of understanding the role of communication in the management process because they are too general. The development of a conceptual model of the *managerial* communication process is discussed by Herbert in "Toward an Administrative Model of the Communication Process" (*Journal of Business Communication*, Summer 1977). Herbert's expansion of the traditional information-based communication model offers a realistic means of observing results of communication attempts in a managerial framework. Because an important function of organizational communication is to "provide information where it is needed,"[1] it is critical to examine communication from an information-task viewpoint. Poole ("An Information-Task Approach to Organizational Communication," *Academy of Management Review*, July 1978) presents a framework for examining the process of creating and utilizing communication channels with organizational work units so that the information task of the organization may be carried out.

Lewis also expands a general communication model to include the managerial perspective in *Organizational Communication* (Grid, 1975); Huseman and Alexander explore this managerial dimension in "Communication and the Managerial Function: A Contingency Approach" (*Readings in Organizational Behavior: Dimensions of Management Action*, Allyn & Bacon, 1979), offering a contingency model that suggests that "the manager's attention should move from one type of communication mode to another as the organizational environment (technology) changes."[2]

Interpersonal Communication

Particular elements of the communication function can also be examined in further detail through the literature. These include the interpersonal dimension of organizational communication, the directions of communication flows (upward, downward, horizontal), the influence of informal processes (i.e., the "grapevine"), and the solution of communication problems. In *Interpersonal Communication in Organizations* (Holbrook Press, 1976), Huseman, Lahiff, and Hatfield use a perceptual approach to delineate the role of individuals in the organizational communication process. Their chapter on "Nonverbal Communication," and Hayes' original essay on "Nonverbal Communication: Expression without Words" (*Readings in Interpersonal and Organizational Communication*, 2nd ed., Holbrook Press, 1973) provide a well-organized, reasoned view of this important aspect of the communication process that has unfortunately become overly diluted through the popular literature.

Message Diffusion

The method of message diffusion in organizations is outlined in Goldhaber's chapter on "Communication Variables in Organizations" (*Organizational Communication*, William C. Brown Publishers, 1974). Melcher and Beller outline a theory of channel selection that is useful in analyzing managerial communication practices ("Toward a Theory of Organization Communication: Consideration in Channel Selection," *Academy of Management Journal*, March 1967). Channel management is also discussed by Lambert and Armitage in "An Information System for Effective Channel Management" (*MSU Business Topics*, Autumn 1979). Harriman describes the upward-downward elements of organizational communication, using the framework of a structured upward communication program in a particular organization ("Up and Down the Communications Ladder," *Harvard Business Review*, September-October 1974). Chase and Gemmill also suggest approaches to upward-downward communication in "How to Make Downward Communication Work" (*Personnel Journal*, June 1970) and "Managing Upward Communication" (*Personnel Journal*, February 1980). Finally, Davis describes the "informal" organization, better known as the "grapevine," and its influences on communication in "The Organization That's Not on the Chart" (*Readings in Interpersonal and Organizational Communication*, 2nd ed., Holbrook Press, 1973). Additional discussions of this vital communication flow can be found in Emery's "The Library Grapevine" (*Assistant Librarian*, January 1971) and Davis's "The Care and Cultivation of the Corporate Grapevine" (*Dun's Magazine*, July 1973).

The structure of the organization can influence and be influenced by communication. Hage, Aiken, and Marrett identify these relationships in "Organization Structure and Communication" (*American Sociological Review*, October 1971). A view of the library as part of the communication structure of the larger organization is presented by Howard's "Innovation in University

Organization: The Communication Model" (*Journal of Academic Librarianship*, May 1980). Changing events in the organizational environment may also influence communication, as seen in Robb's "Changing Loyalties: Effects of Unionization on Communication Patterns in Libraries" (*Canadian Library Journal*, October 1975).

Group Dynamics

Specific communication practices have a strong impact on the outcome of the management process. These include small group dynamics and meeting organization and implementation. The work group is a particular focus of communication activity in most organizations, including the library. Donnelly et al. outline the characteristics of the work group in *Fundamentals of Management* (revised ed., Business Publications, 1976). Huseman discusses specific communications problems in groups in chapters 8 and 9 of *Interpersonal Communication in Organizations* (Holbrook Press, 1976). The committee is often an important library group in terms of communication, and Tarr focuses on this kind of small group setting in "Effective Group Process for Libraries: A Focus on Committees" (*College and Research Libraries,* November 1974). Meetings are often an important communication device in the small group setting, as well as in the larger organization. The value of meetings and their use as a communication device are topics explored by Spaulding ("Undiscovered Values in Meetings," *Journal of Systems Management,* June 1978) and Larson ("The Behavioral Side of Productive Meetings," *Personnel Journal*, April 1980). Suggestions for planning and carrying out effective meetings are provided in "Conducting a Successful Meeting" (McDougle, *Personnel Journal*, January 1981).

Communication Problems

Communication problems can occur at all levels of the organization and for a variety of reasons. Rogers and Roethlisberger's classic article, "Barriers and Gateways to Communication" (*Harvard Business Review*, July-August 1952) illustrates some of the important human communication problems and possible solutions in a work context. Kilcoski also identifies ways of solving communication problems in "Communication: Understanding It, Improving It" (*Personnel Journal*, February 1980). Other approaches to improving the communication function may be found in Samaras' "Two-Way Communication Practices for Managers" (*Personnel Journal*, August 1980), Penley and Hawkins's "Communicating for Improved Motivation and Performance" (*SAM Advanced Management Journal*, Spring 1980), and Kellogg's *Talking with Employees: A Guide for Managers* (Gulf, 1979).

Conflict Resolution and Management

As demonstrated in selection 16, conflict is an ever-present feature of organizational life. Much of this conflict is generated through the communication process. Any reader who wishes to understand the management process fully must therefore develop a clear view of the nature and causes of organizational conflict and methods of management or resolution. Conflict within the library organization is not often discussed in library literature—two exceptions are Bundy's "Conflict in Libraries" (*College and Research Libraries*, July 1966) and Runyon's "Power and Conflict in Academic Libraries" (*Journal of Academic Librarianship*, September 1977). Huseman reviews the characteristics of conflict in the organizational setting, methods of conflict resolution, and role of communication in resolution in "Interpersonal Conflict in the Modern Organization" (an original essay for Huseman, Logue, and Freshley, *Readings in Interpersonal and Organizational Communication*, 3rd ed., Holbrook Press, 1977). In the same volume, Alexander also examines the relationship between communication and conflict by reviewing research on "The Effect of Communication on Conflict Resolution." As an introduction to the Winter 1978 issue of the *California Management Review*, which focuses on conflict in organizations, Filley outlines "Some Normative Issues in Conflict Management"; like Huseman's analysis of interpersonal conflict, a discussion of perception and of problem-solving as an alternative to power-oriented methods of resolving conflicts are included. Brown's *Managing Conflict at Organizational Interfaces* (Addison-Wesley, 1982) explores different relationships—between departments, levels, cultural groups, or even organizations—and presents strategies for managing conflicts in these situations.

Other approaches to conflict resolution included in *Readings in Interpersonal and Organizational Communication* are Burke's "Methods of Resolving Superior-Subordinate Conflict" and Filley's "Conflict Resolution: The Ethic of a Good Loser." Smyth ("The Sources and Resolution of Conflict in Management," *Per-*

sonnel Journal, May 1977) and Labovitz ("Managing Conflict," *Business Horizons*, June 1980) explore these issues as well. Murray, Von Der Embse, and Waggener look at one particular kind of conflict in "Evaluating Disagreement in Committee Action" (*University of Michigan Business Review*, May 1976). Finally, in a thought-provoking essay, Robbins explores the value of conflict to an organization in " 'Conflict Management' and 'Conflict Resolution' Are Not Synonymous Terms" (*California Management Review*, Winter 1978). This author suggests that conflict has value to an organization as a means of fostering a responsive and innovative environment. Some organizations, then, may have levels of conflict that are too low and require stimulation, methods of which are suggested by Robbins. Kelly has also taken this positive approach in "Make Conflict Work for You" (*Harvard Business Review*, July-August 1970).

Evaluation

Like all of the other functions in the library management process, organizational communication should be evaluated through some control mechanism. The execution of such an "audit" or evaluation of communication is outlined by Greenbaum ("The Audit of Organizational Communication" in *Readings in Interpersonal and Organizational Communication*, 3rd ed., Holbrook Press, 1977), who provides the reader with a detailed conceptual and methodological structure for examining the communication processes in the organization. A second introduction to this kind of evaluation, although less detailed, is Gildea and Rosenberg's "Auditing Organizational Communications: Is There Life beyond Print-Outs?" (*University of Michigan Business Review*, July 1979), which offers a sample survey approach. Through these kinds of evaluation, the interrelationship of the functions in the management process is illustrated clearly, and control becomes a part of communication just as communication is essential to the control function.

Staffing

The achievement of every library's objectives is largely dependent on the effective use of its human resources. Because libraries *are* so dependent on people, staffing is a vital part of the process of library management. "Staffing" is not, however, just another term for employment. Rather, it is an integrated management function designed to move personnel "into, through, and eventually out of an organization," matching "skills available with the tasks to be performed."[1] Components of the staffing function include manpower planning, job design, recruitment and selection, as well as placement and orientation of employees. Motivation, training, and development of personnel already on the job, appraisal of performance, and deselection are also parts of the staffing function. Often organizational design is closely associated with staffing as well. The overarching concept of human resources planning links all of these components together and provides a bridge between organizational and individual concerns inherent in the staffing function.

The reading selections in this chapter have been chosen because they assess major components of the staffing function and at the same time illustrate the integrated nature of these components. All of the authors emphasize that the manager must not only consider the needs and goals of the library in developing a sound staffing program, but must also address individual needs and concerns. A positive work climate, a good organizational "fit" for prospective employees, means for development and growth, and an equitable system of appraisal are all devices to enhance employee commitment. Taken together, then, these selections demonstrate that one cannot isolate the components of the staffing function from one another nor consider them only in the organizational context. They must instead be considered as a whole, influencing and being influenced by one another.

What holds all of the components together and keeps staffing from becoming a synonym for "employment" is the concept of human resources planning (HRP). By outlining each of the elements of HRP, Edgar Schein provides the reader with a framework within which to view the other selections in this chapter. His "developmental model of human resources planning and development," in particular, serves the reader as a comprehensive guide to formulate an understanding of the integration of individual and organizational needs in each component area of staffing.

Job design is a vital element in the staffing function—one often overlooked by library managers. Rather than simply reviewing the content of a job at the point of selection, job design efforts maintain a continuing review of organizational task requirements and employee needs, both present and projected. Shaughnessy not only outlines specific steps in the job design process but stresses the need for management to design jobs that reflect both human values and technological change in libraries. This emphasis on human values in turn leads the reader to the Nadler and Lawler selection on "Motivation: A Diagnostic Approach." Surveying the range of motivational theories and practices available to managers, Nadler and Lawler maintain that a new approach, based on "expectancy" theory, represents the most useful tool for understanding motivation in an organizational context because it integrates both individual and organizational goals and values. In outlining the theory and its elements, the authors suggest important implications for applying the theory in organizations.

Nowhere is the importance of a direct link in staffing components better illustrated in the library context than in Berkner's article, "Library Staff Development through Performance Appraisal." In outlining the elements of development and appraisal and describing their connectedness, the author suggests that performance appraisal be used not only as a means of evaluating employees, but also as an integral tool to be utilized in staff development, counseling, and career planning aspects of staffing.

Berkner has carefully chosen examples that draw together both management theory and library practice. The author's emphasis on the library as an interactive system also highlights the theme of integration prevalent in all selections in this chapter. Finally, Berkner's article allows the reader to see the end result of the staffing process as a cycle completed through the appraisal of employee performance on the job.

18. Increasing Organizational Effectiveness through Better Human Resource Planning and Development

Edgar H. Schein

Introduction

In this article I would like to address two basic *questions. First,* why is human resource planning and development becoming increasingly important as a determinant of organizational effectiveness? *Second,* what are the major *components* of a human resource planning and career development system, and how should these components be *linked* for maximum organizational effectiveness?

Much of the research on which this paper is based was done under the sponsorship of the Group Psychology Branch of the Office of Naval Research. Their generous support has made continuing work in this area possible. I would also like to thank my colleagues Lotte Bailyn and John Van Maanen for many of the ideas expressed in this paper.

The field of personnel management has for some time addressed issues such as these and much of the technology of planning for and managing human resources has been worked out to a considerable degree.[1] Nevertheless there continues to be in organizations a failure, particularly on the part of line managers and functional managers in areas other than personnel, to recognize the true importance of planning for and managing human resources. This paper is not intended to be a review of what is known but rather a kind of position paper for line managers to bring to their attention some important and all too often neglected issue. These issues are important for organizational *effectiveness*, quite apart from their relevance to the issue of humanizing work or improving the quality of working life.[2]

The observations and analyses made below are based on several kinds of information:

1. Formal research on management development, career development, and human development through the adult life cycle conducted in the Sloan School and at other places for the past several decades;[3]
2. Analysis of consulting relationships, field observations, and other involvements over the past several decades with all kinds of organizations dealing with the planning for and implementation of human resource development programs and organization development projects.[4]

Why Is Human Resource Planning and Development (HRPD) Increasingly Important?

The Changing Managerial Job

The first answer to the question is simple, though paradoxical. Organizations are becoming more dependent upon people because they are increasingly involved in more complex technologies and are attempting to function in more complex economic, political, and sociocultural environments. The more different technical skills there are involved in the design, manufacture, marketing, and sales of a product, the more vulnerable the organization will be to critical shortages of the right kinds of human resources. The more complex the process, the higher the interdependence among the various specialists. The higher the interdependence, the greater the need for effective integration of all the specialities because the entire process is only as strong as its weakest link.

In simpler technologies, managers could often compensate for the technical or communication failures of their subordinates. General managers today are much more dependent upon their technically trained subordinates because they usually do not understand the details of the engineering, marketing, financial, and other decisions which their subordinates are making. Even the general manager who grew up in finance may find that since his day the field of finance has outrun him and his subordinates are using models and methods which he cannot entirely understand.

What all this means for the general manager is that he cannot any longer safely make decisions by himself; he cannot get enough information digested within his own head to be the integrator and decision maker. Instead, he finds himself increasingly having to manage the *process* of decision-making, bringing the right people together around the right questions or problems, stimulating open discussion, insuring that all relevant information surfaces and is critically assessed, managing the emotional ups and downs of his prima donnas, and insuring that out of all this human and interpersonal process, a good decision will result.

As I have watched processes like these in management groups, I am struck by the fact that *the decision emerges out of the interplay*. It is hard to pin down who had the idea and who made the decision. The general manager in this setting is *accountable* for the decision, but rarely would I describe the process as one where he or she actually makes the decision, except in the sense of recognizing when the right answer has been achieved, ratifying that answer, announcing it, and following up on its implementation.

If the managerial *job* is increasingly moving in the direction I have indicated, managers of the future will have to be much more skilled in how to:

1. Select and train their subordinates,
2. Design and run meetings and groups of all sorts,
3. Deal with all kinds of conflict between strong individuals and groups,
4. Influence and negotiate from a low power base, and
5. Integrate the efforts of very diverse technical specialists.

If the above image of what is happening to organizations has any generality, it will force the field of human resource management increasingly to center stage. The more complex organizations become, the more they will be vulnerable to human error. They will not necessarily employ more people, but they will employ more sophisticated highly trained people both in managerial and in individual contributor, staff roles. The price of low motivation, turnover, poor productivity, sabotage, and intraorganizational conflict will be higher in such an organization. Therefore it will become a matter of *economic necessity* to improve human resource planning and development systems.

Changing Social Values

A second reason why human resource planning and development will become more central and important is that changing social values regarding the role of work will make it *more complicated to manage people*. There are several kinds of research findings and observations which illustrate this point.

First, my own longitudinal research of a panel of Sloan School graduates of the 1960s strongly suggests that we have put much too much emphasis on the traditional success syndrome of "climbing the corporate ladder."[5] Some alumni indeed want to rise to high-level general manager positions, but many others want to exercise their particular technical or functional competence and only rise to levels of functional management or senior staff roles with minimal managerial responsibility. Some want security, others are seeking nonorganizational careers as teachers or consultants, while a few are becoming entrepreneurs. I have called these patterns of motivation, talent, and values "career anchors" and believe that they serve to stabilize and constrain the career in predictable ways. The implication is obvious—organizations must develop multiple ladders and multiple reward systems to deal with different types of people.[6]

Second, studies of young people entering organizations in the last several decades suggest that work and career are not as central a life preoccupation as was once the case. Perhaps because of a prolonged period of economic affluence, people see more options for themselves and are increasingly exercising those options. In particular, one sees more concern with a balanced life in which work, family, and self-development play a more equal role.[7]

Third, closely linked to the above trend is the increase in the number of women in organizations, which will have its major impact through the increase of dual career families. As opportunities for women open up, we will see more new life-styles in young couples which will affect the organization's options as to moving people geographically, joint employment, joint career management, family support, etc.[8]

Fourth, research evidence is beginning to accumulate that personal growth and development is a life-long process and that predictable issues and crises come up in every decade of our lives. Organizations will have to be much more aware of what these issues are, how work and family interact, and how to manage people at different ages. The current "hot button" is *mid-career crisis,* but the more research we do the more we find developmental crises at *all* ages and stages.[9]

An excellent summary of what is happening in the world of values, technology, and management is provided in a recent text by Elmer Burack:

The leading edge of change in the future will include the new technologies of information, production, and management, interlaced with considerable social dislocation and shifts in manpower inputs. These developments are without precedent in our industrial history.

Technological and social changes have created a need for more education, training, and skill at all managerial and support levels. The lowering of barriers to employment based on sex and race introduces new kinds of manpower problems for management officials. Seniority is coming to mean relatively less in relation to the comprehension of problems, processes, and approaches. The newer manpower elements and work technologies have shifted institutional arrangements: the locus of decision-making is altered, role relationships among workers and supervisors are changed (often becoming more collegial), and the need to respond to changing routines has become commonplace. . . .

These shifts have been supported by more demanding customer requirements, increasing government surveillance (from product quality to antipollution measures), and more widespread use of computers, shifting power bases to the holders of specialized knowledge skills.[10]

In order for HRPD systems to become more responsive and capable of handling such growing complexity they must contain all the necessary components, must be based on correct assumptions, and must be adequately integrated.

Components of a Human Resource Planning and Development System

The major problem with existing HRPD systems is that they are fragmented, incomplete, and sometimes built on faulty assumptions about human or organizational growth.

Human growth takes place through successive encounters with one's environment. As the person encounters a new situation, he or she is forced to try new responses to deal with that situation. Learning takes place as a function of how those responses work out and the results they achieve. If they are successful in coping with the situation, the person enlarges his repertory of responses; if they are not successful the person must try alternate responses until the situation has been dealt with. If none of the active coping responses work, the person sometimes falls back on retreating from the new situation, or denying that there is a problem to be solved. These responses are defensive and growth limiting.

The implication is that for growth to occur, people basically need two things: *new challenges* that are within the range of their coping responses, and *knowledge of results,* information on how their responses to the challenge have worked out. If the tasks and challenges are too easy or too hard, the person will be demotivated and cease to grow. If the information is not available on how well the person's responses are working, the person cannot grow in a systematic, valid direction but is forced into guessing or trying to infer information from ambiguous signals.

Organizational growth similarly takes place through successful coping with the internal and external environment.[11] But since the organization is a complex system of human, material, financial, and informational resources, one must consider how each of those areas can be properly managed toward organizational effectiveness. In this article I will only deal with the human resources.

In order for the organization to have the capacity to perform effectively over a period of time it must be able to plan for, recruit, manage, develop, measure, dispose of, and replace human resources as warranted by the tasks to be done. The most important of these functions is the *planning* function, since task requirements are likely to change as the complexity and turbulence of the organization's environment increase. In other words, a key assumption underlying organizational growth is that the nature of jobs will change over time, which means that such changes must be continuously monitored in order to insure that the right kinds of human resources can be recruited or developed to do those jobs. Many of the activities such as recruitment, selection, performance appraisal, and so on presume that some planning process has occurred which makes it possible to assess whether or not those activities are meeting *organizational needs,* quite apart from whether they are facilitating the individual's growth.

In an ideal HRPD system one would seek to match the organization's needs for human resources with the individual's needs for personal career growth and development. One can then depict the basic system as involving both individual and organizational planning, and a series of matching activities which are designed to facilitate mutual need satisfaction. If we further assume that both individual and organizational needs change over time, we can depict this process as a developmental one as in figure 1.

In the right-hand column we show the basic stages of the individual career through the life cycle. While not everyone will go through these stages in the manner depicted, there is growing evidence that for organizational careers in particular, these stages reasonably depict the movement of people through their adult lives.[12]

Given those developmental assumptions, the left-hand side of the diagram shows the organizational planning activities which must occur if human resources are to be managed in an optimal way, and if changing job requirements are to be properly assessed and continuously monitored. The middle column shows the various matching activities which have to occur at various career stages.

The components of an effective HRPD system now can be derived from the diagram. First, there have to be in the organization the overall planning components shown on the left-hand side of figure 1. Second, there have to be components which insure an adequate process of staffing the organization. Third, there have to be components which plan for and monitor growth and development. Fourth, there have to be components which facilitate the actual process of the growth and development of the people who are brought into the organization; this growth and development must be organized to meet both the needs of the organization and the needs of the individuals within it. Fifth, there have to be components which deal with decreasing effectiveness, leveling off, obsolescence of skills, turnover, retirement, and other phenomena which reflect the need for either a new growth direction or a process of disengagement of the person from his or her job. Finally, there have to be components which insure that as some people move out of jobs, others are available to fill those jobs, and as new jobs arise that people are available with the requisite skills to fill them.

In the remainder of this article I would like to comment on each of these six sets of components and indicate where and how they should be linked to each other.

Overall Planning Components

The function of these components is to insure that the organization has an adequate basis for selecting its human resources and developing them toward the fulfillment of organizational goals.

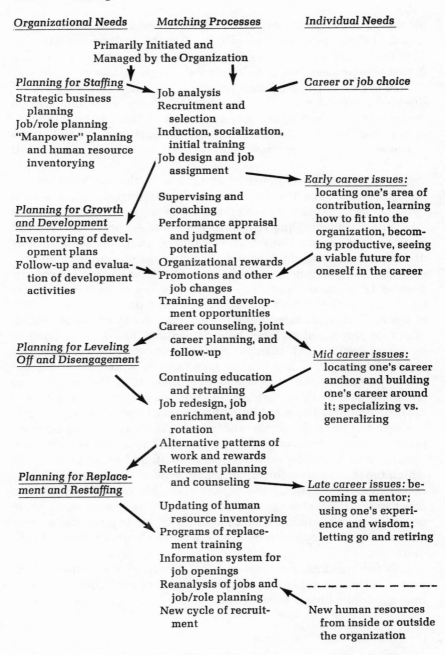

FIGURE 1. A developmental model of human resource planning
and development

Strategic Business Planning. These activities are designed to determine the organization's goals, priorities, future directions, products, markets growth rate, geographical location, and organization structure or design. This process should lead logically into the next two planning activities but is often disconnected from them because it is located in a different part of the organization or is staffed by people with different orientations and backgrounds.

Job/Role Planning. These activities are designed to determine what actually needs to be done at every level of the organization (up through top management) to fulfill the organization's goals and tasks. This activity can be thought of as a dynamic kind of job analysis where a continual review is made of the skills, knowledge, values, etc., which are presently needed in the organization *and will be needed in the future.* The focus is on the predictable consequences of the strategic planning for managerial roles, specialist roles, and skill mixes which may be needed to get the mission accomplished. If the organization already has a satisfactory system of job descriptions, this activity would concern itself with how those jobs will evolve and change, and what new jobs or roles will evolve in the future.[13]

This component is often missing completely in organizations or is carried out only for lower level jobs. From a planning point of view it is probably most important for the highest level jobs—how the nature of general and functional management will change as the organization faces new technologies, new social values, and new environmental conditions.

"Manpower Planning" and Human Resource Inventorying. These activities draw on the job/role descriptions generated in job/role planning and assess the capabilities of the present human resources against those plans or requirements. These activities may be focused on the numbers of people in given categories and are often designed to insure that under given assumptions of growth there will be an adequate supply of people in those categories. Or the process may focus more on how to insure that certain scarce skills which will be needed will in fact be available, leading to more sophisticated programs of recruitment or human resource development. For example, the inventorying process at high levels may reveal the need for a new type of general manager with broad integrative capacities which may further reveal the need to start a development program that will insure that such managers will be available five to ten years down the road.

These first three component activities are all geared to identifying the *organization's* needs in the human resource area. They are difficult to do and tools are only now beginning to be developed for job/role planning.[14] In most organizations I have dealt with, the three areas, if they exist at all, are not linked to each other organizationally. Strategic planning is likely to exist in the office of the president. Job/role planning is likely to be an offshoot of some management development activities in personnel. And human resource inventorying is likely to be a specialized subsection within personnel. Typically, no one is accountable for bringing these activities together even on an ad hoc basis.

This situation reflects an erroneous assumption about growth and development which I want to mention at this time. The assumption is that if the organization develops its *present* human resources, it will be able to fill whatever job demands may arise in the future. Thus we do find in organizations elaborate human resource planning systems, but they plan for the present people in the organization, not for the organization per se. If there are no major changes in job requirements as the organization grows and develops, this system will work. But if jobs themselves change, it is no longer safe to assume that today's human resources, with development plans based on *today's* job requirements, will produce the people needed in some future situation. Therefore, I am asserting that more job/role planning must be done, independent of the present people in the organization.

The subsequent components to be discussed which focus on the matching of individual and organizational needs all assume that some sort of basic planning activities such as those described have been carried out. They may not be very formal, or they may be highly decentralized (e.g., every supervisor who has an open slot might make his own decision of what sort of person to hire based on his private assumptions about strategic business planning and job/role planning). Obviously, the more turbulent the environment, the greater the vulnerability of the organization if it does not centralize and coordinate its various planning activities, and generate its HRPD system from those plans.

Staffing Processes

The function of these processes is to insure that the organization acquires the human resources necessary to fulfill its goals.

Job Analysis. If the organizational planning has been done adequately, the next component of the HRPD system is to actually specify what jobs need to be filled and what skills, etc. are needed to do those jobs. Some organizations go through this process very formally, others do it in an informal unprogrammed manner, but in some form it must occur in order to specify what kind of recruitment to do and how to select people from among the recruits.

Recruitment and Selection. This activity involves the actual process of going out to find people to fulfill jobs and developing systems for deciding which of those people to hire. These components may be very formal including testing, assessment, and other aids to the selection process. If this component is seen as part of a total HRPD system, it will alert management to the fact that the recruitment selection system communicates to future employees something about the nature of the organization and its approach to people. All too often this component sends incorrect messages or turns off future employees or builds incorrect stereotypes which make subsequent supervision more difficult.[15]

Induction, Socialization, and Initial Training. Once the employee has been hired, there ensues a period during which he or she learns the ropes, learns how to get along in the organization, how to work, how to fit in, how to master the particulars of the job, and so on. Once again, it is important that the activities which make up this component are seen as part of a total process with long-range consequences for the attitudes of the employee.[16] The goal of these processes should be to facilitate the employees becoming productive and useful members of the organization both in the short run and in terms of long-range potential.

Job Design and Job Assignment. One of the most crucial components of staffing is the actual design of the job which is given to the new employee and the manner in which the assignment is actually made. The issue is how to provide *optimal challenge*, a set of activities which will be neither too hard nor too easy for the new employee, and which will be neither too meaningless nor too risky from the point of view of the organization. If the job is too easy or too meaningless, the employee may become demotivated; if the job is too hard and/or involves too much responsibility and risk from the point of view of the organization, the employee will become too anxious, frustrated, or angry to perform at an optimal level. Some organizations have set up training programs for supervisors to help them to design optimally challenging work assignments.[17]

These four components are geared to insuring that the work of the organization will be performed. They tend to be processes that have to be performed by line managers and personnel staff specialists together. Line managers have the basic information about jobs and skill requirements; personnel specialists have the interviewing, recruiting, and assessment skills to aid in the selection process. In an optimal system these functions will be closely coordinated, particularly to insure that the recruiting process provides to the employee accurate information about the nature of the organization and the actual work that he or she will be doing in it. Recruiters also need good information on the long-range human resource plans so that these can be taken into account in the selection of new employees.

Development Planning

It is not enough to get good human resources in the door. Some planning activities have to concern themselves with how employees who may be spending thirty to forty years of their total life in a given organization will make a contribution for all of that time, will remain motivated and productive, and will maintain a reasonable level of job satisfaction.

Inventorying of Development Plans. Whether or not the process is highly formalized, there is in most organizations some effort to plan for the growth and development of all employees. The planning component that is often missing is some kind of pulling together of this information into a centralized inventory that permits coordination and evaluation of the development activities. Individual supervisors may have clear ideas of what they will do with and for their subordinates, but this information may never be collected, making it impossible to determine whether the individual plans of supervisors are connected in any way. Whether it is done by department, division, or total company, some effort to collect such information and to think through its implications would be of great value to furthering the total development of employees at all levels.

Follow-up and Evaluation of Development Activities. I have observed two symptoms of insufficient planning in this area—one, development plans are made for individual employees, are written down, but are never implemented, and two, if they are implemented they are never evaluated either in relation to the individual's own needs for growth or in relation to the organization's needs for new skills. Some system should exist to insure that plans are implemented and that activities are evaluated against both individual and organizational goals.

Career Development Processes

This label is deliberately broad to cover all of the major processes of managing human resources during their period of growth and peak productivity, a period which may be several decades in length. These processes must match the organization's needs for work with the individual's needs for a productive and satisfying work career. The system must provide for some kind of forward movement for the employee through some succession of jobs, whether these involve promotion, lateral movement to new functions, or simply new assignments within a given area.[18] The system must be based both on the organization's need to fill jobs as they open up and on employees' needs to have some sense of progress in their working lives.

Supervision and Coaching. By far the most important component in this area is the actual process of supervising, guiding, coaching, and monitoring. It is in this context that the work assignment and feedback processes which make learning possible occur, and it is the boss who plays the key role in molding the employee to the organization. There is considerable evidence that the first boss is especially crucial in giving new employees a good start in their career,[19] and that training of supervisors in how to handle new employees is a valuable organizational investment.

Performance Appraisal and Judgment of Potential. This component is part of the general process of supervision but stands out as such an important part of that process that it must be treated separately. In most organizations there is some effort to standardize and formalize a process of appraisal above and beyond the normal performance feedback which is expected on a day-to-day basis. Such systems serve a number of functions—to justify salary increases, promotions, and other formal organizational actions with respect to the employee; to provide information for human resource inventories or at least written records of past accomplishments for the employee's personnel folder; and to provide a basis for annual or semiannual formal reviews between boss and subordinate to supplement day-to-day feedback and to facilitate information exchange for career planning and counseling. In some organizations so little day-to-day feedback occurs that the *formal* system bears the burden of providing the employees with knowledge of how they are doing and what they can look forward to. Since knowledge of results, of how one is doing, is a crucial component of any developmental process, it is important for organizations to monitor how well and how frequently feedback is actually given.

One of the major dilemmas in this area is whether to have a single system which provides both feedback for the growth and development of the employee and information for the organization's planning systems. The dilemma arises because the information which the planning system requires (e.g., "how much potential does this employee have to rise in the organization?") may be the kind of information which neither the boss nor the planner wants to share with the employee. The more potent and more accurate the information, the less likely it is to be fed back to the employee in anything other than very vague terms.

On the other hand, the detailed work-oriented, day-to-day feedback which the employee needs for growth and development may be too cumbersome to record as part of a selection-oriented appraisal system. If hundreds of employees are to be compared, there is strong pressure in the system toward more general kinds of judgments, traits, rankings, numerical estimates of ultimate potential, and the like. One way of resolving this dilemma which some companies have found successful is to develop two separate systems—one oriented toward performance improvement and the growth of the employee, and the other one oriented toward a more global assessment of the employee for future planning purposes involving judgments which may not be shared with the employee except in general terms.

A second dilemma arises around the identification of the employee's "development needs" and how that information is linked to other development activities. If the development needs are stated in relation to the planning system, the employee may never get the feedback of what his needs may have been perceived to be, and, worse, no one may implement any program to deal with those needs if the planning system is not well linked with line management.

Two further problems arise from this potential lack of linkage. One, if the individual does not get good feedback around developmental needs, he or she remains uninvolved in their own development and potentially becomes complacent. We pay lip service to the statement that only the individual can develop himself or herself, but then deprive the individual of the very information that would make sensible self-development possible. Two, the development needs as stated for the various employees in the organization may have nothing to do with the organization's needs for certain kinds of human resources in the future. All too often there is complete lack of linkage between the strategic or business planning function and the human resource development function resulting in potentially willy-nilly individual development based on today's needs and individual managers' stereotypes of what will be needed in the future.

Organizational Rewards—Pay, Benefits, Perquisites, Promotion, and Recognition. Entire books have been written about all

the problems and subleties of how to link organizational rewards to the other components of a HRPD system to insure both
short-run and long-run human effectiveness. For purposes of this
short paper I wish to point out only one major issue—how to
insure that organizational rewards are linked *both* to the needs
of the individual and to the needs of the organization for effective
performance and development of potential. All too often the reward
system is neither responsive to the individual employee nor to the
organization, being driven more by criteria of elegance, consistency, and what other organizations are doing. If the linkage is to
be established, line managers must actively work with compensation experts to develop a joint philosophy and set of goals based
on an understanding of both what the organization is trying to
reward and what employee needs actually are. As organizational
careers become more varied and as social values surrounding work
change, reward systems will probably have to become much more
flexible both in time (people at different career stages may need
different things) and by type of career (functional specialists may
need different things than general managers).

Promotions and Other Job Changes. There is ample evidence
that what keeps human growth and effectiveness going is continuing optimal challenge.[20] Such challenge can be provided for
some members of the organization through promotion to higher
levels where more responsible jobs are available. For most members of the organization the promotion opportunities are limited,
however, because the pyramid narrows at the top. An effective
HRPD system will, therefore, concentrate on developing career
paths, systems of job rotation, changing assignments, temporary
assignments, and other lateral job moves which insure continuing
growth of all human resources.

One of the key characteristics of an optimally challenging
job is that it both draws on the person's abilities and skills and
that it has opportunities for "closure." The employee must be in
the job long enough to get involved and to see the results of his
or her efforts. Systems of rotation which move the person too
rapidly either prevent initial involvement (as in the rotational
training program), or prevent closure by transferring the person
to a new job before the effects of his or her decisions can be
assessed. I have heard many "fast track" executives complain
that their self-confidence was low because they never really could
see the results of their efforts. Too often we move people too fast
in order to "fill slots" and thereby undermine their development.

Organizational planning systems which generate "slots" to be
filled must be coordinated with development planning systems

which concern themselves with the optimal growth of the human resources. Sometimes it is better for the organization in the long run not to fill an empty slot in order to keep a manager in another job where he or she is just beginning to develop. One way of insuring such linkage is to monitor these processes by means of a "development committee" which is composed of both line managers and personnel specialists. In such a group the needs of the organization and the needs of the people can be balanced against each other in the context of the long-range goals of the organization.

Training and Development Opportunities. Most organizations recognize that periods of formal training, sabbaticals, executive development programs outside of the company, and other educational activities are necessary in the total process of human growth and development. The important point about these activities is that they should be carefully linked both to the needs of the individual and to the needs of the organization. The individual should want to go to the program because he or she can see how the educational activity fits into the total career. The organization should send the person because the training fits into some concept of future career development. It should not be undertaken simply as a generalized "good thing," or because other companies are doing it. As much as possible the training and educational activities should be tied to job/role planning. For example, many companies began to use university executive development programs because of an explicit recognition that future managers would require a broader perspective on various problems and that such "broadening" could best be achieved in the university programs.

Career Counseling, Joint Career Planning, Follow-up, and Evaluation. Inasmuch as the growth and development which may be desired can only come from within the individual himself or herself, it is important that the organization provide some means for individual employees at all levels to become more proactive about their careers and some mechanisms for joint dialogue, counseling, and career planning.[21] This process should ideally be linked to performance appraisal, because it is in that context that the boss can review with the subordinate the future potential, development needs, strengths, weaknesses, career options, etc. The boss is often not trained in counseling but does possess some of the key information which the employee needs to initiate any kind of career planning. More formal counseling could then be supplied by the personnel development staff or outside the organization altogether.

The important point to recognize is that employees cannot

manage their own growth development without information on how their own needs, talents, values, and plans mesh with the opportunity structure of the organization. Even though the organization may only have imperfect, uncertain information about the future, the individual is better off to know that than to make erroneous assumptions about the future based on no information at all. It is true that the organization cannot make commitments, nor should it unless required to by legislation or contract. But the sharing of information if properly done is not the same as making commitments or setting up false expectations.

If the organization can open up the communication channel between employees, their bosses, and whoever is managing the human resource system, the groundwork is laid for realistic individual development planning. Whatever is decided about training, next steps, special assignments, rotation, etc., should be jointly decided by the individual and the appropriate organizational resource (probably the supervisor and someone from personnel specializing in career development). Each step must fit into the employee's life plan and must be tied into *organizational needs*. The organization should be neither a humanistic charity nor an indoctrination center. Instead, it should be a vehicle for meeting both the needs of society and of individuals.

Whatever is decided should not merely be written down but executed. If there are implementation problems, the development plan should be renegotiated. Whatever developmental actions are taken, it is essential that they be followed up and evaluated both by the person and by the organization to determine what, if anything, was achieved. It is shocking to discover how many companies invest in major activities such as university executive development programs and never determine for themselves what was accomplished. In some instances, they make no plans to talk to the individual before or after the program so that it is not even possible to determine what the activity meant to the participant, or what might be an appropriate next assignment for him or her following the program.

I can summarize the above analysis best by emphasizing the two places where I feel there is the most fragmentation and violation of growth assumptions. First, too many of the activities occur without the involvement of the person who is "being developed" and therefore may well end up being self-defeating. This is particularly true of job assignments and performance appraisal where too little involvement and feedback occur. Second, too much of the human resource system functions as a personnel *selection* system unconnected to either the needs of the organization or the needs of the individual. All too often it is only a system for short-run replacement of people in standard type jobs. The key planning functions are not linked in solidly and hence do not influence the system to the degree they should.

Planning for and Managing Disengagement

The planning and management processes which will be briefly reviewed here are counterparts of ones that have already been discussed but are focused on a different problem—the problem of the late career, loss of motivation, obsolescence, and untimely retirement. Organizations must recognize that there are various options available to deal with this range of problems beyond the obvious ones of either terminating the emyloyee or engaging in elaborate measures to "remotivate" people who may have lost work involvement.[22]

Continuing Education and Retraining. These activities have their greatest potential if the employee is motivated and if there is some clear connection between what is to be learned and what the employee's current or future job assignments require in the way of skills. More and more organizations are finding out that it is better to provide challenging work first and only then the training to perform that work once the employee sees the need for it. Obviously for this linkage to work well continuous dialogue is needed between employees and their managers. For those employees who have leveled off, have lost work involvement, but are still doing high quality work other solutions such as those described below are more applicable.

Job Redesign, Job Enrichment, and Job Rotation. This section is an extension of the arguments made earlier on job changes in general applied to the particular problems of leveled off employees. In some recent research, it has been suggested that job enrichment and other efforts to redesign work to increase motivation and performance may only work during the first few years on a job.[23] Beyond that the employee becomes "unresponsive" to the job characteristics themselves and pays more attention to surrounding factors such as the nature of supervision, relationships with co-workers, pay, and other extrinsic characteristics. In other words, before organizations attempt to "cure" leveled off employees by remotivating them through job redesign or rotation, they should examine whether those employees are still in a responsive mode or not. On the other hand, one can argue that there is nothing wrong with less motivated, less involved employees so long as the quality of what they are doing meets the organizational standards.[24]

Alternative Patterns of Work and Rewards. Because of the changing needs and values of employees in recent decades, more and more organizations have begun to experiment with alternative work patterns such as flexible working hours, part-time work, sabbaticals or other longer periods of time off, several people filling one job, dual employment of spouses with more extensive childcare programs, etc. Along with these experiments have come others on flexible reward systems in which employees can choose between a raise, some time off, special retirement, medical, or insurance benefits, and other efforts to make multiple career ladders a viable reality. These programs apply to employees at all career stages but are especially relevant to people in mid and late career stages where their own perception of their career and life goals may be undergoing important changes.

None of these innovations should be attempted without first clearly establishing a HRPD system which takes care of the organization's needs as well as the needs of employees and links them to each other. There can be little growth and development for employees at any level in an *organization* which is sick and stagnant. It is in the best interests of both the individual and the organization to have a healthy organization which can provide opportunities for growth.

Retirement Planning and Counseling. As part of any effective HRPD system, there must be a clear planning function which forecasts who will retire, and which feeds this information into both the replacement staffing system and the counseling functions so that the employees who will be retiring can be prepared for this often traumatic career stage. Employees need counseling not only with the mechanical and financial aspects of retirement, but also to prepare them psychologically for the time when they will no longer have a clear organizational base or job as part of their identity. For some people it may make sense to spread the period of retirement over a number of years by using part-time work or special assignments to help both the individual and the organization to get benefits from this period.

The counseling function here as in other parts of the career probably involves special skills and must be provided by specialists. However, the line manager continues to play a key role as a provider of job challenge, feedback, and information about what is ahead for any given employee. Seminars for line managers on how to handle the special problems of preretirement employees would probably be of great value as part of their managerial training.

Planning for and Managing Replacement and Restaffing

With this step the HRPD cycle closes back upon itself. This function must be concerned with such issues as:

1. Updating the human resource inventory as retirements or terminations occur;
2. Instituting special programs of orientation or training for new incumbents to specific jobs as those jobs open up;
3. Managing the information system on what jobs are available and determining how to match this information to the human resources available in order to determine whether to replace from within the organization or to go outside with a new recruiting program;
4. Continuously reanalyzing jobs to insure that the new incumbent is properly prepared for what the job *now* requires and *will* require in the future.

How these processes are managed links to the other parts of the system through the implicit messages that are sent to employees. For example, a company which decides to publicly post all of its unfilled jobs is clearly sending a message that it expects internal recruitment and supports self-development activities. A company which manages restaffing in a very secret manner may well get across a message that employees might as well be complacent and passive about their careers because they cannot influence them anyway.

Summary and Conclusions

I have tried to argue in this article that human resource planning and development is becoming an increasingly important function in organizations, that this function consists of multiple components, and that these components must be managed *both* by line managers and staff specialists. I have tried to show that the various planning activities are closely linked to the actual processes of supervision, job assignment, training, etc., and that those processes must be designed to match the needs of the organization with the needs of the employees throughout their evolving careers, whether or not those careers involve hierarchical promotions. I have also argued that the various components are linked to each other and must be seen as a total system if it is to be effective. The total system must be managed as a system to insure coordination between the planning functions and implementation functions.

I hope it is clear from what has been said above that an effective human resource planning and development system is integral to the functioning of the organization and must, therefore, be a central concern of line management. Many of the activities require specialist help, but the accountabilities must rest squarely with line supervisors and top management. It is they who control the opportunities and the rewards. It is the job assignment system and the feedback which employees get that is the ultimate raw material for growth and development. Whoever designs and manages the system, it will not help the organization to become more effective unless that system is *owned* by line management.

Additional References

Bennis, W. G. *Organization Development: Its Nature, Origins, and Prospects.* Reading, Mass.: Addison-Wesley, 1969.
Van Maanen, John, ed. *Organizational Careers: Some New Perspectives.* New York: Wiley, 1977.

19. Redesigning Library Jobs

Thomas W. Shaughnessy

Over the past few years, there have been a number of experiments conducted to humanize work, to make it more satisfying, and to improve worker efficiency and productivity.[1] Frequently these studies are undertaken in response to a problem such as employee alienation and dissatisfaction, absenteeism, high rate of turnover, and frequency of errors or defects in products. It has

Reprinted from *Journal of the American Society for Information Science* 29:187–90 (July 1978). © 1978 by John Wiley & Sons, Inc. Reprinted by permission of John Wiley & Sons, Inc.

been discovered, however, that these problems, which seem to be more or less present in all organizations, are often symptoms of some deeper issue, one that is related to the very nature of work and its significance or value in modern society. Although our attempts to diagnose the specific factors which cause these problems have been somewhat inconclusive, one remedy which is frequently prescribed is the redesign and enrichment of jobs. In fact, the recently completed report to the Secretary of Health, Education and Welfare entitled *Work in America* states that the redesign of jobs is its key recommendation.[2] The purpose of this paper is to relate the process of job design to library management, and more specifically to the quality of working life in libraries.

The Need for Job Design

Job design is defined as "the specification of the contents, methods, and relationships of jobs in order to satisfy technological and organizational requirements as well as the social and personal requirements of the jobholder."[3] It differs from job description in a number of respects, significant among which are (1) that job design is a continuing organizational process, whereas job description is static and (2) the former is based on environmental, organizational, and individual worker factors, while the latter is essentially task oriented. Furthermore, job design focuses on the means by which work activities are to be combined into tasks, and the combination of related tasks to form jobs.[4]

There are a variety of changes—environmental, social, technological—which have contributed to the need for the redesign of jobs throughout society.[5] Technology may be viewed as an artifact or product, or as a process by which problems are solved, artifacts produced, or transformations brought about. It plays such an important role in one's work that it has the capacity for determining *what* the work is and *how* the individual and the organization of which he is a part should accomplish it.[6]

At the beginning of the Industrial Revolution, the factory system spawned a deterministic technology wherein workers were assembled, assigned to work (usually simple, repetitive jobs), and then closely controlled by supervision and work flow processes.[7] Prior to the Industrial Revolution, the craftsman or artisan controlled, developed, and utilized the various technologies that were extant. Craftsmen were able, within the range of their competence, to determine not only what should be produced, but also determine the raw materials, tools, and techniques to be used.[8] They were, in effect, the producers or procurers of raw materials, tool designers, manufacturers, distributors, and salesmen—functions which today have become very fragmented and even highly specialized. However, the introduction of the factory system and its concomitant scientific analysis of tasks, gradually led to the displacement of the artisan/craftsman.[9] The worker was often viewed as a mere extension of machinery.

The role and function of the individual worker were further reduced with the advent of the assembly line in factories and its resulting emphasis on mass production. More recently, production technologies developed in the chemical, petroleum, and gas industries have continued this trend. Kast and Rosenzweig[10] have suggested that there is a technology continuum, ranging from a relatively stable or uniform technology to dynamic, rapidly changing technology, which is illustrated in figure 1.

Obviously, the role and function of the worker have undergone considerable change over this continuum. Similarly, jobs have had to evolve to keep pace with technological requirements. New jobs and new careers have developed while others gradually

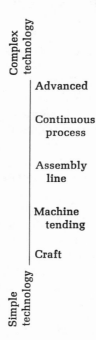

FIGURE 1. Technology continuum

faded. From once having three roles to play in the production of goods, the average worker now has just one, the remaining two having been preempted by machines. His first role as energy supplier is now almost nonexistent in the industrial world. A second role as guider of tools is increasingly being transferred to machines. The third traditional role as controller and monitor of a unit or system is virtually the only one that remains, at least in areas of advanced technology.[11]

Technological change has not only affected the production industries, but the human services and professions as well. It has created specialties within every profession, has modified professional relationships (such as between practitioner and client, and between practitioner and practitioner), and has contributed in some cases to changing the very nature of the profession. For example, sophisticated technology has seen engineering develop from a field which focused on the application of tools and techniques to the actual design of methods and tools. Advances in health care and in the pharmaceutical industries "have helped turn pharmacy practitioners into little more than dispensers of medication—a seemingly routine job."[12]

It is also interesting to note that as specialties develop as a result of technology, there is often a corresponding change in the labor pool. In other words, the characteristics of persons who elect teaching (or librarianship) as a career are probably quite different from those of individuals seeking to become instructional technologists (or information scientists).[13]

The changes discussed above along with the advent of the Post-Industrial Era have brought an extraordinary amount of attention to the significance—social and personal—of one's job and the quality of one's working life. Increasingly, jobs are being viewed not as mere economic activities or adjuncts to one's "real" life, but as being central to the individual's psychological and social well being. Workers at all levels are insisting that the contexts and contents of their jobs be improved. In a word, jobs must be *meaningful*. This has become such an important requirement that even increased leisure time cannot compensate for it.[14]

To the extent that advanced technology has the capacity to absorb many routine, monotonous tasks, it can contribute to the design of more meaningful jobs.[15] It must be recognized, however, that some workers, including professionals, may prefer routine, repetitive work assignments over those which are nonprogrammable and are characterized by decision-making responsibilities.[16] If certain routine, programmable work activities are in fact absorbed by newer technologies, it is quite likely that one of two situations will occur with respect to individual jobs: (1) The worker's role (that is, the set of rules and expectations held by both employee and employer which directs or influences the employee's occupational or "at work" behavior) diminishes or disappears with his job, or he continues working at a "nonjob"; or (2) his role enlarges as his job diminishes.[17] As the worker takes on responsibility for production, quality control, maintenance, and system monitoring, his *role* becomes more complex and demanding as his *job* (which is comprised of a series of discrete tasks) becomes smaller and simpler.[18] In either case, changes in technology by their very nature exert pressures which, sooner or later, modify jobs as well as the structure of the organization. In fact, one writer has suggested that technology is the most important single determinant of what people do at work.[19]

Job Design and the Librarian

For the library professional, the stresses and strains brought about by technological and environmental changes may be particularly disturbing. Some of these have been described by McAnally and Downs[20]: pressure from campus administrators, library staff, faculty, and students coupled with an institutional inability to accommodate to changing conditions.

To the extent that librarianship is a craft technology—one that relies on experience, judgment, and intuition—the more extensive is the impact of technology. To illustrate, there is no doubt that the availability of bibliographic data via computers has affected the jobs of many catalogers. In addition to a reduction in cataloging staff, participation in network cataloging has resulted in some departmental reorganization and in the upgrading of the heretofore routine work done by nonprofessionals.[21] Nor is there doubt as to whether the advent of automated database searching has affected the job of the reference librarian. It is interesting to note, however, that another type of craft position in some libraries—the job of the children's librarian—has been relatively unaffected by changing technology (although there has been considerable change in the market environment for children's library services). This is probably due to the lower priority assigned to this service by the profession, and perhaps by society in general.

The changes discussed above do not at all suggest the demise of the librarian specialist. On the contrary it is quite possible that the *role* of this professional will be enlarged and enhanced as his or her job is redesigned to incorporate changes in library technology. For example, as certain tasks are removed from one's job, responsibilities for staff functions such as coordination and integration of services may be added.

Organizational style and the presence of employee organizations will necessarily modify the redesign process. With regard to the former, some libraries (and individual librarians) appear to be impervious to technological and environmental change. They operate as if libraries were closed systems, insulated from their multiple environments. Others function as open, organic systems which attempt to respond to (and sometimes even anticipate) changing conditions. In regard to library unions, it is perhaps too early to attempt to characterize their posture vis à vis the redesign of jobs. However, there is some evidence that unions tend to be conservative in this area, and may wish to forestall any significant reallocation of tasks, as they have tried to do in the railroad and shipping industries.

Management Theory and Job Design

The concept of job design has been contributed to by a number of theorists. Some of these belong to the methods engineering school of Frederick Taylor; others may be found in the human relations or sociotechnical systems school. Job design which is based more on methods is sometimes called "traditional." Traditionally designed jobs are often characterized by "high specialization, repetitive tasks, short cycle times, low variety and low discretion, and possibly—mechanical pacing."[22] They tend to minimize the dependence of the organization on the individual. In contrast, more recent theories of job design (sometimes referred to as the job enrichment approach) rest largely on the assumption that effective performance and genuine job satisfaction are due to the intrinsic content of the job.[23] In other words, the job itself must provide opportunities for achievement, recognition, responsibility, advancement, and growth. The elements of worker relationships and individual discretion are also held to be very important to the redesign process.[24] Furthermore, enrichment is not to be confused with job enlargement, which consists of merely adding similar elements to the job (job loading), without altering job content.

A number of studies have shown that enrichment has led to reduced absenteeism and turnover, a decrease in worker alienation, and increased job satisfaction.[25]

Some argue, however, that a good deal of job design causes

organizational dysfunction because it is too employee centered, and places far too much emphasis on the human relations school of management and the concept of the employee's need for self-actualization. A more balanced approach is that of Davis who believes that for the redesign process to be effective, it must be job centered.[26] His approach goes beyond the process-centered and worker-centered views and is based on the notion that a job cannot be adequately designed without taking into account all of the essential variables: process or technology, worker, and organization, as well as variables arising from their interaction.[27]

It should be pointed out that the majority of studies conducted in this area focus on blue collar or nonprofessional white collar work. In addition, most of the research has been directed toward business or industry. There appears to be very little analysis of the influence of *professional* job enrichment on productivity or job satisfaction.

It is obviously very difficult to measure accurately productivity or service in the human service professions. So much depends on the quality of the practitioner-client relationship. There is, moreover, some evidence that enrichment may "have an impact on organizational effectiveness criteria that are not reflected by quantity of productivity analyses."[28] Other research has shown that individuals who have a relatively high need for personal growth at work respond more positively to enriched work than people with lower development or growth needs.[29] Apparently the former group places a higher value on the psychic rewards that can be obtained from superior performance on a challenging assignment.[30] But positive employee response may also be due to job-related characteristics which have been built into the redesign or enrichment process. For example, one of the key attributes of redesigned jobs is worker autonomy. According to Eldred Smith, a significant number of professional library functions are "so lacking in autonomy . . . as to qualify far more as bureaucratic rather than professional activity!"[31] It is a measure of autonomy which encourages workers to take on greater responsibility, including functions such as planning and monitoring their own work.[32]

Guidelines for Job Design

The job-design process is both costly and difficult. It requires an ability on the part of management to gain not only the confidence but even the ego involvement of staff. Furthermore, it requires that the redesign be first and foremost a job-centered process, but one that never loses sight of the psychosocial needs of workers and the constraints imposed by technology and the environment. And lastly, it requires that organizations move toward what Likert calls a "System 4" style of management—one which recognizes employees as mature individuals who are capable of self-control and self-direction.[33]

Once the decision to undertake job design has been made, certain guidelines[34] should be observed in the process. First, each job should contain the optimum level of task variety. Redesigned jobs should attempt to keep routineness and monotony to a minimum, for it is the pervasiveness of characteristics such as these that has spawned the so-called blue-collar blahs. In view of the rather large number of routine operations in libraries, it may be inaccurate to limit this phenomenon to just blue-collar workers.

Second, the tasks combined to form the job should entail some degree of skill, care, effort, or knowledge that is worthy of both individual and organizational respect. In addition, the worker should have some discretion or latitude for setting production standards, and should receive feedback on a regular basis concerning the results of his or her efforts.

Third, there should be opportunity for interaction among staff, for a team approach to interlocking or related tasks, and for job rotation, especially if a relatively high degree of stress is associated with the job.

Fourth, a meaningful pattern of tasks should be designed so as to give each job the semblance of modular unity. The job-enrichment approach attempts to take a holistic view of work systems. It attempts to integrate fragmented tasks so that jobs result which enable the worker to not only see the finished product, but also take some pride in it. In other words, each job should make, as far as is possible, some perceivable contribution to the social utility of the organization's service or product.

Lastly, job design, once initiated, should become an on-going, continuous process, one which enables the organization to respond to contingencies brought about by turbulent environments, by advancing technology, or by changing worker values or needs.

Conclusion

By drawing upon recent management literature and research, this paper has attempted to relate the concept and practice of job design to libraries. It is based on the assumption that libraries, along with other complex organizations, have been overtaken in large measure by advancing technology, environmental change, and shifts in worker values, and that to the extent this is true the effectiveness of libraries has been diminished. This condition in turn has resulted in other symptoms of organizational malaise. The redesign of library jobs has been proposed as an important strategy for increasing organizational effectiveness while at the same time improving the quality of working life in libraries.

20. Motivation: A Diagnostic Approach

David A. Nadler and Edward E. Lawler III

What makes some people work hard while others do as little as possible? How can I, as a manager, influence the performance of people who work for me? Why do people turn over, show up late to work, and miss work entirely?

These important questions about employees' behavior can only be answered by managers who have a grasp of what motivates people. Specifically, a good understanding of motivation can serve as a valuable tool for *understanding* the causes of behavior in organizations, for *predicting* the effects of any managerial action, and for *directing* behavior so that organizational and individual goals can be achieved.

Existing Approaches

During the past twenty years, managers have been bombarded with a number of different approaches to motivation. The terms

Reprinted from *Perspectives on Behavior in Organizations*, J. R. Hackman, L. W. Porter, and E. E. Lawler, eds. (New York: McGraw-Hill, 1977). © 1977 by David A. Nadler and Edward E. Lawler III. Reprinted by permission.

associated with these approaches are well known—"human relations," "scientific management," "job enrichment," "need hierarchy," "self-actualization," etc. Each of these approaches has something to offer. On the other hand, each of these different approaches also has its problems in both theory and practice. Running through almost all of the approaches with which managers are familiar are a series of implicit but clearly erroneous assumptions.

Assumption 1: All employees are alike. Different theories present different ways of looking at people, but each of them assumes that all employees are basically similar in their makeup: Employees all want economic gains, or all want a pleasant climate, or all aspire to be self-actualizing, etc.

Assumption 2: All situations are alike. Most theories assume that all managerial situations are alike, and that the managerial course of action for motivation (for example, participation, job enlargement, etc.) is applicable in all situations.

Assumption 3: One best way. Out of the other two assumptions there emerges a basic principle that there is "one best way" to motivate employees.

When these "one best way" approaches are tried in the "correct" situation they will work. However, all of them are bound to fail in some situations. They are therefore not adequate managerial tools.

A New Approach

During the past ten years, a great deal of research has been done on a new approach to looking at motivation. This approach, frequently called "expectancy theory," still needs further testing, refining, and extending. However, enough is known that many behavioral scientists have concluded that it represents the most comprehensive, valid, and useful approach to understanding motivation. Further, it is apparent that it is a very useful tool for understanding motivation in organizations.

The theory is based on a number of specific assumptions about the causes of behavior in organizations.

Assumption 1: Behavior is determined by a combination of forces in the individual and forces in the environment. Neither the individual nor the environment alone determines behavior. Individuals come into organizations with certain "psychological baggage." They have past experiences and a developmental history which has given them unique sets of needs, ways of looking at the world, and expectations about how organizations will treat them. These all influence how individuals respond to their work environment. The work environment provides structures (such as a pay system or a supervisor) which influence the behavior of people. Different environments tend to produce different behavior in similar people just as dissimilar people tend to behave differently in similar environments.

Assumption 2: People make decisions about their own behavior in organizations. While there are many constraints on the behavior of individuals in organizations, most of the behavior that is observed is the result of individuals' conscious decisions. These decisions usually fall into two categories. First, individuals make decisions about *membership behavior*—coming to work, staying at work, and in other ways being a member of the organization. Second, individuals make decisions about the amount of *effort* they will direct *towards performing their jobs.* This includes decisions about how hard to work, how much to produce, at what quality, etc.

Assumption 3: Different people have different types of needs, desires and goals. Individuals differ on what kinds of outcomes (or rewards) they desire. These differences are not random; they can be examined systematically by an understanding of the differences in the strength of individuals' needs.

Assumption 4: People make decisions among alternative plans of behavior based on their perceptions (expectancies) of the degree to which a given behavior will lead to desired outcomes. In simple terms, people tend to do those things which they see as leading to outcomes (which can also be called "rewards") they desire and avoid doing those things they see as leading to outcomes that are not desired.

In general, the approach used here views people as having their own needs and mental maps of what the world is like. They use these maps to make decisions about how they will behave, behaving in those ways which their mental maps indicate will lead to outcomes that will satisfy their needs. Therefore, they are inherently neither motivated nor unmotivated; motivation depends on the situation they are in, and how it fits their needs.

The Theory

Based on these general assumptions, expectancy theory states a number of propositions about the process by which people make decisions about their own behavior in organizational settings. While the theory is complex at first view, it is in fact made of a series of fairly straightforward observations about behavior. Three concepts serve as the key building blocks of the theory:

Performance-outcome expectancy. Every behavior has associated with it, in an individual's mind, certain outcomes (rewards or punishments). In other words, the individual believes or expects that if he or she behaves in a certain way, he or she will get certain things.

Examples of expectancies can easily be described. An individual may have an expectancy that if he produces ten units he will receive his normal hourly rate while if he produces fifteen units he will receive his hourly pay rate plus a bonus. Similarly an individual may believe that certain levels of performance will lead to approval or disapproval from members of her work group or from her supervisor. Each performance can be seen as leading to a number of different kinds of outcomes and outcomes can differ in their types.

Valence. Each outcome has a "valence" (value, worth, attractiveness) to a specific individual. Outcomes have different valences for different individuals. This comes about because valences result from individual needs and perceptions, which differ because they in turn reflect other factors in the individual's life.

For example, some individuals may value an opportunity for promotion or advancement because of their needs for achievement or power, while others may not want to be promoted and leave their current work group because of needs for affiliation with others. Similarly, a fringe benefit such as a pension plan may have great valence for an older worker but little valence for a young employee on his first job.

Effort-performance expectancy. Each behavior also has associated with it in the individual's mind a certain expectancy or probability of success. This expectancy represents the individual's perception of how hard it will be to achieve such behavior and the probability of his or her successful achievement of that behavior.

For example, you may have a strong expectancy that if you put forth the effort, you can produce ten units an hour, but that you have only a fifty-fifty chance of producing fifteen units an hour if you try.

Putting these concepts together, it is possible to make a basic statement about motivation. In general, the motivation to attempt to behave in a certain way is greatest when:

1. The individual believes that the behavior will lead to outcomes (performance-outcome expectancy)
2. The individual believes that these outcomes have positive value for him or her (valance)
3. The individual believes that he or she is able to perform at the desired level (effort-performance expectancy)

Given a number of alternative levels of behavior (ten, fifteen, and twenty units of production per hour, for example) the individual will choose that level of performance which has the greatest motivational force associated with it, as indicated by the expectancies, outcomes, and valences.

In other words, when faced with choices about behavior, the individual goes through a process of considering questions such as, "Can I perform at that level if I try?" "If I perform at that level, what will happen?" "How do I feel about those things that will happen?" The individual then decides to behave in that way which seems to have the best chance of producing positive, desired outcomes.

A General Model

On the basis of these concepts, it is possible to construct a general model of behavior in organizational settings (see figure 1). Working from left to right in the model, motivation is seen as the force on the individual to expend effort. Motivation leads to an observed level of effort by the individual. Effort, alone, however, is not enough. Performance results from a combination of the effort that an individual puts forth *and* the level of ability which he or she has (reflecting skills, training, information, etc.). Effort thus combines with ability to produce a given level of performance. As a result of performance, the individual attains certain outcomes. The model indicates this relationship in a dotted line, reflecting the fact that sometimes people perform but do not get desired outcomes. As this process of performance-reward occurs, time after time, the actual events serve to provide information which influences the individual's perceptions (particularly expectancies) and thus influences motivation in the future.

Outcomes, or rewards, fall into two major categories. First, the individual obtains outcomes from the environment. When an individual performs at a given level he or she can receive positive or negative outcomes from supervisors, coworkers, the organization's rewards systems, or other sources. These environmental rewards

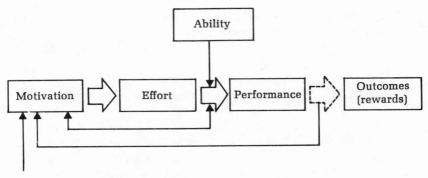

A person's motivation is a function of:

a. Effort-to-performance expectancies
b. Performance-to-outcome expectancies
c. Perceived valence of outcomes

FIGURE 1. The basic motivation-behavior sequence

are thus one source of outcomes for the individual. A second source of outcomes is the individual. These include outcomes which occur purely from the performance of the task itself (feelings of accomplishment, personal worth, achievement, etc.). In a sense, the individual gives these rewards to himself or herself. The environment cannot give them or take them away directly; it can only make them possible.

Supporting Evidence

Over fifty studies have been done to test the validity of the expectancy-theory approach to predicting employee behavior.[1] Almost without exception, the studies have confirmed the predictions of the theory. As the theory predicts, the best performers in organizations tend to see a strong relationship between performing their jobs well and receiving rewards they value. In addition they have clear performance goals and feel they can perform well. Similarly, studies using the expectancy theory to predict how people choose jobs also show that individuals tend to interview for and actually take those jobs which they feel will provide the rewards they value. One study, for example, was able to correctly predict for 80 percent of the people studied which of several jobs they would take.[2] Finally, the theory correctly predicts that beliefs about the outcomes associated with performance (expectancies) will be better predictors of performance than will feelings of job satisfaction since expectancies are the critical causes of performance and satisfaction is not.

Questions about the Model

Although the results so far have been encouraging, they also indicate some problems with the model. These problems do not critically affect the managerial implications of the model, but they should be noted. The model is based on the assumption that individuals make very rational decisions after a thorough exploration of all the available alternatives and on weighing the possible outcomes of all these alternatives. When we talk to or observe individuals, however, we find that their decision processes are frequently less thorough. People often stop considering alternative behavior plans when they find one that is at least moderately satisfying, even though more rewarding plans remain to be examined.

People are also limited in the amount of information they can handle at one time, and therefore the model may indicate a process that is much more complex than the one that actually takes place. On the other hand, the model does provide enough information and is consistent enough with reality to present some clear implications for managers who are concerned with the question of how to motivate the people who work for them.

Implications for Managers

The first set of implications is directed toward the individual manager who has a group of people working for him or her and is concerned with how to motivate good performance. Since behavior is a result of forces both in the person and in the environment, you as manager need to look at and diagnose both the person and the environment. Specifically, you need to do the following:

Figure out what outcomes each employee values. As a first step, it is important to determine what kinds of outcomes or rewards have valence for your employees. For each employee you need to determine "what turns him or her on." There are various ways of finding this out, including (1) finding out employees' desires through some structured method of data collection, such as a questionnaire, (2) observing the employees' reactions to different situations or rewards, or (3) the fairly simple act of asking them what kinds of rewards they want, what kinds of career goals they have, or "what's in it for them." It is important to stress here that it is very difficult to change what people want, but fairly easy to find out what they want. Thus, the skillful manager emphasizes diagnosis of needs, not changing the individuals themselves.

Determine what kinds of behavior you desire. Managers frequently talk about "good performance" without really defining what good performance is. An important step in motivating is for you yourself to figure out what kinds of performances are required and what are adequate measures or indicators of performance (quantity, quality, etc.). There is also a need to be able to define those performances in fairly specific terms so that observable and measurable behavior can be defined and subordinates can understand what is desired of them (e.g., produce ten products of a certain quality standard—rather than only produce at a higher rate).

Make sure desired levels of performance are reachable. The model states that motivation is determined not only by the performance-to-outcome expectancy, but also by the effort-to-performance expectancy. The implication of this is that the levels of performance which are set as the points at which individuals receive desired outcomes must be reachable or attainable by these individuals. If the employees feel that the level of performance required to get a reward is higher than they can reasonably achieve, then their motivation to perform well will be relatively low.

Link desired outcomes to desired performances. The next step is to directly, clearly, and explicitly link those outcomes desired by employees to the specific performances desired by you. If your employee values external rewards, then the emphasis should be on the rewards systems concerned with promotion, pay, and approval. While the linking of these rewards can be initiated through your making statements to your employees, it is extremely important that employees see a clear example of the reward process working in a fairly short period of time if the motivating "expectancies" are to be created in the employees' minds. The linking must be done by some concrete public acts, in addition to statements of intent.

If your employee values internal rewards (e.g., achievement), then you should concentrate on changing the nature of the person's job, for he or she is likely to respond well to such things as increased autonomy, feedback, and challenge, because these things will lead to a situation where good job performance is inherently rewarding. The best way to check on the adequacy of the internal and external reward system is to ask people what their perceptions of the situation are. Remember it is the perceptions of people that determine their motivation, not reality. It doesn't matter for example whether you feel a subordinate's pay is related to his or her motivation. Motivation will be present only if the subordinate sees the relationship. Many managers are misled about the behavior of their subordinates because they rely on their own perceptions of the situation and forget to find out what their subordinates feel. There is only one way to do this: ask. Questionnaires can be used here, as can personal interviews.

Analyze the total situation for conflicting expectancies. Having set up positive expectancies for employees, you then need to look at the entire situation to see if other factors (informal work groups, other managers, the organization's reward systems) have set up conflicting expectancies in the minds of the employees. Motivation will only be high when people see a number of rewards associated with good performance and few negative outcomes. Again, you can often gather this kind of information by asking your subordinates. If there are major conflicts, you need to make adjustments, either in your own performance and reward structure, or in the other sources of rewards or punishments in the environment.

Make sure changes in outcomes are large enough. In examining the motivational system, it is important to make sure that changes in outcomes or rewards are large enough to motivate significant behavior. Trivial rewards will result in trivial amounts of effort and thus trivial improvements in performance. Rewards must be large enough to motivate individuals to put forth the effort required to bring about significant changes in performance.

Check the system for its equity. The model is based on the idea that individuals are different and therefore different rewards will need to be used to motivate different individuals. On the other hand, for a motivational system to work it must be a fair one—one that has equity (not equality). Good performers should see that they get more desired rewards than do poor performers, and others in the system should see that also. Equity should not be confused with a system of equality where all are rewarded equally, with no regard to their performance. A system of equality is guaranteed to produce low motivation.

Implications for Organizations

Expectancy theory has some clear messages for those who run large organizations. It suggests how organizational structures can be designed so that they increase rather than decrease levels of motivation of organization members. While there are many different implications, a few of the major ones are as follows:

Implication 1: The design of pay and reward systems. Organizations usually get what they reward, not what they want. This can be seen in many situations, and pay systems are a good example.[3] Frequently, organizations reward people for membership (through pay tied to seniority, for example) rather than for performance. Little wonder that what the organization gets is behavior oriented towards "safe," secure employment rather than effort directed at performing well. In addition, even where organizations do pay for performance as a motivational device, they frequently negate the motivational value of the system by keeping pay secret, therefore preventing people from observing the pay-to-perform-ance relationship that would serve to create positive, clear, and strong performance-to-reward expectancies. The implication is that organizations should put more effort into rewarding people (through pay, promotion, better job opportunities, etc.) for the per-formances which are desired, and that to keep these rewards secret is clearly self-defeating. In addition, it underscores the importance of the frequently ignored performance evaluation or appraisal process and the need to evaluate people based on how they per-form clearly defined specific behaviors, rather than on how they score on ratings of general traits such as "honesty," "cleanliness," and other, similar terms which frequently appear as part of the performance appraisal form.

Implication 2: The design of tasks, jobs, and roles. One source of desired outcomes is the work itself. The expectancy-theory model supports much of the job enrichment literature, in saying that by designing jobs which enable people to get their needs ful-filled, organizations can bring about higher levels of motivation.[4] The major difference between the traditional approaches to job enlargement or enrichment and the expectancy-theory approach is the recognition by the expectancy theory that different people have different needs and, therefore, some people may not want enlarged or enriched jobs. Thus, while the design of tasks that have more autonomy, variety, feedback, meaningfulness, etc., will lead to higher motivation in some, the organization needs to build in the opportunity for individuals to make choices about the kind of work they will do so that not everyone is forced to experience job enrichment.

Implication 3: The importance of group structures. Groups, both formal and informal, are powerful and potent sources of de-sired outcomes for individuals. Groups can provide or withhold acceptance, approval, affection, skill training, needed information, assistance, etc. They are a powerful force in the total motivational environment of individuals. Several implications emerge from the importance of groups. First, organizations should consider the structuring of at least a portion of rewards around group perform-ance rather than individual performance. This is particularly im-portant where group members have to cooperate with each other to produce a group product or service, and where the individual's contribution is often hard to determine. Second, the organization needs to train managers to be aware of how groups can influence individual behavior and to be sensitive to the kinds of expectancies which informal groups set up and their conflict or consistency with the expectancies that the organization attempts to create.

Implication 4: The supervisor's role. The immediate supervisor has an important role in creating, monitoring, and maintaining the expectancies and reward structures which will lead to good performance. The supervisor's role in the motivation process becomes one of defining clear goals, setting clear reward expectancies, and providing the right rewards for different people (which could include both organizational rewards and personal rewards such as recognition, approval, or support from the supervisor). Thus, organizations need to provide supervisors with an awareness of the nature of motivation as well as the tools (control over organizational rewards, skill in administering those rewards) to create positive motivation.

Implication 5: Measuring motivation. If things like expectancies, the nature of the job, supervisor-controlled outcomes, satisfaction, etc., are important in understanding how well people are being motivated, then organizations need to monitor employee perceptions along these lines. One relatively cheap and reliable method of doing this is through standardized employee questionnaires. A number of organizations already use such techniques, surveying employees' perceptions and attitudes at regular intervals (ranging from once a month to once every year-and-a-half) using either standardized surveys or surveys developed specifically for the organization. Such information is useful both to the individual manager and to top management in assessing the state of human resources and the effectiveness of the organization's motivational systems.[5]

Implication 6: Individualizing organizations. Expectancy theory leads to a final general implication about a possible future direction for the design of organizations. Because different people have different needs and therefore have different valences, effective motivation must come through the recognition that not all employees are alike and that organizations need to be flexible in order to accommodate individual differences. This implies the "building in" of choice for employees in many areas, such as reward systems, fringe benefits, job assignments, etc., where employees previously have had little say. A successful example of the building in of such choice can be seen in the experiments at TRW and the Educational Testing Service with "cafeteria fringe-benefits plans" which allow employees to choose the fringe benefits they want, rather than taking the expensive and often unwanted benefits which the company frequently provides to everyone.[6]

Summary

Expectancy theory provides a more complex model of man for managers to work with. At the same time, it is a model which holds promise for the more effective motivation of individuals and the more effective design of organizational systems. It implies, however, the need for more exacting and thorough diagnosis by the manager to determine (1) the relevant forces in the individual, and (2) the relevant forces in the environment, both of which combine to motivate different kinds of behavior. Following diagnosis, the model implies a need to act—to develop a system of pay, promotion, job assignments, group structures, supervision, etc.—to bring about effective motivation by providing different outcomes for different individuals.

Performance of individuals is a critical issue in making organizations work effectively. If a manager is to influence work behavior and performance, he or she must have an understanding of motivation and the factors which influence an individual's motivation to come to work, to work hard, and to work well. While simple models offer easy answers, it is the more complex models which seem to offer more promise. Managers can use models (like expectancy theory) to understand the nature of behavior and build more effective organizations.

21. Library Staff Development through Performance Appraisal

Dimity S. Berkner

In an effective academic library the professional staff can be the most valuable resource—more important than any other one component: books, card catalog, documents, etc. A good professional staff is the key to all the rest, providing access to information whether through selection, cataloging, reference, interlibrary loan, or administration of others. Giving the level of service that offers total access to information requires a staff that is well trained, highly motivated, and cooperative; and the encouragement of such a staff has been a continuing goal of administrators.

One method of encouraging higher standards of performance that has been popular for about the last twenty years in business is the use of performance evaluation. A variety of appraisal techniques have been used, ranging from essays to absolute rating scales, forced comparisons, or ranking of employees. (An excellent short summary of standard methods and their applicability was provided by Winston Oberg in 1972.)[1]

Performance appraisal is applied for a variety of goals:

1. To improve performance in the present job.
2. To provide a basis for recommending promotion, salary increases, or dismissal.
3. To give the employee a chance to "know where he or she stands" in the supervisor's estimation.

Reprinted from *College & Research Libraries* 40:335–44 (July 1979).

4. To develop an inventory of human resources for the use of management—a record of the available talents and potential among the present staff.
5. To provide a method of counseling and encouraging staff members to grow and to plan for future development.

As early as 1957, however, Douglas McGregor pointed out the dangers of using the same technique to try to accomplish such diverse goals.[2] The evaluation of a subordinate can force the supervisor into "playing God," judging performance on personality rather than on results, employing subjective standards, demanding that one employee be measured against another in a win-lose situation, and requiring an uncomfortable face-to-face interview in which neither manager nor subordinate is prepared to give or receive criticism.

The problems inherent in traditional appraisal systems are summarized in Marjorie Johnson's 1972 academic library survey,[3] and specific psychological errors to avoid when evaluating an employee are described in the Pennsylvania State University Libraries "Management Guide to Performance Evaluation."[4]

These errors include the "halo effect" (an overall or early impression of the employee that affects the rating of the individual work factors); the "central tendency" error (rating most people toward the middle of any scale); unconscious prejudice or partiality based on race, politics, friendship, etc.; "contrast" error (rating an employee on his or her potential, rather than on actual performance); inappropriate upgrading of all ratings (to compete with what the supervisor thinks that other department heads are doing, to prevent unfavorable reflections on the supervisor's managerial ability, or to avoid any direct confrontation with the employee); as well as many others.

Pizam discussed still another intrinsic error, "social differentiation."[5] It has been found that some appraisers have difficulty in evaluating subordinates objectively simply because they never recognize wide differentiations in behavior and do not use most of the scale in rating their employees. "It appears therefore that the act of appraisal . . . merely expresses the appraiser's differentiating ability or style of rating behavior. . . . Low differentiators tend to ignore or suppress differences, perceiving the universe as more uniform than it really is."[6]

The credibility of traditional performance evaluation programs was further undermined by studies done at the General Electric Company, which concluded:

Criticism has a negative effect on achievement of goals.

Praise [relating to general performance characteristics] has little effect one way or another.

Performance improves most when specific goals are established.

Defensiveness resulting from critical appraisal produces inferior performance.

Coaching should be a day-to-day, not a once-a-year, activity.

Mutual goal setting, not criticism, improves performance.

Interviews designed primarily to improve a man's [sic] performance should not at the same time weigh his salary or promotion in the balance.

Participation by the employee in the goal-setting procedure helps produce favorable results.[7]

As one of the few carefully documented, methodologically acceptable management studies on the effect of criticism and mutual goal setting, the study has provided the rationale for many recent performance appraisal programs—including the one proposed in this paper. The conclusions reached at General Electric support current psychological findings about the use of behavior modification to encourage and reinforce positive behavior while extinguishing negative behavior by, to put it simply, ignoring it.

Management-by-Objectives

An important part of the General Electric study was to confirm what Peter Drucker had presented and McGregor had recommended years earlier: the use of management-by-objectives (MBO) as the basis for professional performance evaluation.[8] This system involves the supervisor and employee in the establishment of priorities and goals, with specific objectives to be accomplished (by a certain date) to further these goals. The evaluative process then becomes an analysis with an emphasis on the future and on the strengths and potential of the employee. It should blunt some of the judgmental aspects of appraisal and promote a better relationship between superior and subordinate.

An article by Thompson and Dalton provides a good defense of the management-by-objectives approach because it is future-oriented rather than focusing on mistakes of the past. It is an open system in which employees are compared with their own objectives rather than on a scale where some must be ranked lower than others, and it is a flexible system that can be tailored to promote the strengths of each individual.[9]

The pendulum has now swung away from the old judgmental ranking scales with their emphasis on "traits" (aspects of personality, which are supposed to have a bearing on job performance, such as "dependability," "initiative," etc.) toward management-by-objectives and/or a discussion of observable behavior only (number of books cataloged, reference questions answered). Sometimes this is supported by the use of techniques such as "critical incidents," where the supervisor records actual occurrences that exemplify positive or negative behavior.

We are beginning to recognize the use of performance appraisal as a tool that can be appropriate for counseling, career planning, and staff development. A summary of recent research into the use of performance appraisal, with suggestions for affecting motivation, is found in Belcher's excellent text *Compensation Administration*.[10]

Performance Appraisal for Staff Development

In 1971 Ernest DeProspo[11] applied Kindall and Gatza's five-step program[12] to libraries in an effort to focus on employee growth through appraisal. This program includes discussions by the individual and the supervisor on job content, setting of performance targets by the employee, review of these with the supervisor, establishment of evaluative checkpoints, and appraisal of results at the end of the time period.

At about the same time Harry Levinson sounded a warning against unqualified use of MBO. Levinson called MBO "one of the greatest management illusions" and recommended that an MBO program include consideration of an individual's motivation and personal goals, avoidance of the static job description, which is so often a basis for the objectives, and the recognition that the way in which an individual goes about achieving these goals can be as important as the goals themselves.[13] He makes a point that is particularly applicable to libraries, since supportive working relationships can do so much to improve service and increase motivation.

Every organization is a social system, a network of interpersonal relationships. A man may do an excellent job by objective standards of measurement, but may fail miserably as a partner, subordinate, superior or colleague.[14]

In the library these interpersonal relationships can be even more important because so many areas of professional librarianship cannot be appropriately measured by objective standards. How does one cope with the colleague in the selection department who refuses to buy interdisciplinary material out of his or her departmental book budget, thus keeping carefully within set financial limits and building a narrow, specialized collection in depth, but ignoring new fields of interest to the students and cross-disciplinary faculty? A straight MBO approach to evaluation is unlikely to reveal or discourage this inadequacy.

Current practice in academic libraries, according to Yarbrough's *ARL Management Supplement*,[15] includes much use of mutual goal setting and evaluation by librarian and supervisor (and often library director), along with or as a substitute for other procedures such as traditional appraisals (in checklist or essay form), peer evaluations (mainly to recommend for or against promotion, tenure, or salary increases), and even appraisal of supervisors by their subordinates.

One of the most innovative and detailed approaches to performance evaluation was developed at McGill University Libraries in cooperation with the ARL Office of University Library Management Studies in 1975.[16] The key to its uniqueness is the focus on supervisory training in motivation, evaluation, and counseling that appear to be essential in developing such a program. It then recommends the setting of unit and individual work goals, followed by semiannual performance reviews. Salary decisions are treated as a separate procedure, although a formal, annual evaluation does go into the employee's file.

The bases for the McGill program are excellent, but there seems to be a heavy emphasis upon improving the *library's* performance with too little regard for the individual's motivation and for the General Electric findings that "criticism has a negative effect on achievement of goals" and that *general* praise (which is treated almost as an aside in the McGill program) has little effect either way. While the McGill program does recognize that an individual's performance may be helped or hindered by that of some other unit, it does not deal with a solution to this dependency or with the idea of teamwork.

The "Critical Incident" Technique

Current performance appraisal, as exemplified by MBO, by statements of accomplishments on typical faculty (library) evaluation forms, and by the McGill program, focuses not on behavior but on the results of behavior. This stems from the aversion to judging personality when one should be measuring performance. It is certainly true that goals can be legitimately attained by many means, but there is a danger in considering only quantifiable or

objective achievements in a service-oriented field like librarianship.

In other words, the *way in which* one reaches specified objectives is as important as actually reaching them. However, the
process of identifying appropriate behavior in specific instances
is a difficult, time-consuming one—but one that can lead to genuine
staff growth and to the development of future managers and/or
specialists. One useful technique in describing specific behavior
(such as how to handle the reference interview) is the "critical
incident" process.

Let us suppose that the head librarian of the reference department has two librarians who need to be developed into reference
specialists. In observing the behavior of the first librarian, the
department head might note that individual failed to probe sufficiently when a student inquired about articles on air pollution.
The librarian pointed out *Public Affairs Information Service*; the
student wandered away, and the librarian returned to a project of
selecting books from *Choice*.

The second librarian received a query on behavior modification and, not stopping to find out that the student was a freshman
with a two-page summary to prepare, totally overwhelmed the
student with a half-hour explanation on the use of *Psychological
Abstracts*, on-line access to the ERIC database, and a tremendous
amount of material in the card catalog. During the process, however, the librarian forgot to explain to the freshman how to get
from a bibliographic journal citation to the actual printed article.

Now these descriptions are exaggerated, but they illustrate
that the "critical incident" records actual, specific behaviors,
which can then form the basis for a future learning discussion. It
is also quite important that positive incidents be recorded so that
the employee can recognize and receive reinforcement for appropriate behaviors.

Performance Profiles

Critical incidents can also form the basis for a general list of
important behavior aspects in each department or in general interaction in the library. In order to analyze *how* something was
accomplished or the *quality* of performance, it is necessary to
identify the important behaviors expected of employees and how
those can be recognized in specific situations, for example, in open
meetings, in patron contact, in telephone answering, etc. The actual

process of identifying these is most helpful if everyone participates.

In another example from business of the use of critical incidents, the Corning Glass Company developed a fascinating "performance profile" that isolated behaviors which managers could specifically identify, recognize, and discuss with subordinates to give them concrete ideas on how to improve performance and strengthen managerial abilities.[17] A sample of the behaviors that were isolated by identifying approximately 300 critical incidents and translating these into 150 general behavioral descriptions included:

1. Objects to ideas before they are explained.
2. Takes the initiative in group meetings.
3. Has difficulty in meeting project deadlines.
4. Sees his problems in light of the problems of others (that is, does not limit his thinking to his own position or organizational unit).[18]

Appropriate behavioral descriptions for each individual, depending on his or her position and goals, can be selected from such a general list, to be used as a personal performance profile to reflect strengths, weaknesses, and planned areas of improvement.

Developing Managerial Abilities

At the beginning of this paper I said that the professional staff of an academic library can be its most important resource. I now suggest that positive, constructive performance appraisal can contribute to the development of that resource both for the good of the library and for the personal and professional growth of the individual librarian; and that in the long run these goals are more relevant to the library than concern about using evaluation for salary and promotion purposes per se.

A typical university library has a percentage of librarians who, having served for a few years, have tenure in fact if not in theory. Operating at a level of membership motivation (wishing to continue to belong to the organization) but not sufficiently motivated to perform,[19] they often develop attitudes that tend to encourage mediocrity, until they are working at a decreased level of output, service, morale, and personal satisfaction.[20] This atmosphere can discourage new employees and cause the loss of valuable talent to the library.

A staff development program has the potential to expand both specific service skills and general managerial abilities. By managerial abilities I am not necessarily referring only to the ability to supervise but to organizational and leadership qualities, generally accepted as desirable managerial traits in any organizational setting. Charles Gibbons called them the "marks of a mature manager"[21] and stated that the individual should:

1. Possess well-defined goals.
2. Be able to allocate resources according to priorities.
3. Be able to make decisions, act upon them, and accept responsibility for them.
4. Be willing to compromise.
5. Be able to delegate and to depend on subordinates.
6. Be self-motivated and self-controlled.
7. Be able to organize, plan, and communicate for effective use of resources.
8. Maintain good relationships with others.
9. Possess emotional maturity and the internal resources to cope with frustration, disappointment, and stress.
10. Be able to appraise oneself and one's performance objectively, to admit to being wrong.
11. Expect that one will keep on growing, improve one's performance, and continue to develop.

I would add to this list two qualities that Harlan Cleveland stresses in his excellent book *The Future Executive.*[22] These are a tolerance for ambiguity and an openness to change. A performance appraisal program that is aimed at professional growth should contribute to the development of these characteristics in the professional staff.[23]

The Library as an Interactive System

If libraries are to participate actively in technological developments and cope positively with the information explosion while faced with the pressures of decreasing staff and collection funds, then the best talents of that staff must be recognized, cultivated, and used. An emphasis on teamwork rather than competition, an acknowledgment that each department is part of a cooperative system, is essential.

Discussions and negotiations for participation in national and regional library networks and academic consortia have become commonplace; yet in my experience, true day-to-day cooperation among departments within one organization is less usual.

The need for accountability and performance measures is recognized when dealing with large library projects, and these serve as motivating factors for the project directors. In a similar way, performance appraisal can be used as feedback within a library to keep the system functioning on the highest level and as one organization rather than as fragmented pieces with conflicting goals.

In the establishment of a performance appraisal program for an individual library, the organization and its employees can be considered as an interactive system involved with mutual goals for the library, the department, the unit, and the librarian, including for each a feedback loop where goal setting is one input, performance is an output, and evaluation is used to correct the system and keep it on course. The action of departments and users upon each other should be kept in mind at every stage of the program.

For example, the interdependence of the acquisitions, collection development, and catalog departments in providing access to a book is usually recognized and talked about—like the weather—but little is done to contribute to meaningful cooperation. Goals can be set for such things as the quantity of orders placed in a given time, the length of time for receipt of the book, and optimum use of bibliographic searchers in handling the book before and during cataloging. But much of this is based on the quantity and cyclical flow of orders from the selection librarians into the acquisitions department or the percentage of receipts through standing orders and approval programs, which the cataloging department can then handle. The development of such quantitative goals, therefore, might best be done jointly with an open acknowledgment of the interdependence of these departments rather than with a fruitless competition between them.

A Program Proposal

Let us consider the use of performance evaluation in an interactive system that includes supervisory training, mutual goal setting, peer discussions, and teamwork, with an emphasis on behavior as well as results, as a means of developing future leaders and promoting better library service while providing satisfaction for the individual.

The program outlined below is an attempt to use performance appraisal as a library management development tool. It can be modified to meet individual needs and library situations, and whether it should be implemented formally or informally depends to a great extent on the resources of manpower and time available. It does require the support of the library administration, but the procedures themselves could easily be guided by members of a professional development committee if there is no specific personnel librarian at the institution. In any case, its focus should remain the same: communication training for supervisors, goal setting as part of an interactive system, positive motivation, and the highest utilization of and response to individual needs, skills, and strengths.

Step 1. Training of library supervisors. The goal setting and analysis, both individually and collectively, that this program requires will call for supervisors to act as facilitators, to listen carefully and accurately, to spot nonverbal messages, to keep a discussion on track, and to avert the game-playing that often develops out of self-defense when one's ego is threatened. To prepare them for this, the first step is a workshop for supervisors. This ought best be led by an outside consultant or an internal specialist in communication skills (perhaps from the psychology, public administration, or business department in a college or university) to cover active listening, group discussion leadership, how to reach a consensus, how to motivate positively, etc. An interesting approach might be to make use of *The OK Boss* by Muriel James[24] as background reading to introduce the concept of transactional analysis and then to use this tool as a basis for the communication skills to be developed in the workshop.

Step 2. Goal setting. This involves group meetings for all staff units of the library, to discuss the purposes and responsibilities of the library, the department, and the individual. These discussions ought to begin at the level of the library director and associate directors meeting with their department heads. It is easy enough to say that a library provides information, but what are its priorities?

In a specific academic setting, who comes first—faculty, students (graduate, undergraduate, transfer), community, alumni, university staff, library staff, who? Each has different needs, and the priorities that are established will ultimately have an impact on the type and scope of reference service, the emphasis in book selection, the key hours for staffing public desks or keeping the library open, etc.

What are the priorities in terms of time versus money, expenditures for staff salaries versus books, for automated systems, for cooperative projects? (If any part of the staff is unionized, the union will have to be brought into the discussions at some point too.)

This kind of discussion and planning is so often lost in the day-to-day, crisis management that harried administrators are forced into. I realize that the examples above are issues for which there is no one right answer, but some consideration and thought given to these priorities at the beginning of the project is the best basis for rational and consistent goal setting in each department down the line.

As supervisors next participate in sessions of goal setting for their departments, it will be quickly recognized by the group that each department member has certain strengths that can be most effectively used in particular projects. This does not deny the need for job descriptions and the use of these in setting objectives (as has been generally recommended). However, job descriptions are static and based on past experience and needs. Goal setting, which looks toward the future, optimal utilization of available resources, and an open feeling of cooperation among peers to achieve similar objectives can result in a whole new use of skills.

A traditional reference department, which assigns each librarian to three hours of desk duty a day, might find that the optimal use of manpower would call for a division on the basis of subject expertise (depending on the question asked), with a student assistant to respond to those general queries that are routine (Where's the drinking fountain? What are the hours of the reserve reading room? Where's the latest issue of *Reader's Guide*?). At the same time the reference librarians may realize that their work of interpreting the card catalog to users might be enhanced by a short orientation or refresher course run by the catalog department for the staff. They might wish to be brought up to date on such questions as, What's the best way to locate government documents? How are branch library holdings handled in the main catalog?

These thoughts lead us directly into step 3.

Step 3. System interaction. As each department has a chance to discuss its responsibilities, priorities, and goals internally, the staff members will recognize their interdependence with other departments. The supervisor can keep track of these relationships and the particular points of congruency, to be used as a basis for discussions between departments. The usual procedure, when conflicts of interest arise, has been for the two department heads to meet privately and try to work it out. More often than not, however, a win-lose situation develops in which neither can compromise without losing face. A general meeting between the acquisitions and the catalog departments to discuss bibliographic searching, with the head of technical services as facilitator, can do much to clear the air, promote cooperation, and develop a workable compromise—or at least foster an understanding of the other point of view.

Step 4. Refresher. At this point, if not before, it is time for a one-day refresher workshop for the supervisors. They will have participated in goal-setting discussions with their own superiors, with their own departments, and with related departments (all group sessions) and will now have all kinds of situations to discuss: where their group got off the track, when the expected consensus was not reached, where face-saving or game-playing took the place of constructive negotiations. Role-playing and further guidance in transactional analysis and facilitation are appropriate here.

Step 5. Individual goal setting. Each librarian should now be prepared to list his or her goals—professional, departmental, and personal career or life goals—relating them to the operation of the department and the library, building on strengths in order to best utilize one's talents. Each goal should be accompanied by specific, recognizable means to attain this. For instance, the librarian whose goal is to head the acquisitions department might plan to prepare for this responsibility by:

1. Gaining knowledge of publishers and vendors through regular reading of Publishers Weekly, scanning catalogs, and visiting exhibitors' displays at conventions;
2. Attending acquisitions discussion groups and applicable committee meetings at professional conferences;
3. Taking a continuing education course in out-of-print acquisitions;
4. Assisting with budget and book fund allocations (with the support of the present department head).

The supervisor will then take this list of goals and the specific means to achieve them and discuss these with the staff member, offering guidance, suggestions, and support. The more positive the response that can be given, the better. At the same time, however, the manager has an obligation to see that the goals and tactics are realistic—within the librarian's abilities but requiring a consistent effort.

Specific target dates must be set wherever possible, and if the goal or project is a long-term one, then benchmarks should be established to measure interim achievement. If the librarian's goal is to become a specialist in rare books, this may require courses, conferences, contacts, reading, an internship or exchange, etc. To begin with, a tentative curriculum can be listed, the most relevant conferences targeted, a special collections bibliography prepared in an area that will benefit the library users. Out of this may come an application for a grant, travel funds, or professional leave time, and a structured program to achieve this expertise.

The supervisor must also be realistic with the employee, even encouraging him or her to seek other opportunities if the librarian's goals are not compatible with the library situation at all, or when the librarian is really ready for additional responsibilities but no openings are expected to exist for some time. In all areas, once agreement is reached, the supervisor has an obligation to assist in the achievement of the goals.

By listing individual goals and strategies and then discussing these with the supervisor, the librarian will also begin formulating a performance profile that shows strengths and developmental needs.[25] These are relative to the individual, not on a scale that compares one person with another. As this profile is developed, it can form the basis for future appraisals and then future goals. Figure 1 gives an example of the form that might be used for this purpose.

Step 6. Critical incidents. Another component in building a performance profile is the use of critical incidents, as described earlier. This technique should be used informally to record observable, applicable occurrences, rather than depending upon memory, judgment, and impressions. Emphasis should be placed on

	Strength	Weakness	Improving
ability to set priorities			
organizational perspective			
ability to complete a project			
decisiveness			
accuracy			
willingness to delegate			
ability to follow up			

Name_____ Date Set_____ Interim Follow-Up_____ Review Date_____

FIGURE 1. Performance appraisal form

specific, positive contributions made by the employee and on noting occasions when the librarian does demonstrate improvement in an area of the performance profile as this is developed. The critical incidents will form the basis of private discussions between the supervisor and the librarian, both to specifically praise good performance and to determine individual strengths and weaknesses that both parties recognize are pertinent to goal achievement.

For the library with sufficient time or interest, an extrapolation of performance needs from critical incidents can form the basis for preparing general performance profile characteristics against which each staff member may wish to measure himself or herself.[26]

Step 7. Review and analysis. An essential part of performance evaluation is to establish feedback loops through frequent, supportive, scheduled, and unscheduled work review and analysis sessions, again building on strengths and future potential rather than on past performance failures. The first informal checkpoint should be in three months, with a midyear goal reevaluation after six months. This is the time to redefine goals that no longer seem realistic or where financial or technological developments in the library require new responsibilities or new directions.

At each step—the first unit meetings, the interdepartmental discussions, the individual goal setting and reviews—it is up to the supervisor to keep the conversations focused on the relevant topics (without stifling productive discussions), to come to decisions, and to record progress.

Preliminary preparation by all parties will contribute to productive meetings, but it is easy for busy staff members to forget to prepare lists or goals before the meeting is scheduled to start. To avoid this, it is helpful to allow fifteen minutes at the start of the unit meetings particularly for each person to consider the subject of the meeting and his or her views on it and to make a list of goals and priorities for discussion with the group.

Step 8. Evaluation of the evaluation. Since this is an experimental program, which should be designed and adapted to respond to staff and service needs, an evaluation of its effectiveness is necessary. This can be done in two parts:

1. An attitude questionnaire for staff, management, and client groups (faculty and students, library users and nonusers). The same questionnaire should be administered before the program begins, after one year of activity, and after two.

2. An examination of actual goals achieved after two years—

on each level and through interaction and cooperation among the parts of the library system. All examples of cooperation, improvement of service, or professional development that were not originally specified goals should be noted as well, with an attempt to discover whether these arose in part or in whole out of the performance evaluation program.

Conclusion

The entire process of defining responsibilities, establishing goals and the means to achieve them, developing performance profiles, and then evaluating achievement should all follow a regular cycle. The process should begin again annually with goal setting by the library administration, and a refresher course in communication for the supervisors or the entire staff would also not be amiss.

The proposed program is, indeed, a time-consuming one. The underlying principles of MBO and participatory management, however, have been applied in academic libraries around the country through the Management Review and Analysis Program[27] and its more recent small-library counterpart, the Academic Library Development Program.[28] In contrast, this proposal presents an opportunity to improve communication, performance, and morale through a limited area of library management, which can, however, have broad-reaching effects. With support from the library administration (mandatory for the success of any of these projects), the old concept of performance evaluation will make a positive impact on librarians and library service.

Additional Readings

General Discussions

There are literally thousands of reading selections that in some way represent the staffing function, many of which are to be found under the general headings of "personnel management" or "personnel administration." In order to get an overview of this enormous topic, readers concerned with the overall staffing function as well as the details of each component should examine Burack and Mathy's *Human Resource Planning: A Pragmatic Approach to Manpower Staffing and Development* (Brace-Park Press, 1980). The American Society for Personnel Administration's handbook on *Staffing Policies and Strategies* (Bureau of National Affairs, 1974) should also be on every manager's reading list. This handbook emphasizes the professional and managerial responsibilities inherent in all facets of staffing through the discussion of staffing policies and strategies, development of job information, recruitment, selection, interviewing and testing, performance appraisal, internal personnel maintenance, and equal employment opportunity administration. Most important, the handbook presents the staffing function as being an integrated system, a process made up of both vertical and horizontal dimensions—an important framework within which to view the staffing function and its components.

While in the past the library literature related to staffing has been somewhat fragmented, several efforts have been made in recent years to alter this situation. *Personnel Administration in Libraries* (Creth and Duda, Neal-Schuman, 1981) offers a series of seven essays on all aspects of library personnel management, while Van Zant's *Personnel Policies in Libraries* (Neal-Schuman, 1980) provides a collection of personnel policies from more than fifty public and academic libraries. *Personnel in Libraries* (Library Journal Special Report #10) also assesses the role of the librarian today, while *Public Libraries: Smart Practices in Personnel* (Sullivan and Ptacek, Libraries Unlimited, 1982) offers a handbook approach to personnel management for public library administrators.

Human Resources Planning

Numerous articles in business literature discuss the nature of human resources planning, although few are as comprehensive as Schein. Moore provides an important addition to the Schein article by tracing the evolution of human resources management from the "macro" approach of manpower planning to the broader approach of human resources planning ("From Manpower Planning to Human Resources Planning through Career Development," *Personnel*, May-June 1979). While both the Schein and Zedeck and Blood articles refer to manpower planning as a part of human resources planning, neither provides details about the exact nature of this kind of planning and forecasting. Walker, in "Forecasting Manpower Needs" (*Harvard Business Review*, March-April 1969), provides a more complete description of the ranges of manpower forecasting and the ways in which manpower data can be used by an organization.

In library literature, few current articles adequately develop an overview of human resources planning. Lee and Lee, in their 1971 article "Personnel Planning for a Library Manpower System" (*Library Trends*, July 1971), do give such an overview. This article can be supplemented by a review of the demand for and availability of library personnel through the mid-1980s in the Bureau of Labor Statistics' *Library Manpower: A Study of Demand and Supply* (1975). Simon and Myers's "Supply and Demand" (*Wilson Library Bulletin*, December 1976) and Michael Cooper's "An Analysis of the Demand for Librarians" (*Library Quarterly*, October 1975) help to complete the overview of human resources forecasting and planning for library managers. Dougherty's selection in *Academic Libraries by the Year 2000* (Bowker, 1977) on "Personnel Needs for Librarianship's Uncertain Future" highlights important trends and issues that will affect staffing for academic as well as other types of libraries in the future. Finally, the "Personnel Recruitment and Selection in the 1980s" issue of the *Drexel Library Quarterly* (Summer 1981) highlights both human resources planning issues for the decade as well as actual recruitment practices for library personnel.

Selection

The most critical element in the staffing function is selection, since people and skills must be acquired by the library organization if it is to meet changing manpower requirements and organizational needs. Too often selection is thought of as simply the act of recruiting and hiring an individual to fill a specific job vacancy, when in fact managerial and legal processes make this part of the staffing function the most complex element.

Although selection is a major staffing element, articles that cover the process in its entirety are few in number. Instead, materials that describe one or two activities related to selection must be relied upon to develop a view of the process. One major exception to this lack of comprehensiveness in selection literature is Wanous's *Organizational Entry: Recruitment, Selection, and Socialization of Newcomers* (Addison-Wesley, 1980). In presenting a broad treatment of the nature of organizational entry, Wanous focuses on the importance of integrating individuals and their organizations, the nature of organizational recruitment, selection of prospective employees, and the place of organizational socialization in the staffing process. Another exception is Zedeck and Blood's chapter on "Selection and Placement" (*Foundations of Behavioral Science Research in Organizations*, Brooks/Cole, 1974). In this excerpt, the authors discuss the planned and integrated process in which individuals are brought into the organization. In addition, the survey of selection practices in college libraries by Thomas in "Staffing the College Library" (*Library Journal*, 1 April 1973) and the description of the selection process in "Employee Selection at the University of Houston Libraries" (*Journal of the College and University Personnel Association*, October 1975) also give the reader a practical view of selection in libraries, albeit only in one type of library setting.

The establishment and use of selection criteria is a major part of the selection process. It is clear that in the current decade, the validation of selection criteria will be a major issue to all involved in the staffing process, especially for professional organizations such as libraries. Because this aspect of staffing is of such great concern, the entire "Personnel Selection and Classification Systems" section of the 1979 *Annual Review of Psychology* is devoted to reviewing research and applications in this area. In Zedeck and Blood's excerpt, cited previously, the emphasis on designing criteria that predict successful employment, as well as the discussion of validity and reliability of various predictors of job success, contribute measurably to the reader's understanding of selection criteria. These authors also present a clear and carefully designed "walk-through" of the steps in the validation procedure, and all library managers would do well to familiarize themselves with this procedure as outlined.

Library literature that reports on selection criteria includes Estabrook's "Job Seekers in the Buyers' Market: How Library Employers Judge Candidates" (*Library Journal*, 1 February 1973) and Gaughan's "Resume Essentials for the Academic Librarian" (*College and Research Libraries*, March 1980). In addition, Cottam's recent discussion in *American Libraries* summarizes the particular problems librarianship faces in establishing minimum qualifications for professional positions, given the need to validate selection criteria ("Minimum Qualifications and the Law: The Issue Ticks Away for Librarians," *American Libraries*, May 1980). An important work that clearly summarizes all aspects of selection criteria problems faced by organizations in Arvey's *Fairness in Selecting Employees* (Addison-Wesley, 1979), which covers all of the legal aspects of the selection process, including testing and the employment interview. Simon's article on the library employment application and interview process ("Personnel Selection Practices: Applications and Interviews," *American Libraries*, March 1978) supplements Arvey in providing more specific library-related information. More specific aspects of the interview process are covered by Creth's article on "Conducting an Effective Employment Interview" (*Journal of Academic Librarianship*, November 1978).

The nature of jobs library employees will hold, the quality of library worklife, and the development of a climate for productive work are all interrelated issues. In addition to an earlier Shaughnessy article titled "Technology and Job Design in Libraries: A Sociotechnical Systems Approach" (*Journal of Academic Librarianship*, November 1977), which relates organizational theories to the practice of library work, Ricking and Booth's *Personnel Utilization in Libraries* (ALA, 1974) presents an in-depth analysis of the nature of library work from a systems viewpoint. Finally, the relationships between job evaluation and design and job enrichment are examined by Patten in "Job Evaluation and Job Enlargement: A Collision Course?" (*Human Resource Management*, Winter 1977).

Motivation

The motivation of individuals in the workplace is a highly complex issue, with many different approaches and theories represented in the literature. Lawler's "Developing a Motivating Work

Climate" (*Managment Review*, July 1977) furnishes an excellent overview of the organizational setting and societal framework within which motivation must be examined; a few examples of some of the other approaches to the study of motivation are provided by Frederick Herzberg in his "One More Time: How Do You Motivate Employees?" (*Harvard Business Review*, January-February 1968) and in "New Perspectives on the Will to Work" (*The Personnel Administrator*, December 1979), as well as in Abraham Maslow's "A Theory of Human Motivation" (*Psychological Review*, July 1943) and David McClelland's "That Urge to Achieve" (*Think*, November-December 1966). Goodman in "Employee Motivation" (*Library Trends*, July 1971) reviews the various approaches to motivational theory and practice from a library perspective and discusses the role of the supervisor in the motivational process. Because motivation and the quality of worklife are so directly related, Martell's "Improving the Effectiveness of Libraries through Improvements in the Quality of Working Life" (*College and Research Libraries*, September 1981) offers an important addition to discussions of motivational theory and practice in a library context.

Staff Development

While Berkner discusses the staff development process in the library setting, there are additional sources that provide greater depth of coverage in this important area of staffing. Conroy's two works, *Library Staff Development and Continuing Education* (Libraries Unlimited, 1978) and *Library Staff Development Profile Pages* (Conroy, 1980) give comprehensive coverage to the entire development process as it operates in libraries. Two other articles help to integrate this part of staffing with other staffing elements, and provide a managerial focus on the staff development process. Martell and Dougherty's "The Role of Continuing Education and Training in Human Resource Development: An Administrator's Viewpoint" (*Journal of Academic Librarianship*, July 1978) discusses both the costs and the benefits of staff development as well as its practical limitations. Gellerman, in "Training and Behavior Change" (*Training and Development Journal*, February 1977) links the training function to both organizational and managerial support systems.

Performance Appraisal

In addition to staff development, performance appraisal is a major element in the staffing function. The development of an effective appraisal system that will benefit both the library and its employees requires commitment from all levels of personnel. Because the review of an individual's performance often creates problems for managers, Lefton and Buzzota's discussion of the ways in which performance appraisal can be effectively utilized is a particularly good starting point for further reading on appraisal ("Performance Appraisal: Why Bother?" *Training and Development Journal*, August 1978). Also, Smith and Brouwer's *Performance Appraisal and Human Development: A Practical Guide to Effective Managing* (Addison-Wesley, 1977) presents an integrated view of the appraisal process and provides special insights into the manager's role in the process of human growth and development, thereby supplementing the suggested readings on staff development. Because performance appraisal is a critical factor in any organization's efforts in meeting its human resources needs in the coming decade, Morrison and Kranz's "The Shape of Performance Appraisal in the Coming Decade" (*Personnel*, July-August 1981) should provide insights about the major trends that will affect the role of performance appraisal in organizations.

As Berkner has indicated in her article, there are numerous steps in the appraisal process and many ways in which the methodologies for assessing performance can be approached. In "Developing an Appraisal Program" (*Personnel Journal*, January 1978), Haynes describes the overall issues to be considered in developing a program and the types of approaches possible. Library applications of the methodologies available include a description of subordinate evaluation of supervisors in Martin's "Staff Evaluation of Supervisors" (*Special Libraries*, January 1979), peer evaluation in an academic setting in Thomas Yen-Ran Yeh's "Library Peer Evaluation for Promotion and Merit Increase" (*College and Research Libraries*, July 1973), and Brandwein's description of a public library rating program ("Developing a Service Rating Program," *Library Journal*, 1 February 1975). A fine example of librarywide evaluation that illustrates the integration of organizational development and performance appraisal concepts is provided by Turner in "Why Do Department Heads Take Longer Coffee Breaks? A Public Library Evaluates Itself" (*American Libraries*, April 1978). More specific examples of library applications of performance appraisal systems are provided by the College Library Information Packet (CLIP #I–80) *Performance Appraisal*, developed by the ACRL College Library Section. On a larger scale, Johnson's "Performance Appraisal for Librarians—A Survey" (*College and Research Libraries*, September 1972) and Locher and Teel's "Performance Appraisal—A Survey of Current Practices" (*Personnel Journal*,

May 1977) offer insight into the nature and extent of performance appraisal approaches and methodologies in use during the past decade.

Labor Relations and Collective Bargaining

In some libraries, individuals choose to form and be represented by a formal group for the purpose of bargaining about working conditions and relationships. Thus, in some of these organizations, labor relations and collective bargaining play a vital role in the staffing function. The business literature concerning this area of staffing is again enormous; in recent years, as collective bargaining efforts have expanded in libraries, the library literature has grown as well.

Two general suggestions for reading about labor relations are in order. First, Fossum's *Labor Relations: Development, Structure, Process* (Business Publications, 1979) offers a well-organized overview of the field of labor relations, covering history, labor law, bargaining processes, contract administration and other important topics. The yearly *Guidebook to Labor Relations* (Commerce Clearing House) can serve as a reference for managers who wish to examine explanations and summaries of the general principles of labor relations law.

Within the library setting, Guyton's *Unionization: The Viewpoint of Librarians* (ALA, 1975) provides a good starting point for the development of an understanding of unionization in the library environment. Reading selections illustrating the role of labor relations in each of the types of libraries include Weatherford's *Collective Bargaining and the Academic Librarian* (Scarecrow, 1976), Brandwein's "From Confrontation to Coexistence" (*Library Journal*, 15 May 1979), and Aaron's "The Media Supervisor and Collective Bargaining" (*Drexel Library Quarterly*, July 1978). Two *Library Trends* articles that discuss labor relations from a management perspective are Chamot's "The Effect of Collective Bargaining on the Employee-Management Relationship" (October 1976) and Moss' "Bargaining's Effect on Library Management and Operations" (October 1976).

Directing

At all levels, individuals are the key element in carrying out the operations and processes of the library. The management process depends heavily on certain individuals to coordinate and guide others in the performance of work directed toward organizational goals. The process by which this happens is often referred to as "directing," and relies heavily upon several of the other functions of management to become operational. Especially critical are staffing (to provide the human resources to be directed in achieving organizational goals), communication (to convey directions and share information), and planning (to provide a framework for the efforts of directing). Directing is also influenced by the organizing process, particularly in terms of the organizational structure of the library. Directing is, in turn, a key element in carrying out both the organizing and control functions of the management process (and is of course affected by the outcomes of these).

Directing takes place wherever human and organizational resources are present to be coordinated and guided toward common goals. Thus the process involves managers and employees at all levels, since individuals rarely work totally without some kind of organizational accountability concern-

349

ing the outcome of their work activities. If organizational structures change significantly to accommodate future needs and requirements in the way in which Sayles suggests in selection 13, new approaches to the accomplishment of the directing function may evolve. Thus it is important to look beyond the traditional supervisor-subordinate relationship to understand how personnel and organizational resources may be directed in the future.

Often "directing" is used as a synonym for "leadership." While leadership is an important facet of the directing process, other critical elements such as coordination are necessary to bring together the human and organizational resources within the structural and governance framework of the library. However, of all of the functions of management, leadership has probably been the most often discussed in the literature. The hundreds of research studies and articles on leadership present a confusing array of viewpoints to the reader who wishes to clarify the directing process. Furthermore, a significant portion of this literature represents the "one best way" to the study or execution of leadership and thus falls prey to the "lure of the universal theory."[1]

With all of the changes taking place within the internal and external library environment, it is important to develop a new framework for the examination of the directing function. Establishing this framework means that current and past theories and practices must be carefully examined for their future applicability. The three selections in this chapter represent a different perspective on the examination of the directing process. Rather than repeating tried-and-true approaches, they instead present provocative questions about past views and suggest courses of action for the future.

Schriesheim, Tolliver, and Behling offer the reader a balanced overview of the direction leadership research and practice has taken and a discussion of the process leading to effective leadership. In exploring both organizational and individual implications of these leadership theories for managers, the authors focus on situational factors in the process of directing. They note that this process is "not so much one of changing the characteristics of the individual as it is one of assuring that he or she is placed in an appropriate situation or of teaching the individual how to act to fit the situation."[2] Thus, in the view of these authors, directing and leadership can be improved by having individuals develop skills in analyzing the task and political demands present in various organizational situations.

In the professional service organization, one of the leadership approaches often espoused is the participative, or employee-centered approach. Although widely discussed in library literature, and often viewed as a solution to some of the problems of organizational effectiveness in the library, participative management is cited as a particularly noteworthy example of the "lure of the universal theory."[3] Dickinson's article suggests that a restrained view of this approach to management is in order if real organizational effectiveness is desired in the library. Dickinson points to the need for responsibility on all parts for seeing that the work of the organization is undertaken, the absolute need for shared communication, and the necessity of establishing an understanding among all participants about the amount and type of power that is to be shared in the decision-making process.

Many of the discussions throughout the readings in this book identify the enormous impact that individuals have on organizations and the management process. The enormity of this impact suggests that some degree of self-management is necessary for organizational effectiveness to be achieved, particularly in a professional organization (and especially if the organization chooses to adopt a participative style of management). Manz and Sims suggest that self-management techniques are vital to the accomplishment of organizational and personal goals; self-management also becomes important in cases of ineffective leadership. From a social learning perspective, these authors elaborate on the need for individuals to be encouraged to learn to manage their own work-related behavior, with leaders helping subordinates to develop these self-management skills. Within the professional organization, this self-management becomes particularly important when individuals share in the decision-making process. The success of the entire management process, in fact, can be greatly enhanced through self-management at all levels of the library organization. Even in this context, though, encouragement and enhancement of self-management skills must still be considered a part of the *directing* process.

22. Leadership Theory: Some Implications for Managers

*Chester A. Schriesheim, James M. Tolliver
and Orlando C. Behling*

In the past seventy years more than 3,000 leadership studies have been conducted and dozens of leadership models and theories have been proposed.[1] Yet, a practicing manager who reads this literature seeking an effective solution to supervisory problems will rapidly become disenchanted. Although we have access to an overwhelming volume of leadership theory and research, few guidelines exist which are of use to a practitioner. Nevertheless, interest in leadership—and in those qualities which separate a successful leader from an unsuccessful one—remains unabated. In almost any book dealing with management one will find some discussion of leadership. In any company library there are numerous volumes entitled "Increasing Leadership Effectiveness," "Successful Leadership," or "How to Lead." Typical management development programs conducted within work organizations and universities usually deal with some aspect of leadership. This intensity and duration of writing on the subject and the sums spent annually on leadership training indicate that practicing managers and academicians consider good leadership essential to organizational success.

What is meant by leadership, let alone *good* leadership? Many definitions have been proposed, and it seems that most are careful to separate management from leadership. This distinction sometimes becomes blurred in everyday conversations. The first term, *management*, includes those processes, both mental and physical,

Reprinted from *MSU Business Topics* 26:34–40 (Summer 1978).

which result in other people executing prescribed formal duties for organizational goal attainment. It deals mainly with planning, organizing, and controlling the work of other people to achieve organizational goals.[2] This definition usually includes those aspects of managers' jobs, such as monitoring and controlling resources, which are sometimes ignored in current conceptualizations of leadership. *Leadership*, on the other hand, is a more restricted type of managerial activity, focusing on the interpersonal interactions between a leader and one or more subordinates, with the purpose of increasing organizational effectiveness.[3] In this view, leadership is a social influence process in which the leader seeks the voluntary participation of subordinates in an effort to reach organizational objectives. The key idea highlighted by a number of authors is that the subordinate's participation is voluntary.[4] This implies that the leader has brought about some change in the way subordinates want to behave. Leadership, consequently, is not only a specific process (more so than management), but also is undoubtedly political in nature. The political aspect of leadership has been discussed elsewhere, so at this point it suffices to note that a major implication of leadership's political nature is that such attempts at wielding influence will not necessarily succeed.[5] In fact, other types of managerial tasks may have a stronger influence on organizational effectiveness than those interpersonal tasks usually labeled leadership.[6]

Despite this shortcoming, the examination of leadership as it relates to interpersonal interactions is still worthwhile simply because managers may, in many cases, have more control over how they and their subordinates behave than over nonhuman aspects of their jobs (such as the amount and types of resources they are given). In addition, some information does exist concerning which leadership tactics are of use under various conditions. For this information to be of greatest use, however, practicing managers should have some concept of the direction leadership research has taken. Thus, before attempting to provide guidelines for practitioners, we shall briefly review major approaches to the subject of leadership and point out their weaknesses and limitations.

Basic Approaches to Leadership

Thinking concerning leadership has moved through three distinct periods or phases.

The Trait Phase. Early approaches to leadership, from the pre-

Christian era to the late 1940s, emphasized the examination of leader characteristics (such as age and degree of gregariousness) in an attempt to identify a set of universal characteristics which would allow a leader to be effective in all situations. At first a few traits seemed to be universally important for successful leaders, but subsequent research yielded inconsistent results concerning these traits; in addition, research investigating a large number of other traits (about one hundred) was generally discouraging. As a result of this accumulation of negative findings and of reviews of this evidence, such as that conducted by R. M. Stogdill, the tide of opinion about the importance of traits for leadership effectiveness began to change.[7] In the late 1940s, leadership researchers began to move away from trait research. Contemporary opinion holds the trait approach in considerable disrepute and views the likelihood of uncovering a set of universal leadership effectiveness traits as essentially impossible.

The Behavioral Phase. With the fall of the trait approach, researchers considered alternative concepts, eventually settling on the examination of relationships between leader behaviors and subordinate satisfaction and performance.[8] During the height of the behavioral phase, dating roughly from the late 1940s to the early 1960s, several large research programs were conducted, including the Ohio State University leadership studies, a program of research which has received considerable publicity over the years.

The Ohio State studies started shortly after World War II and initially concentrated on leadership in military organizations. In one of these studies, a lengthy questionnaire was administered to B–52 bomber crews, and their answers were statistically analyzed to identify the common dimensions underlying the answers.[9] This analysis discovered two dimensions which seemed most important in summarizing the nature of the crews' perceptions about their airplane commanders' behavior toward them.

Consideration was the stronger of the two factors, and it involved leader behaviors indicative of friendship, mutual trust, respect, and warmth.

The second factor was Initiation of Structure, a concept involving leader behaviors indicating that the leader organizes and defines the relationship between self and subordinates.[10]

In subsequent studies using modified versions of the original questionnaire, Consideration and Structure were found to be prime dimensions of leader behavior in situations ranging from combat flights over Korea to assembly line works.[11] In addition, studies were undertaken at Ohio State and elsewhere to compare the effects of these leader behaviors on subordinate performance and satisfaction. A high Consideration-high Structure leadership style was, in many cases, found to lead to high performance and satisfaction. However, in a number of studies dysfunctional consequences, such as high turnover and absenteeism, accompanied these positive outcomes. In yet other situations, different combinations of Consideration and Structure (for example, low Consideration-high Structure) were found to be more effective.[12]

Similar behaviors were identified and similar results obtained in a large number of studies, such as those conducted at the University of Michigan.[13] Although the display of highly Considerate-highly Structuring behavior was sometimes found to result in positive organizational outcomes, this was not true in all of the cases or even in most of them.[14] The research, therefore, clearly indicated that no single leadership style was universally effective, as the relationship of supervisory behavior to organizational performance and employee satisfaction changed from situation to situation. By the early 1960s this had become apparent to even the most ardent supporters of the behavioral approach, and the orientation of leadership researchers began to change toward a situational treatment.

The Situational Phase. Current leadership research is almost entirely situational. This approach examines the interrelationships among leader and subordinate behaviors or characteristics and the situations in which the parties find themselves. This can clearly be seen in the work of researchers such as F. E. Fiedler, who outlined one of the first situational models.[15]

Fiedler claims that leaders are motivated primarily by satisfactions derived from interpersonal relations and task-goal accomplishment. Relationship-motivated leaders display task-oriented behaviors (such as Initiating Structure) in situations which are favorable for them to exert influence over their work group, and they display relationship-oriented behaviors (such as Consideration) in situations which are either moderately favorable or unfavorable. Task-motivated leaders display relationship-oriented behaviors in favorable situations and task-oriented behaviors in both moderately favorable and unfavorable situations. Fiedler's model specifies that relationship-motivated leaders will be more effective in situations which are moderately favorable for the leader to exert influence, and that they will be less effective in favorable or unfavorable situations; the exact opposite is the case for task-motivated leaders. (They are most effective in favorable or unfavorable situations and least effective in moderately favorable ones.) According to Fiedler, the favorableness of the situation for the leader to exert influence over the work group is determined by (1) the quality of leader-group member relations (the warmer and friendlier, the more favorable the situation); (2) the structure of the tasks performed by the leader's subordinates (the more structured, the more favorable); and (3) the power of the leader (the more power, the more favorable the situation).[16]

A number of other authors propose similar types of inter-actions among the leader, the led, and the situation. We will not review all these other models, but the situational model of Victor Vroom and Phillip Yetton deserves mention.[17] Their model sug-gests the conditions under which the leader should share decision-making power. Five basic leadership styles are recommended. These range from unilateral decisions by the leader to situations in which the leader gives a great deal of decision power to sub-ordinates and serves as a discussion coordinator who does not at-tempt to influence the group. Which style is recommended depends upon the leader's "yes" or "no" response to seven quality and acceptability questions which are asked sequentially. In those cases where more than a single style is suggested, the leader is expected to choose between recommendations on the basis of the amount of time to be invested. While this model, as is the case with most of the situational models, has not been fully tested, the liter-ature supports the basic notion that a situational view is necessary to portray accurately the complexities of leadership processes.

Organizational Implications

What does this discussion of leadership theory and research have to do with the practice of management?

Selection does not seem to be the primary answer to the organization's need to increase the pool of effective leaders. The results of the numerous trait studies summarized by Stogdill and others indicate that the search for universal personality charac-teristics of effective leaders is doomed.[18] This statement requires qualification, however. It should be recognized that the assertion concerns leadership effectiveness, which is only one aspect of managerial effectiveness. A manager may contribute to organiza-tional effectiveness in many ways other than by being an effective leader. The role of selection in picking effective managers, as dis-tinguished from effective leaders, consequently may be much greater. Furthermore, present disappointment with attempts at leader selection is derived from research which has sought to identify universal characteristics of effective leaders in all situations. Summaries such as Stogdill's demonstrate that leadership effectiveness is highly dependent upon the relationship between leader characteristics and the demands of particular situations, and thus universal approaches will not work. Exploration of leader traits as they relate to performance in particular situations may reveal that careful selection has some potential. Unfortunately, given the many situational factors which appear to influence leadership effectiveness, it seems unlikely that selection procedures will be able to follow typical actuarial (statistical) selection procedures.[19] (It appears almost impossible to gather enough individuals in identical jobs to do this.) However, this does not preclude the use of clinical (judgmental) techniques for selection of leaders.

A further limitation on selection procedures as ways of increasing the pool of effective managers and/or leaders within organizations is the dynamic nature of managerial jobs and managers' careers. If, as research seems to indicate, leadership success is situation-specific, then the continual and inevitable shifts in the nature of a manager's assignment and his or her movement from one assignment to another may make the initial selection invalid.

Another implication is that existing forms of leadership training appear to be inappropriate, based on the evidence outlined here. There are two reasons for this. First, the majority of such training programs are based upon the assumption that there exists one best way to manage. Great emphasis usually is placed on an employee-centered (Considerate) approach or one which combines a concern for employees with a concern for high output (Initiating Structure). For example, the Managerial Grid and its associated Grid Organizational Development Program are popular approaches to management and organizational development.[20] Both are based on the premise that a managerial style which shows high concern for people and high concern for production is the soundest way to achieve excellence, and both attempt to develop this style of behavior on the part of all managers.[21] Rensis Likert's "System-Four" approach to managerial and organizational development, although different from the Grid approach, also assumes that one best way to manage exists (employee-centered leadership).[22] Clearly, these ideas are in conflict with the evidence and with contemporary opinion.

The other limitation of leadership training is that it seems ineffective in changing the behavior of participants. Leadership training aimed not directly at leadership behavior itself, but at providing diagnostic skills for the identification of the nature of the situation and the behaviors appropriate to it, appears to offer considerable potential for the improvement of leadership effectiveness. Obviously, however, additional research is needed to identify the dimensions of situations crucial to leadership performance and the styles effective under various circumstances.

Fiedler's suggestion that organizations engineer the job to fit the manager also has potential.[23] However, the idea is impractical, if not utopian. Application of this approach is limited because we have not identified the crucial dimensions of situations which affect leadership performance. Also, while the overall approach may offer theoretical advantages when leadership is treated in isolation, it ignores dysfunctional effects on other aspects of the organization's operations. Leadership effectiveness cannot be the only concern of administrators as they make decisions about job assignments. They must consider other aspects of the organization's operations which may conflict with their attempts to make good use of leadership talent. Some characteristics of the job, task, or organization simply may not be subject to change, at least in the short run. Thus, engineering the job to fit the manager may increase leadership effectiveness, but this approach seems risky, at least for the foreseeable future.

It should also be noted that it is not unusual for work organizations to use traits and trait descriptions in their evaluations of both leadership and managerial performance. A quick glance at a typical performance rating form usually reveals the presence of terms such as *personality* and *attitude* as factors for individual evaluation. Clearly, these terms represent a modern-day version of the traits investigated thirty years ago, and they may or may not be related to actual job performance, depending upon the specifics of the situation involved. Thus, some explicit rationale and, it is hoped, evidence that such traits do affect managerial performance should be provided before they are included in performance evaluations. Just feeling that they are important is not sufficient justification.

Individual Implications

The implications of our discussion of leadership theory and research for individual managers are intertwined with those for the total organization. The fact that leadership effectiveness does not depend on a single set of personal characteristics with which an individual is born or which the individual acquires at an early age should provide a sense of relief to many managers and potential managers. Success in leadership is not limited to an elite, but can be attained by almost any individual, assuming that the situation is proper and that the manager can adjust his or her behavior to fit the situation. The process leading to effective leadership, in other words, is not so much one of changing the characteristics of the individual as it is one of assuring that he or she is placed in an appropriate situation or of teaching the individual how to act to fit the situation.

Thus, a manager's effectiveness can be improved through the development of skills in analyzing the nature of organizational situations—both task and political demands. Although it is difficult to provide guidelines, some recent research points to tentative prescriptions.[24]

Generally speaking, a high Consideration-high Structure style often works best. However, this approach cannot be used in all instances because dysfunctional consequences can result from such behaviors. For example, upper management sometimes gives highly considerate managers poor performance ratings, while in other instances high Structure has been related to employee dissatisfaction, grievances, and turnover. It sometimes will be necessary for a manager to choose between high Consideration and high Structure, and in these cases an individual's diagnostic ability becomes important.

If the diagnostician (manager) has little information, it is probably safe to exhibit high Consideration. Although it does not guarantee subordinate performance, its positive effects on frustration-instigated behavior—such as aggression—are probably enough to warrant its recommendation as a general style. However, in some situations Structure probably should be emphasized, although it may mean a decrease in subordinate perceptions of Consideration. Although the following is not an exhaustive list of these exceptions, it does include those which are known and appear important. The individual manager, from a careful analysis of the situation, must add any additional factors that can be identified.

Emergencies or High-Pressure Situations. When the work involves physical danger, when time is limited, or when little tolerance for error exists, emphasis on Initiating Structure seems desirable. Research has demonstrated that subordinates often expect and prefer high Structure in such instances.

Situations in Which the Manager Is the Only Source of Information. When the leader is the only person knowledgeable about the task, subordinates often expect him or her to make specific job assignments, set deadlines, and generally engage in structuring their behavior. This does not mean that the leader cannot be considerate if this is appropriate.

Subordinate Preferences. There is limited evidence that some subordinates prefer high Structure and expect it, while others expect low Consideration and are suspicious of leaders who display high Consideration. Other preference patterns undoubtedly exist, and managers should attempt to tailor their behavior to each individual employee, as the situation dictates.

Preferences of Higher Management. In some instances, higher management has definite preferences for certain leadership styles. Higher management sometimes prefers and expects high Structure and low Consideration, and rewards managers for displaying this behavioral style. The manager should be sensitive to the desires of superiors, in addition to those of subordinates. While it is not possible to specify how these expectations may be reconciled if they diverge, compromise or direct persuasion might be useful.[25] Once again, the success of these methods probably will depend both upon the situation and the manager's skill. This leads to the last point—adaptability.

Leader Ability to Adjust. Some managers will be able to adjust their behavior to fit the situation. For others, attempts to modify behavior may look false and manipulative to subordinates. In these instances, the manager probably would be better off keeping the style with which he or she is most comfortable.

Limitations and Conclusion

The situational approach avoids the major shortcomings of both the trait and behavioral approaches to leadership. However, the implicit assumption that hierarchical leadership is always important has recently come into question. Steven Kerr, for example, points out that many factors may limit the ability of a hierarchical superior to act as a leader for subordinates.[26] Factors such as technology (for example, the assembly line), training, clear job descriptions, and the like, may provide subordinates with enough guidance so that supervisor Structure may be unnecessary to ensure task performance. Also, jobs which are intrinsically satisfying may negate the need for supervisor Consideration, since Consideration is not needed to offset job dullness.

Another problem with the situational approach, and with

leadership as a major emphasis in general, is that effective leadership may account for only 10 to 15 percent of the variability in unit performance.[27] While this percentage is certainly not trivial, it is clear that much of what affects performance in organizations is not accounted for by leadership. While studying and emphasizing leadership certainly has its merits, it could be argued that there is much to be gained by treating leadership effectiveness as but one component of managerial effectiveness. As an earlier publication emphasized:

It is necessary to note that leadership is only one way in which the manager contributes to organizational effectiveness. The manager also performs duties which are *externally oriented* so far as his unit is concerned. For example, he may spend part of his time coordinating the work of his unit with other units. Similarly, not all of the manager's *internally oriented* activities can be labeled leadership acts. Some of them concern the physical and organizational conditions under which the work unit operates. For example, the manager spends part of his time obtaining resources (materials, equipment, manpower, and so on) necessary for unit operations. This is an essential internally oriented activity but hardly constitutes leadership. Clearly, the manager must perform a mix of internal and external activities if his unit is to perform well. Leadership is only one of the internal activities performed by managers.[28]

Thus, the manager should not overemphasize the importance of leadership activities, especially if this causes other functions to be neglected.

For managers to be effective as leaders, they must attempt to be politically astute and to tailor their behaviors, taking into account differences in subordinates, superiors, and situations. Leadership should be kept in perspective. Clearly, it is important, but it cannot be treated in isolation; the importance of leadership depends upon the situation, and the practicing manager must take this into account.

23. Some Reflections on Participative Management in Libraries

Dennis W. Dickinson

At least since the 1960s there has been a growing realization that the values, needs, and motivations of the work force in this country have been changing. Persons who make up this force are, on the average, better educated, more politically aware, and more socially and economically demanding than their predecessors, i.e., generally more sophisticated and, therefore, less easily managed by traditional controls.[1] The staffs of libraries, which as institutions have more in common with other service and production organizations than many librarians are willing to admit,[2] certainly have not been exempted from this general trend.

At the same time that library managers have been attempting to devise strategies to deal with the changing nature of their labor force, there have been pressures from other quarters as well, the cumulative effect of which is manifest in a new and growing emphasis on library management. Among the problems with which library managers must deal are serious financial shortages; an increasing concern on the part of institutions in authority over libraries with efficiency, cost-benefit ratios, and accountability; and growing patron dissatisfaction with library services.[3] Concurrently, many library administrators face demands from staff members for a more active role in the administration of the library.

It is perhaps indicative of a failure to cope adequately with the circumstances described above that a number of articles have appeared in recent years deploring the present state of library

Reprinted from *College & Research Libraries* 38:253–62 (July 1978).

management. Blame is fixed variously on library schools that fail to prepare students for administrative duties; the dearth of literature pertaining to the management of institutions employing large numbers of professionals; the fact that library administrators shirk their responsibilities for providing goals, direction, and leadership in library management.[4]

Participative Management

Perhaps the most commonly offered solution for such problems is one or another form of staff participation in the management of libraries. One of the first presentations of the case for "democracy in libraries" was made in 1934,[5] and the number and variety of such arguments have been increasing ever since, resulting in a hodgepodge of disparate proposals generally glossed under the rubric of "participative management." One definition of this chimeric term is given by Flener, who states that participation

basically involves representatives of the staff working in task-oriented groups to recommend possible solutions of library problems to the library administrators, to provide for a prescribed system of communication throughout the library, and to promote the means for orderly change within the library system.[6]

But this is by no means universally accepted and, indeed, many writers on the topic do not define the term at all. This mere lack of definition does not, however, dissuade the proponents of participative management from making a number of claims for its efficacy in improving both the lot of librarians and library service as well.

One problem, of course, with using any term as ill-defined as "participative management" is that it is made to carry a tremendous amount of semantic baggage, and persons using such a term will unpack from it just what they want and no more. This has the unfortunate result that any number of people may use the term in question but mean very different things by it, even though at least some of the definitional sets will intersect to a greater or lesser extent.

Thus "participative management" has been used indiscriminately to mean everything from a situation wherein the library management simply seeks information and/or advice from staff members to one wherein the library is governed by plebiscite. To avoid the ambiguity, confusion, and emotion engendered by the term itself, it is advisable to do as Kaplan has done and speak of power sharing when one intends something less than an autocratic or dictatorial managerial style,[7] realizing that the exact nature and extent of such sharing must be specified on a case-by-case basis.

Power sharing always involves delegation, which may range from merely asking for a presentation of the facts concerning a given matter, on the one hand, to instructing a subordinate to take completely independent action on the other. It is important to bear in mind that even though one must delegate both the responsibility for a particular job and the authority necessary for its accomplishment, the delegator remains accountable for the job being done. Since that individual retains the right to retract this delegation, he or she is not completely divested of authority either. Power sharing or delegation, therefore, results in the division of work between vertical levels of an organization and in shared accountability for such work between the delegators and delegates. Delegation emphatically does not, however, simply transfer accountability from the former to the latter.[8]

Theory Y as a Means of Sharing Power

Power sharing, since it necessarily involves superior/subordinate relationships, may properly be seen as an organizational overlay on the superstructure provided by the traditional, pyramidal, administrative structure of libraries;[9] and it is naive to believe or hope that it can extend to the complete abandonment of traditional, hierarchical structure for a one-person/one-vote rule of management as advocated by some.[10] Put another way, "participatory management must become more than a euphemism for shifting responsibility to the members of a committee, or the science of management will not even be an art."[11]

Fortunately, there is available a managerial theory that is fairly specific and steers a middle course between autocracy and anarchy. This so-called Theory Y is described as a liberalized managerial philosophy predicated on the assumption that most employees are motivated and responsible workers who will more likely respond to opportunities for satisfaction of personal goals and ego needs than to the conventional carrot-stick management approach. The basic tenet of Theory Y is that such internal self-motivation can, in the proper context, satisfy the employer's organizational objectives more effectively than the usual external threats and inducements of conventional management, while increasing job satisfaction at the same time.

The Theory Y environment is said to encourage employees to feel trusted, appreciated, and responsible, and thereby predispose them to motivation toward accomplishment of organizational goals. To a considerable extent this environment is created through the delegation of as much of the organization's decision-making process as possible, i.e., a form of power sharing. However, any assumption that a Theory Y managerial approach represents a laissez-faire type of administration is contrary to fact, since management by Theory Y necessitates the same authority structure required by conventional, hierarchical, and top-down strategies. The difference between the two strategies is that in a Theory Y approach the exercise of administrative authority is more remote, subtle, and carefully planned to insure an optimum balance between authority and freedom so employees do not feel overly constrained in their pursuit of personal and professional goals.[12]

Strengths and Weaknesses of Committees

Although staff morale may improve with the introduction of some form of power sharing, as assumed by Theory Y, it does not follow that high morale will automatically result in improved organizational efficiency; and there is more than a little indication that librarians are experiencing difficulty in dealing with their newfound freedom to participate in library administration, particularly in policy making. In large part, this difficulty may be due to the mechanism often used to achieve such sharing, i.e., the ubiquitous committee.

This is particularly apparent in institutions undergoing a shift from a more or less autocratic regime to some sort of power sharing; for, even though many libraries have traditionally used committees to some extent in seeking solutions to library problems, many librarians are neither familiar with nor comfortable in a group problem-solving situation. The result often is that the product of a committee effort is of lesser quality than what might be desired and what, in fact, could have been more easily achieved through other means.[13]

Even taking what may be the most successful task-group in many libraries, i.e., the personnel or search-and-screen committee,[14] management by committee is not without its drawbacks. It has been suggested that through serving as members or chairing committees individuals are honored and gain the recognition of their peers. But the process not infrequently suffers from lack of interest, knowledge, and administrative ability on the part of committee members. This lack prevents them from carrying their assigned task to a satisfactory conclusion, even though committee members may spend much time at meetings and away from their primary library assignments.

In spite of the acknowledged costs to the library in hours lost and services not rendered, Harvey and Parr admit that they found no evidence that appointees selected by a search-and-screen committee were in any way superior to those selected by some other means. In fact, it is alleged that some search-and-screen committees, rather than selecting the person best qualified for the position to be filled, opt for a candidate who displeases no one.[15]

In addition to slowing down the selection process while ostensibly doing nothing to improve the result, Harvey and Parr remark that, like other committees, search-and-screen committees serve to diffuse responsibility as well.[16] This is especially interesting when one considers this statement.

Unless a person can unmistakably identify with the fruits of his labor, there is little chance that any of his higher-level needs will directly motivate his productivity. Any sharing of responsibilities between employees dulls this motivation and increases the opportunities for dissatisfaction.[17]

The above is of particular importance, for it suggests there is a very real danger that the alleged salutary effects of power sharing (i.e., higher staff morale, job satisfaction, and, hopefully, productivity) may well fall victim to the virtually universal committee structure employed to implement it. This seems likely, since if there is anything they consistently do, it is to diffuse responsibility.

The literature on participative management in libraries seems conveniently to overlook the counterproductive force that governance by committee can exert on a library staff. It does not take adequate account of the fact that the product of committee work often may not completely please anyone on the committee, and no one can—nor in some cases would be willing to—take individual responsibility for the outcome.

Thus the committee structure, while it facilitates consultative and advisory processes between staff and administration,[18] nonetheless, carried far enough, denies the feeling of individual responsibility and accomplishment so important to morale and motivation. But, more than that, it places effective administration in double jeopardy. In addition to increasing opportunities for staff dissatisfaction, such collectivization makes accountability impossible. In the usual case there is no way in which a higher authority, such as a college or university administration, can effectively hold a committee as such responsible for the consequences of its decisions, however unfortunate.

This latter problem is particularly apparent in an especially pernicious model of power sharing whereby the professional staff of a library, acting as an assembly, would set policy but then formally turn over responsibility for its implementation, i.e., accountability, to the library administration.[19] The effect of such a plan is, of course, to create a situation wherein the policy-making body can act with complete impunity since it will not and cannot be held accountable for the policies it sets. I shall not trot out the parade of horribles that contemplation of this proposal brings quickly to mind. Anyone with a modicum of intelligence and imagination can, without effort, conjure up the dire consequences of such a strategy.

Librarians as Professionals

One reason why these arguments seem to have been consistently swept under the rug is that some form of power sharing is, at present, widely believed to be the only means of dealing with problems engendered by the presence of large numbers of "professional" employees in a heteronomous organization. The mystique of professionalism serves as a cornerstone for most recent discussions of managerial style in libraries.

"Professional," like "participatory management," is a term without a clear and univocal definition. Drucker, however, gives what is probably as useful a definition of "professionals" as any when he asserts that they are "people who are more interested, and should be, in their profession than the institution—people who look upon the institution very largely as a place that enables them to practice a profession."[20]

In the same vein, Shaughnessy points out that professionals desire autonomy in matters affecting their work and career and seek to identify with their occupational group as opposed to the institution or organization within which they practice. Attainment of these objectives, he points out, would necessarily give professionals "a real, as distinguished from symbolic, voice in determining some of the policies of the organization in which they work."[21]

If librarians are, in fact, professionals, then it follows that some considerable amount of power sharing will constitute a necessary condition of their successful employment in libraries. However, the major premise is at least open to question. Some authors[22] argue that there are real and significant differences between the training required of a librarian and that of professionals in most other fields; e.g., to be a "professional" librarian one needs only complete a relatively brief formal training program, is not required to participate in an internship, and does not need to pass standardized examinations before being admitted as a full-fledged member of the occupational group.

When one considers the foregoing in conjunction with Drucker's judgment that, in general, many individuals in so-called professions are overtrained given the nature of their actual responsibilities, and specifically that librarianship may well have overdone the formal qualifications for membership,[23] then there is considerable justification for the view that librarianship, along with such fields as education, nursing, and social work, might better be categorized as a semiprofession. This argument is based on the fact that the vast majority of practitioners in these fields work in organizational settings and are not independent, autonomous agents as are those who have traditionally been accepted as professionals.[24]

The claim of librarians to professional status seems still less valid when one realizes that much of the work required to operate a library is little different from that which goes on along most assembly lines. Drucker speaks of the incredible amount of "donkey work" required to maintain order in a library,[25] while others have taken note of the routine, repetitive, detailed procedures that make up the bulk of work in most libraries.[26] Although Drucker's characterization of library work is, perhaps, unnecessarily pejorative and provocative, there is a good deal of truth in his assertion.

Support for this heretical view of library work appears in a recently published study of the ways in which academic librarians are perceived by students. A survey of students at a midwestern university disclosed that they generally associated librarians with a reference function and most often believed that "the librarian is 'trained' or 'skilled' rather than 'educated' or 'professional.' "[27] In addition, the authors learned that although students assume that there are educational requirements for academic librarianship they most often do not perceive librarians as possessing a specialized educational background or subject expertise. Given this view, it is not surprising that the investigators also learned that students generally found it difficult to differentiate between professional and other staff in the library and were indifferent to the distinction so long as their needs were met.

It is also significant that even though the students in this study generally equated librarians with reference librarians—perhaps the paradigm of librarianship in the minds of librarians themselves—they still did not see librarians as "professionals."[28] This sort of evidence lends credence to the view that the professional status of librarians is largely only self-ascribed.

Collegiality

But whatever the merit, or lack thereof, of arguments proceeding from the premise of "professionalism," the movement toward power sharing of some sort in libraries continues. One of the common strategies for achieving this end in academic libraries is that of a collegial organization of the library, wherein it becomes an academic unit of the parent institution and is organized accordingly, usually as prescribed by the faculty constitution or some other like document. While it is easy to understand why academic librarians might want collegiality as an organizing principle—being immersed, as they are, in an institution the most prestigious elements of which are so organized—this approach is nonetheless not without problems. The collegial model represents a radical departure from organizational principles which have governed and continue to govern libraries of all sorts (i.e., a hierarchical, bureaucratic model) and will, therefore, place a good deal of stress on the institution that must adapt to it. [29]

Generally, the push toward collegiality is predicated on the assumption that faculty in academic departments have considerable autonomy and exert a significant and direct effect on the administrative decision-making of the parent institution as well as their own departments. Evidence indicates that faculty members already operate in an environment that is hierarchial and considerably less than completely democratic,[30] and, moreover, that heteronomy in institutions of higher education is increasing.[31]

From this it may be argued that librarians who look to the collegial model as a replacement for hierarchical, bureaucratic structure and a mechanism for assuring individual autonomy in matters pertaining to their employment will almost inevitably be frustrated and disappointed. On the other hand, insofar as the collegial model does facilitate individual autonomy, it has been argued that the effects can be deleterious even to the teaching function of an academic faculty. This comes about since such autonomy can, and often does, result in the student's exposure to an unintegrated body of information that he or she is left to turn into a liberal education.[32]

Consider then for a moment the consequences of imposing a mode of organization on libraries that may have essentially the same effect on their mission as it has on the teaching faculty's. As a group the latter can function, to some extent, in a haphazard and uncoordinated manner, as most students are able to make up for themselves what is lacking in the system; i.e., they can, perhaps with the help of knowledgeable librarians, fill in the gaps in the information with which they are presented in their various courses and integrate the separate elements into what can reasonably be called an education.

The stuff of which libraries are made, however, i.e., nonsentient records of knowledge, are inert in this respect and can do nothing to make up what may be lacking in the library's processing system, for example, nor to coordinate and integrate the manifold subsystems of which a modern library is composed. Libraries are essentially complex and sophisticated logistic systems, and library materials are passive objects, not active subjects. This being the case, either materials are moved through a coordinated and integrated system from publisher to patron, or nothing happens at all.

Libraries, then, are nothing if not organizations; i.e., a library is or should be a "systematized whole . . . a body of persons organized for some purpose."[33] Thus, "organization" as it applies specifically to libraries may be defined as "the means by which management channels and directs work flow through operating units; establishes lines of authority, supervision, and control; and coordinates relationships for the accomplishment of the goals for which the library exists."[34] Such a definition is inherent in the description of library management as "all those administrative and supervisory activities in which goals and policies are formulated for the organization or its subdivisions, in which organizational plans are made, and in which the work of others is directed, monitored, and corrected as needed."[35]

But the above can seemingly only be achieved by centralizing ultimate decision-making responsibility and authority; for, given the complexity of libraries, it is only persons occupying relatively high-level administrative positions who can perceive and understand the organization as an integrated whole. Such perception and understanding are necessary for realistic definition of the library's goals and objectives and for informed assessment of what each element must do to achieve these goals. Therefore, except for very small libraries, only centralized decision-making can provide the consistency, leadership, and direction necessary for the establishment and attainment of a library's goals.

The requisite coordination and integration of the systems which taken together make up a library can only be achieved through a hierarchical authority structure; and it follows from this that collegial organization is inappropriate to libraries since persons filling positions within a chain of authority as is required for effective administration of a library must submit to decision-making, coordination, and control from above in the interest of organizational efficiency.[36] This is, of course, the antithesis of collegiality as usually understood.

Managing Change

Yet another reason for centralizing the goal-setting and decision-making functions in libraries lies in the fact that the setting of goals, if they are meaningful, will necessarily involve some potential organizational change. Such change often poses a threat to staff members since, like many service organizations that need not show a profit, libraries tend to concentrate on adding new activities without giving commensurate attention to the elimination of old ones. Thus, especially in times of declining financial resources, the primary responsibility of an administrator should be to determine which activities in the organization need to be supported more adequately, which can be downgraded or completely eliminated, and where the resources gained through the latter can be most effectively invested.

A cardinal rule of administering service organizations should be that "one doesn't start anything new unless one phases out something old." But if a staff member has spent a significant amount of time performing a particular function, the natural, human tendency will be to argue for its continuance even if it has become obsolete from the standpoint of the organization;[37] and there is reason to believe that an occupational group that considers itself "professional" will be especially vigorous in resisting any change that threatens its autonomy or security.[38]

This understandable but unfortunate tendency to retrench when threatened with change is aggravated by the disparity between the number of possible tasks in a library on the one hand and the number actually necessary to the operation of a library on the other. Gore avers that the possible tasks are infinite while the number of tasks necessary to operate a library efficiently is always less than the staff believes; and that, given this fact, it is not surprising that in a large number of libraries many necessary functions remain undone or done badly because there is no differentiation of what is necessary from what is merely possible.[39]

What it is necessary to accomplish can, of course, only be determined in light of the full scope of the library's goals, operations, and resources; and this decision-making context is, as pointed out above, only available to library administrators. They are paid to be informed in these matters and to have the vision, leadership ability, and practical good sense to direct the library properly, as indeed many chief administrators' titles would imply.

Not only do the various operations, functions, and tasks which constitute elements of the formal structure of a library need periodic review and revision, but persons who fill the positions represented on an organizational chart and perform the tasks displayed in an operations algorithm should likewise be subjected to periodic review. Without the latter, the most carefully orchestrated library system will function at less than maximum efficiency, not due to any design defect in the system itself, but to the fact that some persons on the staff cannot or will not perform in a way required by the position they hold and its relationship to the rest of the organization.

That libraries have not been notably successful in pre-employment screening of applicants, assessing the strengths and weaknesses of incumbents, providing in-service training and development programs, devising strategies for placing employees in jobs for which they are suited, or, as a last resort, discharging those few individuals not suited for library work at all, is an acknowledged fact.[40] To the extent that they continue to be unsuccessful in developing effective programs for recruiting, assessing, and developing a competent staff, libraries will be prevented from achieving their goals or will achieve them only at an excessive cost.

In a recent article, a member of the British House of Commons and management scientist, commenting on the poor performance of British industry, lays much of the blame for the striking inefficiency of the latter on the lack of a systematic review and development program for managers in most British companies and the fact that, once recruited, an individual's promotion too often depends solely on "seniority and performance which is not unsatisfactory."[41] There can be little doubt in the mind of anyone familiar with American libraries that this same analysis, mutatis mutandis, applies equally well to their problems also. As Drucker points out, there is a small number of people on any staff who perform well, and there is, consequently, a pressing need to identify these individuals and place them in positions that will make the most of their abilities.[42] Libraries have, in the main, simply failed to do this.

It seems clear, then, that a fairly strong, centralized administration will be required to plan, initiate, and direct the process of change. However, it is often argued by proponents of participative management that any administrative structure, as distinguished from line librarians, becomes isolated from the realities of day-to-day library operations, that a strong, centralized administrative structure automatically excludes librarians who are not part of the management elite from any voice in setting goals and determining policy for the library, and that such exclusion will and does preclude meaningful change in or adjustment of library policy and procedure to bring the services offered into conformity with the needs of library clientele.[43]

But there are indications that such statements are actually contrary to fact and reasons to believe that in most libraries staff recommendations and advice on a wide range of problems are actively sought and exert considerable influence on eventual decisions, even though there is a high total amount of control.[44] From the evidence available, then, it begins to appear as if the ills that power sharing is designed to cure are very likely only psychosomatic.

There is also a counter argument to be considered that holds that libraries, especially large ones, are not now providing effective information services to their clientele because of a lack of congruence between the aims and attitudes of librarians and what should be the goals of libraries as organizations.[45] The Theory Y approach to management, outlined above, offers one possibility for bringing these into coincidence; but however closure is accomplished it will, again, require significant changes in the situation and status of many librarians.

Hence, the argument that increasing staff participation in management is the best means of improving service to library clientele is of questionable validity since the tendency on the part of staff members will be to make just and only such changes as would not diminish their own autonomy, security, or self-ascribed status. Very little real change and virtually no radical, organizational change would likely come about given the primacy of a desire on the part of staff members to secure the status quo.

This line of thinking is reflected in statements such as that of Pierson, who asserts:

Status comprises roles, symbols, and rewards, not just symbols and rewards. . . . Roles, symbols, and rewards should be judged in terms of institutional goals—not in terms of librarians' aspirations. One possibility is to identify those elements of work which need doing and merit desired symbols and rewards and to confine librarians to those elements, thereby simultaneously achieving institutional goals and raising librarians' status—while, perhaps, reducing librarians' numbers.[46]

It is certainly true that there are even yet many repetitive, clerical tasks necessary to the effective and efficient operation of a library, and, in many instances, these tasks are assigned to librarians who are quite comfortable with them. However, what Pierson is proposing is to propel librarians out of low-level, routine functions and confine them instead to a considerably smaller number of jobs deserving of the perquisites and status they seek. But expecting this kind of change—which would, in spite of Pierson's cautious phrasing, surely result in a substantial reduction of available professional positions—to come about in any library through the actions of just those people who would be adversely affected by it is much like expecting a hog to guard the cabbage patch.

While change is necessary to the continued viability of libraries, care must be taken to provide job security for persons displaced by technological or organizational changes that achieve economies in the library's operations. This would be required for humanitarian reasons if for no others, but there is a practical aspect to such precautions as well. That is, although initially most or all changes that will potentially displace staff may have to be at the initiative of management, the hope and expectation should be that staff members themselves may eventually become secure enough to suggest such changes; and one way—perhaps the only way—of fostering this feeling of security is to create an environment wherein staff members can be sure that they are not crawling out on a limb and sawing it off when they offer a suggestion that will improve operational efficiency but may, in the process, eliminate or significantly alter their own job.[47]

Minimizing Bureaucracy

There is a danger, however, that while overall staff size may be reduced through a strong, central administration, that very administrative structure may grow disproportionately large through the addition of associate and assistant directors, administrative assistants, and specialized staff positions, etc.[48] The effect of such an increase in bureaucratic echelons is, more often than not, to simply remove the director from contact with the day-to-day operations of the library; and, continued long enough, this will indeed have the effect predicted by some advocates of participative management, i.e., the library director will be insulated from the realities of the organization he or she is charged with directing. Therefore, the hierarchical structure should have as few managerial levels as possible but still enough to insure a workable span of control at each level.

The same problems of complexity and scale, which render it impossible for a complete and equal sharing of power in the management of a library to succeed, likewise give the lie to any claim that it can be run singlehandedly. No administrator can know enough about the details of each operation in a library to make informed decisions without considerable advice from persons more intimately involved with the operations in question. Thus to be successful, a minimal administrative hierarchy will require frequent consultation with and considerable delegation of authority and responsibility to subordinates. Such a strategy will avoid the extremes of uninformed autocracy on the one hand and an acephalous, popular democracy on the other, while insuring that ultimate decision-making power and accountability remain squarely with the library administration.

Conclusion

Some library managers are unwilling to admit that they want and need control over the operations for which they are accountable, while subordinates are usually desirous of more influence on the decision-making process in the organization than is actually permitted, no matter what the managerial strategy employed.[49] This combination of a manager's unwillingness to express undemocratic opinions and realization that staff members desire more influence on decision-making within the organization than is or should be allowed combine to create a situation in which management may turn to some form of putative power sharing in hopes of mollifying the staff without granting them any actual decision-making power.[50]

Such duplicity serves no purpose, of course, as staff members quickly see through the sham and become variously disenchanted, cynical, and/or hostile, and with the inevitable result that the attempt at mere passification will not only fail, but will prove dysfunctional for the organization as a whole when staff members' negative feelings manifest themselves in actions or inaction, as the case may be.

The extent to which power will be shared in the organization will be influenced by a number of personal and organizational factors,[51] but it needs to be carefully spelled out to all concerned. The library staff should never be led to believe that they have or will receive more decision-making authority than the chief administrator is, in fact, willing and able to grant. It should be made clear in both policy and practice that the overall managerial style is one of consultation and coordination, with decision-making authority being delegated to particular individuals for specific purposes when dictated by circumstances.

This strategy should satisfy the needs of librarians for participation in the management of their institution as it will perforce require a great deal of delegation on the part of the library administration. It will do so, however, without a full surrender of decision-making authority or abdication of responsibility on the part of the director who will ultimately be held accountable for the performance of the organization as a whole.

None of these remarks should be taken as in any way an argument for a dictatorial, autocratic, or oligarchic management style in libraries. Rather, what I have attempted to do is to provide an antidote for some of the more extreme and sometimes naive interpretations of participative management that appear from time to time in library literature. That is, participative management or power sharing should not—and cannot, if it is to be successful—mean an abdication of responsibility for the library on the part of administrators and managers in the name of democracy. For all of the reasons mentioned above this simply will not work. What seems to be required instead is extensive and intensive consultation between administration and staff, but with the ultimate decision-making authority and attendant accountability unequivocally lodged with the library administration.

24. Self-Management as a Substitute for Leadership: A Social Learning Theory Perspective

Charles C. Manz and Henry P. Sims, Jr.

Within organizations, leadership can be described as a process through which the supervisor structures reinforcement contingencies that modify the behavior of subordinates.[1] It is important to note, however, that a work environment entails many important contingencies of reinforcement that the supervisor does not directly control. The primary purpose of this paper is to focus on a generally neglected substitute for leadership: the capability of the subordinate to exercise self-management. The concept of self-management will be described and evaluated, primarily from a social learning theory perspective,[2] and the role of the organizational leader in the development of subordinate self-management will be discussed.

Kerr and Kerr and Jermier have suggested that, when task demands are well known, then this task-related knowledge, whatever the source, can be regarded as "a substitute for leadership."[3] They have suggested further that when substitutes for leadership are salient, then the causal link between leader behavior and subordinate performance would be weak. In essence, subordinate

Reprinted from *Academy of Management Review* 5:361–67 (July 1980).

The authors wish to acknowledge the contributions of Michael J. Mahoney, who provided inspiration in the early stages, and also Robert House and Steve Kerr, who provided useful comments in the later stages. An earlier, more lengthy version of this paper was presented at the Mid-West Academy of Management, Cleveland, 1979.

performance would be primarily influenced by the substitutes for leadership rather than by any direct action or behavior on the part of the leader.

A social learning theory view of employee behavior recognizes the influence of reinforcement contingencies on the behavior of employees within organizations. A reinforcement contingency refers to the environmental cues that precede employee behavior (i.e., discriminative stimuli), and to the rewards that subsequently reinforce employee behavior. When initiated from nonleader sources, the contingencies can be regarded as substitutes for leadership. If an individual is instrumental in specifying contingencies of self-reinforcement, this self-influence might well be regarded as a substitute for leadership.

The focus of our paper is the role of the individual in managing his or her own behavior. Our goal is to shed light on the what, why, how, and when of self-management, or, more specifically, *what* self-management is, *why* it might be a desirable pursuit for organizations, and *how* and *when* the leader might trigger effective self-management in individuals.

What Is Self-Management?

Definition and Description

Self-management, more often called self-control, has been defined as follows: "A person displays self-control when in the relative absence of immediate external constraints, he engages in behavior whose previous probability has been less than that of alternatively available behaviors."[4] Self-control can be said to include the following major characteristics: the existence of two or more response alternatives; different consequences for the alternatives; and, usually, the maintenance of self-controlling actions by longer-term external consequences.[5]

The administration of consequences plays an important role in both self-management and the management of others. However, the question of who actually administers the consequences is perhaps less important than the determination of who evaluates whether the response requirements for reinforcement have been met. Goldiamond reminds us of Skinner's suggestion that all reinforcement could be described as self-administered because it is the person's response that produces the reinforcement. Thus, an important consideration is the issue of who has the evaluative control in determining if responses have met the criteria for reinforcement.[6]

In summary, several aspects of self-management are potentially important. It can be described as a process whereby a person is faced with immediate response alternatives involving different consequences and the person chooses an apparent low-probability response. Self-management behavior may include personal goals, self-instructions toward achieving goals, self-administered consequences, and plans for one's behavior patterns.[7] The self-management process may be encouraged and maintained by desirable long-term consequences. Finally, its true effects will be mediated by whoever evaluates responses against existing criteria.

The Natural Occurrence of Self-Management

We all exercise self-control over our own behaviors to some degree. Typically we set certain behavior standards and reward or punish ourselves according to judgments we make of our performance in relation to these standards.[8] Bandura indicates that we typically set standards in comparison to three referents: past performance, the observed performance of others, and socially acquired performance criteria.[9] The difficulty of these self-imposed standards is determined by what we see in highly observable models and by our socialization history.[10]

Furthermore, the topography of self-control behavior is itself a function of the resulting consequences. This suggests the existence of two levels of consequences: those directly involved in the self-controlling process, and those resulting from the outcomes of self-controlling behavior. Consider the example of a long-distance runner. Imagine that this individual praises herself for each mile run during training. Then, if she goes on to win a gold medal in a marathon, she has received an external consequence contingent on her performance. Self-praise served as an internal consequence and was part of the self-control process that helped to manage the training behavior. The winning of a gold medal was an external consequence resulting from the effective training that should serve to reinforce such self-controlling behavior in the future. In the absence of long-term external reinforcement, such self-controlling behavior is not likely to be continued.[11] Furthermore, intermediate or sustaining achievements, such as learning and physical conditioning, would aid progress toward winning a gold medal.

In summary, a certain degree of self-control is present even in situations with extremely strong external contingencies. Conversely, in situations where a high degree of self-control is present, long-term external consequences may be critical for maintaining the self-controlling behavior.

The Role of Covert Processes

Social learning theory proposes that an integration of cognitive and environmental determinants yields a more adequate explanation of human behavior than does focus on strictly environmental determinants.[12] This perspective inspires a new focus on the self-regulatory behaviors of individuals in conjunction with the external consequences that now receive major attention. Thoresen and Mahoney point out that covert self-instructions, self-evaluations, and self-reactions are invariably involved whenever an individual alters the consequences of his own behavior.[13]

Furthermore, some have argued that covert activity may be governed by the same basic principles as overt behavior. For example, Thoresen and Mahoney have described what is called "covert behavior modification," which suggests that internal phenomena (i.e., thoughts) can be considered as internal behavior responses similar to those of external behavior.[14]

When one considers the possibility that covert events are capable of the same basic three functions as overt events (antecedents, target behaviors, and consequences), several complex interactions between the overt and covert level are possible. Thoresen and Mahoney conclude that the most successful covert self-control methods typically involve some interaction with external control.[15] All this suggests that careful scrutiny be made of both covert and overt forces, and the possible interaction of the two.

Why Self-Management?

Effective self-management appears to offer potential benefits to individual employees and organizations. For example, a primary assumption of attribution theory is that the way we respond to others is dependent on the attributes (reasons) we assign for others' behavior.[16] One common tendency of individuals is explaining others' behavior by internal personal dispositions, while explaining their own behavior in terms of the external situation. This tendency has been called "over attribution."[17] A manager, for example, may attribute poor performance to internal attributes of the subordinate ("He has a bad attitude") rather than to inadequacies in the structure of external reinforcement contingencies that support desirable employee behavior. If an employee takes responsibility for his own behavior, on the other hand, some observer biases may be limited. A person would not be likely to attribute a decrease in his own performance to a character flaw, when it has, in fact, been caused by situational constraints. Ineffective self-management, however, may result if an individual attributes failures to the situation when they could in fact be prevented with one's own initiative.

Furthermore, from a cost/benefit perspective, self-management can be considered a desirable objective because it involves less expense to the organization, in terms of dollars and time, than having someone else serve as a manager.[18] Furthermore, the employee's manager is free to address longer-term problems and issues that need attention.

Finally, because all individuals appear to engage in some sort of self-controlling behavior, it is too important for organizations to ignore. Indeed, many individuals may engage in *dysfunctional* self-management. For example, a person who sets unrealistically high goals may become frustrated rather than motivated to achieve them.[19]

How to Develop Self-Management

In this section, we will describe strategies and procedures for developing self-management behavior in subordinates. Thoresen and Mahoney suggest two general strategies: environmental planning and behavioral programming.[20] Environmental planning involves changing situational factors before the performance of target behaviors. An employee who is making an effort to cut down on time spent chatting with others might rearrange the office furniture so that the desk does not face the door. Behavioral programming includes the self-administration of consequences contingent on the performance of target responses. An example might be rewarding oneself with a steak dinner and bottle of expensive wine after a sale.

Two important elements of self-management can be delineated in these strategies. First, before a target behavior, environmental cues and personal goals or standards are important. Second, after a target behavior, the consequences of one's performance are important. Following are some specific procedures to implement these strategies.

Self-Management Procedures

Self-observation involves systematic data gathering about one's own behavior, thus establishing the basis for self-evaluation, which in turn provides information on which to base self-reinforcement. The individual who desires to reduce informal conversations might record the number of such conversations in each day and the conditions that existed at that time. Thus a basis is established for self-evaluation and reinforcement as well as possible insight regarding the causes of one's behavior. A long-distance runner, on the other hand, could time her daily practice runs.

Specifying goals is another technique of effective self-management. Latham and Yuki[21] have reviewed research which concludes that specific goals result in improved performance. Furthermore, goal attainment seems to possess strong reinforcing properties, subsequently leading to further goals in the pursuit of organizational objectives. Indeed, Mahoney and Arnkoff[22] suggest that goal setting might be a sufficient self-regulatory strategy in itself. They point out that goals may be more effective if they are publicly stated, focus on behavior change, and are short range instead of distant. The long-distance runner, for example, can set distance and time goals as a part of her training.

Cueing strategies (stimulus control) can be described as the gradual limiting of discriminative stimuli that precede maladaptive behavior while simultaneously increasing exposure to stimuli evoking more desirable behavior.[23] Bandura[24] has suggested that the aim is to regulate the frequency of certain behaviors by altering stimulus conditions. For the individual seeking to reduce informal conversation behavior, rearranging the office removes the visual cue (i.e., viewing of people passing in the hall) that tends to stimulate the undesired behavior (i.e., initiating an informal conversation with colleagues who go by the door). Another cueing strategy might be to close the door. Luthans and Davis[25] provide several examples of successful applications of cueing strategies.

Incentive modification can be divided into self-reinforcement and self-punishment, both of which are based on self-evaluation. There are several factors that apparently influence the execution of self-reinforcement. Bandura indicates that individuals who gain self-control over administration of reinforcers are likely to reinforce themselves in a manner similar to the way that they were initially externally reinforced by socialization agents.[26] An individual who has been liberally reinforced externally for mediocre performance, for example, is likely to continue with internal reinforcement in similar circumstances. Furthermore, Speidel points out that special conditions may mediate the effect of self-reinforcement: the self-control behavior already in an individual's repertoire, the level of aversiveness of the task, and the level of attractiveness of the reward itself.[27]

There is substantial support for the notion that self-reinforcement can be effective for self-management. Mahoney and Arnkoff[28] concluded that self-reinforcement has consistently yielded positive outcomes. In reviewing experimental evidence, Scott and Rosentiel[29] found covert positive reinforcement to be successful in modifying wide varieties of behaviors.

The apparent effectiveness of self-reinforcement does not seem to be shared by self-punishment, which attempts to reduce undesired behavior by self-administering *aversive* consequences. Because the aversive consequence for undesired behavior is self-administered, it can be freely avoided.[30] Successful use of self-punishment requires the consequence to be sufficiently aversive to suppress undesired behavior yet not so aversive that it won't be used.[31]

Rehearsal is the systematic practice of a desired performance.[32] Rehearsal can occur either overtly or covertly (i.e., imagined performance of desired behavior). Kazdin,[33] for example, found that covert rehearsal was effective in producing assertive behavior. Mahoney and Arnkoff[34] point out that covert rehearsal allows an individual to rehearse a desired performance before an attempt at actual overt performance. In addition, Kazdin[35] suggests that the effects of rehearsal may be mediated by the consequences following imagined performance of behavior. In other words, rehearsal might be paired with imagined or actual consequences, or both. A salesperson, for example, could rehearse a sales presentation both covertly and overtly and thereby refine it. Then, through intentionally imagining the desirable consequences of a successful sale, feelings of confidence could be reinforced.

Encouraging Self-Management for Subordinates

How can a leader encourage subordinates to engage in self-management? First, the importance of modeling should not be underestimated. Bandura suggests that individuals who effectively use self-management procedures can serve as models for others to learn self-management.[36] Persons will adopt the standards for self-reinforcement that they observe in exemplary models and then evaluate their own performance according to these standards. In addition, if a leader reinforces self-management in one subordinate, a self-management model is available for other subordinates. Above all, whether intentional or not, the leader's own self-management behavior inevitably serves as a model to subordinates. Consequently, overdependence by the leader on the behaviors of superiors would provide a poor self-management model.

A more directed procedure (originally offered by Meichenbaum[37]) is described by Thoresen and Mahoney[38]: "initial modeling, guided participation, and gradual development of covert self-control." These procedures might be adapted to the "leader-subordinate" situation. For example, in the guided participation phase, the verbal behavior of the leader is critical. The leader attempts to evoke subordinate self-management through a series of directed questions. First, self-observation: "Do you know how well you are doing right now?" "How about keeping a record of how many times that happens?" Second, self-goal setting: "How many will you shoot for?" "When do you want to have it finished?" "What will your target be?" Then, self-evaluation leading to self-reinforcement: "How do you think you did?" "Are you pleased with the way it went?" Finally, rehearsals: "Why don't we try it out?" "Let's practice that." The aim, of course, is to give the employee practice in self-management behaviors.

It is also important that social reinforcement be applied when these self-management behaviors do occur. Unfortunately, some social reinforcement may detract from the development of effective self-management capabilities (e.g., reinforcement by peers that encourages overconformity). Note the elements that seem to be of particular importance: the evaluative and reinforcement functions are gradually shifted from external sources to the individual; the progress made in self-regulatory behavior is reinforced; and a shift is made from external material rewards to self-administered covert consequences.[39]

Finally, the most important requirement is that reinforcing functions and patterns of the leader change as the subordinate becomes more and more capable of self-management. Initially, the leader reinforces specific performance-related behaviors by the subordinate. As time goes by, the reinforcement shifts from the performance-related behaviors to the process of self-management. That is, the primary function of the leader becomes that of encouraging and reinforcing processes such as goal setting and 'self-reinforcement rather than *directly* reinforcing subordinate performance. Some supervisors may resist this shift because it involves less direct control over subordinates. Over the long run, however, this decrease of direct control is desirable because overall subordinate effectiveness should be improved as a result of increased self-management capability.

A note of caution is important. Bandura points out that self-management attempts can fail because of vague self-instructions that have no immediate implications for behavior.[40] Furthermore, self-control behavior may be difficult to sustain without some form of "self-reinforcing operations" for support.[41] Finally, once self-management procedures are established, an individual is faced with both external and self-administered consequences, which at times may conflict.[42] Therefore, care must be taken in developing self-management in subordinates.

When Should Managers Encourage Employee Self-Management?

Overall, we have taken the position that moving employees toward self-management is advantageous to the organization. Nevertheless, it is naive to assume that self-management is *always* appropriate. Indeed, external managerial control will always play an important role in any organization. Also, it is incorrect to assume that self-management and external control are mutually exclusive. Even in the most intensive external control situations, employees always exercise some degree of self-management. Conversely, even when self-management is deliberately encouraged, some external control by management, primarily focused on output measures, or at the task boundary, is commonly found and is typically wanted by employees. In addition, external reinforcement of the self-control process will be necessary to make it work. There are several important situational factors that will likely influence the appropriateness of attempts to develop self-management in subordinates. These include the nature of the task, the nature of the problem, the availability of time, and the importance of subordinate development.

The nature of the task itself has some connection with the potential applicability of self-management. Cummings and Slocum and Sims[43] have attempted to link concepts of technology/task with self-regulation types of control systems. In addition, a managerial decision to "enrich" a job is typically concerned directly with the issue of self-management. It seems clear that when a task is largely creative, analytical, or intellectual in nature, greater self-management would be appropriate.[44]

Self-management might be viewed as falling on a participative decision continuum.[45] Managers must make decisions as to how much self-management to encourage in subordinate employees, and some criteria are available to help enlighten this decision.[46] In general, more participative decision methods are appropriate when (1) the problem is not highly structured, (2) information is needed from subordinates, (3) solutions must be accepted by subordinates to ensure implementation, and (4) subordinates share organizational goals.

The time available for decision-making or problem solving is another element that has bearing on whether self-management should be encouraged. In crisis situations, the time may simply not be available to develop self-management. However, if crisis situations are *likely* to occur in the absence of a leader, then self-management training would be appropriate.

At the extremes are the "development" mode versus the "short-term efficiency" mode. In the latter, self-management will be deemphasized, except as required by the immediate task, in order to speedily carry out the task. In the development mode, subordinate self-management will be emphasized and encouraged and will be regarded as an investment for the future. One might term this mode as "leader investment behavior" from which a return in later time periods is expected. Most managers will operate in some zone between these two extreme modes of encouraging employee self-management. In the end, each manager must evaluate the specific situation. Such factors as individual employees' eagerness, desire, and present capacity for self-management are important. House[47] has even suggested that an individual's Need Achievement[48] "may well be a measure of an individual's orientation/predisposition toward self-management." Furthermore, it would be naive to argue that the self-administration of external rewards such as one's pay would not lead to organizational problems. Many other reinforcers could be tapped, however. (See Luthans and Kreitner,[49] for example, regarding nonmonetary organizational incentives.)

Summary

We have presented definitions and descriptions of self-management (a critical element of social learning theory), as well as examples of specific self-management techniques that can be used by organizational employees. The role of the leader as one who can encourage and develop self-management subordinates has been discussed. Overall, we have taken the position that self-manage-ment by individual employees can be instrumental in achieving organizational goals, and that it is a useful and legitimate role of the supervisor to develop and encourage self-management capa-bilities. Subordinate self-management can reduce the need for close supervision because it can indeed be a "substitute for lead-ership."

Additional Readings

Of all of the functions of management, more has undoubtedly been written about the leadership aspects of directing than any other topic. Fortunately, several works are available that bring together much of this literature for the reader. The most compre-hensive summary of leadership research and study can be found in Stogdill's *Handbook of Leadership* (Free Press, 1974). Barrow ("The Variables of Leadership: A Review and Conceptual Frame-work," *Academy of Management Review*, April 1977) further analyzes the literature of leadership and categorizes it into four interrelated classifications:

1. Leader behavior investigations
2. Situational and reciprocal causal investigations
3. Leadership effectiveness theories
4. Normative leadership approaches.[1]

This author further refines the examination of the variables of leadership by developing a three-factor "Leadership Effectiveness Framework" that will be useful to the reader attempting to com-bine the various approaches to leadership. Barrow's 200-item bibliography provides an important source of further reading as well. In addition, *Crosscurrents in Leadership* (edited by Hunt and Larson, Leadership Symposia Series, vol. 5, Southern Illinois Uni-versity Press, 1979) provides an important overview of current thought in leadership research, and Katz and Kahn summarize approaches to leadership and their applicability to the open social system concept in *The Social Psychology of Organizations* (chapter 16, 2nd ed., Wiley, 1978).

Because the majority of the literature on leadership is reviewed by Stogdill and Barrow, the additional reading selections for this chapter will concentrate on materials in the library literature and supplementary items in business literature that suggest new directions for the future of the directing function.

Participative management is both a leadership style and a means of overall management and decision-making. As selection 23 suggests, this approach to directing has received great attention in library literature (as well as in business and public administration writings). Kaplan has reviewed the literature in this area in "The Literature of Participation: From Optimism to Realism" (*College and Research Libraries*, November 1975). Important questions about this approach to management are raised by Nigro and Bellone ("Participative Management: Making It Work," *The Bureaucrat*, Winter 1979–80), Kelly and Khozan ("Participative Management: Can It Work?" *Business Horizons*, August 1980), McDaniel and Askmos ("Participatory Management: An Executive Alternative for Human Service Organizations," *Human Resource Management*, Spring 1980) and Nyren ("Participatory Management in Libraries: What Is Its Future?" *Library Journal*, 15 May 1976). The importance of the leadership function in collaborative work groups is discussed by Finch ("Collaborative Leadership in Work Settings," *Journal of Applied Behavioral Science*, July-August-September 1977), Kuehl ("Leader Effectiveness in Committee-like Groups," *Journal of Business*, April 1977) and Schmuck ("Developing Collaborative Decision-Making: The Importance of Trusting, Strong and Skillful Leaders," *Educational Technology*, October 1972).

Several specific aspects of the directing process are also worthy of further exploration through the literature. These include delegation, coordination, and the communication of direction in the management process. Delegation is addressed by Lagges's "The Role of Delegation in Improving Productivity" (*Personnel Journal*, November 1979), and coordination by Pugh's "Effective Coordination in Organizations" (*SAM Advanced Management Journal*, Spring 1979). The actual giving of directions is both a function of communicating and directing. Potter's "Speaking with Authority: How to Give Directions" (*Supervisory Management*, March 1980) and Lewis's discussion of instruction-giving tech-

niques ("Communication Stratagems for Accomplishing Organization Objectives," in *Organizational Communication*, Grid, 1975)
are both pragmatic approaches to this vital part of the directing
process. Delegation and coordination often require the resolution
of conflicts between superiors and subordinates. Approaches to
the resolution of these conflicts are outlined by Burke in "Methods
of Resolving Superior-Subordinate Conflict: The Constructive Use
of Subordinate Differences and Disagreements" (*Readings in Interpersonal and Organizational Communication*, 2nd ed., Holbrook
Press, 1973).

Examining the *role* of the library director can be an enlightening
way of exploring the directing function. Two books provide a particularly rich source of information about approaches to the managerial role—Mintzberg's *The Nature of Managerial Work* (Harper
& Row, 1973) and Sayles's *Leadership: What Effective Managers
Really Do . . . and How They Do It* (McGraw-Hill, 1979). Kemper
and Ostrander offer a pragmatic and personal overview of the
library director's role in *Directorship by Objectives* (Libraries Unlimited, 1977). In a more specific vein, McAnally and Downs ("The
Changing Role of Directors of University Libraries," *College and
Research Libraries*, March 1973) and Metz ("The Role of the
Academic Library Director," *Journal of Academic Librarianship*,
July 1979) have examined the director's role and the changes in it.

The dilution of authority of library administrators is examined
by Allison's "Factors Affecting Administration in United States
Academic Libraries during the Period 1971–1975" (*Illinois Occasional Papers*, #138). Role conflicts experienced by library directors are outlined by Lee in "Conflict and Ambiguity in the Role of
the Academic Library Director" (*College and Research Libraries*,
September 1977). Additional views of leadership in a library setting are provided by Dragon ("Leader Behavior in Changing Libraries," *Library Research*, 1979) and Sparks ("Library Management: Consideration and Structure," *Journal of Academic Librarianship*, May 1976).

What is perhaps most important to consider when looking at
the directing function are future approaches that might yield
significant results. Odiorne's "A Management Style for the Eighties" (*University of Michigan Business Review*, March 1978), Gray
and Landrum's "Are You Ready for Tomorrow's Management
Style?" (*Business*, November-December 1979), Appley's "New Directions for Management" (*Supervisory Management*, February
1981), Rieder's "The Role of Tomorrow's Manager" (*Personnel
Administrator*, December 1979), Mueller's "Leading-Edge Leader-

ship" (*Human Systems Management*, February 1980), and Maccoby's *The Gamesman* (Simon & Schuster, 1977) also suggest new approaches for the leadership of tomorrow's organizations. Additions to or substitutes for leadership are discussed by Luthans and Davis ("Behavioral Self-Management: The Missing Link in Managerial Effectiveness" (*Organizational Dynamics*, Summer 1979) and Kerr ("Substitutes for Leadership: Some Implications for Organizational Design," in *Organization Design: Theoretical Perspectives and Empirical Findings*, Kent State University Press, 1977).

Developing these new approaches to directing may also require changes in leadership development. The kinds of skills needed for directing are addressed by Katz ("Skills of an Effective Administrator," *Harvard Business Review*, September-October 1974) and in *Personnel Journal* ("What Successful Managers Say about Their Skills," November 1978). Specific aspects of development for future leaders are outlined by Weihrich ("How to Change a Leadership Pattern," *Management Review*, April 1979), Sinetar ("Developing Leadership Potential," *Personnel Journal*, March 1981), and Guglielmino ("Developing the Top-Level Executive for the 1980s and Beyond," *Training and Development Journal*, April 1979). Finally, McClure's "Library Managers: Can They Manage? Will They Lead?" (*Library Journal*, 15 November 1980) should be examined once again to help in assessing future need for leadership development in the library environment.

Notes

Introduction

1. There are many avenues for educating oneself about library management. Course work, credit-free workshops and seminars, conference programs, observation of managerial behavior in others—all are ways of learning about management. One method of acquiring knowledge about library management is through reading management-related literature. This literature is generally available to all individuals, regardless of level or affiliation, location, or ability-to-pay. Thus, the "student" of library management, at any level—in a first professional or advanced degree program, a continuing education activity, or a self-study endeavor—may undertake an examination of management literature as a means of developing a better understanding of the process of library management. (See Ruth J. Person, "Middle Managers in Academic and Public Libraries: Managerial Role Concepts," Ph.D. diss., University of Michigan, 1980, pp. 104–10, for a discussion of the ways in which library managers learn about the process of management and its interpretation.)

2. Joseph L. Massie, The Essentials of Management, 3rd ed. (Englewood Cliffs, N.J.: Prentice-Hall, 1979), p. 4.

3. Leonard Sayles, Leadership: What Effective Managers Really Do . . . and How They Do It (New York: McGraw-Hill, 1979), p. 7.

4. Henry L. Mintzberg, The Nature of Managerial Work (New York: Harper & Row, 1973).

5. Richard DeGennaro, "Library Administration and New Management Systems," Library Journal 103:2477–82 (15 Dec. 1978); Pauline A. Thomas and Valerie A. Ward, Where the Time Goes (London: Aslib, 1973).

6. Peter Haskell, "Library Administrators and the Need for Continuing Education in Process Skills," College and Research Libraries News 41:388 (Dec. 1980).

7. Jay W. Lorsch, "Making Behavioral Science More Useful," Harvard Business Review 57:171–80 (Mar.-April 1979).

Management in the Library Setting

1. See Frank Harrison, "Towards a General Model of Management," Journal of General Management 5:33–41 (Winter 1979/80).

1. Managing Not-for-Profit Enterprises—Newman and Wallender

1. R. H. Brady, "MBO Goes to Work in the Public Sector," *Harvard Business Review* 51:65–74 (Mar. 1973); F. H. Genck, "Public Management in America," *AACSB Bulletin* 9, no. 3 (Apr. 1973); S. K. Gore and C. E. Floyd, "Research on Higher Education Administration and Policy: An Uneven Report," *Public Administration Review* 35:111–18 (Jan. 1975); M. E. McGill and L. M. Wooton, eds., "Symposium: Management in the Third Sector," *Public Administration Review* 35:443–47 (Sept. 1975); M. A. Murray, "Comparing Public and Private Management: An Exploratory Essay," *Public Administration Review* 35:364–71 (July 1975); B. A. Olive, "The Administration of Higher Education: A Bibliographical Survey," *Administrative Science Quarterly* 11:671–77 (Mar. 1967).

2. Internal Revenue Service, *How to Apply for Recognition for Exemption for an Organization*, and "Activity Code Numbers of Exempt Organizations," (Washington, D.C.: Supt. of Documents, 1976).

3. Amitai Etzioni, "The Third Sector and Domestic Missions," *Public Administration Review* 53:314–27 (July 1973); Theodore Levitt, *The Third Sector: New Tactics for a Responsive Society* (New York: AMACOM Pr., 1973).

4. G. T. Allison, *Essence of Decision: Explaining the Cuban Missile Crisis* (Boston: Little, Brown, 1971), chapters 1 and 3.

5. M. J. Roberts, "An Evolutionary and Institutional View of Behavior of Public and Private Companies," *American Economic Review* 65:415–27 (May 1975); R. L. Satow, "Value-Rational Authority and Professional Organizations: Weber's Missing Type," *Administrative Science Quarterly* 20:626–31 (Dec. 1975).

6. E. E. Savas, "New Directions for Urban Analysis," *Interfaces* 6:1–9 (Nov. 1975).

7. Paul Lawrence and J. W. Lorsch, *Studies in Organization Design* (Homewood, Ill.: Irwin, 1970).

8. W. H. Newman, *Constructive Control: Design and Use of Control Systems* (Englewood Cliffs, N.J.: Prentice-Hall, 1975).

2. Conceptual Dimensions—Nitecki

1. Paul J. Gordon, "All Very Well in Practice! But How Does It Work Out in Theory?" *Wilson Library Bulletin* 42:676–85 (Mar. 1968). Reprinted in Ross Shimmon, ed., *A Reader in Library Management* (London: Clive Bingley, and Hamden, Conn.: Linnet, 1976), pp. 35–47, with linking commentaries by John Allred, K. H. Jones, and Peter Jordan.

2. For a comprehensive bibliography, see N. R. Hunter, *Library Management: Bibliography* (Bradford, England: MCB Publications, Ltd., 1977).

3. Dalton E. McFarland, "Management, Definition of," in Lester Robert Bittel, ed., *Encyclopedia of Professional Management* (New York: McGraw-Hill, 1978), p. 640.

4. Peter F. Drucker, *Management: Tasks, Responsibilities, Practices* (New York: Harper & Row, 1974), pp. 398–400.

5. Ken H. Jones, "Creative Library Management: The Existential Perspective," *The Assistant Librarian* 66:178–82 (Nov. 1973); idem, "Creative Library Management: The Limiting Factors," *The Assistant Librarian* 66:158–62 (Oct. 1973). Reprinted in Shimmon, *Reader in Library Management,* pp. 46–68.

6. Joel de Rosney, *The Macroscope: A New World Scientific System*; trans. by Robert Edwards (New York: Harper & Row, 1979), p. 130.

7. Paul Howard, "The Functions of Library Management," *The Library Quarterly* 10:313 (July 1940). Howard lists seven major functions of management, of which the following are also incorporated in our conceptual management: (1) directing ("establishment of objectives and the formulation of policies"), (2) organizing ("the processes by which relationships within the library are established for the purposes of facilitating management and operation"), and (3) abstract evaluation ("concerned with those intangible elements in library service which are not yet susceptible of measurement"). Not included in our model are (1) ordering ("formulating and issuing orders"), (2) supervising ("seeing whether orders are carried out and seeing that orders are carried out"), (3) controlling ("producing in the workers the willingness and capacity to carry out orders"), (4) concrete evaluating ("those elements in the library which may be reduced to figures"), and (5) representing ("liaison between the public and the library").

8. Paraphrased after A. D. Hall and R. E. Fagen, "Definition of a System," *General Systems Yearbook* 1:18 (1956).

9. Rosney, *Macroscope,* p. 58.

10. Bittel, *Encyclopedia of Professional Management,* p. 1130.

11. Ibid., p. 1131.

12. A. M. McMahon and J. Tydeman, "A System Framework for Literary Analysis," in George J. Klir, ed., *Applied General Systems Research* (New York and London: Plenum Pr., 1978), p. 913.

13. John R. Haak, "Goal Determination," *Library Journal* 96:1573–78 (1 May 1978). Reprinted in Shimmon, *Reader in Library Management,* p. 85.

14. John Walton, "The Administration of Libraries," *Johns Hopkins University Ex Libris* 16:1–2 (Nov. 1957). Reprinted in Paul Wasserman and Mary Lee Bundy, eds., *Reader in Library Administration* (Washington, D.C.: NCR Microcard Ed., 1968), p. 139. Includes a quote from introductory commentary.

15. Dennis C. Fields, "Library Management by Objectives: The Human Way," *College & Research Libraries* 35:346 (Sept. 1974).

16. Louis Round Wilson and Maurice T. Tauber, *The University Library: Its Organization, Administration and Functions* (Chicago: Univ. of Chicago Pr., 1945), p. 98.

17. Wasserman and Bundy, *Reader,* p. 254.

18. James Michalko, "Management by Objectives and the Academic Library: A Critical Overview," *The Library Quarterly* 45:245 (July 1975).

19. This study is an outgrowth of papers developing the concept of a root-metaphor theory in librarianship. For a summary statement and additional bibliography, see Joseph Z. Nitecki, "An Idea of Librarianship: An Outline of Root-Metaphor Theory in Library Science," *The Journal of Library History, Philosophy, and Comparative Librarianship* 16, no. 1–2 (Winter/Spring, 1981).

3. The Management of Libraries—Drake
1. Peter F. Drucker, "Managing the Public Service Institution," *College & Research Libraries* 37:4–14 (Jan. 1976).
2. Harold L. Wilensky, "The Professionalization of Everyone?" *American Journal of Sociology* 70:138 (Sept. 1964).
3. Robert N. Anthony and Regina Herzlinger, *Management Control in Nonprofit Organizations* (Homewood, Ill.: Irwin, 1975), p. 34–38.
4. Mary Lee Bundy and Paul Wasserman, "Professionalism Reconsidered," *College & Research Libraries* 29:5–26 (Jan. 1968).
5. Arthur M. McAnnally and Robert B. Downs, "The Changing Role of Directors of University Libraries," *College & Research Libraries* 34:103–25 (Mar. 1973).
6. Doralyn J. Hickey, "Public and Technical Library Services: A Revised Relationship," in Norman D. Stevens, ed., *Essays for Ralph Shaw* (Metuchen, N.J.: Scarecrow, 1975), p. 180.
7. Philip Kotler, *Marketing for Nonprofit Organizations* (Englewood Cliffs, N.J.: Prentice-Hall, 1975), p. 43.
8. Richard Durbin and W. Herbert Springall, *Organization and Administration of Health Care: Theory, Practice and Environment* (St. Louis: Mosby, 1969), p. 138.
9. Rue Bucher and Joan Stalling, "Characteristics of Professional Organizations," *Journal of Health and Social Behavior* 10:5 (Mar. 1969).
10. Bundy and Wasserman, "Professionalism Reconsidered," p. 14.
11. Drucker, "Managing the Public Service Institution," p. 11.
12. McAnnally and Downs, "The Changing Role of Directors of University Libraries," p. 111.

4. Administration —Martell
1. Peter Drucker, *Technology, Management and Society* (New York: Harper & Row, 1970), p. 12.
2. Sherman Krupp, *Patterns in Organization Analysis: A Critical Examination* (New York: Holt, 1961), p. 80.
3. Ben-Ami Lipetz, "A View of the Special Library of the Future," *Drexel Library Quarterly* 5:195–208 (Oct. 1969).
4. Alvin Toffler, "New York Faces Future Shock," *New York,* 27 July 1970, p. 22.
5. Douglas McGregor, *The Professional Manager,* ed. Caroline McGregor and Warren G. Bennis (New York: McGraw-Hill, 1967).
6. Ibid., p. 7.
7. Thomas J. Sergiovanni and others, "Toward a Particularistic

Approach to Leadership Style: Some Findings," *American Educational Research Journal* 6:62–79 (Jan. 1969).

8. McGregor, *Professional Manager*, p. 67.

9. Philip E. Slater and Warren G. Bennis, "Democracy Is Inevitable," *Harvard Business Review* 42:51–59 (Mar.–Apr. 1964).

10. Chris Argyris, "Today's Problems with Tomorrow's Organization," *Journal of Management Studies* 4:31–55 (Feb. 1967).

11. McGregor, *Professional Manager*, pp. 10–11.

12. Drucker, *Technology*, pp. 15–16.

13. Ibid., p. 21.

14. Chris Argyris, "Management Information Systems: The Challenge to Rationality and Emotionality," *Management Science* 17:B275–92 (Feb. 1971).

15. Paul R. Lawrence and Jay W. Lorsch, in their landmark work, *Organization and Environment: Managing Differentiation and Integration* (Homewood, Ill.: Irwin, 1967), analyzed four variables crucial to the success of any organization: (1) orientation toward particular goals, (2) time orientation, (3) interpersonal orientation, (4) formality of structure.

16. Robert J. Mockler, "Situational Theory of Management," *Harvard Business Review* 49:147 (May-June 1971). Mockler finds a parallel development (situational approach) in the behavioral area of management theory. "Attention has shifted from presenting universal leadership guidelines to studying such situational factors as operating requirements, individual and work-group needs, and the leadership style of individual supervisors."

17. Peter Drucker, *Age of Discontinuity* (New York: Harper & Row, 1969), p. 264.

18. Slater and Bennis, "Democracy Is Inevitable," p. 52.

19. Douglas Davis, "New Architecture: Building for Man," *Newsweek*, 19 April 1971, p. 88.

Additional Readings

1. John F. Magee, "Management: An Evolving Technology," *Human Systems Management* 1:49 (1980).

Decision-Making and Planning

1. John F. Magee, "Management: An Evolving Technology," *Human Systems Management* 1:49 (1980).

2. Ibid.

3. R. L. Ackoff, "A Concept of Corporate Planning," *Long Range Planning* 3:2 (1970).

6. Psychological Aspects—Taylor

1. See R. W. Knoepfel, "The Politics of Planning: Man in the Decision Process," *Long Range Planning* 6:17–21 (1973); R. F. Neuschel, *Management by Systems* (Toronto: McGraw-Hill, 1960); and M. K. Starr, "Commentary," *Management Science* 12:30–35 (1965).

2. R. Ackoff, "A Concept of Corporate Planning," *Long Range Planning* 3:3 (1970).

3. Starr, "Commentary," p. 31.

4. Ackoff, "A Concept of Corporate Planning," p. 2.

5. Ibid.

6. R. N. Taylor and M. D. Dunnette, "Relative Contribution of Decision-Maker Attributes to Decision Processes," *Organizational Behavior and Human Performance* 12:286–89 (1974).

7. K. R. MacCrimmon and R. N. Taylor, "Decision Making and Problem Solving," in M. D. Dunnette, ed., *Handbook of Industrial and Organizational Psychology* (Chicago: Rand-McNally, 1975).

8. See D. E. Ewing, *The Human Side of Planning* (Toronto: Macmillan, 1969); M. Radnor, A. H. Rubenstein, and D. A. Tansik, "Implementation in Operations Research and R&D in Government and Business Organizations," *Operations Research* 18:967–91 (1970); and G. Watson, "Resistance to Change," in Bennis, Benne and Chen, eds., *The Planning of Change,* 2nd ed. (Toronto: Holt, 1969), pp. 488–98.

9. Ewing, *The Human Side of Planning,* p. 44.

10. See J. S. Hammond, "The Roles of the Manager and the Management Scientist in Successful Implementation," *Sloan Management Review* 15:1–24 (1974); R. J. Mockler, *Business Planning and Policy Formulation* (New York: Appleton-Century-Crofts, 1972); and G. A. Steiner, "Contemporary Managerial Planning," in J. W. McGuire, ed., *Contemporary Management: Issues and View Points* (Englewood Cliffs, N.J.: Prentice-Hall, 1974), pp. 325–50.

11. Steiner, "Contemporary Managerial Planning," p. 346.

12. Mockler, *Business Planning and Policy Formulation,* p. 293.

13. Ibid., p. 294.

14. See J. P. Campbell, M. D. Dunnette, E. E. Lawler III, and K. E. Weick, Jr., *Managerial Behavior, Performance and Effectiveness* (New York: McGraw-Hill, 1970); and V. H. Vroom, *Some Personality Determinants of the Effects of Participation* (Englewood Cliffs, N.J.: Prentice-Hall, 1960).

15. C. A. Mace, *Incentives: Some Experimental Studies* (London: Industrial Health Research Board, 1935).

16. Vroom, *Some Personality Determinents of the Effects of Participation* and V. H. Vroom, "Leadership and Decision Making," in M. D. Dunnette, ed., *Handbook of Industrial and Organizational Psychology* (Chicago: Rand-McNally, 1975).

17. N. Kogan and M. A. Wallach, "Risk Taking as a Function of the Situation, the Person and the Group," in *New Directions in Psychology III* (New York: Holt, 1967).

18. Ibid.

19. Steiner, "Contemporary Managerial Planning," p. 33.

20. R. Radosevich, "A Critique of Comprehensive Managerial Planning," in J. W. McGuire, ed., *Contemporary Management: Issues and View Points* (Englewood Cliffs, N.J.: Prentice-Hall, 1974), p. 360.

21. D. I. Cleland, "Planning Processes," in J. W. McGuire, ed., *Contemporary Management: Issues and View Points* (Englewood Cliffs, N.J.: Prentice-Hall, 1974), p. 351.

22. K. Lewin, L. Dembo, L. Festinger, and P. Sears, "Level of Aspiration," in J. M. Hunt, ed., *Personality and Behavior Disorders* (New York: Ronald Pr., 1944); and S. Siegel, "Level of Aspiration and Decision Making," *Psychological Review* 64:253–62 (1957).

23. H. A. Simon, *Administrative Behavior*, 2nd ed. (New York: Macmillan, 1957).

24. A. C. Stedry, *Budget Control and Cost Behavior* (Englewood Cliffs, N.J.: Prentice-Hall, 1960).

25. H. I. Ansoff, *Corporate Strategy* (New York: McGraw-Hill, 1965).

26. See P. Bruckman and D. T. Campbell, "Hedonic Relativism and Planning the Good Society," in M. H. Appley, ed., *Adaptation-Level Theory: A Symposium* (New York: Academic Pr., 1971); and R. M. Steers and L. W. Porter, "The Role of Task-Goal Attributes in Employee Performance," *Psychological Bulletin* 81:434–52 (1974).

27. L. E. Bourne, Jr., B. R. Ekstrand, and R. C. Dominowski, *The Psychology of Thinking* (Englewood Cliffs, N.J.: Prentice-Hall, 1971).

28. Mace, *Incentives*.

29. Steers and Porter, "The Role of Task-Goal Attributes."

30. J. F. Bryan and E. A. Locke, "Goal Setting as a Means for Increasing Motivation," *Journal of Applied Psychology* 53:274–77 (1967).

31. Bruckman and Campbell, "Hedonic Relativism."

32. Ackoff, "A Concept of Corporate Planning."

33. J. G. March and H. A. Simon, *Organizations* (New York: Wiley, 1958).

34. R. N. Taylor, "Perception of Problem Constraints," *Management Science* 22:22–29 (1975).

35. For governmental policy, see C. E. Lindblom, *The Intelligence of Democracy: Decision Making through Mutual Adjustment* (New York: Free Pr., 1965); for military tactics, see R. Wholstetter, *Pearl Harbor: Warning and Decision* (Stanford, Calif.: Stanford Univ. Pr., 1962); for business, see G. Katona, *Psychological Analysis of Economic Behavior* (New York: McGraw-Hill, 1951); and for natural resource management, see G. Kaufman, *The Forest Ranger* (Baltimore: Johns Hopkins Univ. Pr., 1960).

36. G. A. Miller, "The Magical Number Seven, Plus or Minus Two: Some Limits on Our Capacity for Processing Information," *Psychological Review* 63:81-97 (1956).

37. D. G. Elmes, "Short-Term Memory as a Function of Storage Load," *Journal of Experimental Psychology* 81:203–4 (1969).

38. M. I. Posner, "Immediate Memory in Sequential Task," *Psychological Bulletin* 60:346–54 (1963).

39. See J. Block and P. Peterson, "Some Personality Correlates of Confidence, Caution, and Speed in a Decision Situation," *Journal of Abnormal Social Psychology* 51:34–41 (1955); and D. G. Pruitt, "Infor-

mational Requirements in Making Decisions," *American Journal of Psychology* 74:433–39 (1961).

40. Taylor and Dunnette, "Relative Contribution."

41. J. S. Bruner, J. J. Goodnow, and G. A. Austin, *A Study of Thinking* (New York: Science Editions, 1956).

42. S. Fillenbaum, "Some Stylistic Aspects of Categorizing Behavior," *Journal of Personality* 27:187–95 (June 1959).

43. J. Feldman, "Simulation of Behavior in the Binard Choice Experiments," in E. A. Feigenbaum and J. Feldman, eds., *Computer and Thought* (New York: McGraw-Hill, 1963), pp. 329–46.

44. R. H. Doktor and W. F. Hamilton, "Cognitive Style and the Acceptance of Management Science Recommendations," *Management Science* 19:884–94 (1973).

45. H. A. Witkin, "Origins of Cognitive Style," in Constance Scheere, ed., *Cognition, Theory, Research, Promise* (New York: Harper & Row, 1964), pp. 172–205.

46. Ibid.

47. Ibid.

48. J. H. B. M. Huysmans, "The Effectiveness of the Cognitive-Style Constraint in Implementing Operations Research Proposals," *Management Science* 17:92–104 (1970).

49. C. W. Churchman and P. Ratoosh, "Report on Further Implementation Experiments" (Working paper no. 26, Center for Research in Management Science, Univ. of California, Berkeley, 1961).

50. Doktor and Hamilton, "Cognitive Style."

51. Ackoff, "A Concept of Corporate Planning."

52. A. N. Duvall, "Functional Fixedness: Replication Study," *Psychological Record* 15:497–599 (1965); W. S. Ray, "Three Experiments on Functional Fixedness," *Psychological Record* 15:489–95 (1965); and J. P. Van de Geer, *A Psychological Study of Problem Solving* (Haarlem: Uitgeverig De Toorts, 1957).

53. S. Glucksberg, "The Influence of Strength of Drive on Functional Fixedness and Perceptual Recognition," *Journal of Experimental Psychology* 63:36–51 (1962).

54. Y. Ijiri, R. K. Jaedicke, and K. E. Knight, "The Effects of Accounting Alternatives on Management Decisions," in R. K. Jaedicke, Y. Ijiri, and O. Nielson, eds., *Research in Accounting Measurement* (Chicago: American Accounting Assn., 1966).

55. I. Maltzman, "On the Training of Originality," *Psychological Review* 67:229–41 (1960).

56. F. J. Divesta and R. T. Walls, "Transfer of Solution Rules in Problem Solving," *Journal of Educational Psychology* 58:319–26 (1967).

57. I. Maltzman, S. Simon, D. Raskin, and L. Licht, "Experimental Studies in the Training of Originality," *Psychological Monographs* 74: whole no. 493 (1960).

58. A. F. Osborn, *Applied Imagination: Principles and Procedures of Creative Thinking* (New York: Scribner, 1941).

59. W. J. Gordon, *Synectics* (New York: Harper & Row, 1961); and G. M. Prince, "The Operational Mechanisms of Synetics," *The Journal of Creative Behavior* 2:1–13 (1967).

60. Ackoff, "A Concept of Corporate Planning."

61. Lindblom, *The Intelligence of Democracy.*

62. Ackoff, "A Concept of Corporate Planning," pp. 4–5.

63. Simon, *Administrative Behavior.*

64. Katona, *Psychological Analysis.*

65. Ackoff, "A Concept of Corporate Planning."

66. Lindblom, *The Intelligence of Democracy.*

67. D. Braybrooke and C. E. Lindblom, *A Strategy of Decision* (New York: Free Pr., 1963).

68. Ackoff, "A Concept of Corporate Planning"; and K. Weick, *The Social Psychology of Organizing* (Reading, Mass.: Addison-Wesley, 1969).

69. Ackoff, "A Concept of Corporate Planning," p. 8.

7. Libraries at the Turning Point—Davis

1. R. L. Ackoff, "Planning in the Systems Age," *Sankyha: The Indian Journal of Statistics*, Series B, vol. 35, pt. 2, 1973.

2. "Texas Instruments Shows U.S. Business How to Survive in the 1980s," *Business Week*, 18 Sept. 1978, pp. 66–92.

3. J. Eldred, "Strategic Participation" (Dissertation proposal, Social Systems Sciences Program, Wharton School, Univ. of Pennsylvania, 1979).

4. Klaus Musman, "Socio-technical Theory and Job Design in Libraries," *College & Research Libraries* 39:20–28 (Jan. 1978).

5. H. I. Ansoff, *Corporate Strategy* (New York: McGraw-Hill, 1965).

6. E. L. Trist, "Referent Organizations and the Development of Interorganizational Domains" (Distinguished Lecture to the Academy of Management, 39th Annual Convention, Atlanta, 9 August 1979).

7. S. Sarason, *The Creation of Settings* (San Francisco, Jossey-Bass, 1974).

8. Paul Watzlawick, John Weakland, and Richard Frisch, *Change* (New York: Norton, 1976).

9. A. A. Milne, *Winnie-the-Pooh* (New York: Dutton, 1926).

10. Arthur D. Little, Inc., "Passing the Threshold into the Information Age" (Report to the National Science Foundation, reprinted in the abbreviated form as *Into the Information Age: A Perspective for Federal Action on Information.* Chicago: ALA, 1979).

11. T. D. Thompson, *Organization in Action* (New York: McGraw-Hill, 1967).

12. P. Davis and F. Krejs, "The Challenge of Retrenchment and the Future of Research Librarians" (Working paper, Social Systems Science Unit, Wharton School, Univ. of Pennsylvania, 1979).

13. W. F. Lancaster, "Whither Libraries? or, Wither Libraries," *College & Research Libraries* 39:345–57 (Sept. 1978).

14. R. W. Boss, "The Library as an Information Broker," *College & Research Libraries* 40:136–40 (Mar. 1979).

8. Economic Analysis—Prentice
1. Aaron Wildansky, *Budgeting: A Comparative Theory of Budgetary Process* (Boston: Little, Brown, 1973), p. 15.
2. *Spec Flyer*. Systems and Procedures Exchange Center, ARL Office of Management Studies, #36, Sept. 1977, p. 1.
3. J. Victor Baldridge and Terrence E. Deal, *Managing Change in Educational Organizations* (Berkeley, Calif.: McCutcheon, 1974).
4. Ibid., p. 36.
5. Jean B. Wellish, Ruth J. Patrick, Donald V. Black, and Carlos A. Cuadra, *The Public Library and Federal Policy* (Westport, Conn.: Greenwood Pr., 1974); Don Kennington, "Long Range Planning for Public Libraries: A Delphi Study," *Long Range Planning* 10:73–84 (Apr. 1977).
6. Baldridge and Deal, *Managing Change*, p. 297.
7. Peter Phyrr, *Zero Base Budgeting* (New York: Wiley, 1973).
8. Diane D. Cole, "Mathematical Models in Library Management Planning Analysis and Cost Assessment" (Ph.D. diss., University of Texas at Austin, 1976).
9. William F. Massy, "A Dynamic Equilibrium Model for University Budget Planning," *Management Science* 23:248 (Nov. 1976).
10. National Center for Higher Education-Management Systems, *Library Statistical Data Base* (Boulder, Colo.: The Center, 1977).

Additional Readings
1. R. L. Ackoff, *Redesigning the Future* (New York: Wiley, 1974).
2. Charles R. McClure, *Information for Academic Library Decision Making* (Westport, Conn.: Greenwood Pr., 1980), p. 10.
3. Vern M. Pings, "Use or Value of Goals and Objectives Statements," *Journal of Library Administration* 1:56 (Fall 1980).
4. John Haak, "Goal Determination," *Library Journal* 96:1574 (1 May 1971).
5. Dale D. McConkey, *MBO for Nonprofit Organizations* (New York: AMACOM Pr., 1975), p. 13.
6. J. H. Bell and R. B. Keusch, "Comprehensive Planning for Libraries," *Long Range Planning* 9:49 (Oct. 1976).

Control
1. M. Gene Newport, *The Tools of Managing* (Reading, Mass.: Addison-Wesley, 1972), p. 101.
2. William H. Newman and Harvey W. Wallender, "Managing Not-for-Profit Enterprises," *Academy of Management Review* 3:31 (Jan. 1978).
3. See Peter F. Drucker, *Management: Tasks, Responsibilities, Practices* (New York: Harper & Row, 1974), p. 138 and John Rizzo, *Management for Librarians: Fundamentals and Issues* (Westport, Conn.: Greenwood Pr., 1980), p. 76.

9. Control—Rizzo

1. A. C. Filley, R. J. House, and Steven Kerr, *Managerial Process and Organizational Behavior,* 2nd ed. (Glenview, Ill.: Scott, Foresman, 1976).

2. R. F. Mager and Peter Pipe, *Analyzing Performance Problems or "You Really Oughta Wanna"* (Belmont, Calif.: Fearon, 1970).

3. One text offers an excellent example of audits that are designed to cover a wide array of organizational phenomena. See R. F. Thierauf, R. C. Klekamp, and D. W. Geeding, *Management Principles and Practices* (New York: Wiley, 1977).

4. See, for example, R. K. Merton, *Social Theory and Social Structure,* rev. ed. (New York: Free Pr., 1957), and A. W. Gouldner, *Patterns of Industrial Bureaucracy* (New York: Free Pr., 1954) for excellent models of how the need for control creates dysfunctional consequences.

10. The Role of Budgeting—Cherrington and Cherrington

1. John W. Gardner, *Self-Renewal: The Individual and the Innovative Society* (New York: Harper & Row, Harper Colophon Books, 1965), pp. 1–7.

2. Wendell L. French and Cecil H. Bell, Jr., *Organization Development* (Englewood Cliffs, N.J.: Prentice-Hall, 1973).

3. Daniel Kaltz and Robert Kahn, *The Social Psychology of Organizations* (New York: Wiley, 1966), pp. 19–28; French and Bell, *Organization Development,* p. 76.

4. Rensis Likert, *The Human Organization* (New York: McGraw-Hill, 1967); French and Bell, *Organization Development.*

5. Lester Coch and John R. P. French, Jr., "Overcoming Resistance to Change," *Human Relations* 1:512–32 (1948).

6. Reviewed and discussed by Victor H. Vroom, *Some Personality Determinants of the Effects of Participation* (Englewood Cliffs, N.J.: Prentice-Hall, 1960); Coch and French, "Overcoming Resistance"; John R. P. French, Jr., Joachim Israel, and Dagfin As, "An Experiment on Participation in a Norwegian Factory," *Human Relations* 8:3–19 (1960).

7. For example, two authors who have stated this argument are V. Bruce Irvine, "Budgeting: Functional Analysis and Behavioral Implications," *Cost and Management* (Canada) 44:6–16 (Mar.-Apr. 1970); and E. D. Smith, "Human Behavior: A Factor in Accounting," *Management Services* 2:53–58 (Sept.-Oct. 1965).

8. Victor H. Vroom, "Industrial Social Psychology," in Gardner Lindzey and Elliot Aronson, eds., *The Handbook of Social Psychology,* 2nd ed. (Reading, Mass.: Addison-Wesley, 1969), pp. 196–268.

9. Kurt Levin, Tamara Dombo, Leon Festinger, and Pauline Sears, "Level of Aspiration," in Joseph Hunt, ed., *Personality and the Behavior Disorders* (New York: Ronald Pr., 1944), pp. 333–78.

10. Chris Argyris, "Human Problems with Budgets," *Harvard Business Review* 31:97–110 (Jan.-Feb. 1953).

11. David J. Cherrington and J. Owen Cherrington, "Appropriate Reinforcement Contingencies in the Budgeting Process," in *Empirical*

Research in Accounting: Selected Studies, 1973 (supplement to *Journal of Accounting Research*, vol. 11).

12. Argyris, "Human Problems with Budgets."

13. See, for example, J. L. Child and J. W. M. Whiting, "Determinants of Level of Aspiration: Evidence from Everyday Life," in Howard Brand, ed., *The Study of Personality* (New York: Wiley, 1954), pp. 148–58.

11. A Conceptual Basis—Du Mont

1. See, for example, Martna Boaz, "Evaluation of Special Library Service for Upper Management," *Special Libraries* 59:289–91 (Dec. 1969); Charles R. McClure, "The Planning Process: Strategies for Action," *College & Research Libraries* 39:456–66 (Nov. 1978); F. W. Lancaster, *The Measurement and Evaluation of Library Services* (Washington, D.C.: Information Resources Pr., 1977), pp. 2–9; Morris Hamburg, Leonard E. Ramist, and Michael R. W. Bommer, "Library Objectives and Performance Measures and Their Use in Decision Making," *Library Quarterly* 42:107–28 (Jan. 1972); E. Evans, H. Borko, and P. Ferguson, "Review of Criteria Used to Measure Library Effectiveness," *Bulletin of the Medical Library Association* 60:102–10 (Jan. 1972); John R. Haak, "Goal Determination," in Ross Shimmon, ed., *A Reader in Library Management* (Hamden, Conn.: Linnet, 1976), pp. 83–96.

2. See, for example, Richard M. Dougherty, "The Human Side of Library Effectiveness," in Allan F. Hershfield and Morell D. Boone, eds., *Approaches to Measuring Library Effectiveness: A Symposium* (Syracuse, N.Y.: School of Library Science, Syracuse Univ., 1972), pp. 40–47; Ernest R. DeProspo and Ellen Altman, "Another Attempt at Measuring Public Library Effectiveness: Some Methodological Considerations," in ibid., pp. 14–30; Kenneth Beasley, "A Theoretical Framework for Public Library Measurement," in Herbert Goldhor, ed., *Research Methods in Librarianship: Measurement and Evaluation* (Champaign, Ill.: Univ. of Illinois Graduate School of Library Science, 1968), pp. 2–13; R. H. Orr, "Measuring the Goodness of Library Services: A General Framework for Considering Quantitative Measures," *Journal of Documentation* 29:315–32 (Sept. 1973); Richard W. Trueswell, "User Circulation Satisfaction vs. Size of Holdings at Three Academic Libraries," *College & Research Libraries* 30:204–13 (May 1969).

3. See, for example, Dougherty, "The Human Side of Library Effectiveness."

4. See, for example, Barry Totterdell and Jean Bird, *The Effective Library: Report of the Hillingdon Project on Public Library Effectiveness* (London: Library Assn., 1976); Douglas L. Zweizig, "Measuring Library Use," *Drexel Library Quarterly* 13:3–15 (July 1977); F. W. Lancaster, *Measurement and Evaluation*, pp. 299–309; Timothy P. Hays and Concepsion S. Wilson, *A Survey of Users and Non-users of Public Libraries in Region 6, North Carolina* (Greensboro, N.C.: Piedmont Triad Council of Governments, 1974).

5. Rosemary Ruhig Du Mont and Paul F. Du Mont, "Measuring

Library Effectiveness: A Review and Assessment," in Michael Harris, ed., *Advances in Librarianship* (New York: Academic Pr., 1979), pp. 103–41.

6. Such questions were first raised by Richard M. Steers, "When Is an Organization Effective? A Process Approach to Understanding Effectiveness," *Organizational Dynamics* 4:51–54 (Autumn 1976).

7. Du Mont and Du Mont, "Measuring Library Effectiveness," p. 131.

8. See, for example, Larry Earl Bone, "The Public Library Goals and Objectives Movement: Death Gasp or Renaissance?" *Library Journal* 100:1283–86 (July 1975); Allan F. Hershfield, "Measuring Library Effectiveness: A Challenge to Library Educators: Introductory Remarks," in Hershfield and Boone, eds., *Approaches to Measuring Library Effectiveness*, pp. 7–13.

9. Du Mont and Du Mont, "Measuring Library Effectiveness," p. 132.

10. See, for example, the various contingencies identified in the model developed by John L. Davies, "Organizational Effectiveness and Corporate Management: The Implications for Libraries," in P. A. Thomas and Valerie A. Ward, eds., *The Corporate Approach to Library Management* (London: Aslib, 1974), p. 3.

11. See, for example, Chris Argyris, *Integrating the Individual and the Organization* (New York: Wiley, 1964); Frederick Herzberg, *Work and the Nature of Man* (Cleveland: World, 1966); Rensis Likert, *The Human Organization: Its Management and Value* (New York: McGraw-Hill, 1967); Douglas McGregor, *The Human Side of Enterprise* (New York: McGraw-Hill, 1960).

12. See, for example, Klaus Musmann, "Socio-Technical Theory and Job Design in Libraries," *College & Research Libraries* 39:20–28 (Jan. 1978); Charles Martell, "Administration: Which Way—Traditional Practice or Modern Theory?" *College & Research Libraries* 33:104–12 (Mar. 1972); Dougherty, "Human Side of Library Effectiveness"; Maurice P. Marchant, "Participative Management as Related to Personnel Development," *Library Trends* 20:48–59 (July 1971).

13. See, for example, S. Terreberry, "The Evolution of Organizational Environments," in F. E. Kast and J. E. Rosenzweig, eds., *Contingency Views of Organization and Management* (Chicago: Science Research Associates, 1973), pp. 81–100; F. E. Emery and E. L. Trist, "The Causal Texture of Organizational Environments," in Frank Baker, ed., *Organizational Systems: General Systems Approach to Complex Organizations* (Homewood, Ill.: Irwin, 1973), pp. 165–77.

14. For further discussion of these criteria and their relation to libraries, see Beverly P. Lynch, "The Academic Library and Its Environment," *College & Research Libraries* 35:126–32 (Mar. 1974); W. Boyd Rayward, "Libraries as Organizations," *College & Research Libraries* 30:312–21 (July 1969); Arthur M. McAnally and Robert B. Downs, "The Changing Role of Directors of University Libraries," *College & Research Libraries* 34:103–25 (Mar. 1973); Jeffrey A. Raffel, "From Economic to

Political Analysis of Library Decision Making," *College & Research Libraries* 35:412–23 (Nov. 1974).

15. Pauline Wilson's book *A Community Elite and the Public Library: The Use of Information in Leadership* (Westport, Conn.: Greenwood Pr., 1977) is one interesting example of such a study.

Additional Readings

1. Robert N. Anthony and Regina E. Herzlinger, *Management Control in Nonprofit Organizations* (Homewood, Ill.: Irwin, 1975), pp. 16–17.

2. Murray S. Martin, *Budgetary Control in Academic Libraries* (Greenwich, Conn.: JAI Pr., 1978), p. 21.

3. Anthony and Herzlinger, *Management Control*, p. 32.

4. Charles A. Reimnitz, "Testing a Planning and Control Model in Nonprofit Organizations," *Academy of Management Journal* (Mar. 1972), p. 78.

Organizing

1. Joseph L. Massie, *Essentials of Management*, 3rd ed. (Englewood Cliffs, N.J.: Prentice-Hall, 1979), p. 7.

12. An Introduction to Organizational Design—McCaskey

1. Herbert A. Simon, *The New Science of Management Decision* (New York: Harper & Row, 1960), pp. 2, 43.

2. Tom Burns and G. M. Stalker, *The Management of Innovation* (London: Tavistock, 1961).

3. Geoffrey Vickers, *The Art of Judgment* (New York: Basic Books, 1965).

4. Burns and Stalker, *Management of Innovation*.

5. Paul R. Lawrence and Jay W. Lorsch, *Organization and Environment* (Boston: Grad. School of Business Admin., Harvard Univ., 1967).

6. James D. Thompson, *Organizations in Action* (New York: McGraw-Hill, 1967).

7. Paul R. Lawrence and Jay W. Lorsch, "New Management Job: The Integrator," *Harvard Business Review* 45:142–51 (Nov.-Dec. 1967).

8. Arthur H. Walker and Jay W. Lorsch, "Organizational Choice: Product Versus Function," *Harvard Business Review* 46:129–38 (Nov.-Dec. 1968); Jay R. Galbraith, *Designing Complex Organizations* (Reading, Mass.: Addison-Wesley, 1973).

9. Donald Ralph Kingdon, *Matrix Organization: Managing Information Technologies* (London: Tavistock, 1973).

10. Peter M. Blau and Richard A. Schoenherr, *The Structure of Organizations* (New York: Basic Books, 1971).

11. Jay W. Lorsch and Paul R. Lawrence, eds., *Studies in Organization Design* (Homewood, Ill.: Irwin, 1970).

12. Blau and Schoenherr, *Structure of Organizations*.

13. Lawrence and Lorsch, *Studies in Organization Design*.

14. Galbraith, *Designing Complex Organizations*.

15. Robert B. Duncan, "The Effects of Perceived Environmental Uncertainty on Organizational Decision Unit Structure: A Cybernetic Model" (Ph.D. diss., Yale University, 1971).

16. Robert Propst, *The Office: A Facility Based on Change* (New York: Taplinger, 1968).

17. Fred I. Steele, "Physical Settings and Organizational Development," in Harvey Hornstein and others, eds., *Social Intervention: A Behavioral Science Approach* (New York: Free Pr., 1971), pp. 244–54.

18. Thomas J. Allen, "Communication Networks in R&D Laboratories," *R&D Management* 1:14–21 (1970).

Additional Readings

1. Rowena W. Swanson, "Organization Theory Related to Library Management," *Canadian Library Journal* 30:356 (July 1973).

2. Daniel Katz and Robert L. Kahn, *The Social Psychology of Organizations* (New York: Wiley, 1978), p. 20.

3. Fremont E. Kast and James E. Rosenzweig, "General Systems Theory: Applications for Organization and Management," *Academy of Management Journal* (Dec. 1972), p. 462.

4. Swanson, "Organization Theory," p. 362.

5. George P. Huber, Joseph Ullman, and Richard Leifer, "Optimum Organization Design: An Analytic-Adoptive Approach," *Academy of Management Review* 4:567 (Oct. 1979).

6. Janet Schriesheim, Mary Ann Von Glinow, and Steven Kerr, "Professionals in Bureaucracies: A Structural Alternative," *North-Holland/TIMS Studies in the Management Sciences* 5:55 (1977).

7. Robert H. Waterman, Jr., Thomas J. Peters, and Julien R. Phillips, "Structure Is Not Organization," *Business Horizons* 23:7 (June 1980).

8. Charles Perrow, "A Framework for the Comparative Analysis of Organizations," *American Sociological Review* 32:195 (Apr. 1967).

9. Terry Connolly, Edward J. Conlon, and Stuart Jay Deutsch, "Organizational Effectiveness: A Multiple-Constituency Approach," *Academy of Management Review* 5:211 (1980).

10. See also Edward R. Johnson and Stuart R. Mann, *Organizational Development for Academic Libraries: An Evaluation of the Management Review and Analysis Program* (Westport, Conn.: Greenwood Pr., 1980).

11. Robert C. Shirley, "An Interactive Approach to the Problem of Organizational Change," *Human Resource Management* (Summer 1975), p. 11.

12. T. D. Wilson, "Organisation Development in Library Management," in *Studies in Library Management*, vol. 4 (Hamden, Conn.; Linnet, 1977), p. 45.

Communicating

1. Richard V. Farace and Donald MacDonald, "New Directions in the Study of Organization Communication," *Personnel Psychology* 27:1–15 (1974).

2. T. Connolly, "Information Processing and Decision Making in Organizations," in B. Staw and G. Salancik, eds., *New Directions in Organizational Behavior* (Chicago: St. Clair, 1977), p. 205.

3. Chester Barnard, *The Functions of the Executive* (Cambridge, Mass.: Harvard Univ. Pr., 1938).

4. See, for example: T. Burns, "The Directions of Activity and Communication in a Departmental Executive Group," *Human Relations* 7:73–97 (1954); Edward E. Lawler, Lyman W. Porter, and A. Tennenbaum, "Managers' Attitudes toward Interaction Episodes," *Journal of Applied Psychology* 52:432–39 (1968); Henry Mintzberg, *The Nature of Managerial Work* (New York: Harper & Row, 1973). A library application can be found in Pauline A. Thomas and Valerie A. Ward, *Where the Time Goes* (London: Aslib, 1973).

5. Phillip V. Lewis, *Organizational Communication: The Essence of Effective Management* (Columbus, Ohio: Grid, 1975), p. 5.

6. Richard C. Huseman, "Interpersonal Conflict in the Modern Organization," in Richard C. Huseman, Cal M. Logue, and Dwight L. Freshley, *Readings in Interpersonal and Organizational Communication* (Boston: Holbrook Pr., 1977), p. 224.

15. Communication Thermoclines—Huseman et al.

1. Daniel Katz and Robert Kahn, *The Social Psychology of Organizations* (New York: Wiley, 1966), p. 33.

2. Although no one has developed the thermocline concept in organizations, several writers have discussed the effect of stratification on communication. See, for example, Lee Thayer, *Communication and Communication Systems* (Homewood, Ill.: Irwin, 1968), pp. 188–203; Alfred Vogel, "Why Don't Employees Speak Up?" *Personnel Administration* 30:18–22 (May-June 1967); William Read, "Upward Communication in Industrial Hierarchies," *Human Relations* 15:3–15 (1962); and Chris Argyris, "Interpersonal Barriers to Decision Making," *Harvard Business Review* 44:84–97 (Mar.-Apr. 1966).

3. W. J. Buckley, *Sociology and Modern Systems Theory* (Englewood Cliffs, N.J.: Prentice-Hall, 1967), p. 4.

4. H. Dudley Dewhirst, "Influence of Perceived Information-Sharing Norms on Communication Utilization," *Academy of Management Journal* 14:305–15 (Sept. 1971).

5. Ibid., p. 307.

6. Gary Gemmill, "Managing Upward Communication," *Personnel Journal* 49:109 (Feb. 1970).

7. Judson Gooding, *The Job Revolution* (New York: Walker, 1972), p. 66.

8. *Work in America: A Report of a Special Task Force to the Secretary of Health, Education and Welfare* (Cambridge, Mass.: MIT Pr., 1972), p. 40–41.

9. Clearly, the location of the thermocline is relative. Since it results from a combination of structure and process, it could occur at

the vice president level although it is probably more pervasive and serious at lower levels.

10. Perhaps the concept of the "ombudsman," which has been used effectively in some organizations for similar purposes, is the closest analogy to a bubble machine.

11. See, for example, André Delbecq and Andrew Van de Ven, "A Group Process Model for Problem Identification and Program Planning," *Journal of Applied Behavioral Science* 7:466–92 (July-Aug. 1971); idem, "Nominal Versus Interacting Group Processes for Committee Decision-Making Effectiveness," *Academy of Management Journal* 14:203–12 (June 1971); Richard C. Huseman, "Defining Communication Problems in the Organizational Setting," *Journal of Organizational Communication* 2:18–20 (Summer 1972).

12. There is a "trade-off" decision to be made here. If groups are composed of people from the same level, it is likely that the quality and quantity of responses will be greater. If people from different levels (superiors and subordinates) are included and verbal interaction is permitted at later stages, it is likely to create a more favorable "behavior change" climate.

13. Donald W. Taylor, Paul C. Berry, and Clifford H. Block, "Does Group Participation When Using Brainstorming Facilitate or Inhibit Creative Thinking?" *Adminstrative Science Quarterly* 3:23–47 (1958); Victor H. Vroom, Lester D. Grant, and Timothy S. Cotton, "The Consequences of Social Interaction in Group Problem Solving," *Organizational Behavior and Human Performance* 4:77–95 (1969).

14. Delbecq, "A Group Process Model."

15. Taylor, Berry, and Block, "Does Group Participation When Using Brainstorming Facilitate or Inhibit Creative Thinking?"

16. N. R. F. Maier, *Problem-Solving Discussion and Conferences* (New York: McGraw-Hill, 1963), pp. 248–49.

17. David Sirota and Alan D. Wolfson, "Pragmatic Approaches to People Problems," *Harvard Business Review* 51:130 (Jan.-Feb. 1973).

18. Ibid.

19. These as well as other aspects of training consequences are more than adequately discussed elsewhere. See, for example, Robert J. House, "Leadership Training: Some Dysfunctional Consequences," *Administrative Science Quarterly* 12:556–71 (Mar. 1968).

16. Managing Organizational Conflict—Derr

1. Richard E. Walton, "How to Choose between Strategies of Conflict and Collaboration," in Warren Bennis, Kenneth Benne, and Robert Chin, eds., *Changing Organizations* (New York: Holt, 1969).

2. For a more detailed treatment of some of these assumptions, see C. Brooklyn Derr, "Uncovering and Working with Conflicts," in Schmuck et al., *Handbook of Organization Development in Schools* (Palo Alto, Calif.: National Press Books, 1972).

3. For a thorough treatment of third party functions in inducing

collaboration, see Richard E. Walton, *Interpersonal Peacemaking: Confrontation and Third Party Consultation* (Reading, Mass.: Addison-Wesley, 1969).

4. Robert R. Blake and Jane S. Mouton, "The Fifth Achievement," *Journal of Applied Behavioral Science* 6:413–26 (Oct.-Nov.-Dec. 1970); Rensis Likert and Jane Gibson Likert, *New Ways of Managing Conflict* (New York: McGraw-Hill, 1976).

5. Likert and Likert, *New Ways*; Alonzo McDonald, "Conflict at the Summit: A Deadly Game," *Harvard Business Review* 50:59–68 (Mar.-Apr. 1972); Richard E. Walton and John M. Dutton, "The Management of Interdepartmental Conflict: A Model and Review," *Administrative Science Quarterly* 14:73–84 (Mar. 1969).

6. Anatol Rapoport, "Models of Conflict: Cataclysmic and Strategic," in Anthony de Reuch and Julie Knight, eds., *Conflict and Society* (Boston: Little, Brown, 1966), pp. 259–88.

7. See Robert J. Ringer, *Winning through Intimidation* (New York: Fawcett, 1974); L. Z. Bloom, Karen Coburn, and Joan Pearlman, *The New Assertive Woman* (New York: Dell, 1975); Michael Korda, *Power: How to Get It, How to Use It* (New York: Random, 1977); and B. L. Harragan, *Games Mother Never Taught You: Corporate Gamesmanship for Women* (New York: Warner, 1977).

8. See G. W. Dalton, L. B. Barnes, and Abraham Zaleznick, *The Distribution of Authority in Formal Organizations* (Boston: Harvard Graduate School of Business, 1968); J. R. P. French, Jr., and Bertram Raven, "The Bases of Social Power," in Dorwin Cartwright, ed., *Studies in Social Power* (Ann Arbor, Mich.: Institute for Social Research, 1959), pp. 150–67; G. Gilman, "An Inquiry into the Nature and Use of Authority," in Mason Haire, ed., *Organization Theory and Industrial Practice* (New York: Wiley, 1962).

9. Anthony Jay, *Management and Machiavelli* (New York: Holt, 1967); George L. Peabody, "Power, Alinsky, and Other Thoughts," in H. A. Hornstein and others, eds., *Social Intervention* (New York: Free Pr., 1971), pp. 521–32.

10. Daniel C. Lortie, "The Balance of Control and Autonomy in Elementary School Teaching," in A. E. Tzioni, *The Semi-Professions and Their Organization* (New York: Free Pr., 1969); William R. Scott, "Professionals in Hospitals: Technology and the Organization of Work," in B. S. Georgopoulos, *Organization Research on Health Institutions* (Ann Arbor, Mich.: Institute for Social Research, 1972); and Louis R. Pondy, "Organizational Conflicts: Concepts and Models," *Administrative Science Quarterly* 12:296–320 (Sept. 1967).

11. Virginia E. Schein, "Individual Power and Political Behaviors in Organizations," *Academy of Management Review* 2:64–72 (Jan. 1977).

12. See Richard E. Walton and Robert B. McKersie, "Bargaining Dilemmas in Mixed-Motive Decision-Making," *Behavioral Science* 11:370–84 (Sept. 1966); and Roger Harrison, "Role Negotiation: A Tough-Minded

Approach to Team Development," in W. W. Burke and H. A. Hornstein, *The Social Technology of Organization Development* (Washington, D.C.: NTL Learning Resources, 1972).

17. The Psycho-Organizational Approach—Wilkinson

1. I. L. Heckman and S. G. Huneryager, *Human Relations in Management: Text and Readings* (Cincinnati: South-Western, 1960), p. 255.

2. M. D. Abell, "Aspects of Upward Communications in a Public Library," in Mary Lee Bundy and Ruth Aronson, eds., *Social and Political Aspects of Librarianship: Student Contributions to Library Science* (Albany: School of Library Science, SUNY, 1965), p. 91.

3. Richard Emery, *Staff Communication in Libraries* (Hamden, Conn.: Linnet, 1975), p. 9.

4. J. P. Wilkinson, review of *Staff Communication in Libraries*, by Richard Emery, in *Canadian Library Journal*, 33:5 (1 Feb. 1976).

5. Lawrence Kohlberg, "A Cognitive-Developmental Approach to Moral Education," *Humanist* 32:13–19 (Nov.-Dec. 1972).

6. Ibid., p. 14–15.

7. Abraham Maslow, *Motivation and Personality* (New York: Harper & Row, 1970). See particularly chapter 4: "A Theory of Human Motivation."

8. Lawrence Kohlberg, "The Child as a Moral Philosopher," *Psychology Today* 2:24 (Sept. 1968).

9. Maslow indeed makes the bold assertion that "a man who is thwarted in any of his basic needs may fairly be envisaged simply as a sick man or at least less than fully human." Maslow, *Motivation and Personality*, p. 57.

10. Kohlberg, "Child as Moral Philosopher."

11. Ibid.

12. Ibid.

13. Eric Berne, *Transactional Analysis in Psychotherapy* (New York: Grove, 1961).

14. Thomas Harris, *I'm O.K.—You're O.K.* (New York: Avon, 1973), p. 40.

15. Ibid., p. 48.

16. Ibid., p. 57.

17. Kohlberg estimates, for example, that "the final 'principled' stages [stages 5 and 6] are characteristic of 20 to 25 percent of the adult population, with perhaps 5 to 10 percent arriving at stage 6" (Kohlberg, "A Cognitive-Developmental Approach," p. 16); Maslow notes that "it is as if the average citizen is satisfied perhaps 85 percent in his physiological needs, 70 percent in his safety needs, 50 percent in his love needs, 40 percent in his self-esteem needs, and 10 percent in his self-actualization needs" (Maslow, *Motivation and Personality*, p. 54).

18. See, for example, Alex Bavelas, "An Experimental Approach to Organizational Communication," *Personnel* 33:366–71 (Mar. 1951); and

H. J. Leavitt, "Some Effects of Certain Communication Patterns on Group Performance," *Journal of Abnormal and Social Psychology* 46:38–50 (Jan. 1951).

19. The initial work of Bavelas and Leavitt has been questioned to some extent by later researchers such as Arthur Cohen, who points out that "past experience can play a systematic and important part in the development of systems that groups adopt for solving problems. . . . The systems that come to be developed are not simply rote transfers from the past." Arthur Cohen, "Communication Networks in Research and Training," *Personnel Administration* 27:20 (May-June 1964). However, granted that no adult is free from previous pattern socialization, a new organizational (communication) structure *can* reeducate along desired lines; in any case, individuals in an organizational context do not so much adopt a formal system as they are adopted by it.

20. It is not suggested, in other words, that "high level" development coupled with all-points patterns will eliminate productive conflict and responsiveness toward change. Indeed, the increase in data assimilation and critical evaluation typical of such an organizational approach may well increase the dissatisfaction of personnel with remaining imperfections. However, such constructive dissatisfaction is surely a major element in organizational flexibility and adaptablity.

21. M. E. Shaw, "Some Effects of Problem Complexity upon Problem Solution Efficiency in Different Communication Nets," *Journal of Experimental Psychology* 48:211–17 (1954).

22. Amitai Etzioni, *Modern Organizations* (Englewood Cliffs, N.J.: Prentice-Hall, 1964), pp. 75–93.

23. Ibid., p. 77.

24. Rensis Likert, *The Human Organization: Its Management and Value* (New York: McGraw-Hill, 1967), pp. 47–49.

25. Edward Howard, "The Orbital Organization," *Library Journal* 95:1712–15 (1 May 1970).

Additional Readings

1. Marshall Scott Poole, "An Information-Task Approach to Organizational Communication," *Academy of Management Review* 3:495 (July 1978).

2. Richard C. Huseman and Elmore R. Alexander III, "Communication and the Managerial Function: A Contingency Approach," in *Readings in Organizational Behavior: Dimensions of Management Action* (Boston: Allyn & Bacon, 1979), p. 331.

Staffing

1. Dale Yoder and Herbert G. Heneman, Jr., eds., *Staffing Policies and Strategies: ASPA Handbook of Personnel and Industrial Relations,* vol. 1 (Washington, D.C.: Bureau of National Affairs, 1974), pp. 4–2.

18. Increasing Organizational Effectiveness—Schein

1. Paul Pigors and C. A. Myers, *Personnel Administration*, 8th ed. (New York: McGraw-Hill, 1977); Elmer Burack, *Organization Analysis* (Hinsdale, Ill.: Dryden, 1975).

2. J. R. Hackman and J. L. Suttle, *Improving Life at Work* (Los Angeles: Goodyear, 1977); Hyman Meltzer and F. R. Wickert, *Humanizing Organizational Behavior* (Springfield, Ill.: Charles C. Thomas, 1976).

3. Douglas McGregor, *The Human Side of Enterprise* (New York: McGraw-Hill, 1960); W. G. Bennis, *Changing Organizations* (New York: McGraw-Hill, 1966); Pigors and Myers, *Personnel Administration; E. H. Schein, *Organizational Psychology* (Englewood Cliffs, N.J.: Prentice-Hall, 1970); John Van Maanen, "Breaking In: Socialization to Work," in Robert Dubin, ed., *Handbook of Work, Organization, and Society* (Chicago: Rand-McNally, 1976); Lotte Bailyn and E. H. Schein, "Life/Career Considerations as Indicators of Quality of Employment," in A. D. Biderman and T. F. Drury, eds., *Measuring Work Quality for Social Reporting* (New York: Sage, 1976); Ralph Katz, "Job Enrichment: Some Career Considerations," in John Van Maanen, ed., *Organizational Careers: Some New Perspectives* (New York: Wiley, 1977), pp. 133–48.

4. See R. D. Beckhard, *Organizational Development: Strategies and Models* (Reading, Mass.: Addison-Wesley, 1969); Bennis, *Changing Organizations;* E. H. Schein, *Process Consultation: Its Role in Organization Development* (Reading, Mass.: Addison-Wesley, 1969); Jay Galbraith, *Designing Complex Organizations* (Reading: Mass.: Addison-Wesley, 1973); F. G. Lesieur, *The Scanlon Plan* (New York: Wiley, 1958); Theodore Alfred, "Checkers or Choice in Manpower Management," *Harvard Business Review* 45:157–69 (Jan.-Feb. 1967).

5. See E. H. Schein, "How 'Career Anchors' Hold Executives to Their Career Paths," *Personnel* 52:11–24 (May-June 1975).

6. See E. H. Schein, *The Individual, the Organization and the Career: Toward Greater Human Effectiveness* (Reading, Mass.: Addison-Wesley, forthcoming).

7. See Bailyn and Schein, "Life/Career Considerations"; C. A. Myers, "Management and the Employee," in J. W. McKie, ed., *Social Responsibility and the Business Predicament* (Washington, D.C.: Brookings, 1974); John Van Maanen, Lotte Bailyn, and E. H. Schein, "The Shape of Things to Come: A New Look at Organizational Careers," in J. R. Hackman, E. E. Lawler, and L. W. Porter, eds., *Perspectives on Behavior in Organizations* (New York: McGraw-Hill, 1977); R. J. C. Roeber, *The Organization in a Changing Environment* (Reading, Mass.: Addison-Wesley, 1973).

8. John Van Maanen and E. H. Schein, "Improving the Quality of Work Life: Career Development," in Hackman and Suttle, *Improving Life at Work;* Lotte Bailyn, "Career and Family Orientations of Husbands and Wives in Relation to Marital Happiness," *Human Relations* 23:97–113 (Apr. 1970); idem, "Involvement and Accommodation in Technical

Careers," in Van Maanen, *Organizational Careers*; R. M. Kanter, *Work and Family in the United States* (New York: Russell Sage, 1977).

9. Gail Sheehy, "Catch 30 and Other Predictable Crises of Growing Up Adult," *New York Magazine* 7:30–44 (Feb. 1974); L. E. Troll, *Early and Middle Adulthood* (Monterey, Calif.: Brooks/Cole, 1975); R. A. Kalish, *Late Adulthood: Perspectives on Aging* (Monterey, Calif.: Brooks/Cole, 1975); R. F. Pearse and B. P. Pelzer, *Self-Directed Change for the Mid-Career Manager* (New York: AMACOM Pr., 1975).

10. Burack, *Organization Analysis*, pp. 402–3.

11. Schein, *Organizational Psychology*.

12. G. W. Dalton and P. H. Thompson, "Are R&D Organizations Obsolete?" *Harvard Business Review* 54:105–16 (Nov.-Dec. 1976); D. E. Super and M. J. Bohn, *Occupational Psychology* (Belmont, Calif.: Wadsworth, 1970); D. T. Hall, *Careers in Organizations* (Los Angeles: Goodyear, 1976); Schein, *The Individual, the Organization and the Career*.

13. Schein, *The Individual, the Organization and the Career*.

14. Ibid.

15. E. H. Schein, "How to Break in the College Graduate," *Harvard Business Review* 42:68–76 (Nov.-Dec. 1964); idem, *The Individual, the Organization and the Career*.

16. E. H. Schein, "Organizational Socialization and the Profession of Management," *Industrial Management Review* 9:1–16 (Winter 1968); Van Maanen, "Breaking In."

17. Schein, "How to Break in the College Graduate."

18. E. H. Schein, "The Individual, the Organization, and the Career: A Conceptual Scheme," *Journal of Applied Behavioral Science* 7:401–26 (1971); idem, *The Individual, the Organization and the Career*.

19. Schein, "How to Break in the College Graduate"; D. W. Bray, R. J. Campbell, and D. E. Grant, *Formative Years in Business* (New York: Wiley, 1974); David Berlew and D. T. Hall, "The Socialization of Managers," *Administrative Science Quarterly* 11:207–23 (Sept. 1966); Hall, *Careers in Organizations*.

20. Dalton and Thompson, "Are R&D Organizations Obsolete?"; Katz, "Job Enrichment."

21. R. Heidke, "Career Pro-Activity of Middle Managers" (Master's thesis, Massachusetts Institute of Technology, 1977).

22. Bailyn, "Involvement and Accommodation in Technical Careers."

23. Katz, "Job Enrichment."

24. Bailyn, "Involvement and Accommodation in Technical Careers."

19. Redesigning Library Jobs—Shaughnessy

1. See, e.g., R. N. Ford, *Motivation through the Work Itself* (New York: American Management Association, 1969); L. E. Bjork, "An Experiment in Work Satisfaction," *Scientific American* 232:17–24 (Mar. 1975).

2. J. O'Toole, ed., *Work in America: Report of a Special Task Force to the Secretary of Health, Education and Welfare* (Cambridge: MIT Pr., 1973), p. xvii.

3. L. E. Davis, "The Design of Jobs," *Industrial Relations* 6:21–45 (Oct. 1966).

4. G. I. Susman, *Autonomy at Work* (New York, Praeger, 1976), p. 31.

5. The impact of these changes on complex organizations (such as libraries) has been described by the author in an earlier article: "Technology and Job Design in Libraries: A Sociotechnical Systems Approach," *The Journal of Academic Librarianship* 3:269–72 (Nov. 1977).

6. L. E. Davis, "Job Satisfaction Research: The Post-Industrial View," *Industrial Relations* 10:176–93 (Feb. 1971).

7. Ibid.

8. P. G. Herbst, *Socio-Technical Design* (London: Tavistock, 1974), pp. 13–16.

9. Ibid.

10. F. E. Kast and J. E. Rosenzweig, *Organization and Management: A Systems Approach* (New York: McGraw-Hill, 1974), p. 187.

11. L. E. Davis and J. C. Taylor, "Technology, Organization, and Job Structure," in Robert Rubin, ed., *Handbook of Work, Organization and Society* (Chicago: Rand-McNally, 1976), p. 386.

12. R. L. Jacobson, "Pharmacy Education Stirred by Debates," *The Chronicle of Higher Education*, 20 Sept. 1976, p. 10.

13. R. Heinich, "Technology and the Future of the Media Professions," (typewritten; Los Angeles: Univ. of Southern California, 1976).

14. O'Toole, *Work in America*, p. 30.

15. Davis and Taylor, "Technology, Organization, and Job Structure," p. 388.

16. C. L. Hulin and M. R. Blood, "Job Enlargement, Individual Differences and Worker Responses," *Psychological Bulletin* 69:41 (Jan. 1968).

17. L. E. Davis, "Introduction," in L. E. Davis and J. C. Taylor, eds., *Design of Jobs* (London: Penguin, 1972), p. 11.

18. Ibid.

19. Robert Dubin, *Working Union-Management Relations* (Englewood Cliffs, N.J.: Prentice-Hall, 1958), p. 7.

20. A. M. McAnally and R. B. Downs, "The Changing Role of Directors of University Libraries," *College & Research Libraries* 34:103 (Mar. 1973).

21. J. A. Hewitt, "The Impact of OCLC," *American Libraries* 7:268–75 (May 1976).

22. Susman, *Autonomy at Work*, p. 33.

23. Robert Cooper, *Job Motivation and Job Design* (Los Angeles: Center for the Quality of Working Life, Univ. of California, 1976), p. 12. See also Frederick Herzberg and others, *The Motivation to Work*, 2nd ed. (New York: Wiley, 1959), p. 72.

24. N. Q. Herrick and M. Maccoby, "Humanizing Work: A Priority Goal of the 1970s," in L. E. Davis and Albert Cherns, eds., *The Quality of Working Life*, vol. 1 (New York: Free Pr., 1975), p. 64–66.

25. Susman, *Autonomy at Work*, p. 37.

26. L. E. Davis, R. R. Canter, and J. Hoffman, "Current Job Design Criteria," *Journal of Industrial Engineering* 5:5–11 (1955).

27. L. E. Davis, "Job Design," *Journal of Industrial Engineering* 5:2–4 (1955).

28. D. D. Umstot, C. H. Bell, and T. R. Mitchell, "Effects of Job Enrichment and Task Goals on Satisfaction and Productivity: Implications for Job Design," *Journal of Applied Psychology* 61:392 (Aug. 1976).

29. G. R. Oldham, J. R. Hackman, and J. L. Pearce, "Conditions under Which Employees Respond Positively to Enriched Work," *Journal of Applied Psychology* 61:395–403 (Aug. 1976).

30. Ibid.

31. E. Smith, "Service and Housekeeping: Changing Professional and Non-professional Responsibilities in the Academic Research Library," in *Papers Delivered at the Indiana University Library Dedication, October 9–10, 1970* (Bloomington: Indiana Univ. Library, 1971), p. 59.

32. Louis Davis, "The Design of Jobs," *Industrial Relations* 6:21–45 (Oct. 1966).

33. Rensis Likert, *The Human Organization* (New York: McGraw-Hill, 1967), p. 3–46.

34. See O'Toole, *Work in America*, pp. 96–98; P. R. Lawrence, "Technical Inputs," in J. A. Seiler, *Systems Analysis in Organizational Behavior* (Homewood, Ill.: Irwin-Dorsey, 1967), pp. 138–39; L. E. Davis, "The Coming Crisis for Production Management," in Davis and Taylor, *Design of Jobs*, pp. 455–56.

20. Motivation—Nadler and Lawler

1. For reviews of the expectancy theory research see T. R. Mitchell, "Expectancy Models of Job Satisfaction, Occupational Preference and Effort: A Theoretical, Methodological, and Empirical Appraisal," *Psychological Bulletin* 81:1053–77 (Dec. 1974). For a more general discussion of expectancy theory and other approaches to motivation see E. E. Lawler, *Motivation in Work Organizations* (Belmont, Calif.: Brooks/Cole, 1973).

2. E. E. Lawler and others, "Job Choice and Post-Decision Dissonance," *Organizational Behavior and Human Performance* 13:133–45 (1975).

3. For a detailed discussion of the implications of expectancy theory for pay and reward systems, see E. E. Lawler, *Pay and Organizational Effectiveness: A Psychological View* (New York: McGraw-Hill, 1971).

4. A good discussion of job design with an expectancy theory perspective is in J. R. Hackman and others, "A New Strategy for Job Enrichment," *California Management Review* 18:57 (Summer 1975).

5. The use of questionnaires for understanding and changing organizational behavior is discussed in D. A. Nadler, *Feedback and Organizational Development: Using Data-Based Methods* (Reading, Mass.: Addison-Wesley, 1977).

6. The whole issue of individualizing organizations is examined in E. E. Lawler, "The Individualized Organization: Problems and Promise," *California Management Review* 17:31–39 (Winter 1974).

21. Library Staff Development—Berkner

1. Winston Oberg, "Make Performance Appraisal Relevant," *Harvard Business Review* 50:61–67 (Jan.-Feb. 1972).

2. Douglas McGregor, "An Uneasy Look at Performance Appraisal," *Harvard Business Review* 35:89–94 (May-June 1957).

3. Marjorie Johnson, "Performance Appraisal for Librarians—A Survey," *College & Research Libraries* 33:359–67 (Sept. 1972).

4. Pennsylvania State University Libraries, "Management Guide to Performance Evaluation," 15 February 1972. In Association of Research Libraries, Office of University Management Studies, Systems and Procedures Exchange Center, *SPEC Kit: Performance Review* (Washington, D.C.: Association of Research Libraries, Office of University Library Management Studies, 1974).

5. Abraham Pizam, "Social Differentiation—A New Psychological Barrier to Performance Appraisal," *Public Personnel Management* 4:244–47 (July 1975).

6. Ibid., p. 245.

7. Herbert H. Meyer, Emmanuel Kay, and John R. P. French, Jr., "Split Roles in Performance Appraisals," *Harvard Business Review* 43:124 (Jan.-Feb. 1965).

8. Peter Drucker, *The Practice of Management* (New York: Harper & Row, 1954); McGregor, "An Uneasy Look at Performance Appraisal," p. 91.

9. Paul H. Thompson and Gene W. Dalton, "Performance Appraisal: Managers Beware," *Harvard Business Review* 48:149–57 (Jan.-Feb. 1970).

10. David W. Belcher, *Compensation Administration* (Englewood Cliffs, N.J.: Prentice-Hall, 1974), esp. pp. 199–215; an opposing point of view is presented by E. C. Keil, *Performance Appraisal and the Manager* (New York: Lebhar-Friedman Books, 1977). This is an excellent practical summary of performance review, with emphasis on the interview itself, but Keil concludes that a manager is not qualified to become involved in long-range career development; this is better left to an outside consultant. Believing that most libraries cannot afford this luxury, I have proposed an alternative approach in the second half of this article.

11. Ernest DeProspo, "Personnel Evaluation as an Impetus to Growth," *Library Trends* 20:60–70 (July 1971).

12. Alva F. Kindall and James Gatza, "Positive Program for Performance Appraisal," *Harvard Business Review* 41:153–66 (Nov.-Dec. 1963).

13. Harry Levinson, "Management by Whose Objectives?" *Harvard Business Review* 48:125–34 (July-Aug. 1970); Harry Levinson, "Appraisal of What Performance?" *Harvard Business Review* 54:30–36 (July-Aug. 1976).

14. Levinson, "Management by Whose Objectives?" p. 127.

15. Larry N. Yarbrough, "Performance Appraisal in Academic and Research Libraries," *ARL Management Supplement* 3 (May 1975).

16. Association of Research Libraries, Office of University Library Management Studies and McGill University Libraries, *Staff Performance Evaluation Program at the McGill University Libraries: A Program Description of a Goals-Based Performance Evaluation Process with Accompanying Supervisor's Manual* (Washington, D.C.: ARL Office of University Library Management Studies, 1976).

17. Michael Beer and Robert A. Ruh, "Employee Growth through Performance Management," *Harvard Business Review* 54:59–66 (July-Aug. 1976).

18. Ibid., p. 62.

19. For further comments and citations, see the discussion of equity theory and expectancy theory in Belcher, *Compensation Administration,* pp. 50–68.

20. An expansion of these ideas can be found in Edward Roseman, *Confronting Nonpromotability: How to Manage a Stalled Career* (New York: AMACOM Pr., 1977). Part I, "Concerns of the Manager" (pp. 1–148), gives advice on appraising, counseling, and motivating employees.

21. Charles C. Gibbons, "Marks of a Mature Manager," *Business Horizons* 18:54–56 (Oct. 1975).

22. Harlan Cleveland, *The Future Executive: A Guide for Tomorrow's Managers* (New York: Harper & Row, 1972).

23. Practical aspects of the appraisal interview in developing mature behavior (which he calls Q4 attitudes) are detailed in Robert E. Lefton and others, *Effective Motivation through Performance Appraisal* (New York: Wiley, 1977), esp. pp. 282–90.

24. Muriel James, *The OK Boss* (Reading, Mass.: Addison-Wesley, 1975).

25. This is discussed in detail in Beer and Ruh, "Employee Growth," p. 63. However, they suggest that the supervisors use an already developed performance profile and rate each employee. I believe a similar device can be developed by the librarian and supervisor together, even where there is no personnel specialist available for regular assistance.

26. As done at the Corning Glass Company (discussed above) and described by Beer and Ruh, "Employee Growth."

27. Michael K. Buckland, ed., "The Management Review and Analysis Program: A Symposium," *Journal of Academic Librarianship* 1:4–14 (Jan. 1976).

28. Grady Morein and others, "The Academic Library Development Program," *College & Research Libraries* 38:37–45 (Jan. 1977).

Directing

1. Jay W. Lorsch, "Making Behavioral Science More Useful," *Harvard Business Review* 57:171–80 (Mar.-Apr. 1979).

2. Chester A. Schriesheim, James M. Tolliver, and Orlando C. Behling, "Leadership Theory: Some Implications for Managers," *MSU Business Topics* 26:28 (Summer 1978).

3. Lorsch, "Making Behavioral Science More Useful."

22. Leadership Theory—Schriesheim et al.

1. R. M. Stogdill, *Handbook of Leadership* (New York: Free Pr., 1974).

2. A. C. Filley, R. J. House, and Steven Kerr, *Managerial Process and Organizational Behavior,* 2nd ed., (Glenview, Ill.: Scott, Foresman, 1976). See also R. C. Davis, *Industrial Organization and Management* (New York: Harper & Row, 1957).

3. C. A. Gibb, "Leadership," in Gardner Lindzey and Elliott Aronson, eds., *The Handbook of Social Psychology* (Reading, Mass.: Addison-Welsey, 1969), vol. 4.

4. See, for example, R. H. Hall, *Organizations: Structure and Process* (Englewood Cliffs, N.J.: Prentice-Hall, 1972).

5. C. A. Schriesheim, J. M. Tolliver, and L. D. Dodge, "The Political Nature of the Leadership Process" (unpublished paper, 1978).

6. For examples of other types of managerial tasks that may have more of an impact on organizations, see J. P. Campbell, M. D. Dunnette, E. E. Lawler, and K. E. Weick, *Managerial Behavior, Performance, and Effectiveness* (New York: McGraw-Hill, 1970).

7. R. M. Stogdill, "Personal Factors Associated with Leadership: A Survey of the Literature," *Journal of Psychology* 25:35–71 (Jan. 1948).

8. T. O. Jacobs, *Leadership and Exchange in Formal Organizations* (Alexandria, Va.: Human Resources Research Organization, 1970).

9. A. W. Halpin and B. J. Winer, "A Factorial Study of the Leader Behavior Descriptions," in R. M. Stogdill and A. E. Coons, eds., *Leader Behavior: Its Description and Measurement* (Columbus: Bureau of Business Research, Ohio State Univ., 1957).

10. Ibid., p. 42.

11. Stogdill and Coons, *Leader Behavior.*

12. Steven Kerr, C. A. Schriesheim, C. J. Murphy, and R. M. Stogdill, "Toward a Contingency Theory of Leadership Based upon the Consideration and Initiating Structure Literature," *Organizational Behavior and Human Performance* 12:62–82 (Aug. 1974).

13. See, for example, Daniel Katz, Nathan Maccoby, and Nancy Morse, *Productivity, Supervision and Morale in an Office Situation* (Ann Arbor: Survey Research Center, Univ. of Michigan, 1951).

14. Kerr et al., "Contingency Theory."

15. See F. E. Fiedler, "Engineer the Job to Fit the Manager," *Harvard Business Review* 43:115–22 (Sept.-Oct. 1965).

16. F. E. Fiedler, *A Theory of Leadership Effectiveness* (New York: McGraw-Hill, 1967).

17. V. H. Vroom and P. W. Yetton, *Leadership and Decision-Making* (Pittsburgh: Univ. of Pittsburgh Pr., 1973).

18. Stogdill, "Personal Factors."

19. Kerr et al., "Contingency Theory."

20. R. R. Blake and J. S. Mouton, *The Managerial Grid* (Houston: Gulf, 1964) and *Building a Dynamic Corporation through Grid Organizational Development* (Reading, Mass.: Addison-Wesley, 1969).

21. Ibid., p. 63.

22. Rensis Likert, *New Patterns of Management* (New York: McGraw-Hill, 1961) and *The Human Organization: Its Management and Value* (New York: McGraw-Hill, 1967).

23. Fiedler, "Engineer the Job."

24. Kerr et al., "Contingency Theory."

25. See Filley, House, and Kerr, *Managerial Process*, especially pp. 162–80; and George Strauss, "Tactics of Lateral Relations," in H. J. Leavitt and L. R. Pondy, eds., *Readings in Managerial Psychology* (Chicago: Univ. of Chicago Pr., 1964), pp. 226–48.

26. Steven Kerr, "Substitutes for Leadership: Their Definition and Measurement" (unpublished paper, 1978).

27. O. C. Behling and C. A. Schriesheim, *Organizational Behavior: Theory, Research and Application* (Boston: Allyn & Bacon, 1976).

28. Ibid., p. 294.

23. Some Reflections on Participative Management—Dickinson

1. Fred C. Pearson, Howard A. Scilkin, and Wallace G. Lonegran, *Managing Organizational Improvement* (Chicago: Industrial Relations Center, Univ. of Chicago, 1972), p. 2.

2. Louis Kaplan, "On Decision Sharing in Libraries: How Much Do We Know?" *College & Research Libraries* 38:25–31 (Jan. 1977).

3. Ralph M. Edwards, "The Management of Libraries and the Professional Functions of Librarians," *Library Quarterly* 45:150–60 (Apr. 1975).

4. Miriam A. Drake, "The Management of Libraries as Professional Organizations," *Special Libraries* 68:181–86 (May-June 1977); Peter F. Drucker, "Managing the Public Service Institution," *College & Research Libraries* 37:4–14 (Jan. 1976); Daniel Gore, "Things Your Boss Never Told You about Library Management," *Library Journal* 102:765–70 (1 Apr. 1977); Roger Horn, "The Idea of Academic Library Management," *College & Research Libraries* 36:464–72 (Nov. 1975).

5. J. P. Danton, "Our Libraries—The Trend toward Democracy," *Library Quarterly* 4:16–27 (Jan. 1934). Cited by Amy Winslow, "Supervision and Morale," *Library Trends* 3:39–51 (July 1954).

6. Jane G. Flener, "Staff Participation in Management in Large University Libraries," *College & Research Libraries* 34:275–79 (July 1973).

7. Kaplan, "On Decision Sharing," p. 25.

8. Harvey Sherman, *It All Depends: A Pragmatic Approach to Organization* (University: Univ. of Alabama Pr., 1966), pp. 82–84.

9. Flener, "Staff Participation," p. 276.

10. "Library Administrators: Time to Show Them the Door," *Wilson Library Bulletin* 51:636–38 (Apr. 1977).

11. R. Dean Galloway, "Search and Screen Committees," *College & Research Libraries* 37:551 (Nov. 1976).

12. Donald J. Morton, "Applying Theory Y to Library Management," *College & Research Libraries* 36:302–7 (July 1975).

13. Flener, "Staff Participation," p. 276; Galloway, "Search and Screen Committees," p. 551; John F. Harvey and Mary Parr, "University Library Search and Screen Committees," *College & Research Libraries* 37:347–55 (July 1976); Louis Kaplan, "Participation: Some Basic Considerations on the Theme of Academe," *College & Research Libraries* 34: 235–41 (Sept. 1973); "Participative Management Is Working in California," *Library Journal* 100:248 (1 Feb. 1975); Thomas W. Shaughnessy, "Participative Management, Collective Bargaining, and Professionalism," *College & Research Libraries* 38:140–46 (Mar. 1977).

14. Flener, "Staff Participation," p. 227.

15. Harvey and Parr, "Search and Screen Committees," pp. 349–53.

16. Ibid., p. 354.

17. Morton, "Applying Theory Y," p. 305.

18. Kaplan, "On Decision Sharing," p. 29; Shaughnessy, "Participative Management," p. 143.

19. Kaplan, "Participation," p. 239.

20. Drucker, "Public Service Institution," p. 10.

21. Shaughnessy, "Participative Management," p. 141.

22. Drake, "Professional Organizations," p. 182; Daniel Gore, "The Mismanagement of College Libraries: A View from the Inside," *AAUP Bulletin* 52:46–51 (Spring 1966).

23. Drucker, "Public Service Institution," p. 10.

24. Edwards, "Management of Libraries," p. 153; Shaughnessy, "Participative Management," p. 144.

25. Drucker, "Public Service Institution," p. 12.

26. For example, Drake, "Professional Organizations," p. 182; Edwards, "Management of Libraries," p. 158.

27. Peter Hernon and Maureen Pastine, "Student Perceptions of Academic Librarians," *College & Research Libraries* 38:129–39 (Mar. 1977).

28. Ibid., pp. 132–33, 136.

29. Shaughnessy, "Participative Management," p. 142.

30. Kaplan, "Participation," pp. 236–37.

31. Phillip W. Semas, "Collective Bargaining and Faculty Governance," *Chronicle of Higher Education* 5 July 1977, p. 7; "Can an Administrator Find Happiness as the AAUP's New General Secretary?" *Chronicle of Higher Education* 27 July 1977, p. 3.

32. Drucker, "Public Service Institution," p. 9.

33. *Webster's New World Dictionary*, concise ed.

34. Connie R. Dunlap, "Organizational Patterns in Academic Libraries, 1876–1976," *College & Research Libraries* 37:395–407 (Sept. 1976).

35. Edwards, "Management of Libraries," p. 151.

36. Drake, "Professional Organizations," p. 185; Peter F. Drucker, "The Professor as Featherbedder," *Chronicle of Higher Education* 31 Jan. 1977, p. 24; Edwards, "Management of Libraries," p. 153; Gore, "Library Management," p. 768.

37. Drucker, "Public Service Institution," p. 8.

38. Drake, "Professional Organizations," p. 185.

39. Gore, "Library Management," p. 768.

40. Edwards, "Management of Libraries," p. 159; Virgil Massman, "If We Do Our Job Well," *Journal of Academic Librarianship* 2:284 (Jan. 1977); Winslow, "Supervision and Morale," p. 40.

41. Eric Moonman, "The Ineptitude of British Managers," *New York Times*, 1 May 1977, III, p. 3.

42. Drucker, "Public Service Institution," p. 7.

43. "Library Administrators," pp. 636–37.

44. Flener, "Staff Participation," p. 279; Kaplan, "Decision Sharing," pp. 25–26.

45. Drake, "Professional Organizations," p. 181.

46. Robert M. Pierson, "Roles, Symbols, Rewards," *Journal of Academic Librarianship* 2:285 (Jan. 1977).

47. For an example of how this may be achieved, see David W. Ewing, "Participative Management at Work," *Harvard Business Review* 55:117–27 (Jan.-Feb. 1977).

48. Horn, "Academic Library Management," pp. 469–70; "Library Administrators," pp. 636–37; Phillip W. Semas, "Colleges Adding Administrators, Study Reveals," *Chronicle of Higher Education* 11 July 1977, p. 28.

49. Kaplan, "Decision Sharing," p. 28.

50. Harvey and Parr, "Search and Screen Committees," pp. 350, 353; "Library Administrators," p. 637.

51. Kaplan, "Decision Sharing," pp. 25, 27.

24. Self-Management—Manz and Sims

1. H. P. Sims, "The Leader as a Manager of Reinforcement Contingencies: An Empirical Example and a Model," in J. G. Hunt and L. L. Larson, eds., *Leadership: The Cutting Edge* (Carbondale: Southern Illinois Univ. Pr., 1977), pp. 121–37.

2. Albert Bandura, *Social Learning Theory* (Englewood Cliffs, N.J.: Prentice-Hall, 1977).

3. Steven Kerr, "Substitutes for Leadership," in *Proceedings of the American Institute for Decision Sciences* (Atlanta: AIDS, 1976); Steven Kerr and J. M. Jermier, "Substitutes for Leadership: Their Meaning and

Measurement," *Organizational Behavior and Human Performance* 22: 375–403 (Dec. 1978).

4. E. E. Thoreson and M. J. Mahoney, *Behavioral Self-Control* (New York: Holt, 1974), p. 12.

5. Ibid.

6. Israel Goldiamond, "Self-Reinforcement," *Journal of Applied Behavior Analysis* 9:509–14 (Winter 1976); Bernard Bass and Gerald Barrett, *Man, Work, and Organizations: An Introduction to Industrial and Organization Psychology* (New York: Allyn & Bacon, 1972).

7. Walter Mischel, "Toward a Cognitive Social Learning Reconceptualization of Personality," *Psychological Review* 80:252–83 (July 1973).

8. Albert Bandura, *Principles of Behavior Modification* (New York: Holt, 1969).

9. M. J. Mahoney, *Cognition and Behavior Modification* (Cambridge: Ballinger, 1974), p. 155.

10. Mischel, "Toward a Cognitive Social Learning Reconceptualization."

11. Thoreson and Mahoney, *Behavioral Self-Control.*

12. Bandura, *Social Learning Theory;* M. J. Mahoney, "Cognitive Therapy and Research: A Question of Questions," *Cognitive Therapy & Research* 1:5–16 (Mar. 1977).

13. Thoreson and Mahoney, *Behavioral Self-Control*, p. 107.

14. Ibid.

15. Ibid.

16. E. E. Jones, "How Do People Perceive the Causes of Behavior?" *American Scientist* 64:300–5 (May-June 1976).

17. Ibid.; E. E. Jones and R. E. Nisbett, "The Actor and the Observer: Divergent Perceptions of the Causes of Behavior," in E. E. Jones and others, eds., *Attribution: Perceiving the Causes of Behavior* (Morristown, N.J.: General Learning Pr., 1972); Mischel, "Toward a Cognitive Social Learning Reconceptualization."

18. Fred Luthans and Robert Kreitner, *Organizational Behavior Modification* (Glenview, Ill.: Scott, Foresman, 1975).

19. Thoreson and Mahoney, *Behavioral Self-Control*, p. 45.

20. Ibid.

21. Gary P. Latham and Gary A. Yuki, "A Review of Research on the Application of Goal Setting in Organizations," *Academy of Management Journal* 18:824–45 (Dec. 1975).

22. M. J. Mahoney and D. B. Arnkoff, "Self-Management: Theory, Research, and Application," in J. P. Brady and D. Pomerleau, eds., *Behavioral Medicine: Theory and Practice* (Baltimore: Williams & Williams, 1979), pp. 75–96.

23. Ibid.

24. Bandura, *Principles of Behavior Modification.*

25. Fred Luthans and Tim Davis, "Behavioral Self-Management (BSM): The Missing Link in Managerial Effectiveness," *Organizational Dynamics* 8:42–60 (Summer 1979).

26. Bandura, *Principles of Behavior Modification*, pp. 32–33.
27. G. E. Speidel, "Motivating Effect of Contingent Self-Reward," *Journal of Experimental Psychology* 102:528–30 (Mar. 1974).
28. M. J. Mahoney and D. B. Arnkoff, "Cognitive and Self-Control Therapies," in S. L. Garfield and A. E. Borgin, eds., *Handbook of Psychotherapy and Behavior Change* (New York: Wiley, 1978), pp. 689–722.
29. D. S. Scott and A. K. Rosentiel, "Covert Positive Reinforcement Studies: Review, Critique, and Guidelines," *Psychotherapy: Theory, Research and Practice* 12:374–84. (Winter 1975).
30. Thoreson and Mahoney, *Behavioral Self-Control.*
31. Mahoney and Arnkoff, "Cognitive and Self-Control Therapies."
32. Mahoney and Arnkoff, "Self-Management."
33. A. E. Kazdin, "Effects of Covert Modeling and Model Reinforcement on Assertive Behavior," *Journal of Abnormal Psychology* 83:240–52 (June 1974).
34. Mahoney and Arnkoff, "Cognitive and Self-Control Therapies."
35. Kazdin, "Effects of Covert Modeling and Model Reinforcement on Assertive Behavior"; idem, "Effects of Covert Modeling, Multiple Models, and Model Reinforcement on Assertive Behavior," *Behavior Therapy* 7:211–22 (Mar. 1976).
36. Bandura, *Principles of Behavior Modification*, p. 33.
37. D. H. Meichenbaum, "Cognitive Factors in Behavior Modification: Modifying What Clients Say to Themselves," *Annual Review of Behavior Therapy Theory and Practice* 1:416–31 (1973).
38. Thoreson and Mahoney, *Behavioral Self-Control.*
39. Bandura, *Principles of Behavior Modification*; Thoreson and Mahoney, *Behavioral Self-Control*; Mahoney and Arnkoff, "Self-Management."
40. Bandura, *Principles of Behavior Modification*, p. 255.
41. Ibid., p. 256.
42. Ibid., p. 27.
43. Thomas Cummings, "Self-Regulating Work Groups: A Sociotechnical Synthesis," *Academy of Management Review* 3:625–34 (July 1978); J. W. Slocum, Jr., and H. P. Sims, Jr., "A Typology for Integrating Technology, Organization, and Job Redesign," *Human Relations* 33:193–212 (Mar. 1980).
44. R. J. House, 1979: personal communication.
45. C. C. Manz, "Sources of Control: A Behavior Modification Perspective," in *Proceedings of the Eastern Academy of Management, 1979.*
46. N. R. F. Maier, *Problem Solving and Creativity in Individuals and Groups* (Belmont, Calif.: Brooks/Cole, 1970); V. H. Vroom and P. W. Yetton, *Leadership and Decision Making* (Pittsburgh: Univ. of Pittsburgh Pr., 1973).
47. House, personal communication.
48. David McClelland, *The Achieving Society* (Princeton, N.J.: Van Nostrand-Reinhold, 1961).

49. See Luthans and Kreitner, *Organizational Behavior Modification,* for example, regarding nonmonetary organizational incentives, p. 75.

Additional Readings

1. Jeffrey C. Barrow, "The Variables of Leadership: A Review and Conceptual Framework," *Academy of Management Review* 2:231 (Apr. 1977).

DATE DUE

NOV 19 '85			
DEC 10 '85			
JAN 14			
JAN 14 '86			
FEB 11 '86			
FEB 25 '86			
MAR 18 '86			
DEC 9 '86			
DEC 15 '87			
AP 18 '89			
GAYLORD			PRINTED IN U.S.A.